Post-Fascist Fantasies

POST-CONTEMPORARY INTERVENTIONS

Series Editors: Stanley Fish and

Fredric Jameson

Psychoanalysis,

History, and

the Literature

of East Germany

POST-FASCIST FANTASIES

Julia Hell

Duke

University

Press

Durham

&

London

1997

© 1997 Duke University Press

All rights reserved Printed in the United

States of America on acid-free paper ∞

Designed by Cherie H. Westmoreland

Typeset in Times with Frutiger display

by Tseng Information Systems, Inc.

Library of Congress Cataloging-in-Publication

Data appear on the last printed page of

this book.

For George

Contents

Acknowledgments

This study is the product of a shock. In 1989, in the midst of realizing that I needed to change my theoretical approach dramatically if I were to continue working on the subject of East German literature, this very subject suddenly seemed to disappear before my eyes, to "turn into history" like the state to which it was so inextricably linked. I hope this shock proved to be productive, and that this study will help to resist the simplifications arising from the slow death of Europe's Cold War imaginary.

In the course of writing this book, I have realized how indebted I am to many people for intellectual stimulation. I would like to take this opportunity to thank my parents for letting me grow up in a house full of books. I would also like to express my gratitude to my former professors at Madison, the department responsible for making GDR literature an "acceptable" field of research. In particular, I am happy to finally have the opportunity to thank Nancy Kaiser for years of friendship and intellectual exchange, for endless phone conversations, lots of good advice and black humor. And I would like to thank Kit Belgum, whose company I often miss.

I am also indebted to my colleagues at Duke. Ann-Marie Rasmussen's interest in my work, but above all, her very presence have been vital. James Rolleston's comments on my work have always proved helpful, as has Frank Borchardt's quirky humor. Claudia Koonz has been an inspiring reader, and Liz Clark's help with a text I know little about was greatly appreciated. Thanks also to my graduate students, especially Rob Gibson for his last-minute help, and Katja Altpeter, Maura Dillon, and Kai Evers for many engaging post-contemporary discussions. I will also miss the intellectual intensity and precision of Stefan Jonsson and Sara Danius. I would like to thank Fred Jameson for the opportunity to intervene in the debates about the GDR "post-contemporarily."

At Duke University Press, Reynolds Smith has been the funniest, grumpiest, and most efficient editor one could hope for. Candice Ward, who worked hard on my teutonic prose, and Pam Morrison, who patiently assisted me in the final stages of the manuscript, have contributed to a very enjoyable experience. Special thanks also to the anonymous readers of the manuscript, to Marc Silberman for his detailed feedback, to Jürgen Daniel for providing me with much valuable material on the GDR, to Bob von Halberg for access to his unpublished manuscript on GDR intellectuals, and to Jim Steakley for his help with translations. Loren Kruger and Katie Trumpener have been inspiring co-authors.

There is a group of friends who have made life in the theory swamps of North Carolina a memorable experience. Without Sarah Beckwith, Sibylle Fischer, Thomas Lahusen, and Toril Moi, my life and work would be much impoverished. I owe much to Toril's intellectual presence, her obsession with clarity, and her amazing book on Beauvoir; to Sarah's fascinating explorations of the social meanings of Christ's body, her forceful interventions to rescue the political impetus of cultural studies, and her riotous personality; to Sibylle's work on the problems of realism, and her strong convictions; and to Thomas's determination to rethink socialist realism after the cold war, and his "searching melancholy." I would not have written this book were it not for Ingrid Pisetsky. And for George whose presence is so strongly woven into this book that it would be futile to even try to speak about it here—and rather inappropriate. I dedicate this book to you, to years of love and intellectual companionship.

There is no longer an inside or an outside, the revolution is everywhere.

—Christa Wolf, "Der Sinn einer neuen Sache: Vera Inber" (1967)

Our misrecognition constitutes a closed system, nothing can refute it.

—Christa Wolf, *Medea: Stimmen* (1996)

Critical Orthodoxies:

Toward a New Reading of East German Literature

The field of East German scholarship is still adjusting to the dramatic collapse of the German Democratic Republic in the autumn of 1989. Some GDR scholars have reacted with a form of melancholic paralysis, indulging in memories of a lost country in which their dreams of a better society had been so heavily invested—often at the expense of a clear perception of the realities of "real existing socialism." But most of my colleagues still cannot believe their luck: that this fortress opened up during our lifetime, overflowing with materials, with original versions of manuscripts, banned films, Party documents, and so on. This wealth of new material has been accompanied by an outpouring of voices, a veritable flood of post-1989 autobiographies, essays, memoirs, interviews, and documentaries, not the least interesting of which are the new "post-Wall" novels, breathless narratives about a quickly disappearing country and the ways people lived in it. Obviously, both the GDR itself and East German cultural studies need to be reconceptualized.

Where should we begin? What are the core issues that need to be addressed in this effort to rethink the GDR's cultural landscape? At a postunification conference on GDR literature, Frank Hörnigk, one of the leading literary scholars from the former East Germany, polemically drew attention to the fact that an author like Gert Neumann, with his fiercely experimental prose, was not only omitted from the GDR's official literary histories, but was also never "discovered" by Western critics. This seemingly simple observation has wide-ranging implications. First, there are many East German texts which literary scholarship still ignores. Second, the fact that authors like Neumann have been writing since the early 1960s, drawing on Kafka and Joyce (a literature which was anathema to official East German

Kulturpolitik), unsettles the established literary-historical narratives about the East, with their guiding dichotomy of realism versus modernism. Third, Neumann's early decision to write for *a time after socialism* highlights once again the questions raised after 1989: What was the canonical author's relationship to the East German State? Was the oeuvre of Christa Wolf, Heiner Müller, Volker Braun, Christoph Hein, Kerstin Hensel, and others complicitous with this State or critical of it? Does it even make sense to try to understand their texts in terms of complicity versus critique? We have known for some time that the answer to the first question involves the authors' attraction to a Communist Party that claimed to uphold a specific ideal, antifascism; we also know that these authors saw their literary production as part of this antifascist tradition. What lies at the very core of these questions, then, is the relationship of literature to ideology as that site where stories about a collective history become entangled with the history of the subject.

At stake are questions of periodization, of the realism/modernism dichotomy, of literature's complicitous or critical role, and of the role of (un)conscious fantasies in a given ideological formation. And we are confronted once again with the legacy of the German past, the ways in which it is remembered and the ways in which it is repressed. This particular angle, the legacy of fascism in the literature of the GDR, will serve as a starting point in the effort to answer some of the questions raised above. This book has a dual focus: first, it explores a literary tradition centrally involved in the Communist Party's effort to legitimize its power through the discourse of antifascism; second, it traces the ways in which the work of Christa Wolf, East Germany's most prominent author, has interacted with this tradition. The Communists' effort to build hegemony within the power vacuum left by the collapse of Nazi Germany was based on a discourse of antifascism. More specifically, the GDR claimed the legacy of antifascism by presenting the Socialist Unity Party (SED) and its leaders as the sole heirs of the resistance movement. This founding discourse retained its power until the State imploded in 1989. At the center of the Communists' symbolic politics of power was the figure of the (Communist) father as antifascist hero. This book aims to understand from a psychoanalytic perspective the ways in which Wolf's writing is engaged in this reconstruction of symbolic power, focusing on the (un)conscious fantasies about the post-fascist body and the post-fascist voice that suffuse her texts. The book's dual focus thus allows us to trace the production of cultural fantasies across East Germany's entire history.

What is involved in this particular way of looking back at East German literature? First and foremost, by reading literature as part of a culture's production of fantasies, we shed new light on East Germany's dominant ideological narrative, on the ways in which it works on the political and psychic levels, the ways in which stories about the past are woven into the foundations of a post-fascist German state and into the foundations of that state's post-fascist subjects. Second, concerning more properly literary issues, this approach unsettles our firmly established orthodoxies of realism and modernism. To start with, this study includes what many critics consider that literature's most negligible texts, its socialist realist classics. These texts are essential, indeed indispensable, if we want to understand the cultural fantasies at work. Moreover, we will discover that the usual description of these texts as closed and monolithic needs to be revised. Conversely, our understanding of what we are used to thinking of as East Germany's most modernist works will also be transformed. With respect to Wolf, this means, first, that the realism/modernism split allegedly defining Wolf's oeuvre will be fundamentally reconceptualized. And, second, notions of feminine writing, and of feminism in general, that we have come to associate with Wolf's concept of "subjective authenticity" (this concept which for Wolf defines modernist prose tout court) will be thoroughly problematized. Since this approach represents a radical reframing of the prevailing terms of debate, it is necessary to set out in some detail the categories which have hitherto informed and structured scholarly discussions of GDR literature, culture, and politics.

"The GDR never existed," proclaimed East Germany's most prominent playwright, Heiner Müller, after the Berlin Wall fell in November 1989. Is there any truth to this provocative remark? However pompous and cryptic, Müller's statement does convey a fundamental insight: from its beginnings to its sudden demise, this failed experiment in socialism was characterized by a gaping chasm between utopian expectations and German reality and by an utter lack of autonomy, first from the Soviet occupying power and later from the West. Founded in October 1949 on the territory of the Soviet Occupied Zone, the German Democratic Republic had little opportunity to chart an independent "German path" toward socialism.[1] Nevertheless, many communists and noncommunists returning from the concentration camps, from exile, or from the seclusion forced upon them after 1933 were drawn to a social order that announced its beginnings as "antifascist-democratic." They were joined by a younger generation, many of whose members had as adolescents enthusiastically participated in the rituals of National Socialism. Müller belonged to that generation, as did Christa Wolf, Irmtraud Morgner, Brigitte Reimann, Franz Fühmann, Willi Sitte, and many other prominent East German artists and intellectuals. The antifascist-democratic sentiment was supported by a sizable minority and had a strong anticapitalist component.[2] Yet the SED soon instrumentalized this sentiment in the service of a Soviet-style social order, one in which democracy became democratic centralism and antifascism a discourse that legitimated the power of a single party and its state. Thus the German Democratic Republic, this democratic and socialist alternative to West Germany for which many had hoped, never materialized. Such hopes turned out to be "heroic illusions." [3]

Nor did this "other GDR" emerge from the tumultuous events in the fall of 1989, despite the hopes of many leading East German intellectuals, members of the citizen movements, and sympathizers outside the country.[4] Let me briefly review these events. In East Germany, the late 1980s were characterized by stagnation and the widespread feeling that nothing would ever change, given the SED's open resistance to Gorbachev's reforms.[5] Then, in the summer of 1989, Hungary opened its border to Austria and thousands of refugees began to stream out of the country. Beginning in the early fall, East Germans assembled for peaceful marches in Leipzig and other major cities, declaring their intention to stay ("We're staying here") and demanding democratic reforms ("We are the people"). Meanwhile, preparations were being made for the fortieth anniversary celebrations on October 9. Expecting the government to resort to the "Chinese solution," most observers were surprised when the heavily deployed security forces withdrew from the massive counterdemonstration held in Leipzig on October 7.[6] Nearly a million people gathered in Berlin on November 4 to hear speakers drawn from the citizen movements, the country's most prominent writers and artists (Christoph Hein, Steffi Spira, Christa Wolf, Stephan Heym, Heiner Müller), and the Communist Party. Under pressure from the continuing mass emigration and increasing protests throughout the country, Erich Honecker, Head of State and General Secretary of the Party, resigned in the first week of November, followed by the resignation of the government and then the entire Politburo.[7] On November 9, a "colossal misunderstanding" occurred when a rather bewildered functionary accidentally read an announcement that "the borders are now open" at a nationally televised late-night press conference—and the Wall was opened.[8]

The ensuing period is best described by the title of one of the numerous monographs chronicling this process: "History Is Wide Open." [9] When a new Communist government was formed on November 17, the main citizen movements and new political parties formed a "roundtable" in order to negotiate the citizens' demands with the government. The outcome was an agreement to hold elections in March, with the participation of parties and groups other than the SED, for a "government of national responsibility." During this time a euphoric sense of radical democracy prevailed, notably, in a series of town meetings and open debates. Many expected the roundtable, which emerged as the most important site of continuous discussion during this interregnum, to remain a key institution in the future political order. But the elections on March 18, 1990, yielded a surprise victory for the Christian Democrats. This result unequivocally confirmed the majority's desire to merge with the West as quickly as possible, a desire loudly proclaimed in the new slogan "We are *one* people" heard more and more frequently at demonstrations. A second, reformed GDR thus never became a real possibility. The West was too attractive, the East in its post-perestroika paralysis too discouraging, the experience of forty years of state socialism too powerful a deterrent. Instead, East Germany's ruling elite "surrendered the fortress," [10] and in the fall of 1990 the GDR was absorbed by the Federal Republic. Dependent on the Soviet Union from its Stalinist inception to its corroded state under perestroika and facing the possibility of unification, the GDR as a "third path," a democratic-socialist Germany, had never really existed.

Should we then view the GDR retrospectively as two utopian moments in which the hope for an alternative society flared up briefly—an alternative to the Nazi past, to the Soviet model, and to the consumer society of the Federal Republic—and, between these two moments, the dark night of Stalinism?[11] Such an understanding of forty years of East German history is as simplistic and reductionist as the currently fashionable equation of the Nazi regime and the East German *Unrechtsstaat* (criminal state).[12] The other concept which quickly gained wide acceptance as a way of characterizing this state was, predictably, totalitarianism. Besides the inflationary and often oversimplifying use of that concept in the German press, the most influential version was developed by Sigrid Meuschel in her work on East Germany as a society penetrated by the state, a form of blocked modernization.[13] Meuschel maintains that the process of differentiation into various subsystems, which she views as characteristic of modern industrial societies, was reversed in the GDR: instead of reaching ever greater autonomy from one another, the economic, cultural, and social processes were blocked by the all-encompassing political regulation of East Germany's ruling party, which led to a "withering away of society,"[14] to a society suspended and immobilized.

Such an analysis is problematic because, in constructing a unilateral relationship of dependence between state and society, it underestimates the autonomy of the social in the GDR. Furthermore, it collapses transformational *project* and reality, a program and its partially contingent effects. In its emphasis on state repression and control, it cannot account for individual agency, for the intricate pattern of conformity and resistance which characterized the GDR. As Ralph Jessen observes: "The reality of 'real existing socialism' was a highly complex mixture of the ideologically driven dictatorial attempt at social construction, on the one hand, and the countervailing weight of inherited and emergent social structures and processes, on the other."[15] The totalitarianism perspective remains bound to a Cold War mirror logic, figuring socialist state societies as the opposite of modern Western ones without being able to determine the specific forms of domination and resistance in that system. And by positing a teleological development from Eastern "premodernity" to Western "modernity," this model is ultimately unable to recognize the specificity of the GDR. To grasp this specificity, we need to abandon the simplistic dichotomy of premodernity versus modernity. This reductionist analysis, which accompanies the current revival of modernization theory in Germany, owes more to a political rhetoric intent on portraying West Germany as the more advanced part than to a genuine effort to theorize the complexities of the East German state.[16]

One version of totalitarianism theory, however, does capture part of the GDR's discursive and nondiscursive reality: Claude Lefort's rethinking of totalitarianism precisely as a political-ideological *project.* In Lefort's view, totalitarianism is characterized by the propagation of one-party rule and by a fantasy of social homogeneity, that is, a conception of society as essentially unified. This fantasy is metaphorically embodied in the notion of the People-as-One *and* in the image of the leader's body. Lefort's understanding of totalitarianism thus restricts the term to a specific usage: totalitarianism as an ideological project, a project concerning the realm of symbolic and cultural politics.[17] It does *not* aim at an exhaustive description of the nondiscursive reality of state socialism.[18] And it is certainly not an exhaustive description of this discursive reality *at all times.* The move away from a monocausal explanation also entails a more complex model of understanding the forty years of GDR history, one which comprehends the social as a psychically *and* socially organized formation.[19] Lefort allows us to understand totalitarian mass politics as a highly *modern* form of symbolic politics, relying on elaborate strategies to make the fantasy of the social cohere around the figure of the leader.

Similar issues — the question of the "two dictatorships," that is, of the comparability of the Nazi and SED regime, of conformity versus complicity, of the GDR's relationship to Western modernity — were at stake in the controversies about East German literature and culture that arose after 1989 and have accompanied the process of unification since then, representing one of the sites on which a new German identity is being negotiated. For, as one of the participants in the first, most strident debate averred: "He who determines what was, also determines what will be." [20] By now, the list of these cultural debates is rather formidable. Since they have been well documented, I shall limit myself to a brief overview.[21] In the summer of 1990, an initial controversy developed around the publication of Christa Wolf's *Was bleibt (What Remains and Other Stories).* Wolf's short text chronicles one day in the life of a female author living in East Berlin who becomes aware that she is being kept under surveillance by the Stasi, East Germany's secret police. This surveillance causes her to reflect on her writing, the role of self-censorship, and her desire for *another* language, one free of the official discourse. When Wolf published the text, she indicated that it had been written from June/July 1979 to November 1989.[22] It was this piece of information upon which critics seized, accusing her of trying to assume the role of victim. Calling Wolf the GDR's *Staatsdichterin* (state poet), Ulrich Greiner, writing in the weekly *Die Zeit,* argued that Wolf should have published the story in 1979.[23] In a later piece, Greiner elaborated on his revisionist reading of Wolf, arguing that what was at stake in the debate was her "joint responsibility for the second German catastrophe." [24] Others, such as the editor of the influential cultural journal *Merkur,* Karl-Heinz Bohrer, called Wolf's story *Gesinnungskitsch* (kitsch of conviction), arguing that with unification the time had finally come for postwar German literature to separate art from *Gesinnung,* aesthetics from political metaphysics.[25] For Bohrer, any aesthetic linked to a political project, or what he terms *Gesinnungs-ästhetik* (aesthetic of conviction), remains caught in premodern modes of thought. Similar arguments with respect to both Wolf and her West German colleagues from the so-called Group 47, such as Günther Grass and Heinrich Böll,[26] were made by Frank Schirrmacher, editor-in-chief of the literary supplement to the *Frankfurter Allgemeine Zeitung.*

In the fall of 1990, a brief debate flared up around the East German author Anna Seghers (1900–1983) and her role in the trial of Walter Janka, a veteran of the International Brigades in Spain, a member of the SED, and, at the time of his trial for sedition (1957), head of the prestigious publishing house Aufbau-Verlag.[27] In the fall of 1991 another "literary scandal" pulled Wolf and the so-called *Literaturstreit* (literary controversy) out of the cultural pages and onto the front page: in his acceptance speech for the prestigious Büchner-Preis, Wolf Biermann, the dissident East German *chansonnier* forced into exile in 1976, accused the poet Sascha Anderson of having worked for the Stasi as an unofficial informant even after he had left the GDR for West Berlin in 1986.[28] Anderson was part of the so-called Prenzlauer Berg scene, a group of young poets attempting to lead a subcultural existence outside of official East German cultural institutions.[29] What previously looked like a "clandestine" literary scene inspired by the writings of Foucault, Lacan, and Deleuze now suddenly appeared to be Stasi-supported: Anderson admitted, for instance, that he had received money from the Stasi for the "clandestine" journal *Schaden.*[30] While Anderson continued to deny any official affiliation with the Stasi, Rainer Schedlinski, another poet and theoretician of the Prenzlauer Berg scene, admitted his collaboration publicly.[31] By this time, public attention had come to be focused exclusively on the topic of the Stasi, and in January 1993 Christa Wolf publicized the fact that she had met several times with Stasi officers between 1959 and 1962.[32] And, in the fall of 1995, Monika Maron, an author who had left the GDR in the 1980s, was forced to admit that she had consented to routine conversations with members of the state security.[33] The most recent controversy concerned the refusal of the West German chapter of PEN to merge with its East German equivalent.[34]

In these cultural debates, a paradox emerged ever more clearly with each successive contribution: on the one hand, authors such as Wolf were reproached for not having been more politically engaged; on the other hand, they were accused of mixing politics and literature. Moreover, their critics

8

tended to focus increasingly on the issue of Stasi collaboration, treating such important issues as complicity and critique, modes of accommodation and dissent, in sensationalist terms.[35] Fritz J. Raddatz's response to the revelations about Wolf's and Müller's meetings with Stasi officers provides a good example of the impasse reached at this stage. Repeating the accusations of collaboration— "You turned yourselves into helpers in the construction of a system of persecution" —the former head of the *ZEIT* feuilleton exclaimed, rather melodramatically, "It seems to me that both of them [Wolf and Müller] harmed not only their biographies; they damaged their own work. They betrayed us." [36] Raddatz went on to equate the actions of the GDR's most prominent authors with Knut Hamsun's "betrayal" (his support for the Nazis) and reduced the complex question of aesthetics and politics to a somewhat facile pronouncement: "Every work of art [shelters] at its core a bit of innocence, a grain of purity." [37] Raddatz urged his readers to conclude that both the writers and their works had now lost this "innocence."

Following the lead of Bohrer and Schirrmacher, however, literary critics began to discuss the issue on a different level, recasting the question raised in the debate among historians—whether the GDR had ever attained the same degree of modernization as its Western counterpart—in aesthetic, or rather literary-historical, terms. This discussion was advanced most forcefully by the literary scholar Bernd Hüppauf. Just as Wolfgang J. Mommsen, a West German historian, argued that the GDR ultimately resulted from the infamous German *Sonderweg* (peculiarities), the long-term effects of which had produced a state less Westernized, less modern than the Federal Republic, Hüppauf defined East German literature as an example of "aesthetic nonsynchronicity" (*ästhetische Ungleichzeitigkeit*). This is a literature, Hüppauf argues, whose lack of wordplay, of negativity, and of destructiveness radically distinguished it from the literature of the West.[38] In Hüppauf's view, the GDR was a world "in which power continued to be exercised not through anonymous structures but in unmediated form, personally." To this "nineteenth-century" political universe corresponded, according to Hüppauf, a form of aesthetics also inherited from the nineteenth century, one which demanded the primacy of ethics and politics over "the aesthetic." Hüppauf argues that in the GDR premodern society and premodern aesthetics were thus inextricably linked. The campaigns which the SED's cultural functionaries continually waged against "formalism," designed to banish modernism from the East, were just so many attempts to preserve the hierarchical relationship between ethics and aesthetics. According to Hüppauf, these campaigns also represented a ritual defense against the "life forms of modern society." [39] While aware of the "broken" identification of most authors with the East German state, Hüppauf perceives them as tied into this nineteenth-century universe on multiple levels:

"Declarations of loyalty," "engagement," and "worldview" not only assured that writers were *morally* entangled in the system and behaved like members of an extended *family* (Biermann); they also produced an aesthetic "entanglement" in the politically determined system of this extended family. Literature's place was always already defined in advance, and its position vis-à-vis the *Übervater* determined the rules of the game. From the early formulations—Otto Grotewohl flattered the writers at the Second Writers' Congress with the statement that they were the "government's comrades-in-arms"—to the somewhat subtler formulations of later years, literature in the GDR had come a long way without ever having been able to abolish these rules. The authorities' positions remained intact and the patricide did not take place, not even in symbolic disguise. The revolt of the aesthetic never occurred.[40]

Hüppauf essentially refined Bohrer's story, the story of an "epochally outmoded civilization" and its "metaphysical" literature.[41] He did not hesitate to dismiss the GDR's entire literature as "anachronistic" and "eccentric," adding that this verdict was *especially* valid for the GDR's *critical* literature.[42] "The literature of the GDR never existed" would seem to be a fitting summary of Hüppauf's view.

A similar logic sustained Peter Geist's discussion of East German lyric poetry. Less radical than Hüppauf, Geist nevertheless dismisses all but the lyric poetry of the Prenzlauer Berg—again in the name of modernity. In 1991, Geist described the poetry of Papenfuss-Gorek, Anderson, Kolbe, and others as a "land of thought and language beyond authoritarian logics of surveillance," concluding: "They thus represent the only proper 'modernism' within GDR poetry." [43] Like Bohrer and Schirrmacher, Hüppauf and Geist participate in the wholesale dismissal of East German literature as the literary expression of a premodern society. By arguing for this dismissal from the perspective of Western modernism, they contribute to a particular postunification version of what Fredric Jameson has called the "ideology of modernism." [44] As in the debates over the nature of East Germany in the field of history, the nature of East German literature in the realm of literary criticism is defined in accordance with a teleological model of German modernity in which the GDR figures as the premodern society that has to be raised to the level of its fully modernized Western counterpart. The model—and the telos—of this narrative was, and is, Western capitalism and Western modernism. This postunification ideology of modernism is nothing new, even if its triumphalism is: throughout the entire Cold War period, a dichotomy prevailed between Lukácsian realism and Western modernism.[45] Its Cold War logic functioned like a mirror: what was valued on one side of the Iron Curtain was devalorized on the other; what counted as a "good," "realist," affirmative text in the GDR became a "bad" text outside the GDR, and vice versa.[46] This Cold War imaginary certainly did not allow for a differentiated reading of the texts produced *on the other side of the Iron Curtain,* its crude categories being all too often unable to account for the intricacies of a particular work.[47] This approach is especially unable to account for the *formal* intricacies of GDR literature, an inability which led in most cases and on both sides to a concentration on the novel's content and explicit political discourse, and to the often rather desperate effort to establish the text's "political message." [48] It would be easy to dismiss Hüppauf's story on the grounds that he, too, is unable to account for the complexities of individual literary works. We could even enlist Hüppauf himself in doing so, since he does concede the questionability of speaking of a monolithic GDR literature.[49] Moreover, his rejection of all politically engaged literature in the name of modernism is blatantly ideological.[50] But I hesitate to dismiss Hüppauf's argument for two reasons: First, his premise that, *in the case of GDR literature,* ethics and aesthetics are inseparable is important.[51] And, second, Hüppauf's narrative shares its categories and teleology with the most influential accounts of forty years of East German literature: Wolfgang Emmerich's seminal 1988 article "Gleichzeitigkeit" (Synchronicity), which conceptualizes GDR literature as a sequence leading from realism through modernism to postmodernism, and Genia Schulz's critical, feminist appropriation of this account.[52] Both accounts cast the problematic aspects of the realism/modernism dichotomy into even stronger relief.

Emmerich divides East German literature into three distinct periods: that of 1950s socialist realism, which he terms "premodern" literature; that of "modernism," starting in the early 1960s and reaching its apogee in the mid-1970s; and, finally, that of postmodern literature, represented by the poets of the Prenzlauer Berg. Emmerich's story is basically one of convergence theory in literary guise, informed by Adorno and Horkheimer's *Dialectics of Enlightenment.* For Emmerich traces the East German authors' increasing awareness of the destructive potential of instrumental rationality—an awareness, Emmerich believes, that they share with their colleagues in the West.[53]

Emmerich characterizes the first period as one in which the GDR was still a "premodern land, whose life–world is much less thoroughly rationalized than ours," and he defines its literature (the novels of Willi Bredel and Anna Seghers, Eduard Claudius and Marianne Langer; the plays of Friedrich Wolf and Helmut Baierl) as follows: "Almost without exception, the narration is characterized by the authors' belief in progress; they narrate optimistically, all-around positively with the help of conventional, formerly realistic models." [54] In this description, Emmerich is operating with the opposition between closed and open forms, equating them with "premodern" and "modernist" modes of writing, respectively. Sometime between 1963 and 1965, Emmerich maintains, a qualitative change occurred: with the industrial modernization of the GDR, a new literature emerged, one which borrowed its forms from classical modernism and which began to question the modernization process, without, however, abandoning the utopia of a nonalienated society. The text singled out by Emmerich—and by the majority of critics after him—as instantiating the emergence of modernism in the East was Christa Wolf's 1968 *Nachdenken über Christa T.* (*The Quest for Christa T.*). Emmerich thus makes literature's relation to the utopia of (a different) socialism the cornerstone of his periodization, arguing that with the literature of the 1960s the relation to utopia becomes self-reflective, while the fiction and poetry of the Prenzlauer Berg finally abandoned this utopia entirely.

Emmerich's narrative is sustained by a single, yet twofold, teleology: the move from "premodernism" to postmodernism was accompanied by an increasing gap between official ideology and literature, a process that would eventually result in the complete separation of the "best" authors/texts from the GDR's official discourse. At this point, Emmerich clearly privileges the literature of the late 1970s and early 1980s, reading these works as self-conscious reflections on the dialectic of enlightenment, painfully aware of the "collapse of enlightenment modernism" but nevertheless clinging to what he, along with Wolf, calls a "remainder of utopia." [55] It is this particular body of literature which, in his eyes, meets the standards of High Modernism.[56] Emmerich then conceptualizes forty years of East German literature as a moment of "modernism," whose critical potential emerged in the early 1960s and peaked in the late 1970s and early 1980s. This modernist moment is wedged in, on one side, by a negligible period of "pre-modernism" and, on the other, by a more ambivalently theorized period of postmodernism.

Emmerich's reading of GDR literature and literary-historical categories he constructed broke new ground and paved the way for further research. In the late 1980s, several feminist scholars started to rethink the realism/modernism dichotomy in terms of the emergence of an East German *feminist modernism.* Genia Schulz, for instance, argued that the "disputes with the aesthetic norms of reflection-realism" and the concomitant "emergence of deviant, de-ranged modes of writing" represented the rise of a new form of "feminine writing." [57] Looking back at East Germany's "women's literature" in 1990, Dorothea Böck reaffirmed this reading, arguing that from the 1960s on, literature's "detachment" from the directives of GDR cultural politics, from the prescribed lines of tradition and heritage, *and* from the officially sanctioned topics and genres was intricately linked to a critique of the dominant patriarchal structures and thought patterns.[58] Myra Love, among others, suggested abandoning the realism/modernism dichotomy altogether in favor of a model of "feminine writing" fundamentally different from either category.[59] Despite these attempts to retheorize this founding divide between realism and modernism, the predominant view of East German literature—other than its wholesale dismissal—remains that of the slow emergence of a (feminist) modernism.[60]

This feminist story shares several fundamental elements with Emmerich's account: first, the privileging of modernism and the concomitant investment in the period from the 1960s to the mid-1980s as the Golden Age of East German literature; second, the focus on one specific author, Christa Wolf, and her work as successively marking the important turning points of this literary–historical narrative; third, the overt rejection or simple neglect of the GDR's early literature, the "dark" (and embarrassing) age of socialist realism; and, fourth, the underlying teleology: whereas Emmerich saw the emancipation of the author's voice from the GDR's official political and aesthetic discourse in the increasing mastery of modernist techniques and growing awareness of the dialectic of enlightenment, these feminist critics anticipated and proclaimed a liberation from the official patriarchal ideology in the emergence of a feminist consciousness and its autonomous feminine aesthetic. The core notion of *both* stories is modernism's "authentic voice," a voice that succeeded in establishing a critical distance from the GDR's dominant ideology. And in both accounts, this voice is derived from

Christa Wolf's concept of "subjective authenticity," theorized in the late 1960s. With this notion, Wolf postulated the "truth" of the author's *subjective experience* against the objective knowledge of (socialist) realism's third-person narrator, making the author's/narrator's "presence" in his/her writing the precondition of what she called "modern prose." [61]

A more recent attempt at a synthetic cultural history of the GDR has once again reconfirmed this literary–historical paradigm. The chapter treating the GDR in *German Cultural Studies: An Introduction* firmly locates the story of East German literature in a teleology of convergence: the stark differences between the cultures of East and West Germany gradually faded, the authors assert, as both literatures became more concerned with questions of women's emancipation, peace, and ecology. Again, this convergence, and its obvious redemptive role, is celebrated as the result of a long-term process, the modernization of East German literature. Modernism's corrosive effect, the authors argue, forced the SED to "admit" that its rejection of modernism as Western "decadence" was "ill-advised": "A major factor in this volte-face was undoubtedly the fact that, from the late 1960s, the GDR's leading writers simply began to learn from and use the literary strategies of modernism." The ensuing period is one in which a genuine "cultural identity" materialized. This golden age, with its "distinctive GDR culture," no longer suffers from the lack that characterized the earlier era, namely, the "authentic narrative voice of female authors." [62]

In 1991 Emmerich revised his assessment of what he had theorized as the *critical modernism* of the 1960s. He now calls this literature East Germany's *Sinngebungsliteratur*— "the beautiful era of utopian models from the 1960s and 1970s." [63] Emmerich's new reading culminates in the following thesis:

The ever-increasing stagnation and deformation of "actual socialism" (and the recognition of its criminal prehistory in Stalinism) did not induce the majority of writers to renounce socialism *tout court*. They remained . . . partially trapped in the dominant discourse and its rules, paradoxically even when they extensively negated it. . . . Only a few of those born before 1930 were able to accomplish a genuine withdrawal from this value system. But even the authors of Volker Braun's generation, ten years younger . . . only took this step in a few cases. . . . No, the authors of both generations followed a different path. Although they knew that their God no longer existed, they retained the "epochal illusion" of "true socialism" by enclosing its image in the shrine of utopia, that is, what nowhere exists but still should be. . . . This insulation of utopia, precisely, allowed it to shine ever more brilliantly as a promise, while at the same time removing it further and further from real problems and relationships. It became more than ever a metanarrative . . . with hidden repressive and totalitarian traits.[64]

Here, the literary products of the GDR's Golden Age of Modernism thus turn into the Golden Cage of Utopia or, more appropriately, the Iron Cage. Suddenly, modernism loses its critical potential. Emmerich still emphasizes the growing distance of the East German authors' texts from the S E D's official political and aesthetic discourse. And he also emphasizes that this distance expressed itself in an aesthetic counter-discourse, in modes of writing that met the "standards of modern prose." [65] But his guiding question has changed: Emmerich is now concerned with explaining why the East German authors "tied themselves to the system of actual 'real socialism' " and its "antifascist-socialist state program" *despite* their critical distance.

Emmerich's essay is the result of a shock, one that he was not the only critic to register. Having read the texts of Christa Wolf—and Heiner Müller, Stephan Heym, Volker Braun, Helga Königsdorf, and Christoph Hein—as testimony to a gradual "emancipation" from East Germany's dominant ideology, many Western critics were stunned when suddenly confronted with the statements and actions of these authors in the fall of 1989, with their support for a "third way," a "democratic," "socialist," and "antifascist" alternative to the Federal Republic,[66] and other signs of an attachment to the East German project that went far beyond Western constructions of these exemplary "critical modernists." The same shock was felt by those who had read Christa Wolf as *Germany's* foremost feminist author—one who had made the slow but definitive progression *from Marxism to Feminism.*[67] Surprised by Wolf's strong attachment to the GDR's socialist project and her commitment to a reformed East Germany, many critics were forced to rethink their own investment in the utopian promise of an imagined East German feminist modernism.

What conclusions can be drawn from these debates? Surely, we cannot be satisfied with the widespread move to discard previously canonized East German authors in favor of a newly discovered "genuine" (feminist) modernist, whether a Uwe Johnson or Irmtraud Morgner.[68] Instead, I propose that we abandon several traditional assumptions about GDR literature. First and foremost, we must move beyond the ahistorical realism/modernism dichotomy. Even socialist realism, if there is such a thing, is part of twentieth-century modernism.[69] All the critical narratives discussed above, from Hüppauf to Emmerich to Schulz, demonstrate the problems involved in imposing a specific literary-historical paradigm on the GDR's cultural land-scape, either by compressing the transition from nineteenth-century realism to twentieth-century modernism into forty years of East German culture or by topographically dividing it into Eastern realism and Western mod-ernism. Let me first point out several inconsistencies with respect to the formal aspects of this paradigm: Hüppauf, for example, is forced to include works which employ techniques conventionally defined as modernist in his category of East German pre- or nonmodernism. The close reading of any socialist realist classic would have to acknowledge its formal "modernism." For instance, the montagelike structure of Anna Seghers's 1949 historical novel *Die Toten bleiben jung* (*The Dead Stay Young*) is clearly modeled on Dos Passos's *Manhattan Transfer*.[70] The rigorous, almost rigid metaphorical structure of Christa Wolf's early (1963) novel *Der geteilte Himmel* (*The Di-vided Heaven*) clearly owes as much to Russian Constructivism as it does to any nineteenth-century model.[71] Nor is the "content" side of this argument any less problematic. It is imperative to resist all interpretive stances that read these authors' political consciousness in their literary fiction (or their essays on aesthetics, their poetics, or simply their political statements) and then respond by agreeing or disagreeing with their politics.

A rethinking of GDR culture that hopes to contribute to an understand-ing of the vitally important issue of critique versus complicity, which arose in 1989, should strive to determine the specificity of this literature, should attempt to historicize it thoroughly.[72] To do so would mean working against the grain of two teleologies. The first is the idea of a self-emancipating voice associated with some "Westernized" form of modernism. As we have seen, this imaginary trajectory has been halted once and for all by the events of 1989. Second, this rethinking must problematize the privileging of a golden age associated with the trajectory from realism to modernism. Hüppauf does both, yet at the price of simplification and reduction: the literary pro-duction of forty years becomes a "premodern" monolith, and what we learn beyond that is something we already know: that most of East Germany's prominent authors were both "inside" and "outside," that is, socialists who were critical of the SED's politics. To find an answer to the question raised by the events of 1989 (not for the first time, of course, but certainly with more urgency)—why the GDR authors "tied themselves to the system"—it is necessary to move from the level of conscious political philosophy to that of *unconscious fantasy.* This is, after all, the other level on which ideology works. I propose to start with a basic question: What was the GDR's dominant official discourse? For I do not believe that the answer to this question is as self-evident as the scholarly literature tends to assume.

The most powerful ideological discourse in the GDR was that of antifascism. This certainly is and was common knowledge among those working in the field of GDR studies. The various statements made by authors and oppositional politicians after 1989 have merely reconfirmed that knowledge. What we do *not* know is how that discourse was "made," what its precise contours were, its central images, its stories. The specificity of GDR literature cannot be assessed in comparison with "Western" modernism, or what some critics tend to think of as the "most advanced" aesthetic positions. It lies elsewhere — in this literature's particular implication in and contribution to the GDR's dominant discourse, that of antifascism, in the conscious and unconscious fantasies it developed in its engagement with this discourse. Further, a truly historical account of East German literature cannot afford to exclude the early period, since this is the period of East Germany's *foundational narratives of antifascism.*[73] It is from this perspective that I will approach the author most thoroughly implicated in the writing of this discourse, Christa Wolf.

This book is organized in three parts, each of which covers a specific historical period. In Part I, I analyze the ways in which a particular group of novels written between the early 1930s and the late 1950s contributed to this hegemonic project: Willi Bredel's trilogy (1941–53), *Verwandte und Bekannte* (Relatives and Acquaintances), Anna Seghers's *Die Toten bleiben jung/The Dead Stay Young* (1949), and Otto Gotsche's 1959 *Die Fahne von Kriwoj Rog* (The Flag from Kriwoj Rog). These were novels by Communist authors who were either in exile during the Nazi period or active in the German resistance movement. The first two volumes of Bredel's trilogy, *Die Väter* (The Fathers) and *Die Söhne* (The Sons), as well as Seghers's novel, were written in exile, revised upon the authors' return to Germany, and published first in the Soviet Occupied Zone, then, after 1949, in the GDR. The third volume of Bredel's trilogy, *Die Enkel* (The Grandsons), was written in East Germany, as was Gotsche's novel. What these texts have in common is the following: structured as family sagas, they each narrate the "pre-history" of the German Democratic Republic by focusing on a single working-class family. Moreover, they center on the father and set up an unbroken male lineage of Communist fathers and sons.[74] In this respect, they represent an integral part of the Communists' symbolic politics of power.[75] These novels are foundational narratives in a double sense: first, they were consecrated by the SED and its cultural functionaries; and, second, they were promoted with the goal of providing a framework within which to think not only the new order's past but also its present. Neither of these goals was sufficiently appreciated by Eastern or Western critics. Indeed, this literature was far more influential than these critics have allowed.

The second set of novels, written in the early 1960s by a younger generation of GDR authors such as Brigitte Reimann and Dieter Noll, were canonized in East Germany as a new GDR-specific genre, the so-called *Ankunftsroman,* or novel of arrival. The designation derives from the title of Reimann's 1961 novel *Ankunft im Alltag* (Arrival in Everyday Life), which narrates the "arrival" of its three young protagonists in the world of "real existing socialism." This literature has generally been discussed with respect to its immediate context, the beginning of the GDR's socialist era, which Walter Ulbricht, then president of the GDR, announced in 1952. However, I will argue that these novels also participate in the discourse of antifascism, since their protagonists are positioned as sons and daughters vis-à-vis the idealized parental figures of the antifascist family narratives.

Part 3 focuses on Christa Wolf, concentrating first on her earliest texts, *Moskauer Novelle* (1961) and *Der geteilte Himmel/The Divided Heaven* (1963), and tracing the ways in which they contribute to the paternal narrative of antifascism. I then turn to *Kindheitsmuster/Patterns of Childhood* (1976) and *Kassandra/Cassandra* (1983), showing how they can be read as self-conscious reflections upon this antifascist narrative, in which Wolf is the most centrally implicated East German author. In her literary texts that focus on the figure of the daughter, Wolf both accepts the antifascist narrative as her framework and contributes to its elaboration. I will show that this author, celebrated for having broken most radically with socialist realism, paradoxically continued to write its main story and that, indeed, the very formal innovation taken to signal this break—her concept of subjective authenticity—originated in that story.

When I say that I want to trace this discourse of legitimation in a number of literary works, it may sound as if I am primarily interested in tracing the development of a political theme in a particular narrative form, the family narrative. This is certainly not the case. Nor am I interested in whether the texts' more or less explicit level of political discourse is critical of "real existing socialism." [76] As I argued above, this approach, which reduces complex literary texts—and even the "cultural corpses" [77] of East German socialist realism are literary texts, after all—to their political "message," has informed the field of GDR studies for too long. My approach to this literature combines a critical reading of its explicit political discourse (much like traditional ideology critique) with a psychoanalytic reading. I am interested in these texts because they narrate the—conscious and unconscious—fantasies involved in an ideological formation based on the family. They are *ideological fantasies:* texts that narrate the work of the unconscious and its fantasies in ideology. This study thus represents a contribution to the conceptualization of ideology as a bridge between the level of the social and the level of the individual, between history and the psyche.[78] Ideology cannot be reduced to a (more or less coherent) system of ideas. For any hegemonic formation to be even partially successful—and the East German discourse of antifascism did "work," at least for a "morally inclined minority"—it has to "work at the most rudimentary levels of psychic identity and the drives." [79] Any nonreductionist form of ideology critique thus needs to investigate the psychic force of ideological processes, the work of fantasy in ideology. Indeed, if we do not take into account what Freud termed "psychical reality," the core of which is constituted by unconscious wishes and their fantasies,[80] we not only fall into the trap of a positivist conception of reality, but, more importantly, we will continue to think the unmediated dichotomy of public and private, social-political and psychic, life and will remain unable to account for the transactions between the two. It is in the "area" of the unconscious that these transactions take place, and they concern, above all, the operations of fantasy.[81] In the case of a literature concerned with the theme of the family, a psychoanalytic reading is particularly imperative.

In both the exile literature and the later literature, these unconscious fantasies revolve around an identification with the father's body. Or, to recall Lefort's analysis of the totalitarian project, it is around the leader's body that the social is made to cohere. Employing a concept from Slavoj Žižek, I will call this body the *sublime body* of the Communist hero of antifascism.[82] The Oedipal narratives underlying the novel of arrival construct not only new parents but also new bodies. The identification with the father's body results in the fantasy of the *post-fascist body:* in these novels, sexuality is defined as that part of subjectivity which links the subject to its fascist past, and the new subject comes about as a result of the erasure of its material body, its sexual body.[83] Wolf is the writer who links this fantasy of the "pure" post-fascist body to another fantasy of purity—the "pure" *post-fascist voice.*

This connection determines the narrative voice and, ultimately, Wolf's concept of subjective authenticity, a speaking position developed in relation to the maternal one adopted by Anna Seghers after 1945. The psychoanalytic perspective also informs my approach to the texts' formal level, since I read them *symptomatically,* that is, with a view to their formal incoherencies and sudden failures, which relate to unresolved and often unresolvable contradictions. This project thus integrates three critical perspectives: (1) an analysis of political-historical discourse; (2) an exploration of the textual levels that deal with psychic structures and unconscious fantasies; and (3) a formal analysis, in particular of narrative voice. This approach uncovers an ideological inscription of the psychic that a reading confined to the level of political discourse is bound to miss. By linking the reading of unconscious fantasies to a specific discourse on history, it historicizes psychoanalysis. This approach demonstrates the inexorably historical character of these fantasies, their links to both the subject's private history and to the history of his/her country (a merely heuristic distinction, since as this book will demonstrate, it ultimately proves untenable).

This study thus argues against the grain of much recent GDR criticism, which, as I outlined above, celebrates the 1970s and 1980s as the Golden Age of GDR Literature, with Christa Wolf celebrated as its central representative— "golden" because these years are seen as the period during which East German authors increasingly "liberated" themselves thematically and formally from the official literary-aesthetic system. This construction, as we have seen, remained very much in place even after the Literaturstreit.[84] Let me reiterate my critique of this implicitly teleological view of East German literature with an eye to the specific novels I analyze here. First, the privileging of the later literature led to a dismissal of the earlier literature. At best, Western critics have treated these family narratives as Communist historiography in epic form, of interest only to scholars concerned with the immediate postwar period.[85] Similarly, the novel of arrival has been seen as nothing but a "necessary aberration" on the path to the GDR's more "acceptable" (i.e., critical) literature. This view misunderstands not only the importance of this foundational literature but also its very nature. More significantly, this teleological paradigm deprives itself of the means to adequately understand the literature of the later period which it privileges: as I shall argue in the case of Wolf, the conception of a "voice" that gradually frees itself from the official discourse is untenable. There is no one pure voice—indeed, the concept itself is a fantasy—but that does not make Wolf's work any less compelling. And this genealogy of voice does not deny the significance of the "event" *Christa T.* — it simply retheorizes it.

Although this study covers a period ranging from the immediate postwar years to the early 1980s, I have selected a limited number of texts for analysis because understanding how ideology works in these texts *on the level of fantasy* requires extremely close, detailed readings. I have thus opted for a series of exemplary readings of representative texts — representative in the sense that they were canonized either by SED cultural functionaries or by Western critics. This book is a contribution to a cultural history of the GDR, one that also elucidates and debates central issues in psychoanalytic feminism. It deals with the role of literature in the symbolic reconstruction of power in East Germany, and it proposes new ways of approaching what Emmerich calls *Selbstbindung* by rethinking the notion of an "oppositional" voice from a psychoanalytic perspective.[86] This approach forces us to abandon the neat divisions between *affirmative realism,* on the one hand, and *critical modernism,* on the other; between a space *inside* ideology and a space *outside* of it; between *critical* and *conformist* authors, *critical* and *conformist* texts. Focusing on the most celebrated — and recently the most criticized — author of the golden age, it instead lays bare an immensely complex, conflicted, and, ultimately, alienated insertion into the GDR's family narrative.

I

In the Name of the Father:

East Germany's Foundational

Narratives

Ideology, in so far as it seeks to sustain relations of domination by representing them as "legitimate," tends to assume a narrative form. Stories are told which justify the exercise of power by those who possess it, situating these individuals within a tissue of tales that recapitulate the past and anticipate the future. — John B. Thompson, *Studies in the Theory of Ideology* (1984)

1

Specters of Stalin, or Constructing Communist Fathers

East Germany's Totalitarian Project and the Antifascist Hero

Returning from their Moscow exile immediately after May 8, 1945, the members of the German Communist Party (KPD) conceived of their project, the reconstruction of Germany, on two levels: they intended to rebuild the country on the level of political structure, but, more importantly, they also wanted to construct a new ideological order. This construction is best understood in Gramscian terms as an attempt to establish hegemony, that is, as an order in which "a common social-moral language is spoken, in which one concept of reality is dominant, informing with its spirit all modes of thought and behavior." [1] Advocating an *antifascist-democratic order,* which should later prove to be only a transitional phase toward a centralized Communist state, the "Ulbricht group" took advantage of the postwar power vacuum to establish, with the help of the Red Army, structural conditions favoring their own model of reconstruction.[2] Yet their politics also aimed to secure the active consent of the population with respect to the new society's "central zone," the "center of the order of symbols, values and beliefs," which defines any society's core structures of authority.[3] In these early stages of the GDR's political formation, I would contend, the Communist Party and its leading cultural functionaries constructed this central zone by deploying a *symbolic politics of paternity,* a cultural discourse revolving around the antifascist father. The GDR's foundational narratives were an integral part of this project.

History as Family Narrative

Between 1946 and 1959, two of the GDR's most prestigious publishing houses, Aufbau-Verlag and Mitteldeutscher Verlag, published a series of novels on recent German history: Anna Seghers's *Die Toten bleiben jung/ The Dead Stay Young*; Hans Marchwitza's trilogy *Die Kumiaks, Die Heim-kehr der Kumiaks,* and *Die Kumiaks und ihre Kinder* (The Kumiaks, The Return of the Kumiaks, and The Kumiaks and their Children); Willi Bredel's trilogy *Verwandte und Bekannte* (Relatives and Acquaintances), *Die Väter* (The Fathers), *Die Söhne* (The Sons), and *Die Enkel* (The Grandsons); and, finally, Otto Gotsche's *Die Fahne von Kriwoj Rog* (The Flag from Kriwoj Rog).[4]

Bredel's trilogy tells the story of a German working-class family from 1871 to 1948, that is, from the defeat of the "first workers' state," the Paris Commune, to the beginnings of the German Arbeiter- und Bauern-staat (workers' and peasants' state). The first volume was serialized in the Soviet Occupied Zone's first newspapers as early as 1946,[5] thus appearing in the context of the unification of the KPD (Communist Party) with the SPD (Social Democratic Party) in April 1946. *Die Väter's* focus on the Social Democratic "origins" of the family was clearly meant to help this process by remembering the "revolutionary" traditions of the old Social Democracy as well as its "reformist" errors.[6] There were fifteen editions of *Die Väter* between 1946 and 1961, with another ten after 1962, which makes it one of the most widely distributed East German novels.[7] In addition, the book figured prominently among the required readings of the GDR school system: "Better books should be part of the curriculum, not just 'Die Väter' by Bredel, over and over," complains one of the women in Maxie Wander's famous collection of East German interviews from the late 1970s.[8] Cultural functionaries and literary critics did not even hesitate to compare Bredel to Goethe and Thomas Mann: in 1963 Alexander Abusch called Bredel's work the proletariat's answer to *Buddenbrooks,* and in 1954 Annemarie Auer elevated it to "a great cultural deed." [9]

Marchwitza's *Kumiaks* trilogy, the first volume of which was published in 1934, narrates the history of a miner's family in the Ruhr area. Like Bredel and Seghers, Marchwitza articulates his family saga with a specific histori-cal narrative in mind: the progression from the working-class defeat be-tween 1918 and 1922—the years of the November revolution and the "Ruhr battles"—to the Red Army's victory in 1945. In 1948, *Neues Deutschland,* the SED newspaper, announced the reedition of the first volume, casting Marchwitza as one of Germany's "genuine" working-class authors.[10] Similarly, Gotsche figures in the GDR's national literary histories as the incarnation of the dutiful Party cadre turned working-class author.[11] Unlike Bredel and Marchwitza, Gotsche never emigrated. A parliamentary representative of the KPD in Hamburg, he was, like many other Communists, arrested in early 1933 and detained in a concentration camp until the following September. After his release, he returned to the Mansfeld region where he helped build the "Antifascist Workers' Group of Central Germany." His two best-known novels, *Von Nachts bis Morgens* (From Night until Morning) and *Die Fahne von Kriwoj Rog,* are allegedly based on these historical episodes.[12] The latter presents the life of a supposedly typical family in the mining area of Mansfeld between the tumultuous early years of the Weimar Republic and the arrival of the Red Army in the fictional town of Gerbstedt in 1945. The novel's main character is based on Otto Brosowski, one of the leading members of the antifascist group, according to Gotsche.[13] Commissioned in 1957 to celebrate the fortieth anniversary of the Bolshevik Revolution, *Die Fahne* was carefully prepared for publication by the literary journal *Neue Deutsche Literatur,* in which excerpts from the novel's central passages appeared in 1959, with an introduction by Christa Wolf, then one of the journal's editors.[14] A film adaptation of the novel, directed by Kurt Maetzig, was also released that year.[15] Films based on Bredel's novels and on Seghers's *Die Toten bleiben jung* were also made in the GDR.[16]

The Empty Locus of Power

These founding paternal narratives became a crucial component of the Communists' state-driven project of hegemonic formation.[17] But why did this cultural project cohere around the figure of the antifascist hero? The new social order that emerged in the GDR soon after the unification of the Social Democratic and Communist Parties in April 1946 was founded upon the notion of the "People-as-One," [18] on a conception of society as essentially homogeneous and unified. In the East German case, the SED sought to base this unity on a consensus among all antifascists, a move that relegated egalitarian visions of a just society to a subordinated position. This ideological foundation, which categorically denies that division, conflict, and antagonism are constitutive of society, is characteristic of any totalitarian project, according to Claude Lefort. It is a totalitarian *project* in the sense that any study of totalitarianism must distinguish the ideal project and its representations from its actual, historically contingent developments. The totalitarian project itself, like any other political project, is never fully realized; there are only more or less successfully constructed variants of it.[19] These historically specific and contingent variants are necessarily unstable and in constant need of restabilization because they rest upon denied and repressed antagonisms. Among other things, this stability is achieved by the specific ways in which post-democratic totalitarian societies represent the center. Before the "democratic revolution," that *process* set in motion by the French Revolution, the king's body represented the identity and the unity of the ancien régime.[20] This representation was in turn founded on the image of society itself as body, a structured and hierarchical organization of different parts into an organic whole. In this Aristotelian imagery, which was first elaborated in medieval political theology, the king's body, modeled on the body of Christ, was both mortal and immortal, organic and mystical, symbolizing at once a sacred kingdom and a national community.[21] Under the ancien régime, the king's body continued to incarnate the kingdom, understood as both organic and mystical. The identity of the body politic disappeared in the process of the democratic revolution, however, with two main consequences: first, *power is no longer linked to a body,* so it now appears to be *"an empty place"*; second, along with the king's body the representation of a center and of the contours of society disappears as well. The decapitation of the king destroyed not only the body of power but the "corporeality of the social." Modern democratic societies are characterized by the experience of society as "historical," in constant flux—and as marked by social divisions, not homogeneity. With post-democratic totalitarianism, we see the reemergence of an attempt to revitalize the body's *symbolic* function and to *re-present the center.*[22]

If ever a locus of power was empty, it was certainly so in postwar Germany following the collapse of National Socialism and its political imaginary, organized around Hitler's body.[23] In the immediate postwar period, German Communists reacted to this situation by shifting their focus from Germany's present to its past, from the political register to the register of the family, making the family model the privileged model of Communist politics. The particular "symbolic forms" [24] of this hegemonic project, and their specific ways of marking the center as center, raise several questions: First, why this move to the past? Second, why the focus on the father's body? And third, why the use of a specific plot, the family narrative? There are several reasons for the focus on the past. One possible solution, the creation of a hegemonic project based on a popular narrative of Communist nationalism, where the people are represented by the Party—a project precariously realized in other Eastern European countries—was unthinkable in the German context, where the people's body was "polluted" by National Socialism and therefore could not serve as a basis for a national narrative of popular resistance. The alternative, a solution which would encourage diversity and even conflict while leaving the center of power empty (i.e., Lefort's democratic model), was also out of the question. Despite the democratic rhetoric of the antifascist-democratic (re)construction, especially once Cold War politics took hold, this was clearly not what Ulbricht's "Moscow Group" had in mind. But the East German totalitarian project faced yet another unique problem: given that the real center of power was located in Moscow, its symbolic locus could never be unambiguously filled in Germany. Stalin, the leader who embodied this authorizing center, was absent, as was made more than obvious by a rather peculiar ritual developed in the 1950s in the GDR: at all Party meetings, Stalin was voted honorary chair and a seat left empty in his honor. A similar staging is described in detail in an article from 1950 recounting the celebration of Stalin's seventieth birthday in an East German kindergarten:

Soon the great day had arrived. The most beautiful flowers had been placed on the tables. At the head of the table sat Stalin, his picture adorned with flowers and his place framed by seven large white candles. . . . As always on the occasion of our birthday parties we also sang to Stalin. . . . Two children held Stalin's picture in the middle of the circle, and raised it up at the end.[25]

This rather spectral presence left its trace in the many odes to Stalin written by such central political figures as the GDR's first cultural minister, Johannes R. Becher,[26] and culminated in the 1953 issue of *Neue deutsche Literatur* devoted to Stalin's death. Anna Seghers contributed an obituary to this issue, "Das Unsterbliche der Völker war in ihm verkörpert" (The Immortal Soul of the People Was Embodied in Him), which unintentionally expressed the GDR's condition after 1945—the absent presence of the leader/father: "Have you ever been in a family that was suddenly struck by the greatest misfortune? . . . The family's center, its provider, its support is no longer there—he who never failed, who always knew what to do." [27] Years, even decades later, the Soviet leader's mythical status still looms large in the titles of articles trying to come to grips with the GDR's Stalinist past, such as Stephan Heym's "Stalin verlässt den Raum" (Stalin Leaves the Room), or Christoph Hein's "I Saw Stalin Once."[28] Recent studies of the political rituals of the SED only further underscore this continually displaced character of East German politics. Thus, for instance, Dieter Segert describes the SED's May Day celebrations as an event during which the "Ur-stage" of this political culture, the tribune of the Lenin Mausoleum in Moscow, always maintained a ghostly presence.[29]

Yet the SED's turn toward the past was not only motivated by the precarious dependence of its state power on an occupying army; it also had its roots in the KPD/SED strategy of legitimating its rule through its (supposedly leading) role in the antifascist resistance, without, however, disputing the primacy of the Red Army's victory: the legitimatory discourse of antifascism revolved around a core ideologeme, the idea that the Party, its state, and, later, its people were on the side of the "victors" in the battle of history, that they were the *victors of history*.[30] Thus, the Communists attempted to fill the empty center with founding stories about the German past using a narrative structure centered on the antifascist father. From this perspective, the contribution of the monumental historical epics by the former BPRS authors to the SED's hegemonic efforts becomes obvious: First, the novels fixed a specific reading of the German past that privileged the Communist Party's role and its historiography, thus identifying (East) German history with that of the Communist movement.[31] Second, by virtue of their focus on the past, the novels inevitably touch upon what Bernhard Greiner has called the "double claim of break and continuity."[32] On the one hand, the SED asserted that this new society had completely broken with the old structures; on the other hand, the Party claimed continuity with its own heroized antifascist past. Within the specific structural framework of the family narrative, these novels depict the resistance against Hitler's regime as the politically overdetermined legacy bequeathed by (Communist) fathers to (Communist) sons. Even before 1945, this "solution" was envisioned by authors such as Georg Lukács. In his 1944 essay "Schicksalswende" (Turn of Fate), on the condition of Germany, Lukács stated that the deeds of the "fathers" (i.e., the Nazis) created objective preconditions for the decisions of the "sons." However, he continued, the sons might also have to make decisions which would radically break with the fathers.[33] Constituting the center of authority in this particular way sharply distinguishes the GDR and its early literature from postrevolutionary Soviet culture, since Soviet texts from this period "erase" the father, thus participating in a social imaginary that depicts the 1917 revolution as a radical break with the past and this figure in which its traditions were incorporated. Thus in *The Mother,* Gorky's 1908 novel that gradually became a socialist realist classic, the father dies at the very beginning, and the plot focuses on mother and son. And Mayakovsky's poem "Toi storone" (For this Side) is literally an incendiary fantasy:

The father
let's exchange him for some old things
we
will pour kerosene over him
and let him out on the street
for illumination.[34]

Mayakovsky's dramatic gesture, positing the beginning of a new era not only as an unconditional break with the "fathers" but as patricide itself, is echoed in Lukács's statements quoted above. But in the context of postwar East Germany, this revolutionary gesture was not the dominant cultural signifier. Instead, the SED's legitimatory discourse of antifascism advocated severing all ties with "fascist" fathers, but, for the sake of its new paternal order, foregrounded the unbreakable bond with the fathers of "antifascism." [35] Again, this difference was rooted in the specific German context of a socialist state project supported by a conquering state *after* National Socialism, with all the attendant pressures on the Party to legitimate its "leading role" not only for Germany's population but also for its occupying power: only the foregrounding of "another" Germany *in the past* could serve that role.[36]

However, during the 1930s, narratives similar to the German family novels appeared in both Soviet political discourse and novels:

Soviet society's leaders became "fathers" (with Stalin as the patriarch); the national heroes, model "sons"; the state, a "family." . . . The new root metaphor for society provided the state with a single set of symbols for enhancing its increasingly hierarchical structure by endowing it with a spurious organicity. The metaphor also served the needs of the Stalin faction in its "struggles": it provided formulas for a symbolic legitimization of the actual leadership (the succession of generations in the "family" stands in for the succession of political leaders and for Stalin's accession to power after Lenin's death in particular), for the way forward (through the evolution of ever greater sons), and for the unquestioning loyalty of citizens (blood is thicker than water).[37]

The GDR's foundational narratives differ from these narratives of the "Great Family" in that they literalize the metaphor: the father *is* the leader. As we shall see later, this collapsing of leader/mentor with father has a strong decentering effect on the structure of these narratives. Like the East German narratives, the Soviet novels stage the father and his *sublime body*. The Kantian notion of the sublime surfaced as a central category in the discussion of socialist realism after 1945, specifically, the need to subordinate the sublime itself to "the sublime goal of communism." [38] Celebrated as the category that would allow a "fusion of the sublime and the everyday . . . the 'ideal' and the 'real'," the sublime in Soviet aesthetics came to designate, above all, the "image of unlimited power." Thus, in 1950, the Soviet critic G. Nedoshivin declared in "On the Problem of the Beautiful in Soviet Art": "Amidst all the beautiful material of life, the first place should be occupied by images of our great leaders. . . . The sublime beauty of the leaders . . . is the basis for the coinciding of the 'beautiful' and the 'true' in the art of socialist realism." [39] Drawing on this specific context, on Lefort's writings on the body of the totalitarian leader, and, finally, on an associative, yet not accidental, link to the Freudian notion of sublimation, Slavoj Žižek theorizes this *sublime body* as the *Communist leader's "split" body,* a body divided into a sublime part, linked to a transcendent truth, and its mere material, which needs to be constantly steeled.[40]

The Father's/Communist's Body: "People of a Special Mold"

East Germany's fictions of the father obey a rather curious logic: these texts tend to freeze the narrative in statuesque displays of the male body. In this section, I shall trace the ways in which these novels *engender* (in both senses of the word) the *sublime Communist body* as the incarnation of the Party and its order and as the representation of the father's/leader's connection to his historical mission, to a higher truth. As Žižek argues, the body of the Communist is marked by a form of redoubling—a split similar to that effected by the body of the medieval king—a division into the sublime and its material support: The Communists "are the 'objective Reason of History' incarnated, and in so far as the stuff they are made of is ultimately their body, this body again undergoes a kind of transubstantiation; it changes into a bearer of *another* body within the transient material envelopment." [41] Or, in the words of the East German author Erik Neutsch: "This man [the Party secretary] was invincible, the party sat within him like life in the body of an animal, it even outlived consciousness." [42]

Žižek construes the sublime dimension of the totalitarian leader's body as the Lacanian *objet petit a,* this "thing" the subject desires in order to fill the lack that characterizes it after its entry into the symbolic, the moment when the acquisition of language (and thus the "absence" of the thing referred to) coincides with the separation from the mother's body (and thus the absence of the imaginary unity of mother and child). He then connects this "objet petit a" to the idea of the revolutionary as an instrument of History, embodying the "higher truth" of Stalinism's infamous "iron laws of historical progress," by arguing that the totalitarian leader constitutes himself not as *subject* but as *object* of History/the Other.[43] Finally, Žižek argues that, within the Communist imaginary, it is only the material part of the Communist's body—"this fragile materiality charged with a mandate to serve as a transient support of another body"—which can "go wrong and introduce disorder," "disorder" referring, of course, to what perennially lurks in the soul of every Communist: the threat of "deviationism," "revisionism," and so on.[44] Wasn't Lenin preoccupied with Gorky's body, with his health, asks Žižek, when they corresponded about Gorky's continuing (and, in Lenin's view, rather problematic) interest in the philosophy of "God building"? And doesn't the Communists' practice of embalming their leader's body, indeed their whole architecture of mausoleums, betray the same obsessive preoccupation with the body as the precious but always fragile envelope of the sublime thing?[45]

In these novels, the sublime body is "hardened"; disciplined and ascetic, it is the body of what Kluge and Negt call the Weimar Republic's "ideal type of the steel-hard Bolshevik." [46] It is located within a universe which, in the most banal and misogynist way, equates women with sexuality, tediously unfolding the old paradigm of the idealized woman versus the ("bad") sexualized woman in all those mother figures so essential to the SED's moral project of a socialist reconstruction, whose bodies are "purified," that is, desexualized. In my discussion of the staging of the father's/Communist's body, I shall therefore emphasize the *gendered aspect of the material side* of the sublime body, tracing the process by which it arises as masculine only through its demarcation from what is feminine.[47] Finally, within the specific German context of antifascism, the sublime body of the Communist is figured in a religious guise, as the body of the Christian martyr. In the struggle against fascism, the Communist body becomes a body-in-pain, refracted through a register mobilizing a dense network of religious connotations. This peculiar inflection points to an absolutely central element of the SED's official discourse of antifascism: its iconography of martyrdom and redemption.[48]

Furthermore, these narratives involve a doubling of the paternal function in their depictions of a series of more or less prominent Party representatives who function as mentors to both fathers and sons, that is, as interpreters of the historical situation who assist the "positive" hero in his task of acquiring "consciousness." In the Soviet as well as the German context, they are themselves part of a structure of filiation, since their ultimate legitimacy is derived from carrying on Lenin's line.[49] In the GDR's foundational narratives, these mentor figures inspire heroic struggle, sacrifice, and death, thus positing as their imperative the *identification unto death*. At first glance, this doubling might appear to be an attempt to overdetermine or underwrite the authority of the paternal figure; yet, in light of Lacan's theorizing of the "Symbolic" father, it seems more appropriately understood as pointing to another intricacy of the paternal function:

In all strictness, the Symbolic father is to be conceived as "transcendent," as an irreducible given of the signifier. The Symbolic father—he who is ultimately capable of saying "I am who I am"—can only be imperfectly incarnated in the real father. He is nowhere. . . . The real father takes over from the Symbolic father.[50]

As we shall see, the issue of authoritative paternity and its legitimate incarnation is not so simple, since even in these narratives centered on the father, the locus of power ultimately remains empty.

Ideology as Fantasy

As the emphasis on the father's/leader's body indicates, these cultural narratives about fathers and sons do not simply articulate a specific plot structure with a (Marxist) discourse on history. Instead, they are suffused with fantasies about that body. And as family stories, these texts are engaged with deeper structures of subject formation, especially the Oedipal structuring of subjectivity and its unconscious fantasy scenarios. Any close reading of these texts is bound to uncover this thick layer of fantasy production, especially with respect to the many ways in which these texts confront the intricacies of the Oedipus complex—its "positive" and "negative" forms, which Freud discusses in "The Ego and the Id." [51] The (Communist) father is not only the one who, representing the "cultural past," the "symbolic law of order," [52] intervenes between mother and son; he is also the son's object of love. The narrative of fathers and sons thus involves identification *and* rivalry, homo- *and* heterosexual object choice. It is indeed not only fascism which turns "on the image of the father . . . enshrined in the place of the symbolic, all-powerful to the extent that he is so utterly out of reach." [53] I shall read East Germany's foundational narratives on this level, which has so far been entirely neglected, at least with respect to the inscription of unconscious fantasies. As they wrote their narratives, focusing on the family and its center, the father, the Communist authors were also writing about the structures of individual subject formation and the fantasies involved in them—they were writing *ideological fantasies.* Like fascism, East German socialism's ideological structures can thus be analyzed through its ideological fantasies. This explains their power to seize unconscious drives. It is only because they bridge the social and the individual, politics and desire, that the early GDR's dominant cultural narratives are so successful. This specific ideological universe consisting of different, variously articulated layers is yet another example of the "inseparability of history and subjectivity," of the "way fantasy operates inside historical process." [54] The East German hegemonic project is one which demands subjection to the antifascist father and holds up his sublime body for identification.

Since this study covers only a *single* aspect of the symbolic (re)construction of power in the postwar period, it is important to remember that other stories, which may have been in conflict with these particular narratives, were told as well, so any assumption that this postwar imaginary was homogeneous would be grossly misleading. The formation of any hegemonic project is the site of contestation, in the setting of the early GDR no less than elsewhere.[55] But these alternative discourses lie beyond the scope of this work, as do any statements about the material power structures of the emerging East German State.

Decentering Tendencies or The Myth of Socialist Realism

The texts by the GDR's exile authors share a common ordering principle: the family narrative.[56] Structurally, the family narrative easily lends itself to the ideological project of constructing a coherent paternal order, advocating a form of unity centered on the figure of the father, and emphasizing the present's unbreakable connection to the past. The family plot is a narrative of linear succession, based on the underlying structure of law and transgression.[57] The novels by Bredel, Marchwitza, and Gotsche all construct a politically overdetermined lineage from father to son(s). Here, the family narrative's inherent problematic of subordination to the father's authority, with the attendant issue of legitimate succession, is inscribed in the realm of politics.[58] Moreover, this particular form of emplotment thematizes unity in diversity, since it includes all those in the tradition of the Socialist–Communist–antifascist fathers and excludes everyone else. Structurally based on the principle of paternal authority, these founding fictions of the father thus elaborate a very specific "cultural frame" in order to articulate the legitimacy of political authority.[59] Moreover, this early literature of the GDR invents an ideological project that is thoroughly gendered, exhibiting in an exemplary way Joan Scott's thesis about the role of socially constructed categories of gender as "a primary way of signifying relationships of power": codes of masculinity tend to function in a legitimizing way, underwriting positions of power and strength.[60] The code of (socialist) femininity works in a different yet related fashion, for in these novels femininity means, above all, motherhood. This representation of motherhood and its traditional connotations touches upon another crucial but clearly subordinated dimension of the postwar project. In the early years of the Soviet Occupied Zone, women's "moral indifference" was thematized as the most glaring symptom of moral decay, as a "crisis of motherhood," which can be read in the texts of this period as a constant invocation of exactly this quality in women.[61] This ideologically driven appropriation of the family narrative produced texts in which a link is forged between (Communist) politics and a historically specific form of masculinity—these novels breathe the "spirit of masculinity." [62] Masculinity informs even their structural features: they focus unfailingly on male characters, while female characters and their stories remain peripheral. Whether these women are depicted as involved in Party work or as lovers, they are restricted to only two registers, either conflicting with a male character's political mission or supporting it. Rarely do these texts narrate the issue of succession with respect to women as daughters, for instance, but rather cede space only to mother figures and the obsessive thematization of socialist realist motherhood.

Did *Verwandte und Bekannte, Die Kumiaks,* and *Die Fahne von Kriwoj Rog* then succeed in constructing a "disciplined" and cohesive text of paternal authority? Do they support the prevailing image of socialist realism as a monolithic, monological system, one that transparently translates the rigidity of a social system into the realm of aesthetics? Militating against this seemingly inescapable conclusion are the hidden and not-so-hidden instabilities of these texts: first, as my brief discussion of the intricacies of the paternal function indicates, strong tensions pervade the very core of East Germany's textual foundations; second, the novels' narrative structures are themselves deeply unstable. What better indicator of that instability than "real existing socialism's" eternal ritual of criticism and self-criticism, of writing and rewriting—in short, the desperate attempt to fix meaning once and for all in the endless process of revision?[63]

Bredel's reworking of *Die Söhne* provides a particularly instructive example of this process, as well as pointing to one of the main areas of conflict: the articulation of historical narrative with the family-saga structure. Referring to the 1949 edition, Ilja Fradkin, a Soviet literary critic, criticized *Die Söhne* for neglecting major events of 1917–18, arguing that the fundamental conflicts of an epoch could not be treated within the framework of a family narrative.[64] According to Fradkin, the problem is trivially obvious: focusing on a Hamburg family distances the novel from the center of revolutionary activity, Berlin. In a session of the Writer's Union, Bredel reported on the revisions for the 1955 edition. First, he had extended the time frame of the novel (while the 1949 edition covered the period from 1916 to 1923, the 1955 edition took the characters up to 1930).[65] Bredel gave two reasons for this extended coverage: (1) to retain the Hamburg setting but also include events elsewhere that official SED discourse marked as crucial moments of KPD history;[66] and (2) to elaborate on the love story between Walter Brenten, the main character, and his lover, Cat. (The new version of *Die Söhne* also incorporated the Spartacist revolt in Berlin in 1918.) The second reservation voiced about Bredel's novel (and about Marchwitza's as well) pertained to the depiction of Communist Party figures as too weak. Both authors reacted to this standard criticism of socialist realist novels by foregrounding the Party cadres in various ways.[67]

Not surprisingly, these criticisms by "friends" [68] and comrades problematized the socialist realist writing of history, exposing one of the major faultlines running through these foundational texts. The ideological project of these novelists—to write the history of the German Communist movement according to a philosophy of history which conceived of its driving forces as opposing camps—was *aesthetically* decentered,[69] that is, breaking with the established formal conventions of the family narrative. In other words, the novels' ideological project has been *formally* realized in *two different modes,* both originating in the nineteenth century: the family narrative *and* the historical novel (in the tradition of Walter Scott).

What is the effect of this collusion between different narrative modes, different generic conventions? The principle of law and transgression which operates with respect to the family narrative's theme of transmission also operates on the formal level. Regulatory in nature, the family plot tries to control the inherently arbitrary nature of narrative, thereby reducing the multiplicity of history's many potential stories. It imposes an authority-based order on both the act of narration and the text of history. For instance, by deploying writing strategies which lead the reader to identify with those family members who embody the dominant political discourse, *Verwandte und Bekannte, Die Kumiaks,* and *Die Fahne von Kriwoj Rog* attempt to organize the text of history into *one* story. The authority-centered discourse of the family narrative thus duplicates the theme of discipline and paternal authority on the level of form.[70] This family plot collides with another epic imperative, in which a specific genre, the historical novel, confronts a specific philosophy of history. In the tradition of Walter Scott, whose historical novels underwent a remarkable revival during the exile period and formed the basis for Lukács's major work *Der historische Roman/The Historical Novel* (1937), the novels structure their historical universe into *two main opposing camps.* The heroic story of the life and death of Communist Party cadres is part of this alternative emplotment. Thus, like the narrative logic of the family plot, the logic of the historical novel aims at the integration of multiple narrative strands, since both modes are driven by the desire for totality. Yet, in contrast to the family plot, the conventions of this specific genre tend to move the narrative focus away from a single story. Careful reading of the texts' formal integration thus uncovers tensions produced by this articulation of family and historical narrative. A comparison with *Buddenbrooks* helps to clarify the point: in Mann's novel, all narrative strands center around a character who belongs to the family, thereby yielding a particularly tight narrative integration.[71] In these East German novels, however, narrative strands often center around characters other than family members. The authors try to counter this powerful centrifugal tendency in differing ways: Bredel and Marchwitza periodically attempt to recenter the family narrative, while Gotsche writes it in its purest form, diverging as little as possible from the family plot. Do these other forms of textualization undermine or underwrite the novels' central ideological project? Does the doubling of the paternal text by the heroizing story of Party mentors, for instance, produce a decentering tendency?

Verwandte und Bekannte and the Oedipal Refraction of the Family Narrative

As mentioned above, the overarching story of Bredel's trilogy stretches from the grandfather's involvement in crushing the Paris Commune to his grand- and great-grandsons' participation in the construction of a "new" Germany in the Soviet Occupied Zone, with the whole narrative framed in terms of a successful seizure of state power.[72] Despite this specific framing, however, the trilogy flows to the rhythm of repeated defeats before fading out, or reaching its vanishing point—1948 and the beginnings of a German "Workers' and Peasants' State." Thus, the first volume, *Die Väter,* ends with Johann Hardekopf's death at the outbreak of World War I, a war which, according to the text's argument, *his* party, the Social Democrats, failed to prevent. The second volume, *Die Söhne,* ends with the imprisonment of Walter Brenten, Hardekopf's grandson, a Communist journalist and organizer, and the announcement of the first National Socialist government in Thuringia, which, as we learn through Brenten's inner monologue, neither the SPD nor the KPD was able to prevent. The first part of *Die Enkel* closes with the Nazis' attack on the Soviet Union and Walter Brenten's forced escape from Spain, where he fought in the International Brigades, to his exile in Moscow; the second part mainly focuses on the war in the East, following Walter Brenten, who now works as a propagandist for the Soviet Army, and his son Viktor, a Red Army officer. The first segment of *Die Enkel* is entitled "Defeat" and the second "Victory," referring to the Red Army's victory and the return of the Moscow exiles to Germany. In Bredel's trilogy, therefore, German history is a series of defeats that nevertheless culminate in triumph.

What is the novel's overall structure? Or, more concretely, how does the family plot function as an organizing device? Bredel's trilogy opens with the birth of Walter Brenten in 1901, an event through which the novel's basic character system and its Social Democratic setting unfold. Only after the birth of the trilogy's main character—whose development clearly parallels Bredel's own biography—is Johann Hardekopf's story as a Prussian soldier fighting the Paris Commune narrated, a significant narrative infraction, given the text's linear logic. Most of the characters are introduced in the first chapter within the context of Walter Brenten's birth. At the core of the character system are two families, the Hardekopfs and the Brentens, whose connection is established through the marriage of Johann Hardekopf's daughter Frieda, Walter's mother, to Carl Brenten, Walter's father. However, as more characters begin to gradually cluster around these families, a larger, primarily politically differentiated network of actors is generated in accordance with the reductionist logic of two opposing camps which represent the "forces of history" and, through the course of the trilogy, unfold into a fabric of multiple stories.

Driven by the totalizing imperative of this model, *Verwandte und Bekannte* thus tends to move away from its primary narrative mechanism, aligning the family characters with one political camp or the other. As I mentioned above, the structuring of the novel's narrative around a series of model functionaries arises out of this logic of opposing camps. Functioning as mentor figures within the family narrative, these Party cadres embody the various historical "stages" in the emergence of the German Communist Party, from the left-wing opposition within the pre-1918 SPD through the USPD (Independent Social Democrats) and Spartacus. As for their opponents, Bredel first focuses on the "reformist" wing of the SPD, then, with *Die Söhne,* on the Nazi Party, connecting them through a number of different characters. Not surprisingly, Bredel's trilogy thus exhibits a strong leaning toward the "social-fascism" thesis.[73]

The inexorable move away from the family narrative—its aesthetic decentering—increases throughout the trilogy. While *Die Väter* still focuses primarily on the Hardekopf-Brenten family, *Die Söhne* tends to concentrate increasingly on Walter Brenten and his friends and opponents. With *Die Enkel,* the narrative becomes even more centrifugal: different narrative strands are worked out simultaneously, many of them linked to characters outside the family, such as the Nazis Tönne, Wehner, Ballab, and Rochwitz. Thus in the section on the Spanish civil war in the third volume, the focus systematically shifts back and forth between Wehner, who is fighting on the side of Franco, and Walter Brenten, who fights with the International Brigades. Part two of *Die Enkel* narrates the war against the Soviet Union, alternating between Herbert Hardekopf, Walter's nephew (who will eventually desert), and the SA member Tönne. Likewise, parallel narrative strands follow the Red Army soldier Viktor Brenten, Walter's son, and his former teacher, the SA member Rochwitz: while Viktor advances toward Berlin, Rochwitz tries to stop the German soldiers' flight by executing deserters. Their story lines intersect again when Viktor's regiment passes through the village where the deserters were hanged and is attacked by Rochwitz's soldiers. Toward the end of the novel, the different strands converge as the figures representing National Socialism gather at the house of Hamburg's Gauleiter to plan the future of a Germany without Hitler. Likewise, their opponents are reunited as they conquer Berlin: Herbert Hardekopf and Viktor Brenten, the grandsons, march in together, while Walter Brenten arrives a little later as one of the first exile cadres to return from Moscow.

Increasingly, the trilogy's original organizing structure, the family narrative, thus dissolves into a historical narrative which obeys the logic of opposing historical forces. Potentially working against the family plot's coherence, the historical narrative draws attention to characters and stories outside the family confines, yet proves indispensable to the inscription of the political master-discourse. Bredel tries to counter this tendency by mechanically reestablishing the family narrative as the central mechanism organizing the text of history, deploying different textual strategies: thus in *Die Väter,* the family is periodically reunited around the Social Democratic association Maienblüte. Then, starting with the war against the Soviet Union, the family narrative's continuity is sustained by periodic returns to Germany and Frieda Brenten, Carl's wife and Walter's mother. Finally, Walter's reunion with his mother, sister, and nephew in Hamburg in 1948 reconstitutes the family narrative at the very end of the trilogy.

It is here that Bredel's attempt to jointly rearticulate historical text and family narrative emerges most emphatically. As Walter's mother reminds him, his brief visit in Hamburg coincides with his grandfather's hundredth birthday. Within the version of Marxist historiography inscribed in Bredel's text, this centenary also marks both the publication of the *Communist Manifesto* and Germany's failed bourgeois revolution of 1848. At its moment of closure, the trilogy thus links the family's "founder" and the founding moment of Germany's "revolutionary" forces. Yet it is the trilogy's final paragraph which, above all, executes the ultimate ideological closure. Thinking about Johann Hardekopf's birthday, his grandson Walter, the character most closely aligned with the Communist Party (and the trilogy's narrator) expresses what amounts to the definitive recentering of the novel's ideological project:

Your sons Otto and Emil have become true petty bourgeois, your son Ludwig a night watchman. But your son's son, your grandson Herbert . . . fought on the side of the Red Army to liberate their homeland and his own from the enemies of the people. And your great-grandson is studying in Moscow, the capital of the first Socialist state. In one part of Germany, we workers have finally reunited after a long fraternal war, Grandfather Hardekopf, and together we are now building a state of workers and peasants. Nothing was in vain, no disappointment, no defeat, no sacrifice. . . . Not that everything was always good the way it was, certainly not; but nothing was in vain, everything was worth it. Your cause, Grandfather Hardekopf, marches forward and triumphs. (*VB*3b/625–26)

This closing paragraph raises two fundamental questions: How does the trilogy produce the realignment of historical text and family narrative, and how does it reconcile the triumphalism of its moment of closure with the series of historical defeats outlined earlier?

Attributing defeats to the German labor movement's "reformism," the text's historical narrative and its concomitant political master-discourse foreground the vanguard role of the Communists, positing armed struggle (and the seizure of state power) as the ultimate goal, ambiguously deploying the term "struggle" across the metaphorical (class struggle) and literal registers (war). But in the last instance, it is the Red Army's victory which makes the trilogy's last paragraph possible. Within the confines of the family narrative, this problematic — "reformism" and defeat versus vanguard politics and victory — is thematized by means of the trilogy's fathers, Johann Hardekopf and Carl Brenten. Whereas Hardekopf opposes any form of militant struggle because of his experiences during the Franco-Prussian War, Brenten is portrayed as essentially too weak to take any stance. It is only through a fundamental transformation that Hardekopf, Carl's father-in-law and Walter's grandfather, can become the trilogy's founding father.

The first episode thematizing this transformation, on Hardekopf's involvement in the Franco-Prussian War, introduces Dallmann, a soldier who explains to the naive Hardekopf who the "real" enemy is. Yet while Hardekopf joins the Social Democratic movement after the war, he continues to insist on a peaceful transition to socialism. Within the novel's logic, this desire to avoid violence at all costs gives rise to a reformist party and ultimately leads to the First World War, which forces Hardekopf to admit: "We [i.e., the rank-and-file of the SPD] have done too little" (*VB*1/458). His conversion here results from Hardekopf's association with Fritz Mengers, another mentor figure representing the left-wing opposition within the Social Democratic Party. Both Dallmann and Mengers are characterized by their youth, strength, and radical politics, overdetermined by traditional attributes of masculinity. Introducing Dallmann, the narrator insists on his soldierly courage and discipline, while Mengers is described as "bursting with vigor and decisiveness" (*VB*1/294). Only the influence of these "young guys" transforms Hardekopf into what emerges at this point as the trilogy's model of Socialist/Communist virility: the "youthful" militant who understands the inevitable necessity of violent confrontations with state power. This transformation allows Bredel to ground the "basic Socialist insights," the very object of transmission, in Hardekopf as the point of origin within his patrilinear genealogy. Together with the founding of a Socialist state based on the Red Army's military victory, this is *the very premise of the founding ideological closure* of the novel: "Your cause, Grandfather Hardekopf, marches forward and triumphs." Several key aspects are brought together in this closing: it reaffirms the success of a particular form of politics, *the "masculine" vanguard;* in addition, *the authority of the Communist Party* and its state is underwritten by *paternal authority,* collapsing *historical* and *family* narratives, the stories of *cadres* and *fathers.*

However, to fully understand the pressures behind what will prove to be the trilogy's most violent strategy of containment, we have to return to its very origin—to the peculiar narrative ordering of the first two chapters of *Die Väter.* Otherwise following a strictly chronological, linear narrative logic, the trilogy nonetheless begins with the son's story, instead of the father's; the grandson's instead of the grandfather's. This achronological interlacing of story lines can be read as a symptom, that is, as a moment when the text "knows" more than its author: the dislocation at the story's inception thematizes a dimension of the family narrative which the other novels relegate to the background, namely, the potentially conflictual (and latently Oedipal) relationship between father and son(s).

Substitute Fathers, Armored Bodies, Identification, and Death

Verwandte und Bekannte represents a retrospective rewriting of the triangular Oedipal structure along the lines of an ideology which inextricably links virility to its imperative of seizing state power through armed struggle, and which displaces the positive resolution of the Oedipus complex from the biological father onto a series of substitute fathers, thus elaborating a particular identity that is sustained by a series of icons of (Communist) virility and constructed as the opposite of the "real" father, Carl Brenten. Throughout this process, the object—the mother—remains the same, although repositioned into a political framework within which the mother figure acquires different allegorical significations. As we have already seen, the telos of Walter Brenten's journey is Hamburg and his mother. This trope of "returning home" also constitutes another aspect of the trilogy's narrative structure insofar as a large part of the third volume alternates between the mother in Germany and the sons at war. The mother now figures, on the one hand, as the incarnation of some Communist *Mater Germania,* praying to God to prevent the war and lamenting the ravaging of the country, the killing of its sons; on the other hand, she stands for "the Party":

The Party was an omnipresent, caring mother with millions of caring hands. Banned, spied upon, persecuted in Germany, it existed nevertheless in every city, in every factory, in every street. . . . He who did not abandon her was also not abandoned by her. All who defended her and the working-class struggle, she also protected. (*VB*3a/177)

The third component of this Communist imaginary is the mother-as-the-working class. The trilogy thus has the son returning to his origin—to Hamburg, to his mother—after having accomplished his mission. Reunited with her in 1948, Walter responds to her complaint about Germany's defeat: "But we, mother, we have won our war against Hitler" (*VB*3b/609).

I am indeed arguing that *Verwandte und Bekannte* simply narrates an unresolved Oedipus complex. This ideologically refracted rewriting of the Oedipal story eliminates the "real" father and constructs the father(s) with whom identification is possible, while transforming the mother from an object of love to one of allegorical significance and thereby retaining her as the primary object. This reading does not simply uncover a (thinly veiled) Oedipal truth, but aims to uncover the imbrication of desire in politics through the issue of paternity, a move which involves tracing the articulation of different narrative strands in the patrilinear weave of East Germany's "pre-history." *Die Söhne* lets us read the faint traces of an "original" Oedipal scenario in its moments of intimacy and physical closeness between Walter Brenten and his mother. The mother's portrayal is an idealized merging of conventional maternal characteristics with a specific political perspective. For instance, several times Frieda Brenten takes care of young Communists, hiding them and attending to their wounds.

The trilogy's Oedipal subtext also breaks through into the portrayal of the father, which is from the very start tinged with irony. In *Die Väter,* the father's "meager facial hair" is contrasted with the newborn son's rather grotesque, deep and full voice, contradicting, the narrator implies, Carl's newly acquired "paternity" (*VB1*/40–41, 39). *Die Söhne* systematically elaborates upon the political dimensions of this father–son conflict, aligning the father with the "old," reformist Social Democratic Party, the son with the radicalized youth movement and, eventually, the new German Communist Party. Bredel creates this politically overdetermined Oedipal scenario in two key scenes, the first of which attributes the anxiety of being replaced to the father: when Carl returns from his military service, he perceives his son as a threat to his position, complaining that Walter "seems to think of himself as the provider and head of this household" (*VB2*/72). The second scene, a discussion between father and son, translates the conflict into political terms as Walter tells his father, "You old folks laid the foundation stone of the house, and you didn't do a bad job because it can support a large building; but now we have to support the house" (*VB2*/109).

In accordance with this politically overdetermined Oedipal logic, the father is soon replaced by a series of mentor figures. The representation of the 1920 Kapp-Putsch, a right-wing uprising, dramatizes this process of substitution step by step. When Walter and his father meet a group of insurgent workers led by Ernst Timm, one of the trilogy's main Party mentor figures, Walter immediately notices that Timm is armed. He decides to join Timm's group as soon as Timm asks him if he would like to fight *under his command.* Thus Walter's transformation into a "soldier of the Revolution" is predicated upon his identification with and subordination to Ernst Timm, as a result of which, Walter also receives his first gun, a sort of initiation into masculinity:

Walter took a deep breath. Never in his life had he held a gun in his hands. . . . It made him feel like an adult. Full of his new self-confidence, Walter looked around him. Magic powers seemed to emanate from the rifle. . . . There they were sitting or lying in their beds, sleeping. But he, he was driving through the night, a soldier of the Revolution. And a rifle represented power, with a rifle you could impose your will. (*VB2*/350–51)

While Walter follows Timm without any hesitation, Carl decides to return home, recoiling from the dangerous situation. Amused by his father's behavior, Walter thinks that Carl would obviously never be able to cope with a serious fight.

"Becoming a man" means denying this father, with his "empty" attributes of masculinity, and identifying with a series of mentor figures whose "complete" masculinity is signified first and foremost by their possession of a gun, as the passage quoted above so transparently demonstrates. The reader is repeatedly invited to witness a rather curious voyeuristic exercise exhibiting the father's masculinity in all its ridiculousness: standing "stark naked" in front of a mirror, Carl proudly admires the "most necessary attributes of [his] masculinity" (*VB*1/94).[74] This process of substitution, with its concomitant rhetoric of masculinity, leads to the compulsive repetition of alternative images of masculinity, culminating in the depiction of Thälmann, the head of the German Communist Party and the text's ultimate paternal substitute.[75] The semantic network constructed around Thälmann deploys the familiar rhetoric of masculinity: strength, energy, and a determined, authoritative gaze which Walter notes even from a distance. It is in the mirror of those bright, steely eyes that Walter recognizes himself when he personally encounters Thälmann for the first time. Imagining Thälmann in his prison cell, Walter evokes a vivid portrait of his "leader" and "teacher," whose words, he remembers, always struck him like shots forcefully erupting from Thälmann's body: "This powerful figure with the impressive head, the shining eyes, the energetic fists, the volcanic passion" (*VB*3a/109, 47). A similar homoerotic undertone echoes in the description of yet another model Communist, Max Doppler, commanding officer of the International Brigades' "Thälmann Batallion." Upon arriving in Spain, Walter encounters Doppler, whom he describes in the following terms: "Doppler was at least a head taller than Walter, and he looked great in his uniform, Walter thought. He wore his fur-lined coat open, and under it a short, black leather jacket, and he carried a heavy Colt revolver on his side" (*VB*3/239). Again, their encounter deploys the same formulaic elements: Doppler's "shining eyes," which remind him of Thälmann; Walter's willing subordination under the command of the charismatic Communist; his breathless admiration for this "courageous fighter" (*VB*3/270). The Spain episode thematizes some of the core issues: first, as exemplary "battle," it articulates the essence of the trilogy's vanguard politics, constructing the actual armed confrontation between International Brigades and Franco's

Falange as the moment of truth in which the enemy finally has a "recognizable face" (*VB*3/266); second, in dramatizing Doppler's death and Walter's wounding, this episode plays out a crucial facet of the narrative's serial identification, perhaps best described as an *identification unto death.* In the middle of the Battle of Teruel, Doppler is killed and Walter is given the commander's gun and belt, which make him feel less vulnerable. Caught in a seemingly hopeless situation himself, Brenten discharges a machine gun at the enemy, hysterically screaming Doppler's name over and over again. The chapter ends with his losing consciousness as he is shot in the shoulder. Recovering from his injury, Walter is deeply depressed, ostensibly because of the republican defeat; however, a brief digression into Freud's writings on the Oedipus complex may shed a different light on this reaction.

How should we read this scenario of identification, death, and survival? On the surface, it enacts nothing more than the all-too-familiar topos of the fight that must continue, the passing of the torch from (substitute) father to son. But here it is manifested in a most phallic variant as the passing of the gun. It thus touches upon what Freud calls the "intricacy" of the Oedipal situation, which involves the formation of the superego through identification with the father as well as taking the father himself as a love object.[76] According to Freud, this "feminine sexual disposition" toward the father, or "inverted negative" form of the Oedipus complex, normally tends to disappear. The ego ideal which results from this structure exhibits a double aspect: "Its relation to the ego is not exhausted by the precept: 'You *ought to be* like this (like your father).' It also comprises the prohibition: 'You *may not be* like this (like your father)' — that is, you may not do all he does; some things are his prerogative." [77] As a result of repression, this new ego, "fortified" by erecting an obstacle to the Oedipal desire within itself, now "contains the power of the authoritative father." [78]

In *Verwandte und Bekannte* the Oedipal structuring function is inscribed in a specific historical and ideological context, namely, as a political narrative: fighting for something represented by the maternal *against* the biological father but *with* his substitute. Although there is no strong identification with the "original" father, a strong sexual disposition toward the (substitute) father is maintained. This "symbolic father" takes on a specific valence in accordance with the ideological context in which the Communists' military vanguard politics are coded as masculine, thus valorizing masculinity itself.[79]

The textual segment I have singled out for closer analysis lets us read three things: first, a deeply ambivalent attitude toward the "authoritative father,"which is due to the simple fact that the son identifies with the father but also wants to usurp his position. After all, Bredel's mentor figures all die a heroic death: Fiete, Walter's first Spartacist mentor, dies in an armed in-surrection in 1919, Doppler dies in Spain, Timm is shot by Gestapo agents as he leaves prison, and Thälmann dies at Buchenwald in 1944. After Wal-ter is wounded in Spain, this ambivalence surfaces as depression. Moreover, the segment vividly narrates the authoritative father's double legacy. Iden-tification with him means fighting and resisting, but ultimately, the model can only be fully attained through heroic death, for *only a dead son will ever be a father:* to become the father, the son has to die. The final redemption of the "real" father is governed by this logic. A member of the Communist Party since 1918, Carl Brenten dies after having been jailed by the Nazis. It is this death which finally revalorizes him in the eyes of his son.

Second, this identification with the symbolic father as identification unto death involves another aspect, namely, the *steeling* of the body, which re-sults in what I will call, with Klaus Theweleit, the "armored" body.[80] The large portions of the narrative devoted to Walter's imprisonment, focusing strongly on his physical sufferings, highlight the centrality of this armored body and what it represses. The extended segment narrating his solitary confinement in 1933 most explicitly addresses this issue, alternating be-tween passages graphically describing his agony and those in which Walter, thinking about suicide, exhorts himself to remember those who endured torture in the name of progress, their "strength and hardness" (*VB*3a/106). Trying to forget the cold, his thoughts move from the paternal to the ma-ternal, from Timm, Marx, and "LENIN" (*VB*3a/109), to the Party, whose protection he implores, using a discourse which mobilizes connotations of maternity. By the end of the night, Walter's focus is reduced to his body as he desperately tries to move his frozen limbs, admonishing himself not to weaken—a "promise" to his "comrades" (*VB*3a/126).[81] Later, he will proudly remember that despite his suffering, he never wept.[82] "Not to turn into a weakling" (i.e., disciplining and transcending the body) also involves women and sexuality, the mechanisms of projection and denial, sublima-tion and the redirection of libidinal energy. *Verwandte und Bekannte* thema-tizes sexuality only once, as Walter's seduction by an older woman. Feeling both attraction and revulsion, he answers her question, "What kind of a man are you?" (*VB*2/200), by violently pushing her away and fleeing from her apartment. Predictably, Bredel sets up a contrast between the fragility of Walter's friend Ruth and the other woman's "liveliness." This drearily conventional projection of "unruly" sexuality onto women permeates the trilogy. As we saw earlier, libidinal energy is actually directed away from women, becoming—in a more or less sublimated form—an essential component of the relationship between Communist men.

Third, it is this *homosocialist desire* which evinces the preservation of the son's "feminine disposition" toward the father.[83] It refers not only to a constellation in which the father is the love object, but one that places the son in a position of *feminine passivity*.[84] In the context of an oppositional politics that so forcefully foregrounds the concept of "struggle," this component of the inverted Oedipus complex needs to be contained at any cost. The strategy upon which this containment rests is, once again, projection. As I have argued in more detail elsewhere,[85] Bredel's text, along with those by Marchwitza and Gotsche, unconsciously links the threat of National Socialism to woman *as a reminder of castration,* which within a patriarchal order signifies the position of the powerless. Women in these texts signify, above all, the *castrated,* not the *castrating;* their threat resides not in any position of strength but, on the contrary, in their association with weakness. Structurally and thematically, these narratives marginalize and contain what stands as a reminder of castration, namely, women and femininity.[86]

The Hole at the Center of the Paternal Narrative

Let us return once more to *Die Enkel*'s last pages and its final paragraph. The novel ends, as I mentioned earlier, with Walter Brenten's returning home, that is, to his mother. Along with this plot, which makes the mother both origin and telos of the narrative, stands the patrilinear story recounted in the last paragraph, which I will quote again here:

Your sons Otto and Emil have become true petty bourgeois, your son Ludwig a night watchman. But your son's son, your grandson Herbert . . . fought on the side of the Red Army to liberate their homeland and his own from the enemies of the people. And your great-grandson is studying in Moscow, the capital of the first Socialist state. In one part of Germany, we workers have finally reunited after a long fraternal war, Grandfather Hardekopf, and together we are now building a state of workers and peasants. Nothing was in vain, no disappointment, no defeat, no sacrifice. . . .

Not that everything was always good the way it was, certainly not; but nothing was in vain, everything was worth it. Your cause, Grandfather Hardekopf, marches forward and triumphs.

What does this paragraph do? Following the text's dominant logic, it excludes all women characters. Moreover, it concludes the trilogy by reframing it as a family narrative, that form which revolves around the issue of paternal authority. *Yet the actual father* (i.e., the speaker's father, Carl Brenten) *is absent.* On one level, then, this paragraph invites us to read the trilogy as the fantasy of a successful elimination of the father by the son, who, returning to the mother, is finally able to take his place. At the same time, however, this final passage mobilizes the authority of the father in ideological terms by referring to the grandfather's political project as the basis for the new state. It thereby draws attention again to the ideological layer intervening in the process of paternal identification.

Indeed, as we have seen, the speaker's identity rests on his identification with a series of substitute fathers who represent this ideology. And insofar as this identification is governed by the imperative to die, it necessarily remains partial, incomplete—"becoming the father" is forever deferred. What I would argue, then, is that this final paragraph thematizes the "symbolic overpresence of the father," in Rose's phrase. She argues that the structural paradox at the heart of the Oedipus complex—to be and not to be like the father—is sharpened in the case of a father who also assumes the position of an educator: "[I]t is the father as master who encapsulates the paradox at the heart of the paternal function, who most forcefully demands an identification which he also has to withhold or refuse." [87]

The "hole" at the center of the paternal narrative thus points to the difficulties in attempting to fill the empty locus of power by linking it to a paternal tradition, to "stage" the symbolic father: *no one* can represent the figure whom the text offers as the ultimate father—Stalin. Nor, to make matters even more complicated, can anyone replace Lenin—embalmed in his mausoleum and even further removed by his sacred aura. The paradox inherent to the paternal function is doubled: just as the son can never become the father, the symbolic father is located outside of Germany. While in prison, Walter hears of Lenin's death, and Bredel seizes the opportunity to quote from the speech in which Stalin pledged to uphold Lenin's legacy: "When Comrade Lenin died, he bequeathed to us the legacy to uphold, value highly, and honor the sublime name of this member of the Party and to preserve it in its purity. We swear to you, Comrade Lenin, that we will comply with your command" (*VB*2/448). The aforementioned passage about the "people of a special mold" follows immediately after this pledge. We know from Žižek that these "special" people incarnate History/the Party; we now also know that they represent what cannot be represented, that they are identifying with a father whose place can never be taken. On a more abstract level, *Verwandte und Bekannte* "knows" that the actual father figure can never carry the weight of its symbolic function. In this light, we can read the continual decentering of the trilogy's "original" structure, that of the family narrative's regulatory imperative, as highly symptomatic: Just as "real" father and "symbolic" father are kept apart in the concluding paragraph, so are family narrative and historical narrative, the story of fathers and the story of cadres. Or, stated differently, just as father and symbolic father cannot be made to overlap, the seams of the two narratives cannot be made to overlay each other. And in contrast to Kantorowicz's king, or Žižek's Communist, these "special people" with their two bodies, the German antifascist hero could be said to have *four bodies*.

The "Father as Master": *Die Fahne von Kriwoj Rog*

This synthesis of real and symbolic father is exactly what Otto Gotsche tries to achieve in his *Fahne von Kriwoj Rog*. In contrast to Bredel's trilogy, Gotsche's novel gradually abandons its dominant mentor figure to focus exclusively on the father—who assumes the mentoring function himself—thus imbricating itself much more with the symbolic overpresence of the father. This is the story of a family who hid a Soviet flag, entrusted to the father in 1929, throughout the period of National Socialism. *Die Fahne* focuses on this particular family and on this father (figure), a miner named Otto Brosowski. Although Gotsche does not introduce his mentor figure —the Party secretary, Friedrich Rüdiger—within an Oedipal context, he clearly positions him and Otto Brosowski within a hierarchical relationship. The Party representative plays a crucial role as the one who encourages the Mansfeld miners to write a letter to their colleagues in Kriwoj Rog asking them for advice—the novel's most obvious ideological move, easily traced to the context of the 1950s, with its ubiquitous slogan "To learn from the

Soviet Union means to learn to win." Rüdiger then travels to Kriwoj Rog and accepts the flag from the representative of the Russian Communist Party, then passes it on to Brosowski at a May Day meeting in 1929. In 1933, Rüdiger is the first to be arrested.

Besides revolving around a single family, *Die Fahne* is also set in one city, Gerbstedt, a fictional site intended to be representative of Germany between 1927–28 and 1945. Relative to *Verwandte und Bekannte, Die Fahne* is a tightly integrated narrative; although it combines family narrative and historical epic, the focus tends to stay on the family. This effect is reinforced by a sequence of events, turning points in the narrative that concern the Red Flag from Kriwoj Rog. Indeed, it is the family's gradually evolving concentration on preserving the flag which motivates this foregrounding of the family narrative. Gotsche's novel is thus more successful than Bredel's trilogy in bringing this type of narrative under paternal discipline and control.

What are these flag-related turning points in the narrative? The first one is the May Day 1929 meeting at which Rüdiger entrusts the Red Flag to Otto Brosowski as the "most worthy" representative of the Mansfeld miners. After Brosowski takes an oath to always protect "Lenin's flag . . . with his life's blood" (*DF*/87, 89), the meeting turns into a demonstration headed by Brosowski's eldest son, who carries the flag. On two other occasions, the flag is likewise displayed publicly: in 1930 during a strike, and in 1932 as part of a demonstration protesting Hitler's rise to power. Brosowski's eldest son carries the flag publicly one last time in 1933, at the funeral of KPD members who were killed during a raid by the SA. After that, the flag remains hidden until it reemerges triumphantly in the novel's closing tableau, which stages Brosowski and his family walking toward the Red Army as they display "their" flag. The novel's core section dramatizes several scenes in which the whole family or the father in particular are brutally tortured by the SA, who want the flag for a public burning.[88] A new hiding place is found for the flag after every assault in a ritual that at one moment freezes into a solemn tableau, creating an image of total family unity and endowing this object with a sacred aura: "Eight hands laid themselves on the fabric of the flag, before Walter soldered the lid shut" (*DF*/456).

The flag, as the central narrative object, figures prominently in the text's ideological closure with the Brosowski family welcoming the soldiers of the Red Army in 1945 by displaying the Soviet flag:

Then a small group of people walked toward the Soviet soldiers, carrying the flying flag of Kriwoj Rog. . . . With one hand Brosowski held the cloth which his oldest son carried at the front of the group. . . . He had lived for this moment . . . in the dark nights of pain. . . . His wife marched next to him, leaning on a cane and holding little Walter's hand. Tears streamed down her face, a face framed by white hair. . . . She supported her husband, her arm around his shoulders. The triumphant Soviet soldiers thronged around the little group and kissed the fabric of the flag. . . .

"Mother, Mother, you did it . . . Mother!" said her eldest son. His voice was thick, he staggered, and Walter had to support him. . . .

It rose like a storm into the sunny day: ". . . Brothers, toward the light!"

They sang, and Soviet soldiers and Mansfeld miners jubilantly lifted the Brosowskis onto their shoulders and bore them behind the flag at the front of the column. (*DF*/530–31)

This tableau represents the essence of the East German narrative of transmission and authority, especially if we read it against the background of its famous intertext, Gorky's *Mother*—undoubtedly a reference meant to pay tribute to the Soviet Union's fortieth anniversary. Gotsche's palimpsest invokes the memory of Gorky's socialist realist classic, yet as if reflected in a distorting mirror: in Gorky's (and later, Brecht's) version, the father dies at the very beginning and the mother picks up the flag after her son is arrested; while that plot thus emphasizes the absence of the father, *Die Fahne von Kriwoj Rog* restores the paternal order by centering on father and son. This becomes abundantly clear when Brosowski's wife and youngest son are repeatedly shown to be acting "in the name of the father," recalling the father's oath to defend the flag as they remain silent under torture.

Die Fahne thus seems to successfully collapse biologic and symbolic father, family order and Communist order, yet its conclusion displays a father physically weakened, a "human wreck" destroyed by twelve years of National Socialist rule. In the contrast between Brosowski, who now has to be propped up by his wife, and the strong Red Army soldiers, we can hear an echo of an earlier and very different Brosowski, the Communist militant: "His body stiffened rebelliously. . . . The stout man of medium height made a fist . . . and raised it to greet the comrades to whom his letter was addressed across thousands of kilometers" (*DF*/16). The novel explains this constellation of forces as the outcome of the historical defeat in 1933, which it attributes, loyally following the GDR's official historiography, to the "betrayal" by the Social Democratic leadership. A feverish dream that haunts Brosowski after he learns of Friedrich Rüdiger's death in a concentration camp in 1941 fantasizes a heroic act of liberation which obviously clashes with the novel's concluding scene:

In confused, feverish fantasies he struggled with his opponents. He ripped off his shirt, he hid the flag from the henchmen . . . he carried it at the head of Rüdiger's funeral procession, he waved it above the heads of thousands of demonstrators, he wrapped himself in the cloth so that he might die with it, he planted it victoriously as storming workers smashed the Nazi dictatorship. (*DF*/427)

Brosowski's dream thus splits biologic from symbolic father, aligning the paternal function with Rüdiger and, ultimately, the flag with the Soviet state and its army. Metonymically, it establishes the identity of Brosowski/Rüdiger/the Red Flag, deploying a structure of deferred paternal authority whose legacy is ultimately rooted in Lenin. Moreover, it thematizes the identification unto death: the seemingly incongruous image of Brosowski tearing off his shirt identifies him with the victim, whom he remembers as having worn "the flag on his naked body" (*DF*/427). With Brosowski, who is reduced to a "black lump" (*DF*/383) after days of torture, *Die Fahne* takes this identification unto death to its limits. Finally, the dream thematizes the defeat of 1933 as the Communist Party's traumatic experience, alluding to its "unconscious guilt" over *not* having led the German working class in a revolt against Hitler's regime. The discrepancy between the actual weakness of the German Communists and their imaginary power—derived from their identification with the Soviets—is further underscored by the coincidence of the simultaneous death of the German Party representative and Hitler's attack on the Soviet Union: learning of the attack, Brosowski regains his strength, becoming "hard, firm, strong" (*DF*/429) again, because he "knows" that the Red Army will defeat Hitler's forces.

This same guilt surfaces in an inner monologue when Brosowski is forced to go underground in 1933. Berating himself for his feelings of helplessness, Brosowski even turns against himself, against "comrade Brosowski" (*DF*/318). This self-accusatory passage precedes the section that narrates Brosowski's illegal work, his sudden agitational appearances in the weeks after Hitler's rise to power, which end with his arrest. Similar affects, especially shame, are articulated when the family is forced to hide the flag. Finally, the connection between guilt and aggression against the self is described with respect to another character who starts to injure himself while suffering the SA's torture not, as Brosowski observes, because he is ready to talk but because he feels ashamed. This peripheral incident, occurring within the context of Brosowski's own suffering, articulates (and displaces) the nexus between punishment and guilt which the text refuses to acknowledge.

The Flag as Fetish

Like Bredel's trilogy, Gotsche's novel revolves around the essential instability of the paternal function, although at first glance it seems to actually reassert and fix that function. Closer examination, however, reveals not only the split into biologic and symbolic fathers but also the emergence of a feminine disposition toward the symbolic father at the core of its primary structuring scenario—masochistic torture fantasies.[89] And what underlies the novel's repeatedly enacted masochist scenario, I would argue, is more than just a politically articulated "unconscious feeling of guilt." Before elaborating further on this argument, however, I would like to briefly return to Gotsche's primary intertext, *The Mother.* Despite the many literal reconfigurations of the climactic moment of Gorky's text in *Die Fahne,* Minna Brosowski carries the flag only once, at a demonstration organized by women. However, Gorky's novel, with its emphasis on the "revolutionizing of the mother," [90] leaves its traces in *Die Fahne.* For instance, her son's words ("Mother, you did it!") in the novel's final passage reintroduce Minna's story, which, like Gorky's is a coming-to-consciousness story albeit one that is clearly secondary relative to her husband's. This hierarchical relation between the father and mother can also be read as a sign of the instability of the Communist subject, that is, the subject positioned as the one who carries the flag and passes it on. What I would propose is that, on a deeper level, the periodic reemergence of the Gorkian subject position indicates that the male subject of Gotsche's *Fahne* does indeed vacillate between the feminine and the masculine subject position, thus that it is *essentially* unstable. This thesis is supported by the narrative's participation in what Freud viewed as a form of male pathology, namely, feminine masochism: "If one has an opportunity of studying cases in which the masochistic phantasies have been especially richly elaborated, one quickly discovers that *they place the subject in a characteristically female situation;* they signify, that is, being castrated, or copulated with, or giving birth to a baby." [91]

This instability of the Communist subject surfaces, above all, in the prolonged, excessively brutal scenes of torture which constitute the core of the narrative.[92] This fantasy, so integral to the official discourse of antifascism as it developed in the 1950s, points from yet another angle to the inherent paradox of the symbolic function of paternity: the double injunction *to be* and *not to be* like the father. Central to my argument is Freud's insight that masochism essentially acts out the male subject's feminine disposition toward the father, or rather toward the symbolic father incorporated into the superego as a result of the Oedipal crisis: the male subject's ego assumes a position *not like the father* relative to the superego, thereby reactivating the negative Oedipal stage: desire for the father and identification with the mother. It is the regressive wish "to have some passive (feminine) sexual relations" with the father that causes the masochist's "unconscious sense of guilt," his "need for punishment at the hands of a parental power." [93] Freud saw this same structure as sustaining what he called "moral masochism," that is, the desexualized form of masochism:

If we insert this explanation into the content of moral masochism, its hidden meaning becomes clear to us. Conscience and morality have arisen through the overcoming, the desexualization, of the Oedipus complex; but through moral masochism morality becomes sexualized once more, the Oedipus complex is revived and the way is opened for a regression from morality to the Oedipus complex.[94]

According to Freud, what characterizes this form of masochism is the curious fact that the sadism of the superego tends to enter consciousness, whereas the "masochistic trend of the ego" generally remains unconscious.[95]

What is *Die Fahne*'s central masochistic scenario? It can be distilled from three episodes: the SA's initial assault on the whole family and the two interrogations Brosowski suffers at Gestapo headquarters, both described in all their bloody detail. Twice, the violence of the interrogation leads to a climactic moment dramatizing the sublime body of the Communist subject, which splits into body and Communist mind, body and Red Flag, the material and the sublime:

They turned Brosowski like a spindle around himself, so that his joints cracked and blood spilled from his mouth. He remained silent. Did he weaken once? —No. He could say that with a good conscience. His body might fail, his arms, legs, hearing —he did not fail.

He was hanging like a ball of tangled ropes on the wall, he moaned, drawn out and dangling from the window frame, his dislocated joints swollen and red, *he no longer possessed a body.*

What remained of it was the Communist Brosowski. Ribs, bones, sinews—they no longer belonged to him. They could take it and trample it, they could burn it and break it and hang it. Only the brain was still there, and the thoughts—they belonged to the Communist Brosowski. And he remained silent. (*DF*/369–70; my emphasis)

This quote seemingly contradicts the idea of a split body ("he no longer possessed a body"). But there is another level of contradiction, that between what is stated and what is represented. The entire segment draws its affective power from the minutely executed *representation* of a body-in-pain, a representation bordering in its effect, I would argue, on sadism. Far from eliminating this material body, the text instead creates and deploys the body-in-pain and its horrifying dismemberment as the indispensable support of Brosowski, the communist.

The excerpt conveys, I hope, the novel's demonstrative display of suffering, which evokes not only the Christian dichotomy of body and mind, but, in its careful arrangement, the very body of Christ himself. Yet what really implicates this display of the Communist body-in-pain in the discourse of Christianity is the punishment of the body:

[B]ehind all these "scenes" or "exhibits" is the master tableau or group fantasy— Christ nailed to the cross, head wreathed in thorns and blood dripping from his impaled sides. What is being beaten here is not so much the body as the "flesh," and beyond that sin itself, and the whole fallen world.[96]

Like Brosowski, Rüdiger is portrayed as a Christ figure hanging on the cross as he is viciously tortured before Brosowski's eyes—"in vain," of course.[97] The brief paragraph focused on Rüdiger actually precedes the one in which Brosowski's pain is described. The sudden reemergence of this mentor figure is surprising since Rüdiger practically disappears from the narrative after his arrest in January 1933. He functions as the representative of the Party and its "law" against relinquishing the flag, and, during Brosowski's second interrogation, he imagines himself as both, first becoming the Party—"in this cell, he was not Brosowski, *here he was the party*" (*DF*/382; my emphasis)—then the flag: "Brosowski and the flag—both had become one" (*DF*/378). Merging with Party and flag, that is, interiorizing the law under torture, Brosowski comes to represent the law himself. Struggling with the dilemma of whether to surrender the flag in order to prevent the torture not only of his family but also of his "comrades," he decides: "It was the Party which sustained him, which ordered him to remain silent. The Party was more than one man" (*DF*/416). The (sado)masochistic logic could hardly be more explicit: the body is being punished in the name of the father.

At this point, I would like to return to the question which I raised earlier: What underlies this scenario, this need for punishment? Against all appearances of having "loosened its connection with what we recognize as sexuality," [98] the libidinal investments of this moral masochism actually break through in the scene where Brosowski receives the flag. This rather ritualistic act of handing over the flag—its being passed from Soviet Communist Party to German Communist Party to an ordinary member—culminates in a moment of almost mystical communion:

> Brosowski did not know what was happening as he pressed his lips into the red velvet. His eyes grew moist, he struggled in vain to find words. Again and again he saw the wide Ukrainian landscape before him . . . the Soviet comrades. Their proud strength, their fortitude, their will flowed into his body. Victoriously, he felt his own strength grow, he felt the invincibility of the working class, whose sons they all were. (*DF*/88)

This passage ends with Brosowski's oath to remain eternally loyal to "Lenin's flag" (*DF* 189). It emphatically rearticulates the text's leading ideologemes, establishing the flag as the signifier of the ultimate paternal legacy (i.e., Lenin's) and in the process linking it to the exemplary strength of the Soviet working class. Moreover, it again recalls Gorky's classic by evoking the maternal metaphor, thus keeping alive the identification with a feminine position. Above all, it thematizes a strong erotic attachment to an object signifying both paternal legacy and strength.

In Freud's classic essay on fetishism, he claimed that the fetishistic object at once acknowledges and disavows the idea of women's castration.[99] Representing both a "token of triumph over the threat of castration and a protection against it," it produces a divided attitude in the fetishist himself that is expressed in what he does—in reality or in his fantasies—with this particular substitute.[100] A dream Brosowski has after several days of torture makes it quite clear what he does with his fetish: "Brosowski held the flag in his fist, it rested on his chest, he raised it when they [the SA] came over him at night, it covered him when they left" (*DF*/383). Both acknowledging and defying castration, Brosowski incorporates the Soviet flag, uses it for protection and comfort, and raises it once more. Indeed, throughout the whole narrative, this particular object is either being triumphantly raised at demonstrations or being dismantled. Its shaft, which ends in a clenched fist, is broken when Brosowski's son hides it. This central organizing object thus most obviously connects the narrative's different levels of signification.[101]

Not surprisingly, the flag from Kriwoj Rog plays a dominant role in the novel's prologue, which begins with a dedication to Brosowski and his family. This most painful example of Gotsche's "heroizing functionary style"[102] centers on a letter which "the real Brosowski" wrote a few days before his death in 1947—an allusion that establishes Gotsche's novel as a most literal narrative of the Communist variant of identification with the symbolic father (i.e., the identification unto death). It also elaborates further on the flag topos since, in this letter, Brosowski passes on the flag to the miners of Mansfeld, who raise a Red Flag above the mine shaft named after him. Reaffirming the paternal legacy—"Sons who are helping to build socialism, today in the German Democratic Republic" (*DF*/6)—Gotsche raises this symbol of defeat and castration, thus literally enacting the ideological construct of the SED as *Victors of History.* Yet the flag, I would argue, keeps the traumatic memory of defeat alive because "the horror of castration has set up a memorial to itself in the creation of this substitute."[103] Moreover, the very nature of the fetish—oscillating between acknowledgment and disavowal, presence and absence—again alludes to the problematic representation of power in East Germany's postwar fortress, to the structural absence of its center.

The image at the core of *Die Fahne*'s imaginary logic, the "Father as Master," thus turns out to be as problematic as the father figure in Bredel's trilogy: both texts bring to light a lack in the paternal function—the impossibility of ever fully incarnating the symbolic father—and both capture the paradox of the paternal function as a feminine disposition of he who will one day assume the Name-of-the-Father. Both narratives compensate for this with a proliferation of paternal images, particularly of the sublime body of the father. The difference between them is that Bredel consistently equates the sublime body with the masculine body, while Gotsche stages a shifting of the father's body from masculine monumentality to the body-in-pain. In doing so, he touches upon the limits of masculinity, the weak, feminine body which is punished but nevertheless returns as fetish. Yet there is an even more fundamental difference: Bredel keeps the Oedipal conflict alive by constructing a subject potentially in conflict with the

Law, a potential which would later be actualized by someone like Heiner Müller. In *Die Fahne,* however, this conflict is eradicated, the subjection to the father absolute.[104]

The Power of Discourse

The myth of the Communist resisting under torture became one of the core elements of the GDR's official discourse of antifascism as it developed in the 1950s. Brosowski's story was celebrated by Stephan Hermlin in the section of *Mansfelder Oratorium* (1950) devoted to "Die Hitlerzeit" (The Era of Hitler).[105] Even in 1974, Erik Neutsch mentioned the miner's heroic story in his *Friede im Osten* (Peace in the East); it also survives in many songs, condensed into a generic image of paternity, death, and transmission.[106]

This myth did not remain on the surface but sometimes penetrated the reader's subjectivity "all the way into the body's fibers," as Christa Wolf's daughter, Annette Simon, noted in 1993. Scrutinizing the antifascist imaginary, Simon casts a critical eye on this "covertly sadistic" story of "irrational" loyalty and its "quasi-sadistic superego." Analyzing the effect it had on her, the way it invaded her own body, Simon recalls a scene evoked by her antifascist education: "Even today I have an image in my soul of a woman who is being brutally beaten, and who is focusing on a colored spot on the ceiling in order somehow to endure it." The ideal identity tied to this scenario is that of someone who can "withstand torture and remain true to his ideas under the most difficult circumstances," for loyalty to the GDR was rooted in a deep solidarity with the "victims of fascism" and a feeling of "hereditary guilt." This guilt, Simon argues, "often has something to do with 'incest' in the unconscious, and that is how I sometimes experience the GDR retrospectively: as an amorphous, incestuously bound-up structure which had to wall itself in to be able to remain in this condition." [107]

Except for its concern with the masochistic dimension of antifascist identity, Simon's argument has a very familiar ring since a similar version has been recently and repeatedly advanced by Wolf herself. In many essays and interviews, Wolf has described the first FDJ generation's experience as rooted in a break with their own parents, who were guilty of collaboration with the Nazis. The parents were replaced by representatives of the antifascist resistance, thus establishing "father-son" and "mother-daughter relationships" which were constructed around the curious concept of a "potential but not yet realized guilt." [108] The basic components of this explanatory model were already present in her 1959 introduction to the *NDL* excerpts from *Die Fahne,* which Wolf read as the story of a "hero of our times" who remained true to his ideals against a most inhuman system. Focusing on the brutality of National Socialism, Wolf introduced her own problematic into the discussion of this novel:

Otto Gotsche knows that we contemporary readers have no more urgent need than to become closely acquainted with those heroes who—all too easily frozen into monuments—often seem beyond reach, might seem oppressive, in their mute impenetrability. Such a book . . . takes the reader by the hand, a reader who may be aware of his own negligence and guilt during those times, and brings him closer to those figures who become a true model for him.[109]

Here Wolf thematized the weight of the antifascist superego and pinpointed the sentiment which informs identification with the "true model," namely, guilt. Including herself *as part of the successor generation,* she accepted the dominant ideology's construction of social relations as family relations.

In Part II, we will examine the literature of this generation as the product of a confrontation with the SED's ideological discourse on the Communist family lineage and its unconscious fantasies. These texts by writers like Wolf, who conceived of themselves as East Germany's "reconstruction or FDJ generation," rethematize the issue of father–son (or father–daughter) relations and the trope of substitute fathers, narrating the break with the "real" father/parents.[110]

These "new" fathers are model antifascists, but in the 1950s they had to compete with the "father" whose image was displayed everywhere. Thus the main character in Brigitte Reimann's *Franziska Linkerhand* (1974) exclaims: "We were raised by Stalin." This young architect recalls not only the book bound in brown leather with *his* picture which she received for outstanding achievements but also her tears on that particular day in March 1953—the day Stalin died. In this memory of the bronze monument, before which "we" bowed and whose pedestal "we" decorated with flowers, its sudden disappearance—"without a trace"—caused a shock that still resonates quietly.[111] The identification with the paternal image of Stalinism which stands at the core of the 1950s dominant ideology, and its sudden loss, is nowhere more convincingly articulated than in Irmtraud Morgner's monumental 1976 novel *Leben und Abenteuer der Torbadora Beatriz* (The Life and Adventures of Beatrice the Troubadour). The quest of one of the main male characters, whose identity is defined in terms of a lack — "I am a man who has lost a father" — is organized around this traumatic experience. Since his story of "looking for a new father" is typical of a whole generation, it is worth quoting from:

I am a human being who looked for a new father. . . . I learned to hate my biological father after the war, in a very precise way. And then I tore him out of my life and grew up alone, independent. And I looked for a new father, one you could look up to, devote yourself to, believe in. His face was omnipresent, on pictures and monuments, in every city. . . . One could sing and read about him, and some of the people I revered, because they remained true to their beliefs for twelve years under the gallows, referred to him as "little father." [112]

Yet the story of his desire takes a strange and unexpected turn, transforming the protagonist's very identity: "But alone one cannot fill this gaping hole that emerged when we buried God. Alone one is not strong enough to fill the hole. . . . I am a human being who needs a mother." [113]

Morgner's story of the man who lost a father is not the only East German narrative of Oedipal subjectivity where we encounter the image of the mother; indeed, many texts written by this generation during the late 1970s and early 1980s — the literature so enthusiastically celebrated by Western critics as the final breakthrough of a feminist consciousness in the GDR — revolve around images of femininity developed with or against the maternal. The next chapter will examine the work of Anna Seghers, whose foundational texts foregrounded the image of the (Communist) *mother.* The fact that Seghers contributed to this founding discourse of maternal socialism should not be taken to imply that her major work of the period, *Die Toten bleiben jung/The Dead Stay Young,* is not securely anchored within the traditional paternal order of post-fascist socialism. On the contrary, Seghers, like Bredel and Gotsche, grounded the new ideological formation in the power of the symbolic father. And these narratives know all too well that this power is itself most securely anchored "in the place of the *dead* father." As Samuel Weber writes:

The father is guardian of the Law. . . . But if the father can exercise this function, it is less as a person than through his name, which in turn, as signifier, presupposes the radical absence of the signified. This is why it is above all in the place of the *dead* father that this name assumes its structuring power.[114]

Or, in the words of Stefan Schütz, an East German author who left the country in the 1980s:

For a citizen of the GDR, it was absolutely normal to grow up with the dead. We were always being confronted with some corpse as a glowing model to live up to. The SED practiced a massive cult of the dead. After all, we were walled in for years with the great corpses of the working-class movement, and at some point we all turned into ghosts.[115]

As we have seen, Bredel's and Gotsche's narratives of identification—of imaginary merger with the image of the (dead) father—are suffused with tensions crystallized in the paternal function itself. We will encounter similar contradictions in Seghers's work, yet with a different, albeit equally imaginary, resolution: a shift from the Bredel/Gotsche image of the Communist father to that of the Communist mother.

For just as the psychoanalytic subject is able to designate itself as a homogeneous entity over time only by repressing the traces of its unconscious desires, so . . . the state apparatus continually rewrites its own history to expel the traces of its own ruptured, heterogeneous past.

—Terry Eagleton, *Walter Benjamin; or, Towards a Revolutionary Criticism* (1985)

The Dead have not stayed young at all
The things they died for once are dying
The things that drove them—the things they did:
Their childhood beliefs are spoiled
There will never ever be a paradise
I'm scared of this hell in technicolor
Here, where the dead no longer live
The living too are ruined

I think the dead have died
That is, the dead are now forgotten
—my time on earth is getting a bit too long
All the trendy jerks make me puke
I'm doing fine. Have enough to eat
—and gnaw my heart in loneliness
—Wolf Biermann, "Cor ne edito" (1990)

2

Stalinist Motherhood, or the Hollow Spaces of Emotion: Netty Reiling/Anna Seghers

Die Toten bleiben jung/The Dead Stay Young, Anna Seghers's[1] epic novel on German history (to which Wolf Biermann alludes in his melancholic post-1989 lament), played a central role in the East German patrilinear literature of heroic antifascism. However, Seghers's novel differs significantly from Bredel's and Gotsche's. *Die Toten bleiben jung,* in consciously thematizing the problematic nature of the paternal function—the gap between "real" and "symbolic" father—consciously addresses the symbolic overpresence of the father. But even as it points to the inherent instability of paternal narratives, it sustains them with its concept of the maternal on the level of both content and form. In this novel, Seghers constructs the concept of Communist femininity as motherhood—the very concept which played such a significant part in the postwar effort of reconstruction.[2] And Communist, or rather Stalinist, motherhood, as we shall see, acts as a sort of cement for the faltering paternal construction.

I use the term *Stalinist motherhood* to designate a specific version of Seghers's representation of the maternal. As we shall see in exploring the textual materials from this most painful, yet also most productive, period of Seghers's life, this version is the product of a series of denials, repressions, and rearticulations due to biographical and political pressures, both conscious and unconscious. While this chapter is not a study of the author Anna Seghers, which would go far beyond the limits of my project, it does aim for a thorough, in-depth reading of this particular period in Seghers's life (1942/43–1949), the years during which Seghers was writing both *Die Toten bleiben jung* and two shorter narratives, "Ausflug der toten Mädchen" (The Excursion of the Dead Girls) and "Post ins gelobte Land" (Letters to the Promised Land). I propose to use the notion of the author in the sense in which Toril Moi has retheorized it in *Simone de Beauvoir.* Moi understands the author, or more broadly, subjectivity itself, as a text— an overdetermined network of multiple, potentially conflicting discourses. This "personal genealogy" does not involve a return to older forms of author-oriented criticism in which a writer's diaries or letters are read as the truth of "life" over "fiction." Such a strategy of privileging one textual form over another, and its insistence on establishing coherence, inevitably leads to simplifications and distortions. Instead, as Moi argues, it is vastly more productive to read the various texts in relation to each other, thereby abolishing the distinction between "life" and "text": "The point is not to treat one text as the implicit meaning of another, but rather to read them all with and against each other in order to bring out their points of tension, contradictions, and similarities." [3] And tensions and contradictions are certainly what characterize the text *Anna Seghers* at this particular moment.

The Crisis of the Paternal Narrative

Opening with the execution of a young Spartacist by members of the Frei-korps in 1918, Seghers's epic panorama spans the period from the revolutionary turmoil after the First World War to the end of World War II. Seghers had begun work on *Die Toten bleiben jung* while still in exile in Mexico City.[4] Upon her arrival in the Soviet Occupied Zone in 1947, she started revising the novel, which was published in 1949.[5] Although early reviews objected to the "Communist heroes' [lack of] agitational force," Seghers's novel soon acquired the status of "one of the most important works of the post-45 period," as the authors of the GDR's official literary history put it.[6]

While still in exile, Seghers had written an essay in which she asked whether it would ever be possible to reendow the "brothers and sons of murderers and bandits" with even a semblance of human dignity.[7] Her most famous novel, *Das siebte Kreuz/The Seventh Cross* (1942), the story of seven prisoners who escape from a concentration camp, treats this postwar issue in similar terms. An inmate who was present when one of the last fugitives was brought back to the camp to be nailed to one of the seven crosses later remembers the event:

These were our thoughts on that terrible morning; then for the first time we voiced our conviction that if we were to be destroyed on that scale, all would perish because there would be none to come after us. The almost unprecedented in history, the most terrible thing that could happen to a people, was now to be our fate: a no-man's-land was to be established between the generations which old experiences would not be able to traverse. If we fight and fall, and another takes up the flag and fights and falls too, and the next one grasps it and he too falls—that is natural, for nothing can be gained without sacrifice. But what if there is no longer anyone to take up the flag, simply because he does not know its meaning?[8]

Both essay and novel articulate their problematic of transmission within the familiar framework of patrilinear history, and both are written against the menacing rupture conventionally thematized in *Das siebte Kreuz* through the trope of passing the torch. Seghers's grand national epic, *Die Toten bleiben jung,* also participates in this explicitly didactic project, thematizing the threat to political continuity as the literally unbreakable chain of generations of revolutionary fighters.

Seghers's novel is a conflicted text which relentlessly thematizes paternity itself, foregrounding the substitute father but basing its master-metaphor on the "real" father. Simultaneously, but in contrast to paternity, maternity is constructed as unproblematic, as even "natural." Yet this construction of the feminine as maternal also has a strong metaphorical dimension that is central to the text's ideological project—the dimension of hope and a better life. In *Die Toten bleiben jung,* two different imperatives are at work: the paternal law of order and discipline, and what Seghers constructs as the (albeit repressed and contained) feminine imperative of change. This double imperative affects the relation between content and form, with the regulatory and prestructuring function of the text's initial episode thematizing the paternal principle of order and control on the level of *form.* This paternal ordering principle, analogous to the continuity of male genealogy, confronts the second narrative imperative: to unsettle that linear order. This imperative proceeds from the strongly repressed and contained dimension of the text's construction of motherhood—its association with radical rupture. Seghers's narrative of fathers and sons is thus a narrative-in-crisis, at once desperately sustained and peripherally contested.

Die Toten bleiben jung opens with the execution of Erwin, a young revolutionary and Spartacist, by three members of the Freikorps in 1918. This first scene prestructures the entire book by means of five major narrative strands which develop from this establishing scene and its cast of characters: (1) Marie, a Berlin waitress and Erwin's lover, who at the moment of his death is pregnant with their son, Hans; (2) Klemm, a German Army officer and owner of a chemical factory in Mainz, and his chauffeur, Becker; (3) Klemm's brother-in-law, von Wenzlow, the son of a Prussian military family; (4) Lieven, an officer and expropriated landowner from the East; and (5) Nadler, a soldier and poor farmer from the Berlin region.

Carefully interweaving other narrative voices with Erwin's inner monologue, the novel's opening narrates the final minutes before his death as a continual sliding between the present of his impending execution and his past life, making Erwin's story the story of the revolution, their parallel narration ending in the sentence: "The revolution was as young as himself" (*DS*/8; *DT*/8).[9] We learn how he joined the army, how he received the leaflet which radically changed his life, how he became involved in the revolutionary movement—"a sort of schooling between battles"—and how he fought in the streets of Berlin together with his friend Martin, who had given him the leaflet. What sutures this simultaneous (re)construction of revolutionary biography and historiography is the discourse of familial relations. As past and present flow together toward the moment of Erwin's death, he emerges as someone who has lost both father and mother. Unlike Bredel and Gotsche, then, Seghers begins her novel by envisioning the fatherless revolutionary freed from the authority of tradition and bound only by a utopian vision of a new, radically different life.

This vision is explicitly defined as maternal: the fatherless hero searches for something that would represent "mother, home, protection" (*DS*/7; *DT*/7). Remembering how he soon realized that the army had nothing to do with "mother" and "home," Erwin thinks that "the much-lauded Fatherland had by no means proved to be the sanctuary he expected" (*DS*/8; *DT*/7–8). *Fatherland* is replaced by *Revolution*, which has connotations that, as the text strains to clarify, go beyond the narrowly defined political: "By revolution they did not mean merely a change of government, the Soviet system or 'All Power to the Soviets!' They meant the *New Life* that had as little in common with the past as this world has with the Beyond" (*DS*/8–9; *DT*/8; my emphasis). "They" refers to Erwin and his "friend and brother," Martin (*DS*/10; *DT*/9). Both friends are without family: "No mother waited for them, no sister, no sweetheart—nobody but the Revolution" (*DS*/8; *DT*/8).

At the same time, Seghers creates an overarching metaphor for the entire novel—as (revolutionary) fathers die, their sons live: the dead stay young. This master-metaphor narratively enacts the law of the Communist father, *identification unto death,* but leaves paternity itself an "unconscious" fact: Erwin—like Hans, later in the book—dies without knowing that he is a father. Thus, the novel's narrative structure has two different levels: on the horizontal level, a montage of five separate stories; on the vertical level, five "ground narratives" with an overarching narrative, one which is gradually revealed as the text's master-metaphor. I will return to the topic of narrative structure later. At this point, I want to briefly trace the development of that metaphor, which is born at the moment of Erwin's execution. At the end of chapter 1, Erwin's friend Martin receives the news of the Spartacist's death and his reflections culminate in an almost monumental image of his younger friend, thus initiating the process of metaphorization: "He had died for his people, for whom he had fought ever since he could think. More than that no man could do. . . . Erwin was unassailable: he was inviolate" (*DS*/16; *DT*/15; TA).

The second component in the construction of this master-metaphor is a scene set in Saxony in 1923. Wenzlow and his Freikorps are sent to fight the Red Hundertschaften, and, after the battle, Wenzlow orders the execution of a young Communist. The chapter ends with a dream sequence in which the face of this young man merges with Wenzlow's memory of Erwin's face. Finally, Wenzlow sees Erwin's face once more in 1944, as he shouts the order to kill six men who were caught preparing to defect to the Russian Army. Among them is Hans, Erwin's son, now a soldier in the German Army fighting in the Soviet Union. Wenzlow is unaware of this "coincidence," but as he prepares to kill himself—recognizing that the war has been lost—he connects the two executions. It is this final monologue which definitively merges the images of Erwin and Hans, metaphorically realizing the familiar topos of the son(s) taking up the flag from the fathers:

They had put the man in the ground and covered him up. *But how young he had stayed!* Probably all of them who had been there had been dead now for a long time. . . . But that fellow a little while ago, the second from the left, had flung back his head like a young horse. Death seemed not to have touched him. They had ridden roughshod over him, Noske and Lichtschlag, Kapp and Luttwitz. *But how young he had stayed!* The Nazis had promised him heaven on earth, but he had not let himself be fooled. They had crushed him in every mill till his bones had cracked; they had led him to war, from battle to battle. But he had not let himself be killed: *he had stayed young.* (DS/502; DT/447; my emphases)

This massive construction centered on the iconic image of the young proletarian hero and based on the (mis)recognition of father and son, their virtual identity, spans the whole novel, resurfacing once more on the last page, where we learn that Marie now lives with Emmi, Hans's girlfriend. Like Marie at the beginning of the novel, Emmi is pregnant, and the novel ends with the image of "Marie and Emmi face to face, breathing quietly throughout the last hours of the night. And between them was the child that had not yet seen the light of the world" (*DS*/504; *DT*/448).[10] This metaphor engraves paternal authority and its legacy into the novel's historical text, yet its "biological" dimension, so vehemently criticized,[11] points to motherhood as the indispensable, albeit politically unarticulated, ground of history. Rewriting the passing of the torch from father to son as reincarnation, Seghers changes its meaning by placing motherhood at the center of the story. This maternal dimension of her metaphor marks the text's paternal narrative as fragile, needing this "cement" to stabilize a narrative-in-crisis.

The novel hints at this fragility from yet another perspective: the substitute father is a central theme, with respect both to Hans and Martin, Erwin's friend, and to Hans and Geschke (the man Marie decides to marry when Erwin does not return). In a dialogue between Marie and Geschke, paternity is discussed in terms of political legacy: when Marie asks him if she can tell Hans that he is not his "real father," Geschke refuses, saying that Hans, because of his opposition to the Nazis, is more his than his "real" son, a member of the SA. This theme is played out as a scene of "recognition" between Hans and his adoptive father: On leave from the Eastern front, Hans is addressing a clandestine meeting when he realizes that Geschke is in the room. Seghers describes this climactic moment of "recognition" from both Hans's perspective and Geschke's:

Shortly after he entered the room, he was followed by a little grey-haired man and a heavy, big-boned fellow. The two newcomers sat down in a dark corner, and though Hans could not make out their faces the big-boned fellow reminded him slightly of his father, Geschke. The longer he spoke, the surer he was that his father was in the room. (*DS*/469; *DT*/415)

Geschke, in turn, "had recognized the boy at once. Hans, he felt, was his more truly than any of his children" (*DS*/470; *DT*/415). Despite its melodramatic resonance, the scene addresses paternal authority and legacy in a very complex way: for Hans their common political identity functions to eliminate once and for all any doubts about his paternity, while for Geschke it affirms his decision not to tell Hans about his real father.

This scene also echoes one in which Hans "forces" Martin to recognize him. Although they are both unaware of the fact that Hans is Erwin's son, Martin and Hans become very close after they meet by accident. Through Martin, Hans comes to identify with the politics his father died for. Martin thus replaces Erwin, the father, as a mentor. The relationship between Hans and Martin is depicted in four brief segments: their first encounter, Martin's disappearance into illegality, their second encounter, and Martin's second departure, this time to fight in the Spanish civil war. The moment of recognition occurs during their second encounter. Martin, still an outlaw and suspicious of Hans because he is wearing the uniform of the Hitler Youth, pretends not to recognize him. As Hans desperately tries to convince him that he still believes what Martin once taught him, his former mentor remembers: "I loved this Hans; Gerlach used to tease me you might think he was your son. . . . I drummed into him everything I knew" (*DS*/339; *DT*/301).

When Hans finally succeeds in regaining Martin's trust, their father–son relationship is reestablished.

The figure of Hans is thus inextricably tied into a dense network of father–son relationships. I read this obsessive overproduction as a sign of crisis in the paternal institution. Moreover, the tension between biological genealogy and political affiliation that Seghers's text ends up foregrounding ultimately draws attention to the "artificial" nature of the father-son relationship and its core component, paternity. This is underscored by the way in which Seghers constructs the relationship to the mother. To Hans, Marie is a phenomenon of nature: "His mother was like the snow or the sun: she was just there" (*DS*/229; *DT*/206). Simply present "as the sun is always present" (*DS*/153; *DT*/138), Marie is portrayed in the most stereotypical way as a mother. When Hans briefly returns from the Eastern front, Marie becomes mother/home in the most literal sense: "He put his head on his mother's lap. 'Oh mother,' he said. 'I've often wished I could creep back into you again' " (*DS*/468; *DT*/413). Marie instinctively knows right from wrong, even though she does not have a clear understanding of the political issues at stake. As a mother who wants to prevent her son from dying at the front, Marie gets involved in sabotage, and she is repeatedly contrasted with another mother, a convinced Nazi, who calls upon everyone to fight against the Soviets until the bitter end. From this contrast, Marie emerges as the "genuine" mother, the one Seghers claims is buried beneath the Nazi ideology of motherhood. In 1942, she wrote:

There are a number of words which many people can no longer hear without disgust. . . . These include words like "fatherland," "soil of the homeland," "the people." These words actually do have meanings other than those which Hitler conveyed with them in his raving speeches. . . . No matter what Hitler did with the word "mother," no matter how many Mother's Days or Mother's Crosses were given to praise the German woman for bearing sons for this vile war, the authentic concept "mother" could still never be erased because it is one of those concepts which every human being renews in every moment of his own experience.[12]

I will elaborate on Seghers's concept of motherhood later; here, I simply want to emphasize her representation of the bond between mother and son as undisturbed, unproblematic, natural. Despite the interference of political forces which ultimately separate mother and son, their relationship is always beyond question.

To pursue the topic of the paternal story's instability, we need to change the focus of analysis from the thematic register to the narrative structure. In *Die Toten bleiben jung,* Seghers attempted to realize an aesthetic project which she delineated in her correspondence with Lukács concerning the latter's notion of realism.[13] Defending "wild breaks in style," "experiments," and "peculiar mixed forms" as an attempt to come to grips with a new epoch, Seghers drew a parallel between her own era and that of the German Romantics Kleist and Günderrode, characterizing both as epochs of transition whose reality was best expressed not by harmonious "mirrors" but by what she called "splinters." These splinters have a dual quality: they belong to the old artistic conventions but are also something new.[14] Unlike Bredel, much less Gotsche, who, despite his always polemical relationship with Lukács, essentially tried to conform to his model of realism, Seghers attempted to use the new forms developed by other modernist writers in order to "realistically" portray her era.

Seghers's persistent use of experimental, open forms in her writing has preoccupied her critics, especially with respect to *Die Toten bleiben jung.* For scholars committed to Lukács's concept of totality, such as Lutz Winckler, Kurt Batt, and Sigrid Bock, the novel raises the following question: What are the mechanisms that hold this open form together, and do they work? Winckler argues, for instance, that the use of experimental forms like montage and inner monologue does not necessarily lead to the avoidance of a fixed perspective in favor of a pure, "unengaged" description of reality.[15] Bock, however, one of East Germany's leading Seghers scholars, views this structural—and ultimately ideological—problematic as wholly unambiguous:

She works with elements that are in contradiction with one another, and yet they form an inseparable unity. On the one hand, the "unity of the plot" is destroyed by the dissection of the whole into five autonomous, independently developing strands of action; on the other hand, a new coherence is established through the inner unity of the stories narrated in the individual parts.[16]

I want to direct the focus of this discussion away from its obsession with Lukács's reflection theory and the rather unproductive opposition of open versus closed forms. Instead, I propose that the novel's narrative structure and its problems be understood as yet another symptom of the crisis of the paternal order.

To this end, we must return to the very first scene and its controlling potential. While this initial episode narrates the death of the novel's "founding father," its structuring effects realize the paternal ordering principle on the level of form. That is, the scene functions as a source of authority with respect to everything that follows, imposing its regulatory logic on a narrative that threatens to collapse into unconnected stories. After splitting the narrative into five story lines in the novel's opening pages, Seghers deploys various techniques aimed at building a continuous, seamless narrative across the rupture of these different epic threads. Let us look at her use of simultaneous narration and narrative montage. First, each of the eighteen chapters develops all five story lines *one by one*. Following a rigid logic, the narrative structure thus creates the effect of five different stories narrated simultaneously.[17] Another aspect of this attempt to impose linearity is the reference to historical events in all the chapters. In *Die Toten bleiben jung,* each chapter refers to one specific historical event, a nodal point in the Marxist historiography of Germany before 1945. Translating spatial into temporal organization, montage into chronology, Seghers thus tries to organize the narrative by analogy to the principle of successive stages.[18]

Moreover, Seghers attempts to inscribe the politics of the novel's paternal figure across the entire narrative. The techniques deployed in the opening scene all aim to secure the reader's unconditional identification with Erwin. Written as an inner monologue, the event is described almost entirely from his perspective, reducing the distance between reader and character and preparing the reader for an intense identification with the story most closely linked to Erwin. A few authorial interventions establish the parameters within which the reader will henceforth read the history of this period, juxtaposing the old world of Weimar to the new world of the Soviet revolution, as young as Erwin. In addition to these initial moves, Seghers tries to inscribe a dominant ideological discourse through the figure of Martin, inserting an extended monologue by him at a crucial historical moment— the crisis years preceding Hitler's rise to power. Addressing his dead friend, Martin speaks in the collective voice of the Party. He recalls, one by one, the events narrated in the preceding sections, creating an authoritative version of German history from 1918 to 1929. Seghers will not resort again to this particular way of securing the novel's ideological thrust; indeed, since Martin "disappears," the metaphorical narrative remains the only mechanism by which the political text associated with the novel's heroic father figure can dominate the novel. Ultimately, *Die Toten bleiben jung* does not maintain its paternal text across its complex network of multiple narratives, despite the determined effort to found it upon a principle of order and control aimed at repressing "narrative's more . . . dissolute tendencies, that is, its inclinations toward formlessness and incoherence." [19]

There is indeed another subtext at work, the guiding imperative of which is *the disruption of order.* Like the novel's regulatory thrust, it originates in the opening scene, in which *fatherland* is replaced by *revolution* as the guiding signifier, whereby the associations of *mother, home,* and *protection* are displaced from the former to the latter. This semantic shift thus articulates motherhood, or the maternal, as the intense desire for life and sudden, radical change, which is bound to one specific trope: Marie's waiting. Mistaking her son for her lover, Marie exclaims: "Life should be one delirious waiting till you heard happiness hurrying towards you on swift, impatient feet" (*DS*/393; *DT*/347). The significance of this trope clearly exceeds this scene. Instead, the ecstatic moment comes to mean a reintegration of what has been torn asunder, and it thematizes the unfaltering belief in imminent happiness, change, and the possibility of a better life.

Both the novel's beginning and its various figurations of Marie waiting thus make this intense longing for an experience of radical rupture and this belief in another existence the flip side of its representation of motherhood. Seghers's impassioned emphasis on this intense longing has to be read within the context of a specific debate among those in exile concerning the profound and, on the part of the Weimar Left, very unexpected emotional attraction of Nazi ideology.[20] In 1944, Seghers argued that, unlike the Weimar Left, National Socialism had succeeded in tapping into authentic emotional needs; the politics of antifascism therefore had to try to fill what she called "hollow spaces of emotions" (Hohlräume der Gefühle). *Die Toten bleiben jung* was involved in this project through its rearticulation of one of fascism's central concepts—*Mother/Homeland*—in its vision of another Germany.[21]

Essentially, Seghers united two distinct representations of femininity which dominated the political discourse of the Left in the 1920s and 1930s: Gorky's mother figure and Gladkov's Dasha (the female protagonist of *Cement*). The traditional connotations of motherhood in *The Mother* are mobilized here for a revolutionary praxis, together with the disruptive articulation of sexual emancipation and revolution in Gladkov's novel.[22] However, the potentially disruptive force of femininity—the metonymic chain of sexuality, the unconscious, and revolution—is carefully contained by the more conventional aspects of motherhood with which Seghers characterizes Marie. At the end of the novel, the feminine force resurfaces in the guise of a vague utopian desire: Marie is the only one of a group of women working in an ammunitions factory who can imagine what a "new life" might look like once the misery and the bombing are over (*DS*/484; *DT*/430). Femininity as disruptive excess erupts only on the periphery, when Hans, fighting in the Soviet Union, sees something of his mother in an old Russian peasant who is forced to dance by his lieutenant:

She rushed around faster than ever under all the cuffing and stamping that grew wilder and wilder. For the first time her face twitched as if she had caught the contagion of their uproarious laughter. Her toothless mouth puckered up; her breasts shook with silent laughter. "You devils will soon be out-devilled." Hans stared after her; even to him she looked like a witch at this moment. But he felt instinctively that there was a bit of his mother in this old witch and, when he thought of home, a bit of this old witch in his gentle, silent mother. (*DS*/400; *DT*/353)

It is the victory of the Red Army that this "witch" celebrates as the first snow begins to fall.

The paternal order of *Die Toten bleiben jung* is thus unsettled by the submerged component of Seghers's construction of the maternal: the potentially destabilizing power of femininity associated with the concept of revolution. Here, two different narrative imperatives are at work, staging a conflict between what the text constructs as paternal order and what it alludes to as maternal disruption in its uneasy association of femininity, motherhood, and revolution. Its display of the fatherless father as young revolutionary, I would then argue, represents a symptom of this conflict, a compromise formation between the longing for radical change and the imperative to order, control, and discipline. This imperative was treated less ambivalently by Seghers in a 1943 article in which Hitler and Thälmann are contrasted. Celebrating Thälmann's "disciplining" of the antifascist resistance movement, Seghers centers the movement on a strong father figure against the myth of the Führer.[23] At a moment of danger, the disruptive forces of revolution are in conflict with—indeed subordinated to—the order and discipline of Stalinism.

The image of the mother is thus Janus-faced, at once the highly conventional idealized mother and the equally conventional invention of the 1920s avant-garde—the figure of woman as sign of revolutionary disturbance—so similar to the contemporary icon of surrealism, Andre Breton's *Nadja*.[24] There is no doubt that this second dimension is contained, marginalized, and suppressed. Marie is no Dasha, no Nadja; her transgressive energy is safely transcendent and by no means connected to a transgressively coded feminine sexuality. On the contrary, in the course of the narrative, Marie is completely desexualized, her sexuality sublated into maternal love, while a quasi-religious aura gradually builds up around her character, extending from her name to the aureole of light emanating from her hair. This process of purification, the sequestering of the mind or the idea from the body, is the all-too-familiar prerequisite for the feminine allegory central to many national narratives.[25] Ultimately, Marie emerges as the pure incarnation of the idea of motherhood, the *idealized working-class mother.*

This idealized maternal figure dominates Seghers's textual production from the 1950s.[26] With respect to her political writing, for instance, Cettina Rapisarda has characterized Seghers's postwar engagement with the Council for World Peace as based on the belief that "the feeling of responsibility for future generations which characterizes women as mothers" was the starting point for political action.[27] The same held true for her literary writing. For instance, in her 1959 novel *Die Entscheidung* (The Decision), a subplot revolves around Katharina, who at first refuses to join her husband in the East, on religious grounds. But when she becomes pregnant, she finally decides to leave the West. Immediately after crossing the border, she gives birth to a daughter and then dies of childbed fever. Although merely one subplot among many that thematize "the decision," Katharina's story is nevertheless crucial to the novel's metaphoric ideological dimension. Not surprisingly, the portrait of this mother figure differs only slightly from that of Marie in *Die Toten bleiben jung.* Seghers's posthumously published "Frauen und Kinder in der Emigration" (Women and Children in Emigration) participates in the same celebration of the simple working-class mother who, when faced with the difficulties of emigration, mobilizes all her strength: "The force which had been buried inside of her perhaps for her whole life, perhaps for centuries, was now wide awake. . . . Now she was again the woman of the wars, of the exiles, of the mass migrations." It is the women's "natural feeling of solidarity" which helps their families to survive.[28] Finally, two short stories, "Vierzig Jahre der Margarete Wolf" (The Forty Years of Margarete Wolf), of 1958, and "Agathe Schweigert," of 1965, continue this celebration of the idealized working-class mother. The former develops a minor female character from *Das siebte Kreuz,* while the latter recontextualizes an explicitly Gorkian mother figure within the Communist Party's antifascist struggle.[29]

The Other Family's Story

A very different image of the mother appears in two other short stories by Seghers, "Der Ausflug der toten Mädchen" and "Post ins gelobte Land," written between 1943 and 1945 (i.e., while she was also writing *Die Toten bleiben jung*) and first published in 1946 in New York.[30] "Post ins gelobte Land" tells the story of a Jewish family, the Grünbaums, who, at the end of the nineteenth century, escape from a pogrom in Poland. The family flees first to Vienna, then to Silesia, taking with them their son-in-law, Nathan Levi, and their grandson, born just before their daughter died in the pogrom. With the help of Nathan's brother, Salomon, the family finally ends up in Paris. Much of the story focuses on the gradual assimilation of the grandson, Jacques, into what he comes to consider his nation, a process described as the natural fusion of an older with a newer identity, "like two layers of bark." [31] Shortly after Jacques Levi's marriage to the daughter of his father's friend, Nathan decides to emigrate to Palestine. Jacques, now a famous doctor, promises to write regularly. Soon after his father leaves, however, Jacques discovers that he is terminally ill. He begins to write Nathan letters in advance, making his wife promise that after his death she will continue sending them to his father. She keeps her promise even after she is forced to leave Paris in 1940.

As Kathleen LaBahn has observed, the story's political project is to demonstrate successful assimilation into a society permeated by the principles of its bourgeois revolution, an assimilation held up as a model for Seghers's German context.[32] Unlike any of her other stories, "Post ins gelobte Land" is deeply embedded in the orthodox milieu of her upbringing, while secularizing Jewish traditions in the service of remembering.[33]

Just as *Die Toten bleiben jung* incessantly returns to its first scene, Erwin's death, "Post ins gelobte Land" repeatedly returns to the death of the young mother narrated in its first paragraph. It is through the characters of the young woman's mother and her husband that her memory is kept alive throughout the story. Nathan Levi lives in the hope of being reunited with her in death, and her image remains vivid to him: "His wife's pale face, glowing as she died, remained young and pale in his memory" (P/170). His son, Jacques, cannot remember his mother; all he associates with her is the light of the candle lit in her memory, which he sees for the first time when his grandmother takes him to the synagogue in the Marais:

How they glowed down there, the candles that were lit on the holidays for all of the deceased relatives!

Frau Grünbaum recognized her own candle from up above, or thought she recognized it; tenderly she looked for it, as if it were the daughter herself. She also showed it to the little one. (P/159)

This very image returns in Jacques's last letter to his father, who still believes him to be alive. In this letter, the (dead) son recounts a dream in which he accompanies his grandfather to the synagogue to light a candle in memory of his mother:

"My dear father, I dreamed last night that I was walking through the courts and corridors of St. Paul, I was a little boy, I was holding . . . Grandfather's hand. We climbed the spiral staircase to the first floor of the synagogue. From up there Grandmother showed me the candle which was lit for mother."

Now, the memory of the candle takes on a new urgency as he greedily looks down at the candle. (P/174)

"Post ins gelobte Land" obsessively thematizes the connection between writing and memory. And it explicitly connects the theme of writing to the memory of the mother, a connection which, as we will see, appears in "Der Ausflug der toten Mädchen" only as a displacement. Jacques Levi's letter links the act of writing to the act of remembering and, ultimately, to the face of the mother. Through the correspondence between a (dead) son and his father, writing constitutes memory but also denies death: after his death, Jacques Levi's wife assumes the duty of sending his letters to his father because it allows her the illusion that her husband is still alive. For her, Jacques's letters are a "guarantee of life" (P/172). And these letters do keep arriving in the Promised Land long after this young woman and her son have "disappeared" on the way to Southern France while fleeing from the invading German Army. At the end of the story, we simply learn that her friends "received after some time only the news that the woman with the sick child had been deported somewhere" (P/175).

In "Post ins gelobte Land," the mother's face appears in a highly stylized final act of remembrance. Just as Jacques Levi's memory of seeing his mother's candle faithfully lit replays an earlier scene, his letter provokes a dreamlike, almost hallucinatory state in Nathan Levi which allows him to relive this very moment in the Parisian synagogue. As he reads his son's letter in a garden in Palestine, the faces of the friends surrounding him slowly dissolve into the faces of those close to him when he still lived in the Marais. The letter conjures up the face of his wife in almost the same words as before: "The glowing, pale, fragile face of his wife, who had died in the basement during the pogrom, lit up in the little flame" (P/175). The matter-of-fact statement that follows this lyrical passage produces a strong distancing effect: "The young widow had not left in time" (P/175).

Fantasy and Its Identificatory Structures: The Mother's Journey

This carefully composed frame encircling the Jewish mother's face, I would argue, is meant to control a very personal pain which threatens to break through. Both "Post ins gelobte Land" and "Ausflug der toten Mädchen" were written after the most traumatic experiences of Seghers's life: her accident in Mexico City, which left her unconscious for weeks; and the news of her mother's death in a Polish concentration camp.[34] Notoriously discrete about her private life, Seghers never spoke publicly about these events;[35] nevertheless, their enormous impact can be read in her correspondence, although even there the tone tends to be rather subdued. In a letter to her close friend, Lore Wolf, Seghers said only: "My mother was deported to Poland and murdered, even though we did procure visas for her, but too late by a few days." [36] In January 1944, she told friends that she still had only "little scraps of information" about her mother's fate, and, in a rare display of emotion, she wrote in May 1944: "Sometimes I read the five, six letters which I received from my mother, and each time I sink into an indescribable state of rage and mourning." [37] The guilt that can be inferred from Seghers's repeated allusions to her futile efforts to rescue her mother is most evident in her attitude toward the accident that left her comatose: "I now feel that it is a kind of punishment for having been far away from the dangers of war." [38]

Her mother's disappearance was clearly a trauma, if we understand by that a specific structure of experience in which the overwhelming event "is not assimilated or experienced fully at the time, but only belatedly, in its repeated possession of the one who experiences it." Cathy Caruth, from whose essay on trauma this definition is taken, considers "the delay or incompletion in knowing" the "enigmatic core" of trauma: "The traumatized . . . carry an impossible history within them, or they become themselves the symptom of a history that they cannot entirely possess." [39] In Seghers's case, an almost fatal accident coinciding with the news of her mother's death complicated the issue of surviving the Holocaust. As her letters indi-

cate, Seghers's accident familiarized her with the experience of being a survivor, "one who has come into contact with death in some bodily or psychic
fashion and has remained alive." [40] It also involved an identification with
the mother through death, which touches upon what several participants in
the 1985 International Psychoanalytic Congress referred to as "identification and its vicissitudes in the context of the Nazi phenomenon." [41] These
speakers addressed the " 'transmission' of the traumatic potential from one
generation to the next," [42] that is, how the second generation dealt with
their parents' experience by reliving their (often silent, unarticulated) past
in *fantasy*. These analysts also emphasized the multiple, easily transferable
dimension of identification, observing that subjects often take up positions
in the unconscious that are the opposite of those they occupy consciously,
shifting from identification with the victim to identification with the perpe-
trator, for example.

Seghers's case was complicated by the fact that she did not belong to a
generation born after the persecution, but instead barely escaped her own
mother's fate, a situation put into relief by her accident. Moreover, she
was forced to relive a story that was not so much unspoken as unknown
or, worse, partially known. "Post ins gelobte Land," with its focus on the
Jewish mother killed in a pogrom and on the letters exchanged between
father and son, thematizes the nexus between writing and memory, relating
the authorship of "Anna Seghers" to the mother; moreover, the text enacts
an identification *at the level of fantasy* by the one who survived the lost
mother. The most basic structure through which this identification operates
is the trope of *a mother's journey*. It is with Jacques Levi's wife that Seghers
identifies at the end of the story—by merging the story of Jacques's wife
with her own story, her escape from Paris. The flight of Jacques's wife and
son from Paris toward southern France reproduces accounts by Seghers
of her own escape from the advancing German Army, accompanied by
her children. But the story also diverges significantly from Seghers's since
Jacques's wife never makes the "transit." In this figure, then, Seghers has
conflated her own story with that of her mother, about whose fate she never
learns more than that she perished on her way to a Polish camp. By merging her own journey through France and escape from the Gestapo with her
mother's journey and death, Seghers fantasizes the daughter's/survivor's
own death, taking the identificatory process—her "identifying with"—to
its very limits.[43] In "Post ins gelobte Land," loss and the pain and guilt as-

sociated with it translate into the distancing effect produced by the text's aestheticizing strategies.[44]

Returning Home: "Ausflug der toten Mädchen"

The lyrical, deeply mournful image of the lost Jewish mother in "Post ins gelobte Land" is very different from the mother figure we encountered in *Die Toten bleiben jung.* We find traces of it in another story, "Der Ausflug der toten Mädchen," but here we also find Marie. And in "Der Ausflug," we find the same core topics already developed in "Post ins gelobte Land": the duty to write, the quest for the mother, and the identificatory trope of the journey. Together with "Post ins gelobte Land," this story sketches a topography of identification and mourning which reaches from the "most western" point of Seghers's exile to the "most eastern" point of the Jewish mother's death in Poland.

By breaking through reality into dream/fantasy in "Post ins gelobte Land," Seghers transgresses the boundaries of the realist aesthetic; yet, at the same time, she observes its imperative of "objectivity" by staying within the framework of the chronicle and its omniscient narrator. This is not the case in "Der Ausflug der toten Mädchen," Seghers's only fictional text in which the first-person narrator explicitly refers to autobiographical events, mentioning both the author's exile and her accident at the very beginning; the death of her mother, however, is thematized only at the very end. "Ausflug der toten Mädchen" thus repeats the overarching structure of "Post ins gelobte Land" — an encounter with the Jewish mother at the end of a dreamlike process of remembrance. But more importantly, it multiplies the identificatory gestures of the previous text in an explicitly autobiographical context, elaborating much more on the mother's/daughter's journey.

This story, which so masterfully blends the author's present, her Mexican exile, with memories from her German past, works toward one specific moment, namely, when Netty, the girl, returns home from the excursion, longing to be taken into her mother's arms:

[My mother] was already waiting for me. How young my mother looked, much younger than I. How dark her smooth hair was, compared with mine. Mine very soon turned grey, while not a single grey strand yet ran through hers. She stood there merry and erect, destined for a busy family life, with the usual joys and burdens of everyday living, not for an agonizing, dreadful end in a remote village, to which she was banished by Hitler. Now she caught sight of me and waved, as though I had been away on a journey. This was the way she always laughed and waved after outings.[45]

This passage not only conjures up an impossible meeting, but it does so by splitting the narrator's identity into the little girl she once was and the woman she now is. Comparing her hair color with her mother's, the narrator focuses on the difference between her present self and the mother of her memory. The passage thus discursively narrates the mother's death and, at the same time, evokes it in relationship to the daughter who survived.

As this brief passage indicates, the narrative voice and time structure are remarkably intricate. Speaking in the first person, the narrator continually slides from present to past, at some moments reliving the past in an almost unmediated fashion while at others weaving her present knowledge into the memory traces she recovers. This sliding from present to past self and the blurring of boundaries between present and past are most brilliantly established by the story's opening. At first, the narrator situates herself unambiguously in the present context of her Mexican exile as she arrives at a café. Having answered the owner's question—"No, from much further away. From Europe"—she begins to meditate on her situation, suddenly finding the fact that she lives in Mexico as "fantastic" as the owner does (A/13):

I leant back against the wall and into the narrow shade. The refuge I had found in this land was too dubious and too uncertain to be called salvation. Just behind me I had months of illness that had overtaken me here, even though the manifold dangers of the war had been unable to touch me. (O/14; A/51; TA)

Her goal is a ranch she had discovered the previous evening, looking down from the village where she is staying in a small hotel. From her place at the café table, the ranch appears in a "shimmering haze"; she cannot decide whether it is caused by the sun or her own fatigue. As she begins to walk toward a garden, this "cloud of dust or of fatigue" (O/15; A/52) condenses, only to disperse once she "enters" the garden in Germany—her past.

The opening thus establishes the narrator's condition as extremely fragile, both mentally and physically: she is exhausted; the sun hurts her eyes and she cannot see clearly. Her fatigue, with its dreamlike state, marks the dissolution of the boundary between present and past, reality and memory, lending the narrating voice a highly ambiguous quality, as it cannot be clearly located in either its present or its past. Furthermore, the narrator's setting off for the ranch, which will become the garden terrace on the Rhine where the girls and their teachers stop to rest during their excursion, introduces the trope of the journey—both in a "literal" sense and as fantasy—at the very beginning. This journey will end with the appearance of the mother, with the memory of "coming home" from the outing. The desire which drives the journey is again formulated in the ambiguous voice of present/past— "I thought weakly: what a pity, I should so much have liked to be embraced by my mother" (O/44; A/81).

The attempt to reach the mother proves to be an exhausting journey: "I was utterly exhausted, so that I was glad at last to be standing in front of my house. Only it seemed to me an intolerable effort to climb the stairs" (O/42; A/80). Again, fatigue renders the narrative voice, its anxieties and desires, highly ambiguous, expressing the longing of the girl/narrator to be reunited with her mother. Having recognized her mother on the balcony, "I"/Netty, the autobiographical subject, then hurries toward the staircase, but is abruptly overcome by fatigue: "I was suddenly far too tired to run up the stairs, as just before I had wanted to do" (O/43; A/80; TA). This effort to reach her mother at the top of the stairway slides imperceptibly into the effort to return to the Mexican mountain village, her intradiegetic "place of origin": "what a pity, I should so much have liked to be embraced by my mother. If I'm too tired to climb up, where shall I find the strength to reach my village of origin [Ursprungsdorf] higher up the mountain where people are expecting me for the night?" (O/44; A/81). How should this slippage be read? The narrator's journey to her "village of origin," and her possible breakdown on the way there, reproduces the mother's deportation to the village in Poland, the daughter's exile to the Mexican village, "the most westerly point to which I had ever been on earth" (O/15; A/52), an inverted mirroring of the mother's final destination in Poland, the most easterly point she ever reached during her lifetime.

Like "Post ins gelobte Land," "Der Ausflug" merges two lives and, ultimately, two deaths through the trope of the journey. Yet in the former the death fantasy is veiled, indirect, since the mother figure who dies at the end is not part of an explicitly autobiographical narrative even though she retraces Seghers's own escape route from the Nazis; in the latter this survivor's fantasy of her own death becomes a (more or less conscious) wish. At the end of her quest for the mother—that is, when she recalls coming home from the excursion, longing to join her mother at the top of the stairway—the narrator/daughter is suddenly overcome by the fear of her own death: "if I were to break down from exhaustion" (O/43; A/81). The sudden shift into the present tense—"if I'm too tired to climb up"—takes this fear into the narrator's present as fantasy, not memory.

This moment introduces yet another layer into the narrative's dense tectonic formation of memory and fantasy, since it refers at once to the present, as the narrator tries to climb the Mexican mountain, to the fantasized repetition of the mother's journey to Poland and death, *and* to a moment in the narrator's childhood:

Perhaps my mother had already gone into the hall and was waiting for me in the door to the stairs. But my legs failed me. *Only as a very small child had I felt a similar anxiety that some disaster might prevent me from seeing her again. I imagined her waiting for me in vain.* (O/43; A/81; my emphasis)

This passage adds to the adult experience of separation through exile and violent death the archaic anxieties of childhood, of separation and abandonment, so that the final sentence again oscillates between past and present, remobilizing via a childhood memory the narrator's guilt at having abandoned her mother.

The complex entanglement of being abandoned by/abandoning the mother is escaped through yet another fantasy, that of being rescued by the father: "Then it occurred to me as a consolation that if I were to break down from exhaustion, my father could find me at once. He was not dead after all, because he would be home in a moment" (ibid.). This conscious denial of the father's death is followed abruptly by a passage in which the intrusion of the Mexican present into the narrator's childhood memory is slowly registered by a shift from visual to aural perception: she hears the noise of dinner plates and the sound of hands kneading dough in a *familiar* rhythm. Yet the sense of familiarity quickly disappears: "It seemed strange to me that people were making pancakes this way" (ibid.). The perceptual register changes once more as the narrator is suddenly blinded by a strong light shining through the windows in the stairway: "The stairs were swimming in a haze, the staircase stretched out to an impenetrable depth, like an abyss" (O/44; A/81). The thought of loss and abandonment which accompanies this falling into the "abyss" of memory, as we have already seen, is "what a pity, I should so much have liked to be embraced by my mother."

The present persecution and fear of annihilation thus leads the narrator back to the desire of the child she once was, making "Der Ausflug der toten Mädchen" the most profound exploration of loss that Seghers allowed herself. The narrator, after letting herself be drawn into the vortex of a shattered past, returns abruptly to the present, concerned about whether she has the energy to return to her mountain village; then, finding herself once more in the stairway, admonishing herself: "I pulled myself together" (ibid.). Disoriented, she is still moving in a liminal space between past and present, climbing the stairway in her parents' house whose railing turns into a hedge of Mexican cacti. The story's closing is well known: the narrator finally decides to do what her Jewish teacher of German literature had asked her to do after the outing— "carefully describe the excursion" (O/45; A/82; TA). The ending makes writing the duty, even the imperative, to remember—the task that she was "instructed" to do (O/45; A/82).

Communist Femininity and Its Overdeterminations

These stories, with their focus on the image of the *Jewish* mother, allow us to understand another dimension of Marie's allegorical purity, an aspect which emerges when we compare her with the *other* mother figure in *Die Toten bleiben jung,* Elisabeth Lieven. This woman has witnessed Jews being deported and killed: on the way to her estate in the East, she sees a group of Jews being forced into a cattle wagon; and when Ernst Lieven, now an SS officer, returns home, Elisabeth overhears a conversation about the killing of two thousand Jewish women. The text dwells on the image of the naked women on their way to the gas chambers, on the officers' cynical comments. The contrast between this mother figure and Marie is consistently built up over the course of the narrative, with Marie thereby emerging as the allegorical figure of purity described above: Marie is not only "purified" of her body; her purity also comes from the fact that she is untouched by any knowledge of the Holocaust. As the allegorical, idealized working-class mother, Marie conceals the presence of the Jewish mother, thereby pointing to what *Die Toten bleiben jung* and all other paternal narratives of antifascism repress. And the image of Jewish women on their way to their deaths, intensely disturbing but marginal to the central story of the grand historical epic, constitutes the vantage point of both of Seghers's "minor" stories.

In his work on the psychosocial dimensions of mourning in West Germany, Eric Santner theorizes two different textual processes as responses to trauma and loss, narrative fetishism and *Trauerarbeit* (work of mourning):

By narrative fetishism I mean the construction and deployment of a narrative consciously or unconsciously designed to expunge the traces of the trauma or loss that called that narrative into being in the first place. . . . Both narrative fetishism and mourning are responses to loss, to a past that refuses to go away due to its traumatic impact. The work of mourning is a process of elaborating and integrating the reality of loss or traumatic shock by remembering and repeating it in symbolically and dialogically mediated doses; it is a process of translating, troping, and figuring loss. . . . Narrative fetishism, by contrast, is the way an inability or refusal to mourn emplots traumatic events; it is a strategy of undoing, in fantasy, the need for mourning by simulating a condition of intactness.[46]

Die Toten bleiben jung seems to fall unequivocally into the category of narrative fetishism. It clearly relegates the Holocaust to the status of a peripheral plotline and, in its allegorical figure of Marie as post-fascist utopia, "simulates a condition of intactness" that is actually the effect of massive repression.

There is yet another dimension to the work of repression in which this text engages, for it is not only as a gesture of *identification with the victim* that the trope of the mother's journey is deployed by Seghers. Buried deep within the dense fabric of *Die Toten bleiben jung* lies the *identification with the bystander,* developed along the very same plotline: I am referring to the figure of Elisabeth Lieven; fleeing from the approaching Soviet Army, she leaves her estate in Lithuania and, when her car breaks down in a snowstorm, dies with her young son, unable to reach the nearest village after becoming lost in the storm. The description of her frenzied flight through artillery fire closely resembles Seghers's own experience in 1941. The character of Elisabeth is associated with a desperate search for *home,* her longing forever tied to the memory of her family's estate in the East to which she finally returns with her husband. Elisabeth dies fully conscious of the price she has paid for this "home." Haunted by the image of the Jewish women on their way to the gas chamber, she thought about leaving the estate but had no place to go. Resigned to dying in a snowstorm after having escaped from the Red Army, she prays to the God in whose existence she does not believe to absolve her of her guilt. A desperate parody of the Pater Noster, her prayer becomes a question: "As we forgive those who trespass against us—how could those women who were driven like cattle, stark naked, in front of Lieven and Tetzlow and Schulze, forgive us?" (*DS*/457; *DT*/457). This is the only instance in Seghers's entire oeuvre of the Holocaust's being narrated, albeit in a mediated form. But more importantly, this subplot, which again uses the trope of the journey, explicitly depicts the death of the young mother and son as punishment; it establishes a parallel between character and author, allowing us to read this variation on Seghers's dominant literary figure as the fantasy of identifying with the bystander.

In contrast to *Die Toten bleiben jung,* "Der Ausflug der toten Mädchen" seems deeply engaged in the processes of *Trauerarbeit.* In its profound, sustained exploration, the story becomes an extraordinary record of its author's working through the experience of loss. But the mother in "Der Ausflug der toten Mädchen"—"merry and erect . . . destined for a busy family life, with the usual joys and burdens of everyday living" (O/43; A/80)—is more like Marie, the generic working-class mother of Seghers's novel, than like the disembodied and ethereal dead Jewish mother in "Post ins gelobte Land." Describing "Der Ausflug der toten Mädchen" as part of a project of postwar reconstruction and education, Seghers wrote that it was especially significant as a contribution to what she considered one of the most important postwar themes: the "mother of the people." [47] Rearticulating her mother's death with a political narrative in which the Holocaust plays only a minor role, Seghers superimposed Marie onto the Jewish mother. This discourse, informing both the monumental historical novel and the short story, argues for the Communist Party's popular front politics and its reappropriation of the *Heimat*/homeland concept for a new Germany. In Seghers's work, its aim is the explicit inclusion of Jews as part of the German people. Thus, thinking about Marianne, one of the "dead girls," who will betray her best friend to the Gestapo, the narrator questions her right to believe that only she, the Nazi, loves this country. Heimat, she claims, is made of the common history of all the girls; it is not the exclusive property of a few.[48] Yet while Seghers's story insists that its telos, Heimat, might be reconstituted in the political narrative, it remains irretrievably lost in the personal narrative. These two stories clash most violently in the scene which makes the encounter with the mother the core element of a reappropriated German Heimat, that is, when Netty discovers her mother on the balcony. "Except for a few friends I have no one alive left in Germany," wrote Seghers before she returned in 1947.[49]

As "Post ins gelobte Land" shows, the history of Jewish emancipation and destruction had to be told as a separate story; its political discourse could only be partially integrated into the dominant ideological discourses of Seghers's other literary texts of this period. Instead of assigning "Der Ausflug der toten Mädchen" and "Post ins gelobte Land" to the category of either narrative fetishism or work of mourning, we should think of these texts as an inextricable web of both confronting and fetishizing loss, threads tied to writing as both the work of memory and the work of repression. Reading these stories together with *Die Toten bleiben jung* allows us to read the conflicts and tensions lived by a Communist author whose Jewishness was supposed to be merely incidental, overridden by her identification with that class which guaranteed Germany's "progressive history." [50]

Indeed, what this intertextual reading establishes above all is the over-determined nature of Seghers's particular representation of Communist femininity: Communist motherhood is the effect of condensation, a textual element whose determinants can be traced to more than one "cause." In other words, her overtly idealized working-class mother, a figure of almost allegorical purity by which traditional maternal values are articulated to socialism, is the result of a number of different pressures rooted in both the personal *and* the political. These pressures arose from Seghers's personal story, her guilt concerning her mother's death, *and* her implication in a political discourse which tended to subordinate anti-Semitism and its deadly politics to a national narrative of class struggle.

How did Seghers position herself relative to the Communist Party's popular front discourse? In the early 1940s, Seghers's version of the anti-fascist narrative differed significantly from what later became the GDR's official version. Seghers belonged to a group of so-called Western exiles in Mexico City, who, in their intellectual circle—the Heinrich-Heine Club— and in their journal—*Freies Deutschland*—made the persecution of Jews one of their central topics. Among other works that later came to be considered "deviant" was Alexander Abusch's 1946 historical treatise *Der Irrweg einer Nation* (A Nation's Erroneous Path). Reading German history from the peasant wars to National Socialism as a series of "wrong" turns, Abusch admonished his German readers to seize their last opportunity to correct the nation's developmental path by constructing a socialist Germany after the war. Each chapter closes with a discussion of the fate of Jews at yet another historical turning point, premising the work as a whole on the idea that Jews always function as scapegoats.[51] Paul Merker, another member of the German Communist Party in Mexican exile, published a series of articles in *Freies Deutschland* concerning the future relationship between Germans and (German) Jews which differed significantly from the SED's official discourse, since he argued for the special plight of the Jewish victims—and for their special reparation.[52] At the height of East Germany's involvement in the anti-Semitism of the Soviet-instigated postwar show trials, which started in September 1949 in Hungary with the verdict against Lazlo Rajk and culminated with the execution of Rudolf Slansky in 1952, Paul Merker in 1955 was tried, convicted, and sentenced to eight years in prison as a defender of Zionism and "King of the Jews." [53] Anti-Semitic tendencies or simply thoughtless measures were the outcome not only of Soviet pressure, but also of the KPD/SED's legitimatory strategy. As the former East German historian Olaf Groehler shows in his analysis of the 1945 conference "Victims of Fascism," the distinction between "fighters against fascism" and "victims of fascism," so central to the SED's codification of the past, arose in the context of a heated debate during which many participants opposed the recognition of the racially persecuted as victims of fascism.[54] This expression of a "populist" anti-Semitism in the German working-class movement later coincided with the SED's strategy of foregrounding its own antifascist heroes as part of its legitimatory project. In this context, Jewish German Communists could live in the GDR only by repressing not some essential identity but the memory of a traumatic historical experience.[55] "Red" assimilation was fraught with tensions which, it seems, never really disappeared. As Stephan Hermlin observed in a 1992 interview:

I made some very close friends in the Party, but I met even more people whom I count among my worst enemies. These comrades confronted me with a senseless, irrational hostility from the outset. I often asked myself: What is it about me? What is it that has such unpleasant effects on these people? What could it have been? I have a suspicion, indeed a rather uncanny suspicion . . . anti-Semitism? Yes. Why? These are things that one does not want to recognize for a long time. You redecorate reality to suit your needs. Many people with origins similar to mine had quite similar experiences. Anna Seghers, for instance.[56]

Anna Seghers chose to remain silent, indeed even to participate in the marginalization of the Holocaust after the late 1940s.[57]

Seghers's return to Germany was certainly not easy. In 1947, she asked: "How is it possible that others do not form the same associations, do not carry the same inherited burdens as we do?" [58] Historical memory was not the same for those who had lived under the Nazi regime and those who had left. Seghers's question hints at the difficulties that many exiles, especially Jewish Communists like herself, experienced upon their return "home," the gap between themselves and a population that had remained loyal to the National Socialist regime until the very end. The articles Seghers wrote in Mexico deal in depth with the emigrant's relationship to Hitler's Germany. In 1941, she polemically attacked Thomas Mann for his idea of putting the entire German population under tutelage, asking who the new teachers were supposed to be—those "from superior peoples? From more noble races?"—thus insinuating his complicity with the very thinking he rejected. Her own question—"A people who fall upon others in order to annihilate them, can they still be our people?" [59]—she answers in the affirmative. Five years later, after the revelations about the German death camps, her tone had become harsher, as she spoke of Heine's feelings toward the country he was forced to leave: "Heine loved Germany, and he hated it." [60] Seghers's arrival in postwar Germany seems to have been something of a shock. Explaining her desire to participate in the reconstruction of Germany as the duty to prevent a return of the past, she observed in an April 1947 interview: "For those of us who are returning without any prejudice against Germany, it is horrifying to observe that not only those contaminated by Nazism, but also some of the democrats with whom I speak arrive at conclusions which actually still stem from Goebbel's repertoire." [61] In a letter to Lukács in June 1948, she described herself as living through an Ice Age.[62]

The stories Seghers wrote after 1943 indicate that her increasing silence on the Holocaust was a (voluntary) silencing, if not outright repression. As we have seen, these texts generate on their deepest level structures of identification with the lost mother which permeate the entire narrative. In "Der Ausflug der toten Mädchen," Seghers redeployed the structure underlying "Post ins gelobte Land": the encounter with the (dead) mother at the end of a dreamlike journey of remembrance, as well as its more veiled structure of the daughter's reliving the journey and death of the mother. One might be inclined to attribute this silence and the foregrounding of the antifascist popular front discourse to the GDR's political climate under High Stalinism, including the pressures upon Jewish Communists discussed above. However, I do not want to advance a simple dichotomy of political pressure and personal story, whereby the repression of the Holocaust and its traumatic effects are attributed exclusively to Seghers's position within a specific ideological system. On the contrary, as I have shown, *Die Toten bleiben jung,* "Der Ausflug der toten Mädchen," and "Post ins gelobte Land" exhibit a pattern of crisis in which both the need to remember *and* the desire to repress is strongly linked to the guilt of the survivor. The idealized image of the "mother of the people" is thus overdetermined, the product of an ideological project of reconstruction based on maternal values and of a deep, overwhelming guilt.

In this situation, Seghers defined literature's function as attempting to establish a "tacit agreement" about the new Socialist order and Germany's past.[63] In this chapter, we have approached the topic of "missing" associations and the unexplored "hollow spaces of emotion" from a slightly refracted perspective: a simultaneous inquiry into the ways in which Seghers tried to give meaning to such lacunae *and* to the unconscious associations and "hollow spaces" in her own writings. Those were traced to a central act of silencing and repression: the repression of her mother's death in a Polish concentration camp and the inevitable tensions of a (Communist) Jewish German identity after 1945. As we have seen, these tensions arose from the often unarticulated antagonism between exiles and the silent majority, as well as from Seghers's own implication in a political discourse which tended to subordinate the issue of anti-Semitism to a national narrative of class struggle. In the next section, we will encounter some even "older" pressures which bear on the centrality of the maternal in Seghers's writing of the 1950s, with respect not only to the predominant figure of the idealized working-class mother, but also to a reorganization of Seghers's speaking position as one in the tradition of the mother.

Memory and the Act of Writing:
Transforming the Authorship "Anna Seghers"

The impact of her accident on Seghers was profound: "I was so sick that I could no longer remember anything, least of all the books I had written."[64] Overcoming this trauma entailed a reconstruction of her shattered identity, touching upon the very foundation of the author "Anna Seghers," indeed even redefining the East German institution "Anna Seghers": after 1943, she would write as a *motherly* educator *in memory of her mother.*[65]

In one of her essays on Seghers, Wolf describes the older author's role as that of "teacher" and "mentor": "During the final years of her emigration, Anna Seghers prepared herself for the task which would face her upon her return: to be the teacher for an entire people." [66] This institution "Anna Seghers" acquired a specific motherly dimension. In an open letter of 1975 to Seghers, for instance, Alexander Abusch addressed her first as a mother in the context of her writing: "Mother and motherly one, in your writing the struggles over the key decision of our epoch become visible in figures of women and children;" then in the context of her life: "With a mother's un-broken energy you made your way to the concentration camp Le Vernet." He added that she always reacted with "particular sensitivity and mother-liness." [67] This maternal image carried over into Seghers's West German reception. For instance, the critic Frank Benseler wrote in a congratulatory letter: "If I had only one word to express it, I would say 'Mother,' think-ing of Gorky, of Mother Courage, and of the fishermen's wives." [68] While this public identity represented her acquiescence to the limited role she was allowed to play,[69] it also reflected Seghers's reorganization of her author-ship, as a closer analysis of the narrating subject in "Der Ausflug der toten Mädchen" will demonstrate.

"Der Ausflug der toten Mädchen" proceeds from a profound problema-tization of its narrating instance, the "I" who splits into the first-person voice of the narrator's present and that of "Netty," the narrator's past self. The latter name is heard as the present changes into the past, the Mexican ranch into the German garden: "Now my curiosity was awakened, and I ran through the gate. . . . At that very moment, someone called: 'Netty' " (O/16; A/53; TA). This is the name the narrator has been waiting to hear:

No one had called me by that name since I was in school. I had learned to respond to all of the good names and the bad names with which friends and enemies used to call me, the names which had been given to me over the course of many years in the streets, meetings, celebrations, dark rooms, police interrogations, book titles, newspaper reports, protocols, and passports. I had even hoped that I might hear this old, childhood name as I was lying sick and unconscious. But the name was lost, this name which I self-deceptively believed could make me healthy again, young, happy, ready for the old life with the old friends, a life which was irrevocably lost. (O/16; A/53–54; TA)

What does this passage tell us about the name, about its function and sig-nificance? "Netty" refers to the "oldest" and "earliest" layers of identity, separate from the many other identities related to being a politically com-mitted author. Although the simple identity it promises is recognized as illusory from the very beginning, the name nevertheless provides the basis from which the identity of the author Anna is reconstructed, since it is the girl Netty to whom the Jewish teacher turns with her request: "She [Sichel] said to me . . . because I like to travel and because I like to write essays, I should compose a description of our school excursion for the next German lesson" (O/35; A/73; TA).

The dissolution of identity with which "Der Ausflug der toten Mädchen" begins is thus overcome, linking Netty, the child, to Seghers, the Communist author, through her Jewish teacher of German literature—a figure representing a now very problematic Jewish German assimilation. As the narrator picks up the thread of this tradition, writing becomes the "duty" of remembrance (O/22; A/60). Since this teacher's fate is like that of the mother, as she too is deported to Poland, the narrator's acceptance of this task can be said to reestablish her authorship as one which partially reintegrates her Jewish "origin";[70] it also reinforces the reorganization of her authorship as one which is tied to the memory of women, ultimately to the memory of her mother. But there is yet another important dimension to this authorial subjectivity reconstituted out of a profound personal crisis of identity and resting upon the acceptance of a public task.

The section in which the encounter with the mother is narrativized as a multilayered text of memory is the most complex manifestation of the story's epistemological problem, namely, the breakdown of the barrier between reality and dream, reality and fantasy, present and past, the conscious and the unconscious. The story's inaugurating gesture creates this ambiguity with respect to both the reality it represents and the subject it narrates: the moment of transition from the arid Mexican landscape of the present to the lush green garden of the past—the terrace on the Rhine where a group of German girls and their teachers spend a sunny afternoon long before Hitler's rise to power—inaugurates the process of remembrance as a half-conscious step through the white wall encircling a Mexican ranch by a narrator whose fever or fatigue clouds her vision like "haze" or "dust" (O/15; A/52–53)—as a slippage from present to past self, from first-person narrator to "Netty."

In this story (socialist) realism and its epistemological certainties cede to modernism and its preoccupation with doubt, uncertainty, and ambiguity— a rather banal insight, surprising only to those who are intent on reducing Seghers's entire oeuvre to "socialist realism."[71] What is more significant here is the fact that modernism's epistemological uncertainty is tied to a specific historical phenomenon, the destruction of European Jewry by the Nazis. Approaching her parents' house, Netty/the narrator is overwhelmed by a vague, foreboding, a feeling of dread and terror, "as if something nonsensical, something evil awaited me" (O/39; A/76; TA). Projecting her present knowledge of the bombing of her hometown into the past, the narrator then says: "I had unnecessarily dreaded returning home along this path because it was stuck in my memory that this middle part of town was completely destroyed by bombs." This palimpsest of past and present thematizes not only the transformation of the past through the knowledge of the present but the questioning of that knowledge itself: "It also occurred to me that this newspaper photograph, in which all of the streets and squares had been razed and destroyed, might have been wrong" (O/39; A/76-77; TA). It is the National Socialist aestheticization of politics taken to its extreme — the Nazis' simulation of reality — which so radically undermines any position of certainty: "At first I thought that Goebbels might have ordered the construction of a fake town [*Scheinstadt*] in order to disguise the extent of the attack" (O/39; A/77; TA). The Scheinstadt, intended to alleviate other nations' concern about the German government's policies toward its Jewish citizens, was Theresienstadt, the city to which Seghers's mother was supposed to be deported.[72]

Although this story fundamentally questions any aesthetics of representation, it nevertheless works with a narrator who is, if not omniscient, then omnipotent: one who unequivocally judges and, if necessary, punishes her schoolmates as she tells each girl's story of participation in or opposition to National Socialism. Although "I"/Netty reconstructs many different lives here, she focuses on the betrayal by Marianne, who denounces her best friend, Leni — revealing a character belied by her face: "In her face, as noble and regular as the faces of the medieval girls carved in stone at the Marburg cathedral, one saw nothing but cheer and gracefulness. One did not notice in her any sign of heartlessness, guilt, or a cold conscience" (O/18; A/55-56; TA). Creating an image of great intensity, the narrator later states that she will always remember this girl with a red carnation between tween her teeth, "and the way she was lying in the ashes of her parents' house, bits of clothes smoking, her body half charred" (O/38; A/76; TA). Indeed, the narrator does not hesitate to generalize beyond the group of girls as she observes, on her way home (again merging past and present), that the "comfortable" faces of those passing her do not bear any trace of guilt at "having simply looked on . . . out of cowardice before the power of the state" (O/41; A/79; TA). The angry surprise audible in these sentences, which explode the German idyll on the Rhine, can also be heard in the cold descriptions of destruction, the violent language of which lends them an air of punishment fantasies: recalling the fate of Else and her family, she says they were transformed into "dust and bits" (O/31; A/69; TA); speaking of Ida, she describes a bomb that "exploded friends and enemies, and also, of course, her curly head" (O/24; A/62; TA). This authorial pronouncement of judgment and implicit demand for repentance links "Der Ausflug der toten Mädchen" to the public persona that Seghers would assume in East Germany after 1945.[73]

In my view, "Der Ausflug der toten Mädchen" functions as a "refounding" text for Seghers's authorship by structuring it around her memories of her Jewish German teacher and her mother. Yet "Der Ausflug" is not the only text involved in this process, for a series of interviews given by Seghers between 1973 and 1980 should also be read within this context. What characterizes these five interviews with Achim Roscher, for example, is Seghers's fierce insistence on her independence from her family. Of course, this also has to be understood as the insistence by a GDR writer and intellectual on having broken with her bourgeois background. Yet, as we will see, this independence involves other aspects as well.

The first interview begins with Seghers denying an implication that she reads in Roscher's first question, namely, that her father's profession (art dealer) had anything to do with her decision to study art history.[74] She calls herself an "enfant terrible" and describes her parents' home as suffocating, a "typical bourgeois living room atmosphere," which she longed to escape: "And being locked in there was so repugnant to me that the desire to fly out, to fly away as fast as possible, grew ever stronger within me." [75] Asked how she began writing, she tells Roscher about a period during her childhood when she had to stay in bed due to a severe illness. In a 1965 interview with Christa Wolf, however, she was more specific:

As a little child, as a very little child, before I started school and during my first year in school, I was often sick, and I therefore learned to read, and thus also to write, relatively early. And then, mainly because I was alone and wanted to create my own environment, I invented all sorts of little stories, which I told myself.[76]

Seghers's foregrounding of her autonomy notwithstanding, I would understand this memory differently, namely, one that points to the mother's absence as the structure upon which Seghers's writing rests. Her subsequent comments only strengthen this reading: "As a young child I did not have anyone who told me fairy tales. . . . I had to tell them to myself." [77] These memories match the account given in a 1928 *Mainzer Anzeiger* article, according to which as a child Seghers wrote fairy tales which she dedicated to her mother.[78]

Psychoanalysis theorizes trauma as consisting of two moments, the original event and a later one whereby the original event is remobilized; the trauma itself is the effect of this remobilization. In Seghers's case, the "disappearance" of her mother seems to have reawakened an earlier experience, with her mother's death then remembered as her "absence," more precisely, as the childhood experience of having been abandoned—the very experience that had prompted the child to begin writing in the first place. In the postwar context of the interviews, the theme of *writing for the absent mother* was thus extended into the realm of childhood.

When asked directly about her mother's influence, Seghers responded ambiguously. With respect to her literary education at home, she described her mother reciting Faust's "Prologue in Heaven" and mentioned her father's library. Responding to Roscher's comment that she spoke very little about her mother, Seghers offered an apology: "Actually I would have had reason to be grateful to her too, because I owed many of the initial inspirations for my first stories to her story-telling." [79] The preceding paragraph contains the explanation for this revisionist gesture:

For certain reasons I have said little about my mother, and I am not sure whether it is right to do so at this point. In any case, you should know that I did not have a very good relationship with her. My father understood me better, and I also understood him very well. I was a terrible child, always making trouble for my parents; and my father showed more understanding for me than my mother. Therefore, I was closer to him.[80]

Seghers thus framed her access to culture within an Oedipal problematic: although her mother played an important role, she was the excluded third term—a constellation later fraught with guilt. Like the mother's absence, the issue of guilt thus emerged relative to an earlier, more archaic issue: *Oedipal rivalry.*

The author describes her relationship with her father in terms that are hardly less ambiguous than those used about her mother. When Roscher raises this issue at the very beginning of the interview, Seghers categorically denies her father's influence:

Of course, I had more contact with works of art through my father than others had; we also had books about art and architecture at home because my father was an art dealer. I looked at those books occasionally, but my inclination toward art and art history did not come from that.[81]

It is, above all, with respect to the origin of her pseudonym that her father's significance is evinced in this interview. Although she emphatically denies having been influenced by her father's profession here, later she credits his specialization in seventeenth-century Netherlands painting for her own sustained interest in this particular art.[82] However, in discussing her first story, "Die Toten auf der Insel Djal," published in 1924 under the pseudonym Antje Seghers, she avoids the obvious connection between the Dutch painter Hercules Seghers and her pseudonym. Instead, she explains it in a logical, yet naive way:

In [the story], there was a protagonist whose name was Jan Seghers. I had arranged the narrative as a story about my family; therefore, I wrote in the first person. Because I had to give the figure a name that was supposed to sound Dutch, the name Seghers entered my mind, I liked it. And it was then natural that as a narrating descendant of this man I should also call myself Seghers.[83]

Seghers thus presents her own authorship, the origin of a woman writer's pseudonym, as derived from *a male ancestor:* "I wrote it in the I-form, as if this captain were my grandfather." [84] What makes this move so peculiar is that while she eschewed her patronym, her pseudonym positioned her within an equally male genealogy, as Jan Seghers's "narrating descendant." I would argue that this contradictory and ambiguous positioning vis-à-vis the (real or fictional) father and his tradition enacted the very topic of the story—rebellion.

Let me briefly summarize the story before inquiring more closely into its production of the pseudonym "Antje Seghers." In approximately four pages, "Die Toten auf der Insel Djal" tells the story of Jan Seghers, a minister living on the island of Djal, whose mission is to bury the dead sailors washing ashore on his island—and to keep them buried, for

the dead in the cemetery on Djal are a strange people. Sometimes their bones twitch so forcefully that the wooden crosses and gravestones start to shake. Particularly in the spring and fall, when the wind begins to whistle and howl, they can no longer control themselves. This is because they were all sailors who had crossed the open seas, until they foundered on the cliffs of Djal. And just to lie quietly and listen to the ocean roaring and hissing beyond the churchyard wall, that is too much even for the dead.[85]

The minister so committed to keeping these wild sailors in their graves is himself described as a "strange fellow" who has no need of children or siblings, wife or lover, but who longs for "wilder, more grandiose pleasure, raging passions" (I/205). The story slowly focuses in on the encounter between Jan Seghers and the rebellious captain Morten Sise, who refuses to stay buried. Visiting Seghers one night, he presents himself as a cousin of the dead captain and asks to be taken to his grave. As the church bells sound the midnight hour, Sise tells Seghers that it is now his turn to go to the grave. Laughing, Seghers shows Sise a gravestone hidden away in the corner of the cemetery. The stone's inscription reveals that Jan Seghers, born in Altmark in 1548, died in 1625 on the island Djal. The story concludes with Seghers telling Sise:

Such a common Christian as yourself, Captain, should stay patiently under the earth after his death, until his master deigns to announce the resurrection. But as for me, I was not content to stick out my hand, overturn a gravestone, or frighten a minister. Instead, I harangued God with such wild and furious prayers that he had to call me back to life in my old form, after his seven angels pleaded for me. (I/209)

A core dimension of this rather opaque story about life, death, and rebellion against God is the promise of a life beyond the ordinary: Sise sarcastically notes that the Bible seduces people into believing they will experience the most miraculous things "inside and outside" (I/207), things which are but the prelude to events even more grandiose at the end; but in reality, he continues, all they do is sail around on the ocean, die somewhere, and then lie for the rest of eternity in the filthy dirt. Seghers's response claims the possibility of an extraordinary life for the one who rebels: "As for the extraordinary things, everyone experiences exactly as many of them as he can tolerate" (I/208).

As Bernhard Greiner correctly observes, Seghers produced her own pseudonym from her first literary text.[86] What Greiner does not see, however, is the paternal genealogy of this pseudonym or its origin in a context with a single, central signifier, rebellion, which it narrates as a *masculine* act — the conflict between the minister and his God, between the "son" and his "father." Although the relationship between protagonist and author, Jan and Antje Seghers, remains unspecified, the text hints at a genealogical connection. This rebellious genealogy thus reproduces on the level of the story's content what its author's change of patronym implies: her own—rebellious —act of self-transformation, one that also involves another factor thematized in the story itself, religion. At the same time that she was completing a dissertation entitled "Jew and Jewry in the Works of Rembrandt," Netty Reiling was rewriting herself as the descendant of a Protestant minister.

The "Grundtext" [87] (founding text) of the "Antje/Anna Seghers" authorship inaugurated a rebellious, but also very cautious, entry into the patriarchal order of the literary field. Its tenuous constitution of authorship in relation to paternity is located *within,* yet also *outside* of, the tradition of the father: it emerges out of a specific cultural realm, that of Dutch painting, yet derives a *new* patronym from it; it touches upon the realm of art which is the father's domain, yet constitutes itself as *literary.* Finally, in her first published story, Seghers took back her own voice and put it to the service of, first, an anonymous oral tradition and, second, a male protagonist. For this story is rather curiously framed by two lines that follow the title: "A Legend from the Dutch" and "Retold by Antje Seghers." It thus enacts in a most exemplary way what Gilbert and Gubar call the woman author's "anxiety of authorship," [88] or, in Seghers's own words:

I thought this [pseudonym] was an appropriate way of making my friends notice me—indirectly. This name is so unusual that it had to stand out when it suddenly appeared above a story in the newspaper. On the other hand, I could also hide behind it.[89]

Nevertheless, the central mystery of this first story remains the question implicitly raised by Jan Seghers's gravestone: Who is Antje Seghers?[90]

In its complex articulation of narrator and protagonist, ancestor and descendant, paternal tradition and female authorship, "Die Toten auf der Insel Djal" makes no mention of the mother whom Seghers would later concede was a major influence upon her writing. In this sense, the story conforms to those nineteenth-century woman-authored novels which systematically eliminate the heroine's mother, a cultural pattern that Marianne Hirsch analyzes as "maternal repression" and "paternal alliance." [91] The founding text of the "Antje/Anna Seghers" authorship writes the longing for a life of adventure as masculine and tentatively identifies the instance of writing this life as standing within a paternal tradition.

Thus, not only was Seghers's pseudonym another patronym, but the founding text of her oeuvre was centered on the father, albeit in rebellion against him. Similarly, despite the author's strong insistence on her autonomy, the Roscher interviews hint at her actual formation as an intellectual within a triangular configuration, where the alliance with the father facilitated her entry into the cultural field. At the same time, her remarks in the interviews suggest a desire to retroactively foreground, even to revalidate, the mother—a gesture motivated not only by the guilt linked to her death but by a much older guilt linked to an Oedipal rivalry in which the daughter's development as a writer necessitated the mother's exclusion. Therefore, it would not be merely speculative or unreasonable to assume that the guilt rooted in this Oedipal rivalry was reawakened, even intensified, by the circumstances of her mother's death. I would argue that this older *nexus of writing and guilt* contributed to the tendency toward *idealization* in Seghers's mother figures after 1945.[92]

"Die Toten auf der Insel Djal" works with another element that is already familiar to us: the trope of the journey. The story links the concept of a full, passionate life to the dangerous and exhilarating life of sailors on the roiling sea; moreover, in associating such a life and its attendant journey with rebellion, it introduced a trope which would become central to "Anna Seghers's" writing. Yet, as we have seen, this trope lost its connotations of rebellion in Seghers's later texts; where the journey once promised a better, more exciting life, it came to signify death. And where it once entailed moving away from home/the mother, it became identification with her. In "Der Ausflug der toten Mädchen," the longing for adventure has disappeared: "My desire for strange, extravagant experiences, which had troubled me at one time, had long ago been satisfied, to the point of excess. Only one thing remained to spur me on: the trip home" (O/15; A/52; TA). As I argued above, the story that originated in a double desire—"to travel" and "to write"—became propelled by the desire to join the mother on her deadly journey. Seghers's master trope, the journey, thus became linked not to the rebellious son, but to the lost mother.

Overdetermination, Containment, and Repression

The project of this chapter was to inquire into Seghers's participation in the new Germany's symbolic politics of power, particularly in terms of the mother figure, an image to which Seghers so centrally contributed. As we have seen, the genesis of this particular image and the underlying conflicts which produced it can be traced to the "hollow spaces of emotions," a phrase borrowed from Seghers herself. In three literary works written between 1943 and 1948, a vital tension emerges between the antifascist narrative and the representation of the mother, each text's central, overdetermined element. The multiply determined element of the idealized working-class mother can thus be traced, first, to tension between different discourses on the German past and, second, to conflicts both older and more "subjective," that is, touching upon the very origins of Seghers's writing. Underlying this image of the idealized working-class mother which dominated Seghers's textual production from 1943 to 1948 is a network of submerged yet powerful conflicts.

The double processes of repression and memory also had an important effect upon the textual and self-production of the author "Anna Seghers." For her to be able to live in East Germany, these conflicts, the contradictions between the political story she wanted to tell and the personal story she was forced to live, had to be repressed. Reading through the East German scholarship on Seghers, it becomes obvious that part of her public persona as the motherly educator of the German people depended on this willingness to repress, on her willingness not to express any anti-German *ressentiments,* as Christa Wolf so admiringly—and, one might add, so naively—observed.[93] In light of the transformation Seghers's authorship underwent after 1943, this was an ironic, even tragic, position.[94]

In conclusion, I would like to return to *Die Toten bleiben jung,* with its contradictory narrative principles of order and disruption, its Janus-faced figure of Marie and the witch. Having read this conflicted articulation in terms of the Left's double representation of femininity as the Gorkian mother and Gladkov's cipher of revolution, Dasha, it is tempting to read it another way, seeing in the distorted face of the witch triumphantly celebrating the destruction of the German army *the other face* of the mother, the one that does not fit into the narrative of cultural reconstruction based on maternal values of peace and love. This would be to read the linearity of its narrative structure, which prevails over its fragmenting modernist techniques, as a result of containment and repression—of the maternal as revolutionary change within Stalinism, of the Jewish mother within narratives of antifascism. Seghers's pivotal contribution to the GDR's paternal order—the idealized image of the German working-class mother—as the product of the Holocaust's irruption into the paternal narrative of antifascism, points to the elements which this narrative conceals and represses.

This chapter has focused on a very limited period, from when Seghers began to write "Der Ausflug" to the publication of *Die Toten bleiben jung,* and on a specific body of work, literary and nonliterary. It was a period of crisis during which problems erupted in these texts and became readable, problems that would later be carefully contained. Thus, the pale, glowing face of the lost mother, so omnipresent in "Post ins gelobte Land," survives only as a faint afterglow in Seghers's realist epic about the transformations in the new country, *Die Entscheidung* (The Decision). Like the sculpture at Ravensbrück which bears Seghers's admonition not to forget "our" mothers and sisters, the novel's central mother figure, Katharina, no longer bears any trace of the Jewish mother. However, the ethereal Jewish mother of "Post ins gelobte Land" has been rewritten into the pale, glowing face of Celia, the Spanish woman who rescues the three male protagonists, *Spanienkämpfer* who have returned to Germany. It is the memory of this face, "the quiet pale face of the girl in the narrow shaft of light," that would never be forgotten—the "images in his head" and the "feeling of a duty that could not be postponed"—which forces one of these men, the author Herbert Melzer, to continue writing his novel about the civil war in Spain.[95] Are we wrong to recognize in his motivation, indeed obsession, another shadow of a trauma, the full articulation of which remained impossible but that still never ceased to produce its unsettling effects?

II

Mapping the Oedipal Story

onto Post-Fascist Socialism:

New Families/New Bodies

This much is becoming known after so much "Russian formalism" but also after so many biographies confided on the couch: a narrative is, all in all, the most elaborate attempt, next to syntactic competence, to situate a speaking being between his desires and their prohibitions, in short within the Oedipal triangle. — Julia Kristeva, *Powers of Horror: An Essay on Abjection* (1982)

The borders were drawn inside our very bodies. — Barbara Köhler, "A la recherche de la révolution perdue" (1994)

3

The Past in the Present: Sons, Daughters, and the Fantasy of Post-Fascist Bodies

In chapters 1 and 2 I outlined a compelling discourse of power, one so effective that even in the 1980s the experience of living in the GDR was often formulated within its terms. Thus, in a 1991 interview, the Prenzlauer Berg poet Papenfuss Gorek, whose father was an East German general, described his position within East Germany's dominant order in the following way:

My father's father had a lot to do with the Nazis. . . . [My father] was a vehement anti-fascist. . . .

I could have gone on playing the game and opposed my father again. But that seemed too silly. I think it would have been too schematic for my life to bring to light again the same opposition that my father had had towards his father. Of course I was against my father because sons are against their fathers, but not so schematically and narrow-mindedly. Of course I was against the system he represented for me; but I never saw him, for example, as a personal enemy. Besides, I don't know him all that well. He plays a part for me as a representative of the superstructure, but more in a literary way. That's what I have to come to terms with in my writing, not with him personally. If I shoot off things against the system or the hierarchy, they are always aimed at my father but really only in the abstract. . . .

The distance between my father and me is too great for me to be able to look on him as a personal enemy. He is an abstract quantity to me like "the state" or "the system" or "the army." [1]

What is fascinating about this statement is its interweaving of different registers—the personal, the political, the literary—producing a text which resists any effort to untangle its dense and inextricable texture by explaining one level of discourse through another. Its violent "confusion" has to be taken seriously, and the temptation to read it as singular, the case of a Stasi officer's son, has to be resisted: the paternal narrative is still operative, and those in power want social relations to be read through the dominant fiction.[2] At this point, the master-narrative of the paternal family was certainly no longer one of the central organizing narratives of East Germany's post-fascist culture; rather, it had, so to speak, gone underground, where it still had an unconscious effectivity.[3] However, at the very moment of East Germany's dissolution, the paternal narrative reemerged once more as the most forceful story in a number of texts which attempted to retrospectively portray the protagonist's life under "real existing socialism." For instance, Monika Maron's *Stille Zeile Sechs* (Six Quiet Street) is clearly informed by a father–daughter plot, as is Kerstin Hensel's *Im Schlauch* (Inside the Hose). In his novel *Spiegelland* (Mirrorland), Klaus Drawert even draws explicitly on Lacan in reflecting on the individual and the social, the father and the power of the state.[4]

In order to continue historicizing the production of the GDR's discourse of paternal power, we have to return to the late 1950s and early 1960s, and to a specific genre, the so-called novel of arrival. But before focusing on two canonical texts of this genre, Brigitte Reimann's *Ankunft im Alltag* (Arrival in Everyday Life) and Dieter Noll's *Die Abenteuer des Werner Holt: Roman einer Heimkehr* (The Adventures of Werner Holt: A Novel of Homecoming), I want to recapitulate my argument so far. Drawing on Lefort's writings on the symbolic politics of power, I argued that after 1945 one of the SED's hegemonic strategies involved the attempt to fill the empty locus of power with historical narratives centered on the figure of the father. As a reading of Bredel's and Gotsche's texts revealed, these narratives tend to revolve around Oedipal structures, the relationship between (substitute) fathers and their sons. Moreover, they coalesce around the inherent paradoxes of the paternal function: the incommensurability of penis and phallus, the actual and the symbolic father, and the injunction to be/not to be like the father. In both *Verwandte und Bekannte* and *Die Fahne von Kriwoj Rog,* a feminine disposition toward the father prevails, in one case as a result of a negative Oedipal crisis, in the other as a result of a masochistic scenario at the core of its antifascist narrative. In chapter 2, I argued that

Die Toten bleiben jung thematizes the gap between the Name-of-the-Father and the one who holds that position, while at the same time foregrounding the figure of the Communist mother. As foundational texts, *Verwandte und Bekannte, Die Fahne von Kriwoj Rog,* and *Die Toten bleiben jung* proved rather shaky, riven by contradictions involving the paternal instance itself. Seghers's novel, although still organized around the father, shifted the center of the family narrative slightly, producing a text in which the figure of the (Communist) mother, with its diverse and contradictory connotations, is tied to a narrative imperative that tendentiously unsettles the paternal order. But there is little doubt that Seghers's maternal icon is an integral part of the Stalinist paternal order since, as we have seen, its disruptive connotations are vigorously suppressed. The figure of the Communist father, staged as a disciplined body, and the figure of the Communist mother, with its multiple connotations, were the poles between which the early GDR's Oedipal stories developed. These family narratives produced images of (ideal) parental figures toward which the protagonists of the 1950s and early 1960s *Ankunftsroman* would position themselves.

This GDR-specific genre might be defined as the "Bitterfelder Weg" version of the classic novel of formation, that is, the version developed in the context of the Communist Party's attempt to initiate a "second, Socialist stage of the Cultural Revolution." [5] This broad cultural movement took place between two conferences (1959 and 1964) that were held in a chemical factory in the industrial city of Bitterfeld. Artists were encouraged to work in factories, while workers were called upon to become cultural producers. Bitterfeld has been analyzed by critics from both East and West as yet another effort to involve East Germany's authors in projects oriented toward the "new" reality of socialism rather than dwelling on the catastrophe of the immediate past. The novel of arrival was part of this political–aesthetic program. A narrative in which the protagonist finds his or her place in the emerging Communist order, this plot often entailed the character's integration into the work collectives of the vast construction sites of steel and coal, the mythical "Wild East" of the GDR's heroic "era of construction." The genre's designation was derived from Reimann's *Ankunft im Alltag* (1961). Standard literary histories in both East and West Germany distinguished a subgenre of the novel of arrival, the *Entwicklungsroman* or novel of development, which chronicled the transformation of young former Nazi soldiers into—more or less ardent—supporters of the new order. The canonical novel of development was Noll's *Die Abenteuer des Werner Holt:*

Roman einer Heimkehr (1963). While the master-plot of the novel of arrival, as described by German critics, involved the protagonist's evolution from "idealism" or "romanticism" to "realism," the central transformation of the novel of development is from the ideology of National Socialism to an East German version of Marxism-Leninism.

In my reading of *Ankunft im Alltag* and *Die Abenteuer des Werner Holt,* these founding texts of the new genre share a common story, an Oedipal narrative that is deeply implicated in the German past. Thus, instead of reading them as narratives of changing consciousness, I focus on the conscious and unconscious fantasies inscribed within them, highlighting the textual level on which the (often problematic) integration is depicted as the protagonist's situating him- or herself toward parental figures—particularly, of course, the father. As in Bredel's trilogy, this often involves the replacement of the "biological" father; yet unlike Bredel's story, these plots actually focus on the conflict with this "new" idealized representative of the Law. The resolution of this conflict is then the very motivation of the story, once more affirming Roland Barthes's famous statement that storytelling is a way of searching for one's conflicts with the father as the representative of the law.[6] This shift from "conscious" to "unconscious" text provides access to a level of psychosocial meaning beyond the genre's explicitly inscribed political discourse, the project of integration into the collective.[7]

In this chapter we will thus pursue the problematic of hegemony addressed at the beginning of chapter 1, in particular the question of how ideology works at the most "rudimentary levels of psychic identity and the drives."[8] In my readings of two canonical East German novels of arrival as participating in the construction of the paternal order, the image of the Communist body will remain central. Concentrating on their version of the "dominant fiction,"[9] I will examine the ways in which they position their protagonists as "sons" and "daughters." Both of these cultural narratives revolve around a conflict between young Communists and their "new" parental figures, a conflict which takes place on the terrain of psychosexuality, that is, the pleasure involved in producing conscious and unconscious fantasy scenarios.[10] The conflict is resolved by the subject's final submission to the (Communist) father's Law. This subjection takes a very specific form: the production of the *sublime Communist body* as a *post-fascist body.* In *Die Abenteuer des Werner Holt* and *Ankunft im Alltag,* the sublime Communist body appears in a slightly refracted form signifying the "transient material envelopment" of the sublime body through sexuality.[11] In these texts sexuality, as that which is most tightly tied to the fascist past, must be split off, disciplined, contained. This "containment" is an integral part of the protagonist's entry into the GDR's new paternal order, which holds up the father's sublime body—the disciplined and ascetic body of the Communist fighter—as the image for identification. And this process of identification is a key mechanism in the production of the *sublime* body: "Hegemony hinges upon identification, it comes into play when all the members of a collectivity see themselves within the same reflecting surface." [12]

At this point, we have to resist the seemingly compelling slippage from "sublime" to "sublimation": the weight of my argument rests on the fantasy of the "purified," "asexual" body, not on any act of sexual repression per se. The novels by Noll and Reimann textualize this emergence of the post-fascist body by devising whole scenarios for the workings of fantasy, staging a veritable "mise-en-scène of desire." [13] And, as we will see, these fantasies take on a very specific form where the body has already been "polluted" by the protagonist's involvement in the ideological universe of National Socialism. The Oedipus complex is thus the mechanism through which the subject is inducted into a hegemonic project that symbolizes power as the power of the father. And it is the fantasies involved in the process of identification with the father's sublime body that will be central to this chapter.

My approach to the novel of arrival thus radically shifts the focus from the familiar narrative of "consciousness" to one revolving around fantasy and its scenarios. Moreover, this focus requires us to explore *in detail* the identificatory processes involved in these fantasy scenarios. To clarify, this is not a Reichian argument about East German puritanism, about the repressive character of Stalinism's libidinal economy and its "sexual–moral–authoritarian regulation" of sexual energy. [14] On the contrary, I am attempting to break through this all-too-familiar paradigm which reduces the unconscious to a libidinal, ultimately biological, force to be liberated or repressed. What I want to investigate are the conscious and not-so-conscious *fantasies about the body* at the core of the new paternal order. [15]

But this new paternal universe is not an order which is ever fully stabilized, without room for subversive positions. The Oedipal crisis is a structuring moment, positioning the subject as having/not having the phallus, that is, a structure which produces sexual difference. The identification with the ideal image of the respective parent follows upon this initial positioning as feminine or masculine. Yet, as Juliet Mitchell and others continue to emphasize, masculinity and femininity are never fully achieved but only "precariously" adopted, since each inevitably implies the repression of the other.[16] It is in the realm of unconscious fantasies that the "deviation" from these forced identities must be read, an issue I will explore in chapter 4 in relation to Christa Wolf's *Der geteilte Himmel* (1963).[17]

Maldoror (Berlin, East):
"A dead father might have been/A better father"

Induction into the GDR's dominant discourse, its paternal order, follows different plots, different patterns, one of the more complex and sophisticated being Heiner Müller's 1959 short story "Der Vater" (The Father), which we can read as a pre-text for the novel of arrival.[18] But unlike the novels by Noll and Reimann, "Der Vater" actually articulates the impossible desire that would drive the Oedipal novel of arrival—the desire to replace the biological parents, who happened to be Nazis, with Communist parents—and thereby unveils its ideology. Also in contrast to *Ankunft im Alltag* and *Die Abenteuer des Werner Holt,* "Der Vater" does not constitute sexuality as the past. Nevertheless, it is precisely because of its explicit inscription of the Oedipal story that it can shed light on East Germany's Oedipal narratives.

In "Bericht vom Grossvater" (Report about Grandfather), a 1950 story of only three pages, Müller had already used the family history to narrate the GDR's founding moment. Although more of a report or chronicle, as its title indicates, than an autobiographical story, "Bericht vom Grossvater" is a first-person narrative, its epigraph positing the grandfather's past as a haunting problem for the story's "I": "When his cemetery spills over the wall / the old cobbler comes to me." [19] "Der Vater" is also a story about the narrator's relationship to the past.[20] It strings together episodes related to a father who, as a victim of Nazi repression, is perceived as helpless, and whose weakness ultimately leads to what the narrator views as betrayal: "In 1951, to keep himself out of the class war, my father walked across Potsdam Square into the American sector" (V/25). Although like "Grossvater" a first-person narrative, the narrator of "Der Vater," unlike that of the earlier story (who adopts a distant stance of historical knowledge and omniscience), participates in the story he tells.[21]

"Der Vater" revolves around the tension between father and son—identification and dis-identification, continuity and discontinuity—a tension that also colors its formal aspects. The linearity of the conventional family narrative is disrupted by the juxtaposition of a number of key scenes, with no attempt to create a seamless sequence; on the contrary, the linear family narrative is pushed toward disintegration into unrelated scenes.[22]

The very first episode, a flashback in the form of a Benjaminian *Denkbild,* narrates the father's arrest in 1933 from the son's perspective. Since this scene, a very precise, almost crystal-clear memory, determines the entire narrative, I will quote it in full:

On January 31, 1933, at 4:00 A.M., my father, a functionary of the German Social Democratic Party, was arrested in his own bed. I awoke, the sky on the other side of the window black, noise from voices and steps. . . . I heard my father's voice, higher than the strangers' voices. I climbed out of bed and walked to the door. Through the crack I saw a man striking my father in the face. Frigid, the covers pulled up to my chin, I was lying in bed when the door to my room opened. My father stood in the doorway, behind him the strangers, big, in brown uniforms. There were three of them. One of them held the door open with his hand. The light was at my father's back, I couldn't see his face. I heard him softly calling my name. I did not answer and lay very still. Then my father said: "He's asleep." The door was closed. I heard them leading him away, then the quick step of my mother, who returned alone. (V/20)

The scene thematizes weakness, not only the son's but also the father's, a man whose son perceives him as small compared to the tall, threatening figures of the men in brown uniforms. The child's gaze, falling upon the defeated father, as Genia Schulz correctly observes, is split into the identification of the weak child with the father, the disdain of the child who needs protection, and the empathy of the adult who recalls the scene.[23]

What I would like to emphasize here, however, is the moment of disidentification, when the son can no longer recognize the father's face—no longer recognize himself in his father's face. Müller repeats this scene—the son's gaze on the father's pale face—twice more. Thus, the narrator recalls the moment when mother and son visit the father, who is now a prisoner in a concentration camp: "Then we stood in front of the wide gate with the wire fence until they brought my father. . . . I had to step up close to the wire fence to see his gaunt face" (V/21, 22). Similarly, when the son comes face to face with his father one last time, in a hospital in the West: "We stood there, the glass pane between us, and looked at each other. His gaunt face was ashen" (V/26). As in the very first episode, the son's gaze is fixed on the father's face in these two subsequent scenes. Yet the trope of identification, the gaze between father and son, changes significantly from scene to scene: in the traumatic first moment, it is the son who longs to recognize the father's face, while in the final scene it is the father who desires the recognition which the son withholds by refusing to return his gaze:

> He rattled the locked door and called for the nurse. She came, shook her head, and left. He let his arms drop, looked at me through the glass pane, and was silent. . . . When I left I saw him standing behind the glass door, waving. (V/26)

The traumatic dis-identification leads to a separation signified first by the wire mesh, then by the window pane, and finally by the *son*'s leaving the *father.*

The first scene creates a desire which is belatedly voiced in a second epigraph, inserted between scenes 3 and 4:

> I wished my father had been a shark
> Who had torn forty whalers to pieces
> (And I would have learned to swim in their blood)
> My mother a blue whale my name Lautreamont
> Deceased in Paris 1871 unknown. (V/22)

The first two lines express the desire for a strong father, a desire that takes on a political dimension in the story's last sentence. A reference to the Russian Revolution, it constructs a different origin outside of German history: "Outside was the ice grey light of the October day" (V/26). The last two lines of the epigraph, with their reference to the Paris Commune, further develop this son's fantasy of erasing his origins by attempting to link himself with a different tradition, a different history: first the 1871 Commune, then the October 1917 Revolution.

The futility of this attempt, the impossibility of cutting off oneself (the present) from one's origins (the father) — from history — is formulated in the enigmatic opening epigraph:

> A dead father might have been
> A better father. The best
> Is a stillborn father. (V/20)

Yet the desire is still there; it finds partial fulfillment in the fantasy of replacing the father's tradition by another, revolutionary history.[24] Let me return to that second epigraph, which introduces Lautreamont's *Chants de Maldoror* as "Der Vater's" intertext.[25] Permeating Müller's story both structurally and thematically, the poem gives voice to another, guilty desire which is only hinted at at the end of the first scene: "I heard them leading him away, then the quick step of my mother, who returned alone" (V/20). The father's arrest leaves the son alone with the mother, lets him take the father's place. A fantasy that *Maldoror* touches upon, it is enacted in the next-to-last scene of "Der Vater."

Maldoror has disavowed father and mother, and Müller narrativizes his battle cry — "I made a pact with prostitution in order to sow disorder within families"[26] — in the scene where the son takes the father's place by inviting a prostitute into his parents' bed. This section's first sentence announces the father's escape to the West. After recalling that his mother had accompanied his father to the train station, the narrator states: "I was alone in the apartment" (V/25). He leaves for a bar, where he notices a woman drinking alone. Müller's language suggests a strong undercurrent of repressed violence:

I sat down next to her and ordered a drink. We drank. After the fourth drink I touched her breast and said that she had pretty hair. Because she smiled encouragingly, I ordered more liquor. . . . I pressed teeths and lips against the woman's mouth. (V/25)

In a typically Brechtian move, Müller avoids any false romantic note — "In the adjoining dance hall . . . the violins were screaming" — reducing the meeting to a basic exchange which leaves out the act itself: "A rigid smile was on the woman's face as she undressed without further ado next to the double bed in my parents' bedroom. After intercourse I gave her cigarettes or chocolate" (V/25). With this gesture, I would argue, the narrator attempts not only to take the father's place, but to eradicate his origin, a gesture similar to Artaud's declaring, "I, Antonin Artaud, am my son, my father, my mother/and myself."[27]

However, this desire for "discontinuity" is overshadowed by two fundamentally disturbing insights: first, the radical break with the father/past is impossible; and second, the "act of replacement" implies its own contradictions. When the "rebellious intellectual son" finally occupies the place of the father, he also assumes his position of power.[28] "My rather polite question: 'When will we meet again?' she answered with: 'Whenever you wish' and nearly bowed before me, that is, before the position which she thought my father still held" (V/25, 26). And he does so vis-à-vis a prostitute, a figure not only of Brechtian antisentimentalism but also of women's exploitation.

When the narrator takes over the father's place in this scene, the prostitute takes the place of the mother. The break with the father's politics is thus narrated as an Oedipal scenario in which the son becomes the father and the mother becomes a whore. The mother/whore dichotomy can be read on two levels: first, within the context of the story's Oedipal fantasy itself and, second, on an allegorical, or political, level. In an interview with Sylvere Lotringer, Müller emphasized the importance of the opening scene of "Der Vater": "That's my guilt. I pretended I was asleep. This really is the first scene of my theater." [29] But as we have seen before, this act of "treason" [30] involves more: the fulfillment of a desire to be alone with the mother, a desire which turns her into the whore whom the son invites into his parents' bed. "Der Vater" thus narrates, I would maintain, a very familiar Oedipal fantasy that splits the desired object into two—the sacred and the profane—the "incestuous object," which retains its overvalued quality, and the "debased" whore.[31]

But the Oedipal fantasy accruing to the mother carries yet another meaning. In her discussion of "Der Vater," Schulz draws attention to the photograph of Rosa Luxemburg, which follows the text in *Germania,* Müller's 1977 collection: "the 'mother' after the father." [32] She reads this textual/photographic montage politically, as the contradictory image of the Communist Party's Stalinist history *and* utopian potential, referring to Müller's later play *Germania: Tod in Berlin* (Germany: Death in Berlin), where the Party is both "whore" and "holy virgin," and where a young prostitute appears in Hilse's feverish dream as "red Rosa." [33] I would argue, however, that in relation to "Der Vater," Rosa Luxemburg represents the "pure" mother, on the level of political discourse.[34] "Der Vater" thus generates a political fantasy which positions the son between a new historical origin, the Russian Revolution, and an alternative German history signified by the figure of Rosa Luxemburg.

In summary, what is significant about this particular text in my reading is Müller's deliberate use of the Oedipal scenario, his problematizing of the son's taking the father's place, and his foregrounding of the fantasmatic desire for another origin, another father, another mother.[35] "Der Vater" thus establishes some distance from the very Oedipal narrative that, as we will see, sustains the novels by Noll and Reimann, marking them as ideological fantasies.

Not His Mother's Son:

Die Abenteuer des Werner Holt: Roman einer Heimkehr

One of the most canonical, officially celebrated East German novels, Dieter Noll's 1963 bildungsroman features a young protagonist, Werner Holt, who returns from the war sick, exhausted, cynical, and disoriented to face a world that seems like "utterly foreign territory." [36] The novel's three "books" chronicle Holt's quest for his place in the new postwar order. There could be no stronger contrast to Müller's short story, with its modernist technique and Brechtian laconic tone than Noll's tediously conventional bildungsroman. But the crucial disparity between them which I want to highlight is that while Müller problematizes the (inevitable) identification with the paternal instance—indeed, questions the son's desire to take the father's place—Noll unconditionally celebrates the son's subjection to the father(s) and the new paternal order.

Noll's novel, spanning the period from April 1945 to September 1946, narrates the protagonist's quest as an Oedipal story, mapping the son's trajectory onto the ideological landscape of East German socialism and celebrating his subjection to the father, thus to the new paternal order. Here, however, with the father/son constellation doubled, the identification is also doubled: Holt occupies the position of the son relative to both his "real" father and another figure constructed as paternal authority, Müller, the Party secretary, while the double identification, which emerges with the post-fascist body, is with both the father and Schneidereit, a young Communist who occupies the "son's" position vis-à-vis the Party representative and also functions as the protagonist's ego ideal. Holt's identification with the "real" father involves a body/mind dichotomy that yields not only an identification with his father as an intellectual, but also, more importantly, an erasure of the body of both father and son through a gesture that exiles the mother/the body to the fascist past. Holt's identification with the "other" son, Schneidereit, however, revolves around the latter's ascetic, disciplined body. Together, these identificatory processes generate Holt's new identity, one based on the sublime body as a post-fascist body.

In contrast to other texts analyzed here, *Die Abenteuer des Werner Holt* does not sacrifice the "biological" father to his substitute(s). Instead, the whole narrative is aimed toward the moment when the son's identification with his father is reaffirmed. Here, the Oedipal narrative underwrites other structures of authority, insofar as the son's identification with, and submission to, the authority of the father serves as a model for other relations — just as it should, we might be tempted to add. Holt desires recognition by the father, but the dynamic of Oedipal identification with the one who represents the Law also sustains the desire vested in the Party secretary. When Müller dies, Holt says to himself, "Just admit it: you would have given anything to be this man's friend *and to be like him*" (*WH*/334; my emphasis). However, we must go "beyond" the structuring crisis of the Oedipus complex to explain the association — and violent expulsion — of the past/mother/body. To this end, Kristeva's concept of *the abject* will be of crucial significance.

At the very beginning of the novel, Holt overhears Müller, who runs a chemical factory together with Holt's father, interviewing prospective workers. Every interview leads inevitably to the question of the applicant's involvement in the National Socialist regime. Witnessing Müller's lenience toward some former Nazis, Holt experiences a glimmer of hope but retracts the thought immediately, believing that, as a former soldier, he is nothing but "jetsam" (*WH*/10). This brief moment of vacillation between hope (of integration) and despair (at exclusion) establishes the basic poles of his story.

Noll's narrative is constructed so as to ensure that the reader measures Holt's "progress" against the standard set by its most authoritative figure, the Party secretary. Müller's archetypal life story as a Communist resistance fighter raises him to mythic proportions in Holt's eyes. His own story has two intertwined plots: one revolves around Holt's rivalry with Schneidereit, the head of the Communist youth organization, for the love of a woman named Gundel; the other centers on the conflict between Holt and his parents. What propels both story lines is the experience of loss, namely, of the ideals which once guaranteed an (imaginary) unity between subject and world, Nazi soldier and Nazi regime. A single phrase, Holt remembers, once captured his life's meaning: "pro patria mori" (*WH*/97). These "ideals" provided him with an identity which has been utterly shattered: Holt, now "jetsam" or "dirt" (*WH*/443), is experiencing an irreparable gap opened up between himself and a world that has been radically transformed.

Throughout the course of the novel, the theme of "dirt"—the subject in his "condition of waste, reject, abject"[37]—resurfaces obsessively, grounding the protagonist's subjectivity in self-loathing and hatred.

Holt thinks of his condition as a choice between two solutions: to resign himself to loss or to find a new source of unity, alternately signified by *Heimat* (homeland), *Sinn* (meaning), *Wahrheit* (truth), or a collective *wir* (we), but one that continues to elude him in any case. The experience of loss is described as intolerable "rupture":

The world and I: isn't that the topic? The world is knowable and changeable; it will stop being a cesspool of civilization and will become what it is capable of becoming: a home for a satisfied, unified human race. So much for the world. And the ego, what will become of the ego? Is the ego also knowable? And will the ego—this ego—ever in its lifetime stop being an instinctual, driven thing, torn by contradictions, homeless between the social classes, a mere thinking, laboring, speaking animal; and will it become what it could be: a truly human ego? (*WH*/465)

Yet the new humanism to which he ultimately aspires conflicts with Holt's experience of betrayal, his visceral aversion to any new ideology.[38] Much is made of his suspension between two different modes of being. Yet I would like to pursue another, more pressing question: Why does the Oedipal story figure so prominently in this novel and how is it inscribed in this narrative? From its inception, the novel focuses on the conflict between father and son, which Noll motivates through Holt's rebellion against both paternal authority and a generation he holds responsible for his personal catastrophe. Following a rather hostile confrontation with his father (the director of a chemical factory now run by the Communists), Holt decides to join his mother in the American Zone. After many "detours," however, Holt returns to his father and the territory of the future Socialist state. The conflict between father and son thus ends with Holt's subjection, with their reunion, a rather melodramatic scene in which the prodigal son seeks the father's forgiveness.

Holt is thus forced to choose between the worlds of his father and his mother, with the mother representing Holt's bourgeois origins and the father his "will to change." And while the father becomes a *figure of identification,* the mother figure is savagely excluded from the narrative. Why this violence, and what is it directed against? I would argue that it is his own past as bourgeois *and* Nazi which Holt attempts to eradicate by violently expelling his mother since origin, particularly class origin, is conceptualized in this novel as a tie to the mother, not the father. It is the most abject elements of himself—this past which makes him "dirt" and is still part of him—that are projected onto the figure of the mother.

Holt's self-loathing runs like a thread through the whole narrative but most explicitly in connection with Gundel, the novel's idealized woman figure. After he leaves for Hamburg, where his mother lives, Holt falls ill and screams in his feverish state: "Go to Schneidereit, go, my hands are too filthy" (*WH*/128). In a later conversation with Schneidereit and Gundel, he reminds her of something she had told him earlier: "You once said to me: 'You also have a bit of that inside of you.' . . . Which meant: a bit of fascism" (*WH*/290). And he tells Schneidereit that Gundel was right.

Part of Holt's projected self-loathing involves his associating motherhood with Nazism. During the final meeting between mother and son, Holt's thoughts drift toward the conventional "ideal: security, home, harmony between mother and son" (*WH*/268), which he then discards as embedded in Nazi ideology:

A faultline divided the world. Could it separate two people who had once been more intimate than any other two: mother and son? He recalled all the words he had read concerning "the maternal," perhaps in Wiechert: that no eternity is possible without the mother, but this disastrously recalled a certain "Gospel of Women" and in general this whole seductive, incomprehensible rotten magic. (*WH*/269)

Linked to National Socialism through its idealization of the maternal, the figure of the mother thus comes to unambiguously represent what is most abject, the Nazi past. A long passage narrating Holt's separation from his mother conveys the enormous difficulty of finally relinquishing the "dream" of "motherly love" (*WH*/268, 271). The passage reaches its climax when Holt defines himself as *the son of his father,* an identity which he understands as one of opposition to his mother and her family: "I have nothing to do with you, I do not belong to this widespread family Rennbach. *My name is Holt*" (*WH*/264; my emphasis). Choosing his "father's path" (*WH*/263), he discovers the force which will liberate him from those foul emotions of National Socialist motherhood—hatred.

Assuming the Name-of-the-Father and separating himself from the mother leads to Holt's identification with the father as an intellectual: he now wants to become "a scholar of my father's stature" (*WH*/297). This post-Oedipal subject position is further reinforced by Holt's transformation in a process which essentially recapitulates the story of his father's life. Like his father, he will now strive to find happiness in his work, after having been, again like his father, "once deeply unhappy" (*WH*/499); just as his father lost his mother, Holt loses Gundel. Reliving his father's life also means, of course, experiencing the loss not only of Gundel but of the mother herself (a point to which I will return).

Now Holt's quest, grounded in his identification with his father and centered on Marx's "cold, critical revision" of the past, becomes a "path to Gundel" (*WH*/355, 471) as he tries to win her back. Holt thinks of Gundel as the one who will be able to save him from his past, to redeem this thing inside him which is "distorted, warped, and frozen" (*WH*/388). But his quest soon develops into another story, that of Holt's identification with Schneidereit. For despite their rivalry, Schneidereit emerges as not only the idealized heroic worker but Holt's ego ideal, who, according to Holt, could have saved him from becoming a Nazi. Holt is both fascinated and threatened by the overpowering physical appearance of this worker who commands everyone's attention as soon as he enters the room:

Everyone turned their heads.

A man stepped into the barracks, a young person, tall and broad-shouldered. He stopped in the doorway and scrutinized the room. . . . As he asked with a deep voice: "What's up?" and planted himself before Holt and Gundel, taller than everyone else, something decisive and irresistible emanated from him, something with a threatening and violent effect on Holt. (*WH*/16)

Noll has Holt fixate on Schneidereit's physical strength; each appearance by him entails some comment on his muscular build, which is complemented by his exemplary biography, notably, his imprisonment in 1941 for sabotage, together with his father who is later executed. Schneidereit soon emerges as the idealized heroic worker, Holt's ego ideal who could have saved him from the deadly mistake of following Hitler, but "back then Schneidereit was in prison, and someone else came along, and thus it came to pass that he became ever more deeply involved in the deadly error" (*WH*/337).

Holt's "becoming" Schneidereit is played out on the terrain of the erotic body, the body as "the agent and object of desire." [39] Because Gundel refuses to choose between Holt and Schneidereit, Holt turns to other women. These encounters characterize him as a "bourgeois" who divides women into wives and whores, driven by the "dirt" he harbors within. Noll's novel thus ultimately poses the question of a new, nonfascist, and "truly human self" as a moral issue. Its testing ground is constituted by Holt's relationships with women and, ultimately, his control over his sexuality. For instance, when Holt first meets Judith Arnold, a young woman who spent several years in Ravensbrück,[40] he thinks of her as "a dream image, unreachable" (WH/418), but then he destroys their platonic relationship by brutally assaulting her. Recalling her furious resistance, Holt thinks: "I can't escape from the filth. There is something inside of me, it's like a demon, an evil spirit, that destroys everything" (WH/440). Significantly, the Communist worker Schneidereit functions as a counter-model in the scene in which he overcomes his desire for Gundel, who teaches him the new socialist morality that she has learned from her mother. This scene, which mixes the steamy atmosphere of a Harlequin romance with the sentimentality of Gundel's account of her mother's teachings, reduces the narrative to a rather pious version of Communist soft-core porn. It opens with Schneidereit sweeping Gundel into his arms, ready to carry her off to bed, and ends with him kneeling before her, reflecting on the "radical overthrow of all existing order" (WH/399). Remembering his father and Müller, he realizes that this revolution also involves a transformation of all his personal habits—and he tears himself from Gundel and his desire.

In this scene, the sublime Communist body is "disciplined" to serve a higher historical mission, a process replicated by the novel's protagonist: at the end of a series of encounters with various women, Holt identifies with the image of Schneidereit's strong, masculine but disciplined, body. Moreover, following the narrative's fierce logic of exclusion, the making of this post-fascist "body without dirt" occurs within the Oedipal triangle: when Holt visits his mother, she encourages him to spend time with prostitutes and to have an affair with their maid. The world of the mother is a world of whores, which Holt rejects for that of his father(s), a "pure" world of idealized women figures. Ironically, Noll thus relies on the very same dichotomy that one of his characters had earlier denounced as "bourgeois."

One might, therefore, be tempted to read this novel as the story of a former Nazi soldier's coming-to-consciousness, securely underwritten by the Oedipal structuring of subjectivity which positions the son in *his place* in the symbolic order. Such a reading seems to be supported by the novel's closing scene: before leaving to take up his studies, Holt meets with Angelika, the woman who has come to replace Gundel, and promises to continue their relationship even after his departure. Is this not the perfect moment of closure? Holt has submitted to the Law of the Father and has replaced his mother with a substitute who provides him with an identity and a task. Yet this is not the end of the story, for that same day Holt also meets again with another woman, Judith Arnold, the Ravensbrück survivor.

There is something deeply disturbed about this text, something which has to do with the magnetic force that emanates from the figure of the excluded mother. To put it simply, Holt's exact relationship to each of these three women remains unclear even at the end of the novel. For instance, one can read the merging of Gundel's "indelible face" (WH/502) with Angelika's in the last scene as Holt's continued attachment to Gundel as a mother or a lover. And the same can be said about his relationship to Judith. When they meet again, Holt asks her for help. Judith's response is the novel's very last sentence: " 'As long as you struggle, as long as you do not let yourself go,' she replied and looked into his eyes and nodded to him, 'as long as you are of good will' " (WH/503). The novel thus ends with Judith slipping into the position of the proletarian mother, a transformation which had already started earlier: when Holt leaves his father's office, he decides to follow the example of his father *and* of Judith—like her, he will struggle for the emancipation of the working class. Holt's quest has thus led him back to the father—and to a new, Communist mother figure who will help him overcome the dirty remnants of the past within him (unlike the mother from whom he separated earlier). Does not *Die Abenteuer des Werner Holt* then generate a fantasy that mimics the very universe Holt rejects when he rejects his mother—the ideology of National Socialism and its idealization of motherhood? And, by the same token, is not the maternal an overwhelming presence here, even if it is radically split into "bad" and "good" mothers?[41]

One could read this proliferation of women/mother figures as a "breakdown of objects of desire," a sign of a narcissistic crisis which, according to Kristeva, involves the fragility of the symbolic function and the emergence of what she calls abjection:

There looms, within abjection, one of those violent, dark revolts of being, directed against a threat that seems to emanate from an exorbitant outside or inside, ejected beyond the scope of the possible, the tolerable, the thinkable. It lies there, quite close, but cannot be assimilated. It beseeches, worries, and fascinates desire, which, nevertheless, does not let itself be seduced. Apprehensive, desire turns aside; sickened, it rejects.[42]

This ambiguity of inside and outside, and ambivalence of revulsion and fascination, is implicated in the dichotomy between purity and filth, which Kristeva traces to a moment prior to the Oedipal crisis, even prior to the mirror stage. Abjection is related to the stage when there is neither a subject nor an object, neither the "I" of the symbolic order/of language nor the ego of the imaginary, but only something "opposed to I," the maternal body which is/is not yet different. Abjection preserves the "immemorial violence with which a body becomes separated from another body in order to be"; it is thus related to the archaic mother and takes the "ego back to its source on the abominable limits from which, in order to be, the ego has broken away." The experience itself is located in the superego. An unshakable identification with the Law and its prohibitions is necessary to hem in the "perverse interspace of abjection." [43] When the ego loses its Other (the order by which it is constituted and in whose representatives it recognizes itself) and its objects, the boundaries of this space are threatened and need to be reinforced.

Kristeva allows us to better comprehend why loathing and self-loathing, and their connection to a National Socialist past, are tied to a *maternal* origin, indeed to the body, in *Werner Holt*. The breakdown of the National Socialist regime is thus the narcissistic crisis that has shaken the subject's very foundations, leaving it in a condition of abjection, experienced as the death of the ego, an archaic moment characterized not by its "triumphant" recognition in the image of the (m)other but by its experience, both fascinating and frightening, of one body's difference from another. With the collapse of paternal law, which the defeat of Nazi Germany represents for Holt, emerges the sense of this "pre-objectal" relationship and the threat it poses to the ego. Noll's Oedipal narrative not only resettles the subject firmly in its superego(s) on the condition of separation from the mother, that is, in response to the father's symbolic threat of castration, but it also redeploys this act of separation in response to the experience of abjection, which has its roots in the pre-Oedipal mother—the "excluded ground"— that Kristeva calls the "magnetized pole" from "which he does not cease separating." [44] It is this experience that precipitates the violence with which the mother is excluded, literally ex-territorialized and banished, since she recalls the painful and fragile origin of that ego/subject now in crisis. This same logic ultimately accounts for the ideological fantasy of the post-fascist body, the necessary exclusion of that part which is not sublime but merely material, not pure but filthy.

Noll's well-intentioned but also painfully simplistic Oedipal story may not exemplify Barthes's famous aphorisms that "as fiction, Oedipus was at least good for something: to make good novels, to tell good stories." [45] I have included this novel in my discussion not on the grounds of its literary merits, however, but rather because it so sharply inscribes the Oedipal narrative into the ideological construction of East German socialism. This is not, as I indicated above, an idiosyncratic move on the part of one particularly neurotic writer.[46] On the contrary, this story emerges in many different variations. Reading Müller and Noll, the Freudian notion of the family romance—the fantasy of revising one's family origins—asserts itself forcefully. In the context of the GDR, this fantasy, in which "the child's imagination becomes engaged in the task of getting free from the parents of whom he now has a low opinion and of replacing them by others, who, as a rule, are of higher social standing," [47] repeatedly entails the desire to separate from parents involved in National Socialism. The fantasy of replacing the "real" father is most openly and directly played out in Brigitte Reimann's first novel.[48]

Arriving in a Country without a Father

Reimann's *Ankunft im Alltag* (Arrival in Everyday Life) centers on three protagonists, the students Recha, Nikolaus, and Curt, who postpone their studies to spend a year on one of the GDR's most colossal and legendary construction sites, the "Black Pump" at Hoyerswerda. Canonized as a coming-to-consciousness story in which the young protagonists accept the daily routine of socialist production, socialism's "everyday life," as their generation's "struggle"—a struggle no less heroic than their fathers' legendary resistance to the Nazi regime—this is indeed one of the stories that Reimann's novel tells. Although clearly planned as a kind of "collective" bildungsroman, the novel tends to focus on its female protagonist, often focalizing the narrative through her. Recha's story follows the normative pattern of a daughter's Oedipal trajectory but with more than a slight twist: her parents are dead, so the paternal figure has to be reconstructed, and the daughter's identification with "the ideal parent of the respective gender" leads her to identify with the dead mother. This accords with the logic of a "politics of identification," [49] since the production of the postfascist body again involves the mother, but this time in an act of identification with the Jewish victim of fascism.

However, in its last chapters, the novel's narrative focus shifts radically from Recha's perspective, which functions as a unifying focal point for the collective narrative, to Curt's. This sudden shift massively derails the narrative impetus toward a symmetrical, harmonious closure; moreover, the novel suddenly breaks out of its realist form with the startling eruption of a long, protracted inner monologue. It is this distortion, with its fixation on the father, which alerts us to a problematic that, while never openly thematized, ultimately structures the entire narrative, namely, Stalinism and the dilemma produced by the revelations of the Twentieth Congress. The SED slogan "No Discussion of Mistakes" not only silenced any critical discussion of Stalinism, its crimes, and the GDR's involvement, but also blocked any inquiry into the effects of losing a paternal figure once so highly valued.[50] This problematic is inextricably linked to Curt's personal/Oedipal narrative. *Ankunft im Alltag* is not just a familiar story of three young people's coming-to-consciousness, for accepting the daily routine of socialist production, socialism's *everyday life,* as their generation's "struggle" is only one of the stories it tells. The protagonists' Oedipal fantasies constitute another story, as does their experience of loss, a story that might not even be conscious.

The novel opens with the protagonists' arrival at the train station. Recha, who is introduced first, articulates the two major themes of the novel of arrival: she experiences the very emotion whose overcoming constitutes the telos of the narrative, "homesickness"; moreover, she is disappointed because the "young city" seems much less "grand," much less "glowing" than she had imagined. Disappointed and lonely where she had expected a "new home," Recha remembers that her favorite teacher at the "red fortress" had warned her that she was not balanced and mature enough for this adventure.[51] Straightforward and not too subtle in her approach, Reimann thus immediately confronts the reader with the major flaw that Recha has to overcome to achieve socialist maturity, and with the two central themes of the story: the transformation of foreign territory into home (through the protagonists' integration into the site of production), and the overcoming of "a fantasy image painted by [Recha's] vivid imagination" (*AA*/6) to attain a more realistic view of socialist life. Also established in this very first chapter is the central organizing plot of Recha's bildungsroman, the successful resolution of which will depend on her choosing the "right" man. Reimann constructs this choice as a *rejection* of the father of the past: Recha Heine's mother, a Jew, had died in Ravensbrück, while her father, "the Aryan," disappeared at the front. Recha holds him responsible for her mother's death because he divorced her in 1941—under pressure, as the narrator informs us. Recha herself grew up a "bastard" in a Nazi orphanage and bears her mother's name: Recha Deborah Heine. But there is yet another story behind this one:

She did not know how her mother had looked, what kind of hair and eyes she had had, but she was convinced that she resembled her.

A Polish comrade . . . once said that—with her dark eyes and small, prominent nose—she looked like the young Rosa Luxemburg, and Recha experienced this comparison as a compliment ever since she had read her wonderful prison letters. (*AA*/16)

Ankunft im Alltag is the only canonical East German novel from this period in which a Jewish character plays a central role. This, of course, problematizes—raises the stakes in—a genre which propels its characters toward their integration into a community representing the new German state. In *Ankunft im Alltag,* both sides are suspicious, the protagonist and the collective. Recha's new roommate, a working-class girl named Lisa, reacts with distrust to this "strange foreigner with her dark origin" (*AA*/14); and Recha herself, because of her upbringing in the orphanage, tends to be unstable and oversensitive. Within this particular framework, her Jewish background is a challenge, and her successful integration into a post-fascist German society a triumph over the past.

Against her better judgment, Recha becomes involved with Curt, whom Reimann portrays in a relentlessly negative light. The son of an upper-level functionary, Curt constantly boasts about his father's high status and his heroic past—without, however, believing in any of his father's principles. He has come to Hoyerswerda only to escape military service, and he tries to avoid any difficult work. Already a rather unlikely hero for any novel of arrival, Curt is also negatively characterized with easily recognizable Western traits: he listens to American radio (predictably bursting into "Don't Fence Me In" as he recklessly races around in his father's fancy car) and wears a silver chain around his neck—in short, he corresponds perfectly to the stereotype of the Americanized 1950s West German "greaser" (*AA*/8). Within a few days of their arrival, Curt has seduced Recha into taking advantage of the "unlimited freedom" their new environment represents, encouraging her to drink heavily and adopt a rather lax attitude toward the socialist work ethic. Recha is torn between the need to make a good impression on the brigade leader, Hamann, who functions as the novel's paternal authority, and the new freedom she enjoys with Curt. (Reimann quaintly signifies Recha's "wildness" through her shoes, bright red and high-heeled, in which she occasionally totters through the mud of the Black Pump.)

Recha's story slowly evolves toward its turning point. In her case, the students' "test," which comes when Hamann asks them to volunteer for a special night shift—an effort described in the heroic register of the Soviet production novel—is only of secondary importance. While Nikolaus immediately agrees to work the additional shift, Curt and Recha pretend to be too exhausted. Instead, they go to a nightclub where Recha is suddenly overcome with guilt feelings and runs in her high heels to the construction site to join her brigade. Completely exhausted, Nikolaus recalls the promise he and Recha had made to do their best and thinks: "Today, for the first time, I feel like I really belong here" (AA/226).[52]

For the female protagonist, however, there will be a more significant turning point having to do with her "correct" romantic choice, not her commitment to socialist production. Although she has already abandoned Curt for Nikolaus, Recha quarrels with Nikolaus over their staid, "virtuous" life and allows Curt to persuade her to meet him again. At this meeting, Curt assaults her; only Nikolaus's intervention prevents him from raping Recha. What is important about this passage is the way in which sexuality and the body are once again constructed as the link between the subject and the fascist past, although here the link is different from the one forged in *Werner Holt:*

Recha remembers her father's face whenever she looks at Curt. Frightened, she thinks: whenever I thought about my father during the last weeks (this happened rarely, however, and against her will), he was no longer anonymous. Suddenly, I can imagine him: he is like Curt, blond and victorious and ruthless. (AA/174)

Earlier, Recha had told Curt: "I despise your blond victor's face" (AA/51), so we are not surprised when the attempted rape culminates in her horrified recognition of a "strange terrible face," that of her "Aryan" father, in Curt's "victor's face" (AA/247). Recha's relationship to Curt is highly ambivalent. He represents what is most forbidden—both the fascist father/past *and* the proto-fascist West/present—and Recha's physical attraction is as strong as her moral revulsion.

This brief scene, a rather explosive example of the work of fantasy in ideology, represents an intricate, complex entanglement of desires and prohibitions, its transgressive power drawing as much on the political domain as on the psychic. Reimann's ideological fantasy transgresses not only the prohibition against incest but also those accruing to the fascist past: it is a fantasy of incest with the fascist father in which the daughter takes the place of the Jewish mother, her body merging with that of the dead mother. The mother's story—and the daughter's identification with the mother's history of persecution—has already begun to intrude into the daughter's story as Recha and Curt leave for the forest: bothered by Curt's behavior, Recha remarks that he acts as if he were arresting her and bringing her in. Through the metonymic displacement from Curt to the fascist father, this scene once again signifies the subject's relationship to the past via the Oedipal triangle, implicating her body and her sexuality. It is a fantasy rigidly policed, delimited, and contained: Recha's desire for what is most forbidden—the fascist father—and its sadomasochistic scenario is interrupted not once, but twice: first literally, with Recha's rescue by Nikolaus, who had followed her and Curt into the woods; and, second, by a rather unexpected move on the author's part, as the dramatic narration of the attempted assault suddenly shifts into an account of Hamann's life story, contrasting old and new, negative and positive, fascist and antifascist father figure.

This peculiar Oedipal story results in a number of expulsions and substitutions which distance Recha from the Nazi past (and, by implication, from the temptations of the West). Through her decision to finally separate from Curt, ending a relationship dominated by sexuality, Recha replaces her father, first with Hamann and then with Nikolaus.[53] The Communist subject thus emerges as a daughter who chooses the man sanctioned by the Communist father figure. She also emerges as the Communist whose body is no longer tied to the past by either desire for the father or identification with the mother's body. However, the identification with the Jewish victim is maintained on the spiritual level in Recha's imaginary identity with the figure of Rosa Luxemburg. This identification defines Recha in her relationship with Nikolaus, who notices her resemblance to Luxemburg when they first meet and who feels compelled to reassure her that the Nazi past will not be repeated: "In our country, there will never again be crematoria, you know that as well as I do" (AA/39). Together with Nikolaus, Recha is now prepared to put into practice the idealistic principles she learned at the "red fortress." [54] Of course, the narrative deployment of sexuality and the body is overdetermined: by choosing Nikolaus, Recha also accepts her place as a Communist subject of production in a novel that explicitly thematizes the Communist discourse on the nexus between sexuality and the work ethic, the "revolutionary sublimation" of the Soviet Freudian *Zalkind*.[55] In Recha's case, this discourse is clearly subordinated to the fantasy of the post-fascist body, but it enters prominently into Curt's story, on which *Ankunft im Alltag* starts to concentrate once Recha has found her appropriate place in the new order. His story revolves around two issues, his "undisciplined" attitude and his conflict with his father.[56] The latter, depicted as protest against authority, occurs when Curt screams at his father that he will not join the N V A because he does not want to take orders from him or any other officer.[57] It is also formulated as a discrepancy between the father's "heroic" past and his "unheroic" present:

He had been a textile worker. . . . At eighteen he joined the Communist Party, and he stayed with it, even after 1933. Under the Nazis, he spent a few years in the penitentiary, and they tortured him . . . but he never squealed. In '43 he became a soldier, but after barely two days at the front he deserted. . . . He must have been a great guy, back then. . . .

Curt fell silent for a moment, he was surprised and a bit disconcerted as he imagined this man whom he had just called a great guy: the way he sat at the table . . . already overweight . . . often tired and irritated . . . a man who lived only for his work. (*AA*/29)

When Curt complains to an older worker about this, he receives the standard answer: that his father is fighting a different but no less heroic battle today, that the present task of building socialism is as great an adventure as the struggle against the Nazis. *Ankunft im Alltag* thus casts the father–son conflict of Curt's story in terms similar to those structuring Recha's and Nikolaus's stories: idealism versus reality and romanticism versus reality, respectively.

Yet what Curt's story touches upon is the delegitimation of the heroic paternal narrative. And the problem it only briefly brushes against on its margins is an experience of loss, since his father no longer represents a model for Curt. When he describes his feelings to Recha, he speaks of a "feeling of utter emptiness," a sense of not having any "firm center" (*AA*/96, 176).[58] Curt's problem is not the presence of an unheroic father but the absence of any father. This lack can be read from a different angle, one that links it to a scene which does not even involve Curt. One evening, when Recha and Nikolaus visit Hamann, their brigade leader, they find him dead drunk. Recha is appalled, and the narrator explains why: "Her impassioned spirit had transformed the human being Hamann into an iron statue; she had provided him with an immaculate armor of virtue, and now fissures showed in this armor, and she was sincerely and painfully disappointed" (*AA*/188–89). Recha expresses her disappointment succinctly: "Yet another statue that has fallen from its pedestal" (*AA*/190). With Nikolaus's help and a ready explanation for Hamann's behavior, however, Recha soon overcomes this trauma, deciding that she needs to reexamine her image of Hamann and then to reassemble it anew.

The image of a monument toppling from its pedestal is familiar; we encountered it at the end of chapter 1, for example, where I summarized the description in *Franziska Linkerhand* of the day Stalin died. Remembering the memorial service, the narrator of this later novel recalls that she put a wreath at the "brass feet of his statue" and goes on to say that the statue "had disappeared one morning without leaving any trace except for the black lines of dirt between the patches of grass, which were still glowing with a fresher green than the lawn around them." [59] The absent father whom Curt mourns is this monument which vanished overnight.[60] Reimann's novel deals with the fundamental dilemma of a society in which it is both forbidden to criticize Stalin publicly and impossible to admit that he was once the desired object.[61] For *Ankunft im Alltag* makes it abundantly clear that Stalin, or the mythic and heroic time associated with this name, is what is desired and what is lost.

This heroic era of Stalinist construction is narrated in East German novels with such opening lines as "It was August 18, 1950," that is, before Stalin's death in 1953—and certainly before 1956.[62] This was a time of legendary efforts, as told in such novels as Marchwitza's *Roheisen* (Iron), the production novel from which this opening line comes, which is about the construction of the GDR's largest collective combine, the Eisenhüttenkombinat Ost, and its newly built model city named after the Soviet leader, Stalinstadt.[63] It is the romantic period that Nikolaus longs for; "those hot August days of the year 1955" (*AA*/33) that his new colleagues still dream about when they recount the celebration of their first achievements in Hoyerswerda, the period now called "the era of gold diggers" (*AA*/31), imbued with a Communist pioneer mentality that still echoes in Hamann's speech: "We are making history here" (*AA*/59). Of course, the three protagonists of *Ankunft im Alltag* are there to learn that those times are over, that "cowboys" are no longer in demand, that the "hooligans' construction site" (*AA*/31) no longer exists. But the novel is steeped in nostalgia for this era and for the man with whom it is associated: Stalin. On the one hand,

Stalin's "death" is the unspoken cause of the paternal narrative's delegitimation, around which Curt's story revolves; on the other hand, what the narrative cannot really articulate at all—the taboo around which it develops its solutions—is Stalinism as the lost, and forbidden, object.[64]

In Recha's case, the problem is readily solved, for its real locus is Curt's story. Like Recha, Curt will reconstitute his father's image. At a political meeting, which he attends against his will, Curt hears workers singing the *Internationale* for the first time in his life. Suddenly, he feels close to his father, not the man he knows but the man "whose image he first has to put together for himself" (*AA*/263): the father of the heroic antifascist past. After this moment of recognition, Curt wants to prove himself, an effort which ends in minor disaster when he tries to lift a motor with a crane and destroys it. Hamann confronts him, demanding that he appear before a meeting of their brigade. Instead, Curt takes the next train out of Hoyerswerda. The novel's last chapter consists of Curt's long-winded inner monologue, in which he finally decides to return to the Black Pump and face the brigade. The turning point comes when he thinks about how his father may react to his flight and remembers his "new image" of his father (*AA*/279), suddenly experiencing a sympathy for his father that he has never felt before. However, the resurfacing of the father's new image is only the consequence of another event, Curt's sudden recognition of Hamann's authority. He now recalls their argument and the "suddenly changed, suddenly strange Hamann" (*AA*/276). We are supposed to understand that Hamann's reaction, first furious, then firm, caused Curt's transformation.

If the loss of Stalin is the novel's unspoken problem, then the figure of Hamann is the solution to this silence. This model father figure with a "minor" flaw fills the absence thematized by Curt's story, but Hamann also acts as a stabilizing force for the whole narrative, for each protagonist's "novel of education." Introduced early on as a "natural" authority figure, a "source of tranquility . . . around which the others congregate" (*AA*/45), Hamann has the obligatory set of sharp, observant, ironic eyes, and he intervenes as a kind of "parental guardian" in the stories of all three protagonists. Hamann, always present, fills an absence felt not only by Curt. However, Curt's story, or more precisely, its narrative "derailment," is the symptom which alerts us to the "real" problem with which the novel struggles. Bursting through its own narrative parameters, the novel's last chapter implodes into a panic-stricken inner monologue revolving around the father. Entirely unlike the mode of narration in the preceding chapters, this one is as much a "Fremdkörper" (foreign body) in the novel as the problem which it can never acknowledge, but nevertheless desperately strains to solve.

In 1987, two years before the collapse of the East German State, the protagonist of Wolfgang Hilbig's novel *Die Weiber* (The Women) hallucinates a rather baroque allegory about his own conception:

Because he [the State] had created me . . . O, an act of procreation of immense intensity had taken place. Surrendering, spreading her legs most devotedly, my mother allowed Father-State to come over her in all his powerful beauty. The grand symbol of Reconstruction was standing erect before her; it thrust itself firmly into her body, and to celebrate her blessing an ocean of flags was unfolded, the young guards of the Party let them float over the ceremony of this pure coitus. I was immaculately conceived and I stayed immaculate in this life which was being constructed; my mind grew strong, I seemed to embody hope . . . but then a summer set my mind on fire. Oh, only later did I become jealous of this pure act. And Generalissimo Stalin, the friend of all good people, had created me; I had the honor of owing him my life; I obeyed, and there was weeping in the world, and tears on my mother's face, when he passed away. And I was scared to death . . . but savage and glaring summers enflamed me. . . . I closed my eyes—I must have slept—and terrible was the state of unbelief in which I awakened.[65]

Here, more than twenty years after the Oedipal narratives of the late 1950s and early 1960s, Hilbig resurrected their key components: the interweaving of personal and political history in the family narrative, the ideal of purity, and the centrality of the father. Hilbig's novel zoomed in on the topic that Reimann's could only address obliquely: the loss of Stalin. Hilbig's novel, like those by Hensel, Papenfuss Gorek, and Drawert, demonstrates how, for the later generation of writers, East Germany's paternal narrative disintegrated around the figure of Stalin. This third generation, born after 1945 and therefore less affected by the guilt that suffuses the work of the earlier generation,[66] has achieved a degree of distance from their state's founding narratives that enables them to focus critically on Stalin. The fantasies of the generation of Reimann and Wolf, on the other hand, by remaining preoccupied with Stalinism's antifascist hero,[67] remained mired in loss and identification.

A New Generation

At the end of chapter 1, I mentioned Christa Wolf's reflections on her generation and its substitute parents. It is appropriate at this point to quote Wolf in full:

At the age of fifteen, sixteen, under the crushing realization of the full truth about German fascism, we had to distance ourselves from those who in our eyes had become guilty during those twelve years by simply being present, by collaborating, by remaining silent. We had to discover those who had become victims, who had resisted. We had to learn to empathize with them. Of course we were not able to identify with them, we had no right to do so. That means that when we were sixteen, we could identify with no one. . . . We were then presented with an attractive offer: You can rid yourselves of your potential, not yet realized participation in this national guilt by actively participating in the construction of the new society, a society which represents the exact opposite of the criminal National Socialist system, the only radical alternative. . . . In my specific case, but not only in my case, one also needs to consider the close relationship to Communists and antifascists through my work in the Writers' Union beginning in 1953 . . . a teacher–student relationship emerged; they were our models, absolutely and in every respect; we were the ones who were supposed to listen and learn, in every respect. . . . Those of us who were young then were bound up for too long in father–son, mother–daughter relations which made it difficult for us to become adults.[68]

As I have shown in this chapter, the construction of these "father–son, mother–daughter relations" was indeed a broad cultural phenomenon. Modifying Jameson's compelling characterization of nineteenth-century realism, we might want to speak of these cultural narratives as a postwar mode of *psychic reality construction*.[69] What these narratives also show, however, is that the constitution of a post-fascist identity went far beyond the fantasy of new parents, for it involved the production of entirely new bodies, making sexuality the privileged terrain of subject constitution. Thus, at a time when "petty bourgeois subjectivity" emerged as one of the master signifiers and the slogan "From the I to the We" was repeated ad nauseam, both subjects and their bodies were overhauled more thoroughly than Brecht, the author of *Mann ist Mann,* a play about the disassembling and reassembling of the Irish packer *Galy Gay,* would ever have thought possible.

Returning now to this chapter's epigraph, what Barbara Köhler wrote in 1994—"The borders were drawn inside our very bodies"—we would read as a reference to the Wall and its existence in people's minds: "We dreamed about going too far, but we did not know where that might be." [70] The analysis of the novel of arrival in terms of its unconscious dimensions now compels us to see that statement from a different perspective: the border that was "embodied" was the boundary with the past.

III

Inscribing the Daughter in

the Paternal Narrative

But I did not want to speak like my father (or my grandfather, for instance). This must have been an early feeling, which may have arisen just in time. It was the feeling of a borrowed and worthless language, a language which I resisted almost bodily, such that I unlearned it; for a shadow of perceptible invalidity and of my father's (or, for instance, my grandfather's) claim to power lay over the words, and to use this language would have been a form of submission. I forgot how to speak, and threw my father, in front of everyone, into a state of distress, forcing him to confront this offense: his son, his very image, without language, a blind mirror. — Kurt Drawert, *Spiegelland* (1992)

4

Post-Fascist Body/Post-Fascist Voice: Christa Wolf's *Moskauer Novelle* and *Der geteilte Himmel*

The Age of Reform: "Bathed in a Milder, More Humane Light"

By both accepting the new father-centered cultural narratives as a framework for her early texts *and* contributing to the writing of this ideological story in her own novels, Christa Wolf established herself as the writer most fully implicated in East Germany's paternal order. Wolf's novels invariably revolve around a young woman, a daughter figure, and they gradually develop Wolf's own unique tone, one which deliberately blurs the boundaries of fiction and biography, of author, narrator, and protagonist. As we saw at the end of chapter 1, in 1959 Wolf celebrated Brosowski, Gotsche's antifascist father figure in *Die Fahne von Kriwoj Rog,* as a model for the GDR's postwar generation, calling him a "hero for our times." [1] Her introduction to *Die Fahne* was also published that year. At this time, her journalistic and editorial work already overlapped with her literary writing. In 1959, Wolf moved to Halle, where she became involved in the Bitterfeld movement, advising workers on their writing efforts and beginning to work on her own Bitterfeld novel, *Der geteilte Himmel/The Divided Heaven.* In a short piece entitled "Dienstag, der 27. September 1960" (Tuesday, September 27, 1960), Wolf sketched the circumstances under which the novel arose, her own involvement as author and Party member within a railcar factory (the main setting of *Der geteilte Himmel*), and the difficulties she encountered in writing the book.[2] Wolf published her first literary work, *Moskauer Novelle,* in 1961,[3] followed by *Der geteilte Himmel* in 1963.

Retrospectively, the period between 1959 and 1965 emerges as an extremely complex time in Wolf's life: a member of the SED since 1949, she became a candidate for the Central Committee following the success of *Der geteilte Himmel*. After her critical intervention at the Eleventh Plenary session of the SED in 1965, the infamous conference which abruptly ended the brief era of reform that began with the building of the Wall in 1961, her name disappeared from the list of candidates.[4] Wolf also met from 1959 to 1962 with officers of the Stasi, reporting under the name of "Margarete." In 1993, when these activities first became public, Wolf claimed to have repressed any memory of them.[5] In an extended interview with Günter Gaus, Wolf characterized her situation in those years as follows:

> I had already overcome the high point—or rather, the low point—of my attachment to, or more precisely my dependence—that's the right word for it—on the ideology. It was precisely in Halle that I started to change; I was criticized seriously for the first time there, it had to do with my attitude towards the Twentieth Party Congress of the CCCP.[6]

At this time, she told Gaus, she was already starting to think critically. That memory of herself clashed with the person she encountered while reading the Stasi documents: "That is not me."[7] In a newspaper article, she described this "other" person as "steeped in ideology, a well-behaved comrade, her own past burdening her with a deep sense of inferiority vis-à-vis those who seemed to be historically in the right, and were legitimated by their past."[8] Around the same time, Wolf was involved in critical discussions of Stalinism with Walter Janka and Friedrich Schlotterbeck, both Party members and victims themselves of Stalinist purges.[9] These discussions, she later claimed, taught her a deep distrust of any sort of "hope of salvation."[10]

In an April 1985 speech commemorating Schlotterbeck, Wolf described those years rather nostalgically as a time of heated debates, times more engaging than the decades that followed.[11] Finally, in her lengthy essay on the Eleventh Plenary, Wolf identified the years before 1965 as a period of "reform communism" which brought together people from all different social groups interested in changing the status quo.[12] Clearly, despite the accusations of "bourgeois individualism" leveled against her first book, Wolf experienced the years prior to 1965 as positive ones: she supported what she saw as developments toward a more democratic socialism; she believed that the reform wing of the SED was strong and that the ruling party was truly interested in cooperating with its critical intellectuals; in short, she found herself in a position of what she later often characterized as "identifying while contradicting [*Identifikation im Widerspruch*]." [13]

With the publication of *Nachdenken über Christa T./The Quest for Christa T.,* a book she started working on in 1963, Wolf discovered that those in power were indifferent to her collaboration. Severely criticized and nearly banned, this novel made her persona non grata for several years, unable to appear in public and never mentioned in newspapers or journals.[14] In 1969, she told Brigitte Reimann that her most "fundamental experience" during the preceding years was "the slapping away of hands." [15] Wolf herself called the *Christa T.* controversy a "test case" and claimed in 1991 that, from this moment on, a group of authors began their "life in opposition [*Leben im Widerspruch*]." [16] In interviews and articles since 1993, Wolf has returned to this controversy as the key moment in her growing critical distance from the SED and its state, a slowly developing crisis which made her third novel a "breakthrough of sadness." [17] Wolf thus recalls the period between 1959 and 1965 as a "golden age" of critically engaged intellectuals, with dusk slowly descending after the Eleventh Plenary, yet reading her files in 1992, she also discovers a person who was "steeped in ideology," much less critical, and "well-behaved."

But there is absolutely no need for us as literary critics to assume a "pure" voice.[18] There are only layers of different, often contradictory voices. And no one is more aware of this than Wolf, the author so fundamentally concerned with the writing of memory as the interaction of the voices of the past with those of the present. But there is more to this issue of *voice* in Wolf. Indeed, as I will argue here, Wolf's literary work represents a relentless exploration of the inescapable historicity of voice, of its thorough imbrication in ideology. Any search for a "pure" voice unencumbered by ideology reads Wolf's work through her own theoretical essays, and thereby fatally reduces a project which is characterized by the *tension* between a desire for a "pure" voice and the painful knowledge of the complex link between history and voice. As Wolf herself said in *Was bleibt/What Remains:* "I myself. I couldn't get past those two words for a long time. I myself. Who was that? Which of the multiple beings from which 'myself' was composed?" [19] To do justice to the significance of Wolf's work means not mimicking this search for a "pure" voice or subject; it means resisting the metaphysics of a voice outside of history, "above" history—and the body—since the most dramatic insight of Wolf's project lies in its having revealed the historicity of voice as a set of inextricable ties between voice and ideology, on one hand, and voice and body, on the other.

The Moment of *Christa T.*

Let us then look at the issue of *voice* in Wolf from this perspective. In a famous 1972 interview on her notion of "subjective authenticity," Wolf stated: "I think that it is an essential aspect of modern prose that behind all the fiction and illusion one can hear the author's voice and see his face." [20] Close to autobiographical writing, Wolf's fiction nevertheless successfully avoids any naive notion of a self-authorizing, self-identical authorial subject. [21] On the contrary, her work has become more and more concerned with exploring the very notion of the writing/speaking subject and its constitution in the act of writing. This chapter will scrutinize a specific aspect of this highly self-conscious assumption of voice, namely, Wolf's foregrounding of the act of speaking in writing. My inquiry into voice will focus on Wolf's early novels and address the topic in relation to the post-fascist body, an approach based upon the idea that voice is located between body and language.

Within the context of the normative aesthetics of socialist realism, with its omniscient, but hidden, nineteenth-century narrator, Wolf's insistence on the presence of the author/narrator in the text signifies an appropriation of the right to *speak in one's own voice*—or, in Wolf's terms, reintroducing the figure of the (female) narrator voices the claim to say "I." [22] In most recent literary histories of the GDR, Wolf's *Nachdenken über Christa T.*, a novel in which a "remembering narrator-I" inquires into the life of the protagonist she *remembers*, [23] is now granted a pivotal position. As the authors of these histories argue, this novel signaled an epochal change, a moment of rupture: with *Christa T.*, the GDR's younger generation of authors started to speak in its "own" voice, shedding the conventions of (socialist) realism, particularly the omniscient narrator's universal voice. [24] The novel itself obsessively turns on the theme of writing, referring to the narrator's difficulties in recreating the figure of Christa T. and to the significance of her loss, which is the loss of someone who refuses to adapt and to give up her ideals. More importantly, however, the novel thematizes Christa T.'s attempts to write: "The Big Hope, or, The Difficulty of Saying 'I' " (*QT*/169; *CT*/188). This theme is complexly interwoven with her characteristic gesture—which fascinates the narrator from the moment they meet—of "blowing a trumpet" (*QT*/6; *CT*/13). This uninhibited scream, Christa T.'s "HOOOHAAHOOO" yelled through a rolled-up newspaper, which "for a fraction of a second lifted the sky up higher," takes on a fundamental significance for the narrator: "Suddenly I felt, with a sense of terror, that you'll come to a bad end if you suppress all the shouts prematurely" (*QT*/9, 10, 11; *CT*/16, 17, 18).

Wolfgang Emmerich's account of the "moment" of *Nachdenken über Christa T.* has probably been the most influential. According to Emmerich, in the early 1960s interest in the "self-realization" of the socialist subject and "remarkable innovations in the mode of narration" converged. At the end of this slow and barely visible evolution of a new mode of reality construction stood *Christa T.,* with its ostensibly "visible" narrator:

Retrospection, the layering of time, inner monologue and stream-of-consciousness, ironic refraction and change of narrative perspective—those and other means of representation, hitherto disapproved but common in the West for decades, are not yet prevalent, but they have started to lose their stigma of decadence because they define the officially accepted, remarkable works of the years 1963–1965—C. Wolf's *Der geteilte Himmel,* Strittmatter's *Ole Bienkopp,* Kant's *Die Aula* [The Auditorium]. . . . Overall, the prose that is breaking free of the status quo is marked by the appearance of reflexive moments (*noticeable particularly* in the rediscovery of the figure of the narrator), of subjectivization, differentiation, and perspectivization. . . . This "secret appropriation" of modern means of narration up to 1965 does not yet entail the complete abandonment of the closed form, which is indebted to a conception of totality and a "rational idea." In general, [this form] is preserved, but hairline cracks have emerged in the stone-hard concrete, and the possibility exists that they will expand.[25]

Having accentuated the "rediscovery of the figure of the narrator" in *Christa T.,* Emmerich then turns to Wolf's 1965 short story "Juninachmittag" (June Afternoon) as the actual beginning of GDR modernism.[26] Emmerich's reading focuses almost exclusively on the role of the first-person narrator, presenting the story as a process of impressions, reflections, and memories, an inner monologue which expresses the narrator's uncertainty, doubt, even ignorance.[27]

Wolf herself decisively contributed to this reading of East German literary history, marking the appearance of the author's/narrator's voice as the key element of the teleological narrative of East German literature in her "Lesen und Schreiben"/"Reading and Writing." [28] In this theoretical reflection on the possibilities of modern prose, Wolf argued against the two central categories of Lukácsian realism, the plot (*Fabel*) and the omniscient narrator. On the latter, Wolf stated:

Let's let mirrors do what they were made to do: to mirror. That's all they *can* do. Literature and reality do not stand to each other in the relation of mirror to what is mirrored. They are fused within the mind of the writer. The writer, you see, is an important person.[29]

Focusing on this "important person," Wolf proposed a new category, narrative's "fourth dimension," or authorial subjectivity:

[The] narrative space has four dimensions—the three fictive coordinates of the invented characters, and the fourth, "real" coordinate, the narrator. This is the coordinate which supplies depth, contemporaneity, unavoidable commitment, which determines not only the writer's choice of subject but also its characteristic coloration.[30]

Using the example of Georg Büchner, the nineteenth-century prose writer and playwright, Wolf developed this model of the writer's "own voice that is like no other." She attributes the haunting quality of his novella *Lenz* to the author's "presence": "With 'few means' he has added himself, the insoluble conflict of his life, his personal peril, of which he is well aware." [31] Preempting the charge of "subjectivism," Wolf insisted in her 1973 interview with Hans Kaufmann on the social validity of the author's "experience": "The reservoir writers draw on in their writing is experience, which mediates between objective reality and the authorial subject. And it is highly desirable that this should be socially meaningful experience." [32] Wolf opposes the pressure to speak in the collective, universal voice of the Lukácsian narrator—a voice that supposedly represents the most advanced epistemological position (i.e., that of the working class)—arguing that she does not have the experience on which this voice is founded: she is not from the working class.[33] Instead, Wolf defends the author's right to say "I" as long as it is based on "socially valid" experience.[34] Wolf often characterized this experience in generational terms: "All I can do is trust that my whole life, my experience, which grows out of an intense concern for the development of our society, will evoke problems and questions in me that are important to other people, too." [35] This stance by Wolf and others against the omniscient, "objective" yet veiled, voice of Lukács's nineteenth-century narrator implies, of course, both the "gesture of doubt and questioning" *and* the attempt to authorize one's own voice.[36]

Going beyond Emmerich's Benjaminian framework, which sees Wolf's willfully subjective narrator as a key element of the transition from premodern to modern forms, other scholars have attributed different meanings to this "event," the collective attempt to seize (narrative) authority and to introduce a relativizing perspective. Relative to *Kindheitsmuster/Patterns of Childhood* (1976) and with a psychoanalytically informed approach to ideology critique, Bernhard Greiner has treated subjective authenticity as a questioning of the *Siegersubjekt*—Freud's "victorious" conscious subject— a process of writing which "touches on things that the ego has excluded." [37] Wolf's work turns on a shattering of the subject, a project that, while certainly not new in the West, was of seminal importance in the GDR.[38] Others interpret Wolf's "introjection of a self-reflexive consciousness in the text" [39] from a feminist perspective, understanding it as the first signs of a gradually developing East German women's literature. Myra Love, for instance, reads *Christa T.* as undermining the author as the "ahistorical absolute patriarchal subject" who, even in modernism, stands outside of his creation.[40] Instead, *Nachdenken über Christa T.* "demystifies authorship by removing it from its traditional position of depersonalized authority"; performing a "process of self-constitution in intersubjective relationship [*sic*]," it represents the "coming-into-being of subjectivity free of domination." [41] Similarly, Sonja Hilzinger isolates the increasing "subjectivization of narration," emerging fully with *Christa T.,* as one of the signs of Wolf's new feminine aesthetic— an aesthetic that Hilzinger, too, understands as a break with (socialist) realism: "The strategy of producing realities perceived and described from different subject sites within one narrative space breaks the dominance of a perspective that understands itself as the only 'correct' one." [42]

Concentrating more on the thematic than the formal elements of Wolf's novel, Dorothea Böck, another feminist critic, also assigns *Nachdenken über Christa T.* a central role in the development of women's literature in the GDR.[43] Böck argues that the new literature by women which emerged at the end of the 1960s linked emancipation from traditional normative conventions of realism with a critique of the dominant patriarchal patterns of thought and behavior. Although supposedly foregrounding thematic aspects, Böck isolates the negation of realism's monoperspective as the key issue of this process of emancipation, thus again centralizing the issue of subjective authenticity:

The topic "woman," that is, "gender relations," emerged hesitantly at first, rather subliminally, within the framework of a more general discussion of the individual's chances for development in socialist society (the so-called self-realization debate at the end of the 1960s) and within traditional forms, in particular that of the novel of development. The concept of individuality congealed in this literary model is questioned, however, from the very beginning. It is countered and sublated, either through content (*Nachdenken über Christa T.,* 1968) or through form (*Franziska Linkerhand,* 1974). In Christa Wolf's *Kindheitsmuster* (1975), but especially in Irmtraud Morgner's *Trobadora Beatriz* (1974) . . . the "break" with patterns of narrative and genre which had hitherto prevailed is already obvious. . . . These novels [are] anything but closed, organically structured works of art. . . . They play and experiment with the "realist model of the novel" that has by now become a cliché. Be it in a humorous ironic mode or in a serious elegiac one, in each case, a monoperspective aiming for totality, authority, indeed omniscience, is being called into question. With no respect. Without restraint. Wholeheartedly. Subjective authenticity, and not some "objectively" legitimated consensus, now counts as the guarantee of aesthetic truth.[44]

The entry of the (female) narrator onto the East German literary scene is thus variously understood as a sign of the transition from realism to modernism (Emmerich); as the marker of one particular form of writing, a "psychologically oriented narration" (Greiner) which traces the project of a psychoanalytically informed ideology critique in Wolf's texts; and, finally, as the symptom of a new women's literature.[45]

Toward a Genealogy of Voices:
Moskauer Novelle and Der geteilte Himmel

Several critics have traced the first timid beginnings of this "new" voice back to Wolf's early *Moskauer Novelle* and *Der geteilte Himmel,* retrospectively "discovering" a teleological, often feminist, narrative of Wolf's gradual emancipation from the collective and its omniscient authorial voice in *Der geteilte Himmel*'s curious oscillation between first- and third-person narration.[46] In contrast to this liberal teleology which celebrates Wolf's gradual emancipation from a collective voice and privileges her "mature" texts, I will engage in a genealogy of this "voice," focusing on the determinants of its emergence in her early texts. Not *Christa T.* but *Moskauer Novelle* and *Der geteilte Himmel* are crucial to any project interested in the issue of *voice* in Wolf's work, since it is those particular texts that create a link between post-fascist body and voice. This genealogy implies a rethinking of Wolf's much-acclaimed "break" with Lukácsian realism for a more historically specific reading of her texts and their underlying problematic. Of course, it would be ludicrous to deny the historically specific significance of the act of speaking in one's own voice; nevertheless, in my view, the significance of this break needs to be radically reconceptualized. Rather than seeing it in the generic models of literary history or the feminist privileging of an authentic feminine voice, I propose to understand Wolf's so-called subjectivization of narration, with its foregrounding of the author's/narrator's voice, as that nodal point in the fabric of Wolf's work at which the interrelated themes of history/memory, voice, and body converge in a new speaking position. But I want to emphasize again, since the term "new" might be misleading, this speaking position is *not* a "pure" voice; what it represents, rather, is the very acknowledgment that voice is always layered with, and steeped in, history.

In *Nachdenken über Christa T.,* the narrator speaks about the paradise of communism as the province of those who are "pure." Recalling the early years of the German Democratic Republic, she writes:

We were fully occupied with making ourselves unassailable. . . . Not only to admit into our minds nothing extraneous—and all sorts of things we considered extraneous; also to let nothing extraneous well up from inside of ourselves, and if it did so—a doubt, a suspicion, observations, questions—then not to let it show.

. . . . .

The idea of perfection had taken hold of our minds . . . and from the rostrums at meetings came in addition a great impatience: verily, I say unto you, you shall be with me today in paradise! Oh, we had a presentiment of it . . . we were . . . arguing whether or not our paradise would have atom-powered heating. . . . *Who, but who would be worthy to inhabit it? Only the very purest, that seemed a certainty. So we subjected ourselves afresh to our spiritual exercises.* (*QT*/50, 2; *CT*/61, 62–63; TA; my emphasis).

The notion of purity refers us back to 1959, to Wolf's reading of Gotsche, and to the "purified" post-fascist body, whose production in identification with the steeled body of the antifascist hero I analyzed in chapter 3. As in that chapter, my textual readings here shift the focus from the story of consciousness to the story of the fantasies about the body, a level which, as we will see, is also implicated in the production of the novel's "new" voice.

Moskauer Novelle: The Daughter's Sublime Body and the Songs of the Past

Moskauer Novelle occupies an odd position in Wolf's oeuvre. Since it is now so hard to find, the novella is effectively excluded from the corpus of her work, and the author herself explicitly censored, indeed seemed to loathe, it in her 1973 essay "Über Sinn und Unsinn von Naivität" (The Sense and Non-Sense of Being Naive).[47]

Moskauer Novelle focuses on Vera, a young doctor from East Berlin who travels to the Soviet Union in 1959 as a member of a delegation. The delegation's translator, Pawel Koschkin, is a former officer of the Red Army who fought in Germany in 1945. Vera and Pawel have met before, in a small village in Mecklenburg where Vera worked as the mayor's secretary immediately after the war. It was Pawel's influence that had made her abandon National Socialism for communism. Now, both are married, yet they are immediately drawn to each other again. Vera's extended inner monologues make it clear that their relationship involves massive guilt on her part not only because she is married, but also because she is the daughter of a Nazi and, most of all, because in 1945 she had failed to denounce a couple of former Nazis who severely wounded Pawel as they burned the Red Army's local headquarters. Only now, in Moscow, does she learn that his wounds prevented Pawel from studying medicine. The story of their relationship and Vera's decision to return to Germany is framed by two scenes, conversations between Vera and two figures representing the older generation: Vera's Party school instructor Walter Kernten, who happens to be the delegation's leader, and Lidia Worochinowa, a Soviet doctor, both of whom play the roles of parental figures.

After the brief recognition scene that opens the novella, a paragraph follows which implicitly motivates the narrative structure, its timid departure from realism's linear narration: "Everyone knows that in the few seconds it takes to stand up, to take someone's hands and to press them firmly — that in those five or so seconds you may also blush, turn pale, have tears in your eyes, and see an unbelievable number of images shoot past before your inner gaze" (*MN*/147). Wolf focalizes the story through Vera, having her alternate between living the present and remembering the past, at times adapting Büchner's strategy of abrupt shifts from third- to first-person narration—techniques which Wolf would use more decisively in *Der geteilte Himmel*. The narrative focus remains on the development of Vera's relationship with Pawel and its implications. Nevertheless, even this early work tells several stories: the story of a forbidden love, the story of a young woman's inscription into new family relations, and the story of her own past. My thesis is that the "real" transgression explored here is not Vera's brief experiment in "Red love" but rather her Nazi history. This transgression is linked to the more mundane one of Vera's "illicit" love through a discourse on disciplining the body. Like the novels of arrival analyzed in chapter 3, *Moskauer Novelle* narrates the making of the *sublime post-fascist body*—the "purification" of the body's *material* part, which is linked to a *sublime* part connecting the subject to a higher mission—as an act of separation from the past and the result of a paternal prohibition.

Walter Kernten, the man who replaces Vera's father figure, represents the Communist with an exemplary biography: one of the first members of Spartacus, he spent years in a concentration camp and, toward the end of the Nazi period, fought in the antifascist resistance. His past life, like Vera's, gradually becomes part of the narrative, with each retrospective fragment reconfirming his status as a model Communist. With no children of his own, Kernten took over the function of Vera's father after the latter's death, when, "at the age of twenty-one, she began to orient herself toward this simple, inconspicuous, gray haired man" (*MN*/174). Vera remembers this identification as complete, the narrative expressing it metaphorically through the gaze: "Every time they met, one look into the other's eyes [was enough] to know what the other was thinking" (ibid.). Kernten's eyes function like a mirror, reflecting back to her not only her own image but her very identity as a Communist.

Reflecting upon Kernten's significance in her life, Vera remembers the emptiness he filled, which had been created not only by her father's death but by his silence under Hitler. Her father, Vera thinks at one moment, had "lived his life wrongly," as he himself told her on his deathbed: "The worst thing was that she had to agree with him, although she shook her head vigorously. At that time, she was already a member of the Party" (*MN*/166). The man who had "lived correctly," Walter Kernten, now functions as Vera's conscience, as she herself states after a confrontation with him. Addressing Walter as a parental figure, she turns her love affair into an act of rebellion, a conflict with socialist ethics: "It bores me, do you hear me, I am fed up with always being well behaved. What you demand is not even human" (*MN*/197).[48] Walter assumes the role of the parental superego—in a most comprehensive fashion: after observing her with Pawel, he offers her his "protection":

"I will be like a mother to you."
"Like mother and father, Walter."
"Good. Mother and father." (*MN*/150)

With Walter's help, Vera realizes that Pawel's passion for her is his way of avoiding painful decisions. When she learns from Sina, Pawel's wife, that he turned down a university position in Siberia, she interprets his reaction as fear, as unwillingness to let go of a life that lacks any higher goal. As soon as she realizes this, Vera decides to end their relationship. Wolf thus presents the resolution as an independent act on Vera's part, an act which Lidia Worochinowa, a Soviet doctor of the same generation as Walter Kernten and the plot's "other" mother figure, nevertheless has an opportunity to approve. At the end of her last meeting with Vera, Lidia declares:

You know that I was secretly a little bit curious to see how it would work out between you two? We old people tend to see young people critically because we envy you. I am always happy when I see young people being as strict and uncompromising toward themselves as we were. (*MN*/210)

Having renounced Pawel, Vera now embodies what she herself believes to be the most important characteristic of the "New Socialist Man": "strength of character, self-discipline" (*MN*/183).

Thus far, the story seems quite transparent: no more than the pious story of a young Communist woman who submits to paternal authority, gives up her lover, and returns to her husband and child. What is less obvious is the other transgression touched upon, Vera's past. As soon as Pawel appears, her father's face (that is, the past) also reemerges, pursuing her in her dreams. With Pawel, Vera is forced to remember what she has so successfully forgotten. He is the only one who knows her from "that time" when she was a sixteen-year-old girl, "disturbed, mired in fanaticism" (*MN*/165). With this particular history, being in love is dangerous since it means being spontaneous and uncontrolled, being "driven" by something: "She was running and looked and learned and talked and laughed and moved" (*MN*/159). For the protagonist of *Moskauer Novelle,* desire generates anxiety. Sitting in her room at night, motionless, Vera experiences a "flood" which rises and falls, comes and goes, as she realizes that "for the first time, she was afraid" (*MN*/175). This is the moment when Vera remembers the evening, her dance with Pawel:

He forced her to return his gaze. He pulled her close to him. . . . She felt his warmth throughout her whole body. . . . Then she stopped dancing and let her arms fall weakly to her sides. "I can't go on," she said. (*MN*/174–75)

Vera's anxiety is associated with the loss of control over her emotions: "She could not be sure of her feelings and thoughts; therefore, she had to learn to hide them" (*MN*/175). She overcomes her lack of control and discipline by making herself "cold" and "calm," with a "mask" to pull over her face, "which has seemed naked to her since that night" (*MN*/176).

Separating from Pawel means cutting herself off from the past once more—and from that part of her which is tied not only to Pawel but to the past: her body. Speaking to Pawel about the curious fact that one seems deliberately to forget so much of one's own life, Vera asks herself when it was that she had burned her diary, which bore the inscription "Loyalty is the German's honor." And she tells Pawel that the most difficult thing to control is the impulse to sing Nazi songs: " 'The songs were the worst,' she told Pawel. 'They were very difficult to forget. *Can you imagine suspiciously watching every sound that wants to escape your lips?*" (*MN*/166; my emphasis). Here, Wolf analogizes guarding one's voice and guarding one's body, both involving the strictest discipline: "She encased herself in armor. . . . She watched herself keenly, when she was with him" (ibid.).

When Vera and Pawel finally sleep together, the tone of the narrative is curiously altered. Their affair takes place outside time, during the five days when the group leaves Moscow for Kiev. In the opening passage of this section, an unbearably kitschy tone is introduced. But not only does the text's style radically change, sexuality itself—the body and its desire—suddenly vanishes, leaving only a dreadful travesty of desire rendered as socialist realist kitsch:

Not only the sky of the first morning, everything in this green, vital city seemed favorable to them. . . . The birds in the avenues and parks were singing for them, the peoples' laughter and their songs were for them. The earth was round and surrounded itself with a slight frosting of perfection, that air which only the happy ones can feel. . . .

Each of them found in the eyes of the other happiness about the green trees' contrast with the white houses . . . and that everything stood out so nicely and fittingly against this light blue sky, slightly veiled by the mist of clouds. (*MN*/184)

This is as close as we get here to the body and the issue of desire—unless the following is read as a kinky metaphor for what the narrative so adamantly represses: "Pawel bought a small green melon and cut it with his pocket knife. The melon was overripe, sweet, its flesh red, and its juice ran down their chins and hands as they bit into it. Each let the other taste a bit of their piece" (*MN*/188). This is one of the textual moments where Bitterfeld's mass literature introduces elements from melodrama. And it is precisely due to the melodramatic convention of thematizing sexuality in veiled yet insistent ways that the body comes to play such an important role.

Under such "innocent" conditions, it comes as no surprise that Vera suddenly begins to sing, and in public. In a scene that grotesquely perverts the traditional literary idyll, Vera and the other members of her delegation visit a collective farm where, predictably, everyone starts dancing and singing in the evening, after a meal under the kolkhoz oak, with the obligatory stream of vodka. At the very center of this country idyll stands Vera, who sings a German folk song about love, never taking her eyes off Pawel:

Leaning against a tree, she softly began to sing. "I heard a little creek murmur. . . ." The simple, long-forgotten verses resurfaced in her, up to the last ones, during which she looked at Pawel:
Let it murmur, love, let it murmur
I do not know how I feel
the creeks always murmur
and never lose themselves. (MN/194)

The logic that motivates this rather stunning episode of hardcore socialist realist kitsch is, on the one hand, the granting of absolution: Vera is absolved of her guilt, namely, the past, because the delegation's sojourn at the collective farm has explicitly reconciled Germans and Russians; on the other hand, the scene is aimed at eliminating a "body out of control," a kind of love that, in Vera's song, is signified by a German fairy-tale brook that quietly murmurs and never loses itself.

The plot of *Moskauer Novelle* thus constructs ideal parental figures, brings the daughter into conflict with its central father figure, and develops a resolution which eliminates the daughter's past by eliminating the only character who knew her "in those times" — together with any part of her that is associated with him. When Vera first reflects back upon her past, she remembers that she and Pawel were once allied together against "the girl Vera" (*MN*/161). The plot changes this alliance, setting Vera against Pawel and *her own body*. Vera now incarnates the sublime body, one whose "fragile materiality," to recall Žižek,[49] has been subjected to the strictest discipline, has been indeed all but erased. At the end of Vera's story, feminine desire is brought to submission to the (Communist) father's prohibition. What at the beginning seems likely to be the engine of the plot — the desire to "remake her entire life" (*MN*/152), which Vera voices after meeting Pawel so unexpectedly — undergoes a strange narrative displacement, since it is Pawel's life, not Vera's, that changes radically. Without any hint of irony, Wolf sends him to Siberia, now no longer a simple translator but an instructor of German literature. Yet Vera does undergo a radical transformation nonetheless, for she is now *a woman without a past,* a woman who, having nothing to hide, is rendered transparent and maskless.

More explicitly than either Noll or Reimann, Wolf posits sexuality, in a truly Foucaldian move, as the truth of the (ideological) subject. Throughout *Moskauer Novelle,* she uses the metaphor of the eyes as the mirror of the soul, the face as the transparent reflection of the character's innermost ideological "core": when Vera and Walter meet, a look into the other's eyes is enough to know what the other is thinking; when Walter stands in front of the Kremlin, Vera looks at him and reads his expression as totally transparent — "his innermost being shone through" (*MN*/158); and when Vera understands that she must capitulate to this force stronger than herself, she decides that she will then have to wear a mask to hide her feelings — the mask that she no longer needs at the end of her story.

Even more explicitly than Reimann, Wolf has her protagonist live the past at the level of her body, but in a rather contradictory way. As in the other novels, the post-fascist, desexualized body requires the production of what it denies; it needs the act of transgression. But in *Moskauer Novelle,* the sexual act signifies not only transgression but also redemption. While Vera redeems herself through her desire for a Red Army soldier, she subsequently renounces desire. When Vera explains to Walter why she has stopped resisting Pawel, she claims to be acting out of guilt for having destroyed his future. To herself, she admits that she did not prevent the attack because she wanted to be able to hold on to her hatred, the hatred of the Nazi girl toward the victors. Thus the love affair between Pawel and Vera belatedly enacts a reconciliation between former enemies, demonstrating, again *at the level of the body,* Vera's transformation from a fanatic Nazi, who panics when she meets the Red Army soldier for the first time, into a Communist—and Pawel's transformation from an object of terror and hatred into an object of love. In *Moskauer Novelle,* the sublime Communist body is thus a construct which emerges as the result of a process of separation from (feminine) sexuality and *thereby* from the National Socialist past. Thus the production of the post-fascist body as an asexual one here follows from an act that represents both transgression *and* reconciliation, an act we might be tempted to call sacrificial. This same sacrificial gesture also colors the rape scene in Reimann's narrative. It is here that we recognize the masochistic dynamic so prevalent in Gotsche's celebration of the antifascist hero, the same nexus of guilt and desire carried into the next generation as it models its sublime post-fascist body on the body of the Father.

Through Vera's singing, the post-fascist body is then linked to a *"new" voice* born in the very process of finally separating from her past. As we have just seen, this process is highly contradictory: to separate from a past that is signified as sexuality, Wolf's protagonist must surrender to the sexual act itself; she must *sacrifice* herself in order to acquire not only a post-fascist body but a *post-fascist voice* as well. As if this "new" voice has to be reaffirmed, the section narrating the delegation's sojourn on the collective farm—organized around Vera's song—closes with yet another scene that thematizes singing. On the train which takes them back to Moscow, a few members of Vera's delegation start humming German and Russian songs until finally they all join in singing "Brüder, zur Sonne, zur Freiheit!" After a brief silence, Walter tells them about his years in Buchenwald, and about a clandestine meeting of the Communist cell that ended with the very same song:

At the end, Paul said: "Now let's sing our song: 'Brothers, Toward the Sun, Toward Freedom!' " We stood up and moved even closer together. Paul gave the sign. We sang without making a sound. It was dark. We couldn't see each others' lips moving. But you could feel the other comrades' breath on your face. The silent song roared in our heads as if thousands were singing it. (*MN*/195)

152

Like the previous scene, this one rethematizes guilt, reconciliation, and re-demption—this time a reconciliation between the antifascist hero and the generation of former Hitler Youth members that is sealed by the repetition of a particular song. Listening to Walter, Vera thinks that he has just de-clared all of them his friends by sharing this memory with them. In my view, this passage finalizes the *realignment of voice* from National Social-ism to communism, from the fascist father of the past to the Communist father of the present.

Voice in Psychoanalytic Theory

So far, little psychoanalytic work has been done on the question of voice per se.[50] Didier Anzieu, Guy Rosolato, and Paul-Laurent Assoun have writ-ten about the role of the voice, both the mother's and the child's relative to the periods before and after the child's entry into the order of language. Beginning with Assoun's observation on the vocal nature of the superego, I shall then backtrack to the very early stages of the child's development. Both Anzieu and Rosolato are concerned with the role of voice in the formation of the child's *body ego,* the first experience of not being a frag-mented, uncoordinated collection of body parts, prior to the actual mirror stage. Anzieu deals with this stage before the difference between mother and child, subject and object, is established. He argues that the "sonorous bath" in which the child exists from the very beginning provides it with a first, albeit unstable, experience of not being fragmented—if it works "cor-rectly." This "sonorous envelope" consists of the mother's voice, her words or songs and her other sounds. Although the child does not yet understand any words, it can discern patterns and begin to respond to them:

Before the mother's gaze and smile . . . return to the infant an image of itself that it can visually perceive and that it internalizes in order to reinforce its self and to sketch out its ego, the melodious bath . . . puts at its disposal an initial sonorous mirror that it uses first to scream (screams which the maternal voice quiets in re-sponse), then to babble, and finally to create its phonemic games of articulation.[51]

This first experience of the self as in a "sonorous envelope," surrounded by sounds, precedes another primary formation of the body ego, the *Moi-peau,* or "Ego-skin." The first body image thus emerges when the infant experi-ences its skin as a barrier and point of contact with another object; like skin, the sonorous envelope works toward both the interior and the exterior because it "is composed of sounds emitted alternatively by the environment and by the baby itself." Given the traditional arrangements of child care, voice has a primarily feminine character, and it produces "a real bond of fusion with the mother." [52]

Guy Rosolato's argument is similar, although he focuses more on the impact of the mother's periodic absence on the constitution of the " 'accoustic' mirror," a term he uses analogously to Lacan's "visual mirror." [53] Furthermore, Rosolato understands voice as located *between body and language.* At first, the child's own voice relates to its bodily excitations, painful or pleasurable, both the sounds the child emits and the sounds emanating from within its own body. Like Anzieu, Rosolato emphasizes that the mother's/parents' adequate reaction to these cries or sounds is extremely important. However, Rosolato draws attention to another aspect: from emitting its first screams, the child soon proceeds to imitate the mother's voice, "hallucinating" the familiar but *absent* maternal environment. In this process, voice becomes, first, a marker of an imaginary experience of primordial corporeal harmony. Then, when this voice is received by the mother and returned to the child, it acts like a mirror—establishing a body ego or unitary body image *within the auditory realm.*[54] Like the effect of the mirror stage—the child's coherent gestalt—this bodily ego is, however, ultimately the product of an act of misrecognition. Continuing his exploration of the link between body and voice, Rosolato then discusses the child's entry into the symbolic. Voice, he argues, from the very beginning signals both union and separation: in the mother's absence, the child "makes her present" by reproducing her voice; it also recognizes the agent of separation in the father's voice; and, finally, with the child's entry into the symbolic order— with the recognition of language as anchored to the recognition of the Name-of-the-Father—the association of lack with voice is fixed.

The relationship of voice to the superego and its formation is explored in more detail by Assoun. He begins with a clinical observation: the psychotic who hears voices finds himself "at the center of a host of voices that are aimed at him" and experiences his auditory hallucinations as invocations of the Other. The regulatory instance of the superego thus not only deploys the visual register, but is also involved in the auditory register. Assoun then sets out to explain the interiorization of those voices, which the psychotic hears as *external voices,* in nonclinical cases as the superego. He calls this process the "mise-en-voix," or "putting-into-voice of the parental super-ego." [55] Its climax is the institution of the superego as the identification with the father—and with his voice, as Rosolato argues.

Assoun's theory of voice calls for a brief summary of the formation of the ego prior to the Oedipal crisis and of the Oedipal crisis itself, with its complicated set of identifications, which was partially covered in chapter 1. Elaborating on Freud's insight that "the ego is first and foremost a bodily ego; it is not merely a surface entity, but is itself the projection of a surface," [56] Rosolato and Anzieu draw attention to the effect of voice on the first, early and tentative formation of this ego as a "sonorous envel-ope." Assoun focuses on a different, possibly later aspect of ego formation: the incorporation of the parents' not-yet-understood voices into that ego. But let us first recall Freud's definition of *identification* as opposed to *object cathexis*. In attempting to explain the "metamorphosis of the parental relationship into the super-ego," Freud refers to his definition of identifica-tion: "the assimilation of one ego to another," where the "first ego behaves like the second" and in a sense "takes it up into itself"; in contrast to ob-ject choice, identification means that "the ego is altered." [57] Ego formation occurs prior to the Oedipal crisis. At first, in the infant's relationship with its mother, there is no distinction between object love and identification. But as the need for objects grows so does the realization that they have to be relinquished, since they are not always present.[58] The infant abandons them only partially through a form of identification, incorporation: "The ego is thus formed by this setting up of objects inside itself." [59] Explaining the genesis of the ego as a "vocal interweaving of paternal and maternal imagoes," Assoun points to Freud's discussion of the ego in "The Ego and the Id." [60] Here, Freud refers to a "cap of hearing" worn by the ego, which involves it in auditory perception.[61] These first prelinguistic identifications with the ideal images of the parents, the infant's early ego ideals, are thus literally the result of hearing: the infant takes in not the meaning but the tone of parental voices. According to Assoun, the infant's long period of dependence on its parents means that "the human being is subjected to voices." [62] This also applies to the next stage in the genesis of the superego.

As we saw in chapter 1, Freud posited the following elements as central to the Oedipal crisis: the child's bisexual predisposition, which can result in either a negative or a positive resolution to the crisis, entails in both cases a complex set of identifications at the moment of resolution. In the Oedipal crisis, the child's giving up the intense object cathexes of the parents leads to compensatory identifications with these lost objects. What occurs at the resolution of the Oedipal crisis, according to Freud, is a "strong intensification of the identifications with the parents," identifications that have long been "present" in the ego.[63]

Two things need to be stressed at this point: first, according to Freud, the superego is not simply the residue of earlier object choices; instead, it represents a "reaction formation against these choices." Indeed, the most significant aspect of superego formation is the identification with the figure of the father.[64] The ego is thus an earlier system of identifications along the vocal register which serves as a prelude to the most significant identification, with the Oedipal father. Nevertheless, as Freud himself repeatedly emphasized, these structures cannot be kept entirely separate. In explaining the genesis of the superego, Assoun differentiates between the parental and the paternal superego, the latter being the ultimate formation. The parental part of the superego consists of those prelinguistic parental voices, or "vocalises," which are then restructured through the intervention of the "Name-of-the-Father." Like the ego, the superego originates in what has been heard: "The voices of the superego, its 'vocalises,' are thus literally the voices of parents once actually perceived." [65] Quoting Freud, Assoun argues that the superego represents the "sedimentation" of the "primitive 'parental authority' ": "The incitement to the formation of the ideal ego . . . is originally the effect of the critical influence of the parents, mediated by the voice." These internal voices function from the beginning as a "mediator" between parental influence and subject: "Voice is a kind of intermediate 'schema' between the parental reality and the reality of the subject." [66]

Second, the superego and the ego ideal are inheritances of the Oedipal crisis. The prelinguistic parental voices are restructured, and the identification with the father and his voice becomes central. Nevertheless, these other, prelinguistic voices are still present.[67] In them, the subject still carries the echo of the libidinal object cathexes it was forced to abandon in the course of the Oedipal crisis. According to Freud, the superego therefore expresses the most powerful impulses of the id.[68] The phenomenon of voice is not exclusive to the superego, however, as the psychotic's voices might lead one to conclude, because the superego emerges from a complex process of identification with objects to which strong libidinal impulses were attached. According to Assoun, voice always rests on what he calls *soubassements pulsionels,* instinctual or libidinal foundations:

In contrast to gaze, [voice] is not located on the side of the drives, but on the side of the super-ego's ideal. . . . This does not mean that voice . . . might not *touch on drives*—as on a "root" which has suddenly become "sensitive," but that [process] passes through the "vocalises" of the superego. However, there is no more precise *vector* of the *drive* than the superego: that which "speaks" thereby, through the superego, is the voice . . . of the drive.[69]

This is the case because the superego is both a structure and a kind of "operator of the drives," which reinvests the utterances once perceived with the energy of the unconscious. The superego is, indeed, a contradictory instance, both "interdictory and 'jubilant,' " as it simultaneously limits desire and commands pleasure.[70] "Jouissance," as the impossible desire for a lost unity with the pre-Oedipal mother and its pleasure,[71] is involved in another aspect of the question of voice. With his concept of *voix-corps,* or body-voice, Assoun joins Anzieu and Rosolato in their preoccupation with voice and the imaginary. Citing the myth of the sirens, Assoun suggests that the voice of song—the excess of sound over linguistic content—belongs to the pre-Oedipal realm, to a time before the Law. That is, song, as the stylized form of a "primitive scream," is related to a "jouissance that has not yet suffered . . . symbolic castration." Assoun calls this a "body voice." [72] The way in which voice is theorized in psychoanalysis thus makes it a phenomenon which is limited neither to a specific stage in the subject's development nor to any specific structure, such as the superego. Instead, voice emerges as an area or space, cutting across these separate temporal stages and psychic structures, and always touching upon desire.

Body Ego, Acoustic Mirror, and the Voice of the Superego

The first conclusion to be drawn about *Moskauer Novelle* is rather general: Wolf's novella revolves around two core phenomena, voice and sexual desire, both of which emerge, according to psychoanalytic theory, in the same "space" at the same moment—in the presymbolic realm during the mother's absence. Because of this distinctive focus, the text draws attention to the glaring absence of the maternal figure. In psychoanalytic theory, absence is also the very foundation of sexuality as fantasy. Freud defined fantasy most basically as the means by which the subject "attempts to replace a disagreeable reality by one which is more in keeping with the subject's wishes." [73] Following Freud, Jean Laplanche and Jean-Bertrand Pontalis link the experience of absence not only to fantasy but to the very emergence of sexual desire. They argue that autoeroticism originates at the moment of disjunction between nonsexual function and sexual desire. When the object that provides satisfaction—the breast, for instance—is absent, it becomes an object of desire as the signifier of the lost object—*in fantasy:* "The origin of auto-eroticism would therefore be the moment when sexuality, disengaged from any natural object [such as the breast], moves into the field of fantasy and *by that very fact* becomes sexuality." [74] In its emphasis on Vera's singing and the whole complex tie between voice and the sexual body—the fantasy of controlling what threatens to break through (Vera's desire for Pawel and her fascist past, sexuality and song)—*Moskauer Novelle* draws our attention to the fact that both sexual desire and voice originate in an "empty space," an absence.

Does this mean that we ought to read *Moskauer Novelle* as organized around the pre-Oedipal mother, as Rosolato's and Anzieu's theorizing of voice suggests? The mother is, indeed, conspicuously absent from the story, in which Vera's "real" mother is never mentioned. Moreover, *Moskauer Novelle* also prominently figures the singing voice, this excess of voice over content related to the imaginary and its jouissance, the pleasure attributed to a state of completeness before the separation from the mother. One might thus be inclined to argue that Vera's *voix-corps,* retaining the traces of the pre-Oedipal symbiosis with the mother, marks the daughter's difficult transition from the first object of desire, the mother, to the father. Does Wolf's focus on voice illustrate Juliet Mitchell's apt phrase about the aftermath of this "massive act of repression" demanded of the girl: "What has been displaced remains highly vocal"? [75]

This line of argument does not seem to fit *Moskauer Novelle,* however, because there is a mother figure here, one who constitutes a rather looming presence and plays a primordial role: Lidia Worochinowa. For it is Worochinowa who utters the sentence that gives meaning to Vera's transgression ("I am always happy when I see young people as strict and uncompromising toward themselves as we were"). In contrast to Walter Kernten, Lidia Worochinowa represents the law in all its strictness, and thus, ultimately, the voice of the superego. Under the imperative of the superego, *Moskauer Novelle* produces the post-fascist body—separation from Vera's sexuality, as the element linked to the past—and this body's new post-fascist voice.

Let us approach the problem from a different angle: like Noll's *Abenteuer des Werner Holt,* Wolf's *Moskauer Novelle* revolves around a narcissistic crisis—a loss of identity resulting from the breakdown of National Socialism. This loss is formulated with respect to the figure of the fascist father. Vera is introduced with a patrilinear genealogy, as the daughter who always loved her father, already "resembling him as a child" (*MN*/166)— her mother is never mentioned. *Moskauer Novelle* creates a substitute for this father, Walter Kernten, the antifascist hero. Like Lidia Worochinowa, Walter Kernten represents the Law, to which Vera ultimately submits through the splitting off of her fascist, that is, her sexual, body. Yet Walter's voice also functions as an "acoustic mirror," making him a highly ambiguous father figure—the father as pre-Oedipal mother. In the scenes outlined above, the imaginary unity of mother and child, of child and world, is recreated in the "attunement" (*Übereinstimmung*) of Vera's voice with Walter's.[76] Voice and song function as acoustic mirror, recreating wholeness in the mimesis of Walter's voice, for Vera finds her new identity affirmed in the songs she shares with her friends, but, above all, in those she shares with Walter. Although Vera, as we recall, asks him to act as both *father and mother,* we should not read this as a neat division of his character into the father/symbolic and the mother/imaginary. Instead, with this mother/father figure, *Moskauer Novelle* constructs the figure of the pre-Oedipal mother as both mother and father. Once the imaginary symbiosis between the antifascist hero—the text's father/mother—and the daughter is fixed along the vocal and the visual register, along voice and gaze, Vera recognizes herself in the eyes of Walter *and* in his voice. Vera's new post-fascist voice represents a voice in mimesis of its superego, located in the Communist Walter Kernten; the fact that this voice also carries the traces of its abandoned object cathexes—the pre-Oedipal mother and her voice in the acoustic mirror—accounts for the ambiguous figure of Kernten as father/mother.

As we have already seen, the acoustic mirror represents both the imaginary synthesis with the mother and her body *and* the first stage in the formation of the self as a complete and separate entity, the first stage in the genesis of a *body ego*. What are the implications of Vera's new identity being signified through her singing voice? First and foremost, it locates identity between the development of the superego and the earliest moments of subject formation in the stage of the acoustic mirror. Second, voice designates both the desire for symbiotic merger with the pre-Oedipal mother *and* the desire for separation, for an identity independent of that mother. And, as we have just seen, this mother is represented in *Moskauer Novelle* as the mother/father. Third, positing identity in terms of voice focuses identity around the archaic emergence of *the first contours of a body ego* in the acoustic mirror, a focus that accounts for the novella's connection between (post-fascist) *voice* and (post-fascist) *body*. Thus the realignment of Vera's voice from the fascist father to the Communist father/mother finalizes the transition from the sexual body of the past to the asexual body of the present: just as the post-fascist body is produced through the splitting off of sexuality as the part of subjectivity that is linked to the past, the post-fascist voice emerges from replacing the songs of the past with the songs of the present—and from displacing the father of the past with a father/mother of the present. Fourth, the fact that *Moskauer Novelle* thematizes this early connection between body ego and voice forces us to modify the earlier statement that Vera's "new" voice arises out of a separation from the body. Indeed, this thematization forces us to argue against Wolf's own textual logic of a voice "purified" of desire, for the logic of the post-fascist voice collides with the paradoxical nature that characterizes the phenomenon of voice: it belongs, as Rosolato argues, to the realm of the body and the realm of language. Assoun's discussion of the singing voice as voix-corps, related to the lost jouissance of the imaginary, and Rosolato's thesis that voice has a "corporal source, a source in the organic and in excitation," [77] lead us to understand voice as always carrying the trace of the body, its fantasies, and its desires. But, more specifically, the fact that identity in *Moskauer Novelle* is formulated around voice both as a first experience of separation and as implicated in the imaginary and its lost jouissance makes voice a highly contradictory phenomenon. We thus actually have to read Vera's "new" voice as highly ambiguous—at once the marker of a *sublime* post-fascist body, whose "fragile materiality" has been submitted to the strictest discipline, *and* the very trace of this material body, the proof of its indelible *presence*. What clearer symptom of the ambiguous status of Vera's new post-fascist voice could we find than the highly contradictory status of the sexual act here, representing at once redemption and transgression, necessary sacrifice and illicit love?

Wolf's novella, thus linking body and voice, organizes a whole fantasmatic field around an absence. The absence of the text's "real" mother is now all the more telling—but not as a sign of the daughter's difficult transition from the pre-Oedipal mother to the father. *Moskauer Novelle* revolves around a different stage of development: the acoustic mirror stage, which reaffirms both the imaginary merger with the mother and her voice *and* the first experience of a body ego and an identity separate from the pre-Oedipal other. It is the periodic absence of the mother which first produces the infant's scream. And it is her response which establishes the acoustic mirror and the infant's first body ego, based on the (mis)recognition of the infant's own voice in the voice of the other. This Lacanian approach renders voice—like gaze—an *objet a*. Originating in the absence of the pre-Oedipal other and seeking its reconfirmation in the other's voice, it is also potentially a fetish.

The Postwar Family Romance

At first glance, the role of the Oedipal plot in *Moskauer Novelle* contrasts with its function in *Die Abenteuer des Werner Holt,* where it structures the entire novel, and in *Ankunft im Alltag,* where the decisive moment in the protagonist's development arises from an Oedipal fantasy. Yet the Freudian family romance, the fantasy of revising one's family origins, effects *Moskauer Novelle* more forcefully. The postwar variant of this fantasy elaborated here involves the desire to separate from parents identified with National Socialism via the substitution of the "real" father first by Pawel, the Red Army officer, and then by Kernten, the hero of German antifascism. It repositions Vera toward a new center, shifting her away from the fascist father of the past and toward the Communist father/mother of the present. Vera's subsequent separation from Pawel can then be understood in turn as the elimination of a competing father figure, centering the whole narrative on the figure of the German Communist.

Thus Wolf's novella participates in the new paternal order on several distinct levels: first, it positions its protagonist as a daughter within the Oedipal triangle of the family, without ever problematizing the fantasmatic nature of its family romance; second, it centers its conflict on the daughter's choice of the father's successor; third, and most importantly, it demonstrates in an exemplary fashion the making of the sublime Communist body. *Moskauer Novelle* focuses even more exclusively than *Die Abenteuer des Werner Holt* does on the nexus of sexuality and the National Socialist past, and it demonstrates the very process by which the post-fascist body comes into being in a much more contradictory fashion than the latter. But, more importantly, it establishes the first link between this post-fascist body and a new voice ostensibly produced in the very act of the separation from the body of the past.

As we have seen, this centers the narrative on the acoustic mirror stage and its implications for identity. The issue of voice is therefore more complicated than Wolf leads us to believe. Against the logic of her narrative, which strains to establish the nexus between a "pure" post-fascist voice originating in a "purified" body (i.e., a sublime body linked to the laws of History and a new mission, one whose material support has been "cleansed" of its attachment to the fascist past, conceived of as sexuality), we read Vera's new voice as the trace of a material body that is sexual, a body of desire. First, voice is inextricably bound to the emergence of the body ego and, second, voice is bound to the imaginary jouissance of union with the pre-Oedipal mother. *Moskauer Novelle* demonstrates that voice, in being linked to identity, to the body and the pre-Oedipal mother, is linked to the past—the past of the pre-Oedipal mother, who reemerges in the guise of the antifascist hero as mother/father. We should keep in mind, however, the total exclusion of Vera's "real" mother from a narrative whose very structure rests upon the substitution of one set of parents by another. What this text puts into relief is that both Walter Kernten and Lidia Woroshinow are replacements without an original, but replacements whose power cannot be understood, I would argue, without the force which emanates from the figure that has been completely foreclosed.

In this narrative's particular construction of the dominant cultural icon of antifascism, the articulation at different levels of the individual psychic story with the social–historical story becomes most salient. The link between voice and past has to be understood on two levels: first, with respect to the character's individual problematic, the focus on identity as linked to the acoustic mirror stage; second, with respect to the character's social problematic, her link to the National Socialist past, which remains stubbornly present in her new voice.

The issue of *Moskauer Novelle's narrative* voice then also appears in a new light: on the one hand, the timid use of first-person, retrospective narration at the beginning prefigures Wolf's later move to seize narrative authority; on the other hand, this voice is symptomatic not only of an early liberating shift away from the collective but of a problematic specifically located on the level of voice itself and rooted in the problematic of the body and the past. These same relations would later be reworked in *Der geteilte Himmel,* albeit in a significantly refracted form with the legacy of the past displaced on the novel's male protagonist and its female protagonist purified not only of this past but also of its body, creating yet again the fantasy of a "pure" voice. This new permutation of the same fundamental "fantasy master narrative" [78] requires a more sustained inquiry into the symptomatic nature of narrative voice.

Beyond the Opposition of Subject and Object:
Oedipal Subjectivity in *Der geteilte Himmel*

Like Reimann's *Ankunft im Alltag,* Wolf's *Der geteilte Himmel* was written in the Bitterfeld context, a context that made it difficult for the novel to rise above mere "reportage," the other dominant genre of the Bitterfelder Weg.[79] Calling it a mere "brigade story," Wolf lamented the novel's lack of any overarching idea which would make this "banal material narratable and worth narrating." [80] However, with the completion of the Berlin Wall on August 13, 1961, Wolf found her overarching idea and turned her production novel into the story of Germany's division.[81] Focusing on Rita, a young woman who leaves her village to become a teacher, the plot also has her joining her lover, who lives with his parents in the city where Rita will attend university. As part of her education, Rita spends some of her time in a wagon factory, where she is drawn ever more deeply into the daily struggles of "her" brigade. The novel's central conflict, however, revolves around her decision not to follow her lover, a chemist disappointed by what is not so much an oppressive system as an ineffective one, to the West.

Der geteilte Himmel is an overtly allegorical work that endows Rita's story of love and separation with a political dimension whereby the master-metaphor of a (divided) heaven links love story and allegory. This metaphor develops from a whole network of tropes of harmony and synthesis that are disseminated throughout the narrative. It originates with a description of Rita's village as a perfectly harmonious arrangement of red-roofed houses "surrounded by just the right amount of woods, meadows, fields and open sky." [82] Recalling her first Christmas with Manfred, Rita speaks of a moment when "the two halves of the earth perfectly fit together" (*DH*/11; *gH*/16; TA). She employs a similar trope to express her strongest desire: "One skin to cover us both, one breath for both of us" (*DH*/77; *gH*/80). When Rita and Manfred part, Manfred says that at least "they" cannot divide the sky, but Rita thinks otherwise: "The sky? This whole arch of hope and longing, love and grief? 'Oh yes,' she murmured. 'The sky divides first' (*DH*/198; *gH*/187). Although the trope is shattered as the couple breaks up, this unity is reconstituted in the epilogue as the complementary structure of femininity and masculinity upon which the novel's ideological project—the reconciliation of individual and social order—ultimately rests. The emblematic image at the epilogue's very core, a family at dinner, makes this complementary configuration of gender the explicit metaphor for socialism's utopian community. Rita sees this portrait of the simple life from the outside as she walks around the city, gazing through the "squares of light" that suddenly appear in the dark walls of the houses (*DH*/212; *gH*/199). Problematizing what the epilogue then posits, namely, Rita's integration at some point in the future ("And she was not afraid that she would miss her share of kindliness"), this topography renders the novel's resolution—and one of its most basic ideological paradigms—rather tenuous.[83]

While *Moskauer Novelle* was not widely reviewed, *Der geteilte Himmel* caused one of those heated debates that would partly fix the meaning of a work at the outer limits of the SED's normative theory of socialist realism.[84] The official criticism accused Wolf of "bourgeois decadence," seizing upon the novel's formal "deviation"—its logic of remembrance. After returning from a brief visit to West Berlin during which she leaves Manfred for good, Rita breaks down on the railway tracks that run through the wagon factory. This "unconscious" suicide attempt, of which she has only a dim memory (a recurring image of two railway cars bearing down upon her), and the ensuing period of unconsciousness, from which she awakes in a hospital, prompt a process of remembering that will eventually lead to Rita's recovery. Her recovery process unfolds by means of a peculiar three-fold narrative structure: the overt deployment of the "divided sky" master-metaphor; the continual shifting between narrative present and epic past; and the parallel shifting between first-person and third-person narration. It was the latter aspect, above all, particularly the first-person narrator, that critical reviews of the novel targeted for accusations of a lack of "objectivity" and a slide into "bourgeois subjectivism."

How should we read this particular mode of narration, or rather from what angle should we approach the issue of *voice* in *Der geteilte Himmel?* Wolf's "Wall novel" represents a highly conflictual engagement with the classic totalizing mode of narration of the East German novel of arrival. As we have seen, this genre merged the Bitterfeld focus on production with the classic German novel of formation, in which what Hegel termed the "problematical" individual was integrated into society. In narrative terms, this means that Wolf was writing in the context of Lukács's concept of realism and its very specific formal requirements, notably, the supposedly "objective" mode in which the third-person voice of an omniscient narrator under-lines and emphasizes this process of integration.[85] In her attempt to write the story of becoming a socialist subject, that is, a story whose ultimate goal is the full integration of the problematic subject into the socialist collective, Wolf thus confronted a system of literary conventions *whose very form* purported to represent the dialectical unity of the universal and the particular.[86] However, despite the novel's tendency toward this canonical realism (i.e., its inexorable movement toward the moment when the subjective per-spective is discarded for "objectivity" of third-person narration), it never freezes into the realist mode. In *Der geteilte Himmel,* realism never happens.

To pursue our guiding question of the relationship between post-fascist body and post-fascist voice, we need to get beyond the novel's involvement with its normative aesthetic context—and to go beyond the interpretative grid of Emmerich's realism/modernism dichotomy or Love's feminist read-ing of the emergence of the first-person narrator for example. Instead, this novel's peculiar narrative voice has to be understood symptomatically as the expression of an *internally* split voice. This reading will take us beyond the Hegelian–Marxist problematic of the individual and society that is not only formally inscribed in this novel's relation to the normative conventions of socialist realism, but also allegorically thematized in its excessively struc-tured, highly constructivist use of its master-metaphor. Instead, it will raise the question of the narrating subject itself: the fantasy of the post-fascist body and its production through the splitting off of sexuality, as well as the problem of Rita's potentially contradictory imaginary and symbolic iden-tifications—identifications that themselves involve the issue of the "pure" body/"pure" voice. By separating from Manfred, Rita also separates from the fascist body of the past, which in *Der geteilte Himmel* is displaced to Manfred. This suppression of the body is reconfirmed in Rita's identifica-tion with Wendland and her mimesis of masculinity for Rita's imaginary identification is a feminine one, her symbolic identification a masculine one. In *Der geteilte Himmel,* the subject itself is fundamentally unsettled, and it is this disturbance which ultimately prevents the stabilization of the shifting narrative perspective: Rita's subject positions correspond to both Rita/"she" and Rita/"I"; they correspond to the basic structure of hysteria.

But there is another level to this adamant pursuit of the "pure" voice: a particular kind of acoustic mirror involving the mimesis of Seghers's voice. The novel's prologue and epilogue both continue Seghers's ideologi-cal work. Through their polyvalent master-signifier "life," Wolf's novel is set within the ideological horizon of a maternal socialism in the tradition of Seghers. This horizon is gradually developed through a string of metaphors:

The city . . . basked in the hot sun after long weeks of rain; its breath, coming faster than usual, puffed up through hundreds of factory chimneys into the clear sky. . . . The unaccustomed brilliance struck people as incongruous and almost unbearable in those uneasy days. . . . But the earth was still firm and would bear them as long as it remained beneath them.

. . . A shadow had fallen over the city; now it was warm and alive again, bearing and burying life, giving and taking it away. . . .

We learned to sleep soundly again and to live our lives to the full, as if there were an abundance of this strange substance—life—as if it would never be used up. (*DH*/1; *gH*/7)

Through these metaphors, the prologue produces strong parallels with the beginning of Seghers's *Das siebte Kreuz,* particularly in terms of *the common people's daily life.*[87] Wolf herself called the tension between the poles of "ordinary" and "dangerous" life the basic structure of Seghers's epic of resistance.[88] In the passage quoted above, the notion of "material life" emerges from a network of maternal connotations accruing around "city" and "earth," at the center of which stands the trope of a city giving and taking life. In both prologue and epilogue, this highly ambivalent maternal metaphor works as a master-signifier which assures ideological closure— "life" in socialism as the sublation of the maternal and its imaginary structure in the new symbolic order. Wolf's novel thus partakes of a specific social imaginary, one to which, as we saw in chapter 2, Anna Seghers forcefully contributed. Why, then, the dramatic ambivalence of its central metaphor, the city, which gives birth and buries, gives life and takes life? By mobilizing "life" and its maternal connotations as the central signifier of the socialist order, Wolf reintroduces the material body that her protagonist obsessively puts at a distance. Thus, the prologue relies on an ideological move—the embedding of the novel's ideological project of reconciliation within a wider ideological universe of a socialist order in the image of the mother—that erupts into ambivalence around the signifier, which also stands at the core of the other ideological narrative, the story of the post-fascist body. Wolf's appropriation of Seghers's work thus problematizes her own project, that of the post-fascist body, but it seems to offer the conditions for a "pure" voice through the mimesis of the voice of one of National Socialism's victims. As I shall argue in a reading of Wolf's theoretical essays on Seghers, however, the particular ways in which Wolf constructs Seghers's voice, and the particular ways in which she inserts herself into that construction, reproduce the same structure encountered with respect to Rita's subject positions. By appropriating the narrative mode of Büchner, the alternation between first- and third-person narration, for *Der geteilte Himmel,* Wolf adopts the position of "son" toward Seghers's maternal, "classical" speaking position. Again, we are thus confronted by a voice at odds with itself, both recognizing and not recognizing herself in the image/voice of the other. That the suppression of the body is a violent act is therefore something this text "knows" — as Wolf's theoretical texts "know" about the faultlines of a voice produced in an act of (mis)recognition.

"Where they will meet, there she is lying. There I am lying."

Let us look first at the narrative voice of *Der geteilte Himmel* with the problematic of realism in mind. Wolf's novel is framed by a prologue and an epilogue, each clearly set off from the main text. In the prologue, the narrative voice shifts from an omniscient, anonymous narrating instance to a collective voice, the pronoun "we." Here again is the first paragraph, a classic example of realist narration establishing the broad panoramic view of its narrator's perspective: "The city, on the threshold of autumn, basked in the hot sun after long weeks of rain; its breath, coming faster than usual, puffed up through hundreds of factory chimneys into the clear sky. . . . The unaccustomed brilliance struck people as incongruous and almost unbearable in those uneasy days." The second paragraph shifts into the collective voice, which is maintained until the end of the prologue: "So we returned to our daily work. . . . We learned to sleep soundly again and to live our lives to the full, as if there were an abundance of this strange substance — life — as if it would never be used up." In contrast to the prologue, the epilogue begins with Rita's personal perspective: "The day, the first day of her new-found freedom is almost over" (*DH*/212; *gH*/199; TA). Yet at the end the epilogue also shifts into the collective voice as it echoes, without quite repeating, the prologue's last sentence: "That we live our lives to the full, as if there were an abundance of this strange substance, life" (ibid.; TA).

The actual text can be broadly divided into two main parts, the first one covering the period Rita spends in the hospital and then in a sanatorium. During this period, she thinks back on the experiences which led to her breakdown, up to the unconsciousness from which she awakens as the novel

167

opens. The following passage, from chapter 1, exemplifies the sudden shifts in narrative voice:

In those late August days in 1961 a girl called Rita Seidel wakes up in a small hospital room. *She* had been unconscious, not asleep. As she opens her eyes, it is evening. . . . She is coming from far away. She still has a vague feeling of great breadth, depth also. But *one* rises swiftly from the infinite darkness into . . . the light. Oh yes, the city. Even narrower: the factory. . . . The point on the tracks, where *I* collapsed. (*DH*/3; *gH*/9; TA; my emphases)

The gradual change from *she* to *one* to *I* in this passage parallels a shift between present and past tense.

In the opening paragraphs of chapter 2 the change from "I" to "she" is even more abrupt. First, Manfred's arrival in Rita's village is narrated in the first-person voice: "When he arrived in our village two years ago I noticed him immediately" (*DH*/4; *gH*/11; TA). Then, in the second paragraph, the narrative voice slips into the third person: "Every morning, as she pushed her bicycle up the hill to the main road, she used to see Manfred at the pump" (*DH*/5; *gH*/11). The shifting of the narrative modes—and thus the splitting of the narrative voice—is most abrupt when Rita recalls the traumatic moment of her breakdown or suicide attempt. Remembering the two freight cars rushing toward her, she states: "At the place where they will meet, there *she* is lying. There *I* am lying" (*DH*/4; *gH*/10; TA; my emphases).

The transgression of the boundaries between first- and third-person narration, between narrative present and epic past, thus functions to thematize Rita's experience of being a mere object of historical forces beyond her control, of being alienated from the community to which she had seemed to belong until the moment of her separation from her lover and, on a deeper level, the moment when joining him in the West is no longer even an option due to the Wall. The strangely split and ruptured voice which results from these shifting narrative modes also characterizes the moment when Rita seems finally to have overcome her alienation and is about to become a subject within "actually existing socialism." During this sequence, Rita remembers a dream in which she saw herself walking down a long, deserted street in the company not of Manfred, her lover, but of Wendland, the factory's director—as she notes with some surprise. While the dream itself is narrated in the third person, Rita's reflections conclude with the following sentences: "The astonishment lingered. It can be compared only with the astonishment of the child who thinks, for the first time: *I*" (*DH*/98; *gH*/99; TA; emphasis in original). By now familiar with the repeated shift from "I" to "she" and its immanent logic, the reader expects the passage to continue in the first person. Instead, it shifts into the impersonal "one": "One looks around. . . . Silently, many things had become clear. On this morning, one accepts that one will have to taste it all: the tart, the bitter, the pleasurable and the sweet" (*DH*/98–99; *gH*/99; TA). Just as Rita seems to have reached her Hegelian moment of self-consciousness and reconciliation, then, the narration shifts from her limited perspective to the "objective" voice of an omniscient narrator. But this perspective does not hold, as Rita's voice soon fragments again into *I, she, one*.

There does, however, seem to be a decisive and final transition to the realist mode, notably, when the narration becomes consistently objective after Rita leaves the sanatorium: "The day when Rita returned from the sanatorium to the sooty town was cold and indifferent" (*DH*/200; *gH*/188). Has her moment of self-consciousness merely been deferred until the very end of the novel? In the last chapter, the "objectivity" of third-person narration and the metaphor of the mirror do indeed appear to coalesce in a scene in which the (socialist) subject finally recognizes herself. At first, the traumatic experience is remembered, but this time, significantly, without transgressing the convention of the third-person voice: "She still sees the two heavy wagons rolling towards her, inexorably, calm, certain. They are aiming precisely at me, *she felt*" (*DH*/202; *gH*/189–90; TA; my emphasis). Then Rita looks at herself in the mirror, unconsciously smiling as she discovers something new in her eyes: experience.

One might be inclined to call this moment overdetermined, insofar as the "objectivity" of third-person narration and mirror metaphor converge to produce the effect of integration through recognition:

She reaches for her hand mirror at the bottom of her suitcase. *She* sits down on the edge of the bed, holds the mirror so that it has enough light, and looks into it. For too long, *I* have not looked into any mirror, *she* thinks. That will not happen again. It makes one ugly. . . . *She* looks at her face, centimeter by centimeter . . . unconsciously, *she* begins to smile. The expression in the eyes, which is new to *her,* remains. That's where experience has withdrawn to.

She is, *she* notices, still young. (*DH*/202; *gH*/190; TA; my emphases)

However, once again, this realist mode does not last. On the contrary, fragments of the first-person voice which the narrative finally seemed to have "overcome" reappear on the very last pages. The first instance of this re-emergence occurs when Rita hears about the breakdown of Meternagel, the model worker and one of Rita's father figures. The sentence that notes her reaction to the news is in the first person, yet with no quotation marks— "If that is true, I must go to him immediately" (*DH*/203; *gH*/191; TA)—thus once more disrupting the conventions of realism. The second relapse into the register of subjective narration occurs when Rita sinks into a long inner monologue as she listens to Meternagel's wife tell the story of her ruined life. The novel thus ends with an insistent first-person voice *within* a realist narrative mode.

What remains is the question of whether the epilogue's collective "we" contains the subjective feminine voice after all. As noted above, the epilogue begins with a description of Rita's walk through the city from her perspective, thus claiming the successful sublation of subjectivity through the realist mode. Then comes the following image:

People are coming home from work. . . . Now the private and public ceremonies of the evening begin. . . . Sometimes a man follows his wife with his eyes as she clears the table, without her realizing how surprised and grateful his look is. Sometimes a woman touches a man's shoulder. She has not done it for a long time, but at the right moment she senses: he needs it. (*DH*/212; *gH*/199; TA)

The last paragraph of the epilogue is narrated in a different voice, the collective "we" ("And that makes up for everything: that we . . . fully live our life" [ibid.; TA]), thus once more exploding the novel's realist teleology. But to whom does this collective voice refer? By the story's own logic, to an absence, a moment of not-being-conscious. The epilogue's "we" cannot stabilize, or fix, the multiple narrative voices at either the beginning or the end of the text because the question it necessarily raises—to whom does this "we" refer?—takes it back into the past: the past of the prologue. The *"we" of the prologue* speaks during the crisis of the Wall's erection, that is, while Rita is *unconscious.* This voice belongs to a collectivity which does not include her. The same is true, ultimately, of *the epilogue's "we."* Thus the collective voice is itself deeply problematic, with Rita and the "we" just as "divided" at the end of *Der geteilte Himmel* as they were at the beginning.

Wolf's novel, the central project of which is recovering the lost unity of individual and society, is thus formally in active conflict with the narrative conventions of Lukácsian realism. Yet while *Der geteilte Himmel* is precisely *not* narrated in Lukács's "objective" mode, neither can it be assimilated to what this tradition defined as its "bad" other, namely, subjective narration. Instead, Wolf has constructed a sort of hybrid narration which constantly shifts between the subjective and objective modes, thereby problematizing both *subject* and *object,* the individual to be integrated and the collective. But in order to fully understand the problematized subject and its voice, we need to move to the level of fantasy and the body.

The Displacement of the Post-Fascist Body

There is a moment—a decisive moment, as we will see—when *Der geteilte Himmel* drastically violates its own narrative system, that is, its carefully constructed time frame. Thus the scene in which Rita and Manfred finally separate is narrated from an "impossible" perspective: " 'Goodbye, little brown girl,' he said tenderly. Rita rested her head on his chest for a moment. Weeks later, he still felt the light pressure every time he closed his eyes" (*DH*/199; *gH*/187–88). This brief and rather irritating intrusion of Manfred's perspective represents a clear violation because this is the only moment when Manfred's voice is heard *after their separation.* Since Rita cannot possibly know what Manfred is thinking "weeks later," the narrative logic of remembrance is disrupted. This disruption can be traced to the densely overdetermined nature of this particular passage, in which multiple discursive strands converge. In my view, however, what occurs here is a transfer of the body's emotions and the memory of them from Rita to Manfred—a "delegation" of sexuality and the material body. Indeed, that is precisely the goal of Rita's process of recovery, which involves the splitting off of those memories relating to Manfred and her own sexual body. Rita remembers the beginning of their relationship as a violent shock—"His look sent a quiver through her" (*DH*/11; *gH*/16)—which leaves her trembling. Passages such as the following erupt throughout the whole novel: "A wave of memories rushes toward her, swells, when she closes her eyes, painfully-sweet it breaks over her at night. His face, again and again his face. . . . And the touch of his hands" (*DH*/62; *gH*/62; TA).

Recovery means having to repress these intense, already fragmenting memories and to withstand the sudden assaults of "bodily weakness" and "longing" that they produce. In the last part of the novel—which covers Rita's trip to West Berlin, her last meeting with Manfred, and her decision to return to the East—the erotic, "material" body and its desires are opposed to *Sinn* and *Besinnung,* meaning and consciousness. This opposition emerges in the dialogue between Rita and Schwarzenbach, the Party representative, which frames most of the Berlin episode, producing a fragmented, dreamlike interlude in which their dialogue is interspersed with the bits and pieces of what Rita remembers from her day in the West. On the train to Berlin, Rita worries that Manfred's touching her arm might rob her of the "consciousness" she has barely recovered since he left for the West without informing her about his move or his plans for their future. Her paradoxical way of formulating this fear indicates that this "consciousness" which she might lose through a mere touch does not even exist yet: "He should let me think about things together with him. When I will finally have recovered the consciousness of which he robbed me with his departure. If only I don't lose it again when he puts his hand on my arm" (*DH*/171; *gH*/162–63; TA). It is a "consciousness" yet to be gained in the experience of her separation from Manfred, for as long as she is in his presence, it is threatened, as her memory of their last stop on their way back to the train station shows:

They smiled. Manfred rubbed his face against her hair. He pressed her hands. Rita began to tremble. She craned her head back until she could see the hot, bleached summer afternoon sky through the sparse leaves. Everything is still there. This is his hand. This is the smell of his skin. This is his voice. (*DH*/195; *gH*/182; TA)

This passage describes Rita's last moment of doubt before she summons up the "coldness" needed to execute her decision. The meaning of her decision is constituted in the dialogue between Rita and Schwarzenbach, the character who is not only the novel's most prominent party representative but clearly Rita's most significant father figure as well. In response to Schwarzenbach's questions, Rita explains that the West had felt like a foreign place, "familiar, yet horrible" (*DH*/184; *gH*/174). She recalls being faced with an overwhelming display of commodities whose names she did not even know and asking herself: "What is the meaning of [life]?" (*DH*/183; *gH*/173; TA). Pressed by Schwarzenbach, she finally explains, in strongly emotional terms, why she decided to return from West Berlin: "That which is foreign remained foreign to me, and all of this here hot and familiar" (*DH*/194; *gH*/181; TA). Schwarzenbach analytically reformulates this emotional reaction in terms of historical necessity and the "objective laws of history": "Yes, it's the attraction of a great historical movement" (*DH*/194–95; *gH*/181). Here, the "heat" of the passionate body is sublated to the novel's allegory, the body to the idea.

The opposition of meaning/consciousness to the body produced here is reinforced by the passage in which Manfred realizes the price he will have to pay for his defection. When Rita tells him that Wendland will never forgive him for it, Manfred explodes:

> He knew at that moment that the life he had left behind him would never leave him alone, and this was what infuriated him. All he wanted now was to shift the blame onto someone else for the despair he felt at having failed to stand up to the pressure of that harder, sterner life. (*DH*/193–94; *gH*/181)

The logic underlying this crucial section of the novel is that of revolutionary asceticism, which denies the body in the name of a greater cause. Or, to recall Žižek, in the name of a historical mission that, he argues, "resides" in the Communist's sublime body. When *Der geteilte Himmel* uses the ideal of perfect harmony between man and woman as part of its political allegory, this ascetic discourse generates images of rather astonishingly bad taste—an effect we already encountered in *Moskauer Novelle*. For instance, when Wolf deploys the master-metaphor of the "divided sky," together with a sexual metaphor, the narrative's two main strands—its political allegory and its love story—climax, so to speak, in consummate kitsch:

> The little room hung like a swing somewhere in the blue-black sky, swinging so high and so smoothly that they could only feel it move when they closed their eyes. They closed their eyes.
> They swung up to the stars, down over the lights of the town and up again towards the sickle moon. Back and forth they swung until they were dizzy, holding each other close and caressing each other as lovers do. (*DH*/20–21; *gH*/24–25; TA)

This saccharine passage, in which we can barely detect the most minimal vestiges of sexual passion, is extremely important as it includes a core image embodying what will be lost: the couple's unconditional oneness and its utopian dimension—the seamless identity between subject and world, subject and social order. Yet "embodying" is certainly the wrong word in this context, at odds with the ascetic strand's obsession with "sublating" the very bodies it needs for its story to a higher level of meaning.

Moreover, in all but one of the scenes thematizing the sexual body, Wolf uses the pronoun "she," not "I," when Rita speaks about her body, further distancing Rita from her body. It is from Manfred's perspective (before it becomes "impossible") that we see Rita's body:

He often got her to talk just to be able to look at her. . . . He felt he must make sure of her again and again. He ran his finger lightly over her face, her forehead and temples, from her eyebrows to the down of her cheeks. She knew the path his hand would take, for she had first become conscious of herself through his lips, his eyes, his hands. (*DH*/77; *gH*/79)

It is this male perspective—and male voice—that reappears in the passage which constituted the starting point for our investigation into the metaphorical economy of the body in *Der geteilte Himmel*.

What does all of this have to do with the post-fascist body? Clearly, unlike Vera, Rita is a character born after 1945, thus "untouched" by National Socialism. However, in the passage quoted above, the delegation of the material body to Manfred indicates that *Der geteilte Himmel* reconstitutes the sublime post-fascist body in a *displaced form* ("displaced" because Manfred is the counterpart of Vera as a member of that generation spanning the divide of 1945). At one point, Manfred even thinks, "It's a queer thing, the new generation starts somewhere between us" (*DH*/42; *gH*/44). In *Der geteilte Himmel,* however, Rita is fatherless, while Manfred struggles to break free of a father whom he hates for having been a Nazi, for now being a member of the SED.[89] One of Manfred's earliest memories is of his father admiring his new SA uniform in a mirror, exchanging a triumphant look with his wife. While Vera successfully breaks with this past, Manfred lets himself sink back into it, following his mother's desire to go to the West. As the passage that I have singled out here indicates, it is Manfred who retains the memory of the sexual body, a body that now "belongs" to Manfred and no longer to Rita. In *Der geteilte Himmel,* the female protagonist's *sublime* body is produced through separation and transfer, locating the material, the sexual, and, ultimately, the fascist body on the other side of the border.

Oedipal Subjectivity and the Failure of Identity (Imaginary versus Symbolic Identification)

While *Der geteilte Himmel*'s violation of its own narrative system, its logic of remembrance, alerted us to the splitting off of the sexual body, the overdetermined passage in which this infraction occurs also alludes to the novel's most fundamental taboo: the transgression against the daughter's normative Oedipal trajectory. Rita's story is not only one of separation from her lover, but also one of separation from the realm of the mother: that is, it narrates the transition from the imaginary to the symbolic. Less obvious is the second aspect of this Oedipal trajectory, Rita's identification with a brother figure. It is this "violation" which lies at the root of the text's conflictual engagement with the normative aesthetics of (socialist) realism; it is what underlies the divided voice.

Let us turn to the novel's Oedipal narrative. One of the more obvious dichotomies here is between city and country. The countryside is the realm of the village and the tiny house at the edge of the woods where the fatherless Rita lives with her mother and her aunt. At a moment of crisis, Rita will later nostalgically remember this realm, emphasizing all those aspects that make it more than a mere metaphor of totality. It has the qualities of the pre-Oedipal period, the maternal realm preceding the father's order: the permanence and stasis of being home, of being centered, and, above all, of no sense of separation. Fleeing the city after an ideological dispute at her institute, Rita arrives at her village in the early morning hours. Here, Rita's longing for her mother is written into her panoramic view of the village, with the fantasy of nonseparation zeroing in on the mother's house:

Dawn came slowly. . . . Then came colours . . . and at last a touch of blue above the dark zigzag of the woods at the edge of which, whatever else might happen, there was always the wind-swept meadow and the path turning off to the right, rising slightly and then falling steeply down into her village, which was still firmly in its place. *She had only to walk through it to find the little house and all she needed just then.* (*DH*/127; *gH*/126; my emphasis)

Not surprisingly, the master-metaphor reappears, with the wide dome of the sky ordering everything beneath it — "wie von selbst," around a "natural center" — so that no feeling of "Being-Outside-of-Oneself" can arise (ibid.; TA).

However, Rita's experience of this realm is highly ambivalent. A sphere of perfect harmony (as in the passage quoted above), it is also a realm of utter boredom and stasis to which she is bound by duty and self-sacrifice; ignoring her teachers' advice to continue her education, Rita goes to work as a secretary instead because she wants to repay her mother, who worked in a factory to support her. The novel opens at the moment when she can barely tolerate her condition any longer, the ennui of a seemingly endless series of uneventful days in a country permeated by a sense of "unrest and the atmosphere of departure": "She knew no one at that time who could help her to direct her insignificant—but to her important—existence into the great stream of life" (*DH*/9; *gH*/15). Two men, and two projects, will enable her to escape this stasis: Manfred and his love, and Schwarzenbach with his invitation to enroll in one of the new teaching institutes. Rita experiences her recruitment by Schwarzenbach and the Party as the intervention of a "hand from above" which plucks her from the periphery and catapults her into the center: "Why, this sleepy little town might even wake up, it could be thrown from the periphery of the world to its center" (*DH*/17; *gH*/21; TA). Rita's mother reacts with alarm, since for her anything new is worse than the old.

In *Der geteilte Himmel,* Wolf thus opposes the maternal realm to the order of the father(s) in terms of margin versus center, old versus new, past versus present. Accordingly, her protagonist moves from the margin to the center, from the past to the present, from the realm of the mother to that of the (substitute) fathers: Rita thus lives in the city with Manfred, works in the factory where she meets Meternagel, and studies at the institute where she is taught by Schwarzenbach, with the two mentor figures assuming paternal roles in different domains, production and politics. The separation from the mother, and transition to the symbolic, leads to a narcissistic search, the trajectory of an ego trying to bolster a fictive sense of identity by finding a series of images with which it can identify. The first step in this process is Rita's relationship with Manfred, which at the beginning thematizes the subject's constitution in the other by the first of a series of mirror scenes. After they meet, Manfred has to leave the village, and Rita waits for a letter. When it finally arrives, she regards herself in the mirror: "She knew, there was enough about her that he liked and would always like" (*DH*/7; *gH*/13; TA). Rita recognizes herself in her image, confirmed in her identity by Manfred's gaze.[90] The pivotal mediating role of the other's desire in the constitution of an imaginary unity remains constant in the representation of this relationship, such as in the frequently recurring image of their faces reflected, side by side, in water, or in the image of their eyes meeting: "She caught his gaze and returned it, challengingly, without any reserve. A new expression was in her face, which she herself did not recognize yet. She owed this face to him, and she showed it only to him" (*DH*/63; *gH*/63). The same trope of recognition and identity dominates the descriptions of Rita's relationships with the father figures Schwarzenbach and Meternagel, the Stakhanovite model worker. Early on, Rita realizes that Meternagel's eyes have always provided her with a sense of security and identity: "Sometimes, when she felt most desperate, those eyes were what kept her going" (*DH*/69; *gH*/72). Rita's separation from Manfred is accordingly narrated as a breaking of the gaze. About to part from him in Berlin, Rita, paralyzed and silent, keeps looking at Manfred, losing consciousness as soon as the gaze breaks: "She did not sleep, but she was not fully conscious, either" (*DH*/200; *gH*/188). Losing her image in the mirror of the other's eyes evokes the mirror itself: "The first thing she really saw was a quiet, shining little lake which caught the waning light in the sky and reflected it back more strongly" (*DH*/200; *gH*/188). This passage vividly exemplifies the role of the mirrored image in the constitution of the ego's imaginary identity. It also reconstitutes the novel's imaginary narrative—Rita's drive to find yet another reflecting surface—immediately after her separation from Manfred and after this very moment when her identity dissolves.

As Rita gradually grows apart from Manfred, who lets himself be persuaded by his mother to "go West," she slowly comes to identify more and more with an ideological universe represented—she thinks—by the principles of Meternagel, Wendland, and Schwarzenbach. Does Rita's story then reach closure in a deferred but nonetheless imaginary relationship with the "other" man, Wendland, the committed Communist and brilliant young director of the factory in which she works? Or to put it differently: Is the story of fatherless Rita that of a daughter who, after separating from the mother, seeks an appropriate father substitute, finally choosing between two men whose political and philosophical views—Manfred's existentialism, Wendland's dialectical materialism—are carefully distinguished? This reading would see the "positive" solution as merely deferred: Rita, after separating from Manfred, after gazing on the Communist family from the outside, would finally give in to Wendland who, as Rita and the reader know, is in love with her. From this perspective, *Der geteilte Himmel* would then be the—ideologically—successful resolution of the Oedipal situation, that is, the "normative" version of the daughter's destiny in the paternal order.

Rita's Dream

But such a utopian reading along the lines of a second love plot would not work—not simply because it would ignore the persistent splitting of the narrative voice, but rather because it would fail to consider the passage in which this split is born, when Rita refers to herself as "I" for the first time after her "accident." Moreover, such a reading would also fundamentally misread the function of Wendland's character in this very passage, in Rita's dream:

She can still see this uncannily long road which she does not recognize. But she recognizes her feelings as she walks along it—a curious mixture of fear and curiosity—and strangely enough it is Ernst Wendland, not Manfred, who walks beside her, and even in her dream she wonders why he is there. But he behaves quite naturally and keeps insisting that she should forgive him but not Manfred. Then, before she is able to answer or ask him what he means, they are sitting in Rita's little room at home in the village (she knows it must be her room because the air wafting in through the open window smells like fresh fields). She and Wendland had never been here together, and her astonishment grows.

She woke up at that point and the dream began to fade at once, retreating like a wisp of fog when she tried to grasp it. But her astonishment lingers. It can only be compared to the child, who thinks for the first time in its life: *I.* (*DH*/97–98; *gH*/98–99; TA; emphasis in original)

Whom, we are forced to ask, does this "I" represent? The answer seems obvious: the ideal image guiding Rita's process of recovery, that of the independent young woman, self-confident and convinced that she will find her place in this society after leaving the hospital. We have seen this young woman, in love with Manfred, regarding herself in the mirror; she is also the "queen of the ball," who shies away from the intense, naked longing in Wendland's eyes; but, above all, she is the young woman who studies the traces of her suffering in a mirror the day after she leaves the sanatorium, satisfied with her new, mature self and newly optimistic: "*She* is, *she* notices, still young" (*DH*/202; *gH*/190; TA; my emphases). Rita has realized an ego ideal formulated early on in the novel, namely, the desire to become "older but not harder" (*DH*/28; *gH*/31; TA). Although she has made herself "cold" in order to separate from her lover, this woman, we are assured, has not turned into a man—as has the figure who functions as the narrative's negative pole, Manfred's "hysterical" mother, whose portrait emphasizes sharp, "almost masculine" features "on which powder and make-up seemed almost unnatural" (*DH*/31; *gH*/34; TA).

In this new incarnation, Rita resembles Reimann's Recha and the young women figures featured in the production novels of the 1950s, as well as those in both films and literary texts of the early 1960s. For instance, two highly controversial films, *Das Kaninchen bin ich* (I am the Rabbit) by Kurt Maetzig and *Spur der Steine* (The Trace of the Stones) by Frank Beyer, end with long shots lingering on their young heroines, who are leaving the sites of their troubled relationships and frustrating entanglements with the Party apparatus for a new, radically different life, and who bear a powerful, vibrant utopian aura. Like these films, Wolf's own film project from that period, *Fräulein Schmetterling* (Mademoiselle Butterfly), was never shown publicly.[91] Through its main protagonist, Wolf's film too articulated a particular concept of femininity to a utopian desire for change and transgression that Therese Hörnigk links to Ernst Bloch's "concrete utopia."[92] Closing the door behind her as she leaves Meternagel at the end of *Der geteilte Himmel,* Rita joins these "daughters" who walk away without a "backward Oedipal glance."[93]

But perhaps we should first take a look at the other components of Rita's dream, which might serve as points of entry into the different layers of its densely textured fabric. Besides the initial moment of self-identity here, there is the double astonished recognition registered by the dreaming subject, first when she recognizes Wendland at her side, then when she recognizes the dream's most fundamental effect—the experience of identity; there is the constellation mother–Rita–Wendland; and, finally, there is the return to the "little house" and the long dark road. Moreover, the novel offers us an "original" of this dream: the encounter between Rita, Manfred, Wendland, and their common acquaintance, Rudi Schwabe. As the four of them walk home together along a dark, quiet street after leaving a bar where they danced and exchanged memories of their time as students, Rita and Wendland separate themselves from the other two. Lowering her voice so as not to be overheard by Manfred, Rita tells Wendland about the difficulties in her brigade. As they discuss the wagon factory, Rita suddenly experiences a feeling of "openness," whose source she has trouble explaining: "The old dark street favored them, and this day, which lay behind them" (*DH*/67; *gH*/70; TA). Their brief moment of confidence ends when they arrive at the "tiny cottage" in which Wendland lives with his son. In *Der geteilte Himmel,* this signifier—the little house—stands metonymically for childhood. When Wendland tells Manfred about his life, we learn that he comes from a small village to which he returned at the end of the war after a grueling, fourteen-day march. Having been demobilized as a *Luftwaffenhelfer,* he longs only to reach this "tiny little house, where he is at home" (*DH*/105; *gH*/105; TA). Thus, for Wendland as for Rita, the little house is a refuge at a moment of crisis. It is no wonder, then, that it appears in Rita's dream—"they are sitting in Rita's little room at home in the village (she knows it must be her room because the air wafting in through the open window smells like fresh fields)"—to ground their relationship in the maternal realm and thereby make them brother and sister.

Identity, the "I," is what Rita gains from returning to her place of origin, the mother's house, with a male figure to whom she is not attached by the kind of narcissistic love that bound her to Manfred. Wendland himself knows that Rita will never return his love; as he reflected earlier, "We're too much alike" (*DH*/161; *gH*/154). Rita's dream works on this "similarity," turning it into a narcissistic desire *to be Wendland*. The "I" at the end of the dream is the subject constituted in the image of the other. However, it's not the mother who functions as mirror in this dream, but Rita's "brother"—the one whose presence seems so incongruous and yet is so tightly linked to everything that represents childhood: the house, Rita's "girl's room," the astonishment of the child first saying "I." As a matter of fact, both the mother and the father are expelled from this narrative, leaving only the aunt and the house. As we have already seen, later on in this passage, Rita's voice disintegrates again into *I, she, one*. The subject of this narrative is thus indeed split—into "I" as Wendland and "she" as Rita—into, I would argue, the *daughter as son*.

Rita's identification with the one who comes to represent her brother has a certain quality that may be best grasped through Žižek's concept of *symbolic identification,* which involves the subject's ego ideal and the gaze of the subject who embodies the other.[94] Here we identify, on the symbolic level, with a place from which we are observed—the place from which, looking at ourselves, we appear likeable. Žižek distinguishes this particular identificatory process from *imaginary identification,* in which the identification is with an image in which we appear likeable *to ourselves*. Symbolic identification, Žižek argues, is a structural issue, since it concerns the place taken by the subject in the intersubjective symbolic network, the symbolic "mandate" s/he assumes by acting in a specific way (in Rita's case, by staying in the GDR, like Wendland).[95] In her symbolic identification with Wendland, Rita becomes what the symbolic order prefers her to be—the son, not the daughter—with the symbolic identification thus dominating the imaginary identification at this level.

Wendland becomes this figure for Rita by representing the very position from which Rita wants to be seen as "likeable," the position of one who fully assumes his symbolic ideological mandate. It is Wendland, the Party representative in charge of economic planning and production, who engages her in serious discussions concerning the future of their country. (And, in the novel's productivist logic, this future ultimately depends on producing an ever-greater output, making Wendland the central Party representative.) At the height of her crisis, before leaving for her native village, Rita rehearses in her mind the positions taken by Wendland and Manfred in their dispute over their respective philosophies of history: Wendland's optimistic belief in the essential goodness of people, Manfred's deeply pessimistic view of people being motivated not by morality but by "greed, selfishness, distrust, envy" (gH/147). She will, we know, ultimately side with Wendland. A scene early in the novel nicely illustrates the latter's gaze—what Žižek calls the external "superego gaze." [96] When Rita's brigade celebrates their leader's birthday, some of them, more than a little drunk, start to sing Nazi army songs. Then Wendland enters the bar: "The noise at the table did not die down after he joined them, but something changed. . . . Rita suddenly saw them all as if from a distance, sitting there at the table in the dim public-house light, as if she were looking back into the past, and she heard their voices more distinctly" (DH/48–49; gH/50). Wendland unmistakably incarnates this place from which the post-fascist subject is judged—and in this case, through identification with the gaze, judges itself.

The significance of Rita's dream is further underscored by the fact that it provokes the novel's other major narrative failure. Rita remembers her dream about Wendland twice, first in her fourth week at the sanatorium, then when she attends the funeral of Manfred's mother. In the second passage, Rita recalls her dream as she walks behind the mother's coffin; it functions as a déjà vu experience, accompanied by a sense of relief: this too— the funeral, but even more so Manfred's departure—may also be a dream, may not be reality. Within the narrative logic of remembrance, however, this does not work since the dream occurred *after* Rita's suicide attempt, that is, *after* the funeral. Therefore, the dream cannot be recalled *at the moment of the funeral,* as the passage implies:

But one thing did worry her; she felt she had been through it before. Perhaps not this smell of decay. But the long street. Ernst Wendland beside me, where Manfred should have been. . . . Finally she remembered: the dream. She felt relieved. So she was dreaming now, too? (DH/167–68; gH/159–60; TA).

At most, Rita could superimpose these two events as she remembered, in the sanatorium, the funeral. But that is clearly not what is being conveyed here. In this passage, then, the novel's narrative structure completely collapses. Now more than ever before, the question of who speaks and when cannot be answered. Whereas up to this point Wolf has carefully distinguished the different time levels—the narrated past from the present of narration (even when alternating between present tense and epic past), the voice of the past from the voice of the present (even when switching from "I" to "she"), and the register of dream from that of reality—here these distinctions disappear. There is no way to determine who speaks, for instance, the following sentence: "Later on, when I wake up, I will have a good laugh over it" (*DH*/168; *gH*/160; TA). Is it the protagonist attending the funeral or the protagonist remembering the scene in the sanatorium? Why is this so important? Because this transgression against the daughter's normative Oedipal trajectory seems to constitute the narrative's most fundamental taboo, the "violation" at the root of its conflictual engagement with the normative aesthetics of (socialist) realism.

These two major moments of narrative collapse—the one that served as the starting point for our inquiry into the "delegated" body and the one concerning Rita's dream—thus relate to the tension between Rita's symbolic masculine identification and what on the surface seems to be the ego ideal necessary to Rita's recovery: the image of the self-confident, independent young woman. The protagonist of *Der geteilte Himmel* is therefore feminine *and* masculine, "I"/"he" *and* "I"/"she." When Rita reaches the point in her recovery where she can say "I," that pronoun signifies Rita in both her imaginary and her symbolic identification: Rita as her ideal ego, the young Communist woman, and Rita as Wendland, the figure who functions as her ego ideal. And this ego ideal is located in the paternal narrative's archetypal figure of the son. As a successor to the antifascist father, Wendland has the same biography as, for instance, Werner Holt, and a number of other "sons" in the GDR literature of the 1950s and 1960s.

Rita's identification with Wendland explains the novel's deeply unsettled narrative voice. The narrating subject's division into "I" and "she" goes beyond the problematic of the narrative's conflicted engagement with the regulatory aesthetics of (socialist) realism. I read this truly innovative mode of narration as the expression of a divided subject *not* because I understand the novel as an (East German) illustration of Lacan's concept of the divided subject, but because I locate the split on the level of gender identifications.

How does this division relate to the issue of the novel's basic gendered ide-ologeme, the complementary synthesis of man and woman as an allegory for a (re)constituted totality? It explains, I would argue, why the gendered complementary structure upon which the novel's ideological project rests cannot function. This is what I meant by reading the narrative voice *symp-tomatically*, relating the moment of its utter collapse to the moment that, on the level of fantasy, explodes the novel's most basic ideological paradigm: not *man and woman* but *woman as man*.

Der geteilte Himmel thus exemplifies Jacqueline Rose's insight that the "concepts of fantasy and the unconscious rule any notion of pure imposition or full acquisition [of feminine identity] out of bounds." [97] Instead, the novel enables us to understand that Rita's tenuous fantasmatic identifications are at odds with the daughter's normative Oedipal trajectory. Yet how are we to read this division? Is the split subject of Wolf's novel an Oedipal subject in protest against the father's injunction to be one or the other, embodying what Rose designates as subjectivity at odds with itself? Does Wolf's text articulate the most intensely contradictory and contested insertion into the discourse of the paternal family, at its outer and inner limits? In 1962, Wolf wrote: "August 13th [1961] allowed us to expand the borders of our country, [the borders] inside of ourselves." [98] *Der geteilte Himmel* begins when the Wall is erected, at a moment of "danger" that casts a deadly shadow over the city and over Rita's consciousness. Nevertheless, like many of those committed to the construction of an alternative socialist Germany, Wolf understood the building of the Wall as a means of giving reforms a chance within the GDR, so we might read this beginning—Rita's moment of not-being-conscious—as a stepping outside of the historical continuum (i.e., the GDR's history), or of its Oedipal narratives and the history of the gendered Oedipal subject. Conversely, we could read the novel as a response to an unformulated trauma, as the sudden recognition of being firmly inscribed in a specific narrative and locked into its limited subject positions. Yet the way in which Rita is locked into these positions recalls one of the found-ing concepts of psychoanalysis: hysteria, or the hysterical stage, as defined by Gregorio Kohon: "I think that in the development of the Oedipal drama of the woman there is a hysterical stage, in which the subject—caught up in her need to change object from mother to father—can get 'fixed,' unable to make the necessary choice." [99] Kohon understands "hysterical stage" not only in developmental terms but as a "place where something happens, on which a performance takes place, a drama is developed." We can read this performance as the subject's wandering back and forth from one object to the other, displaying a "gesture of apparent resolution." [100] For Žižek, what is being enacted is the conflict between imaginary and symbolic identification:

[The] gap between the way I see myself and the point from which I am being observed to appear likeable to myself is crucial for grasping hysteria . . . for so-called hysterical theatre: when we take the hysterical woman in the act of such a hysterical outburst, it is of course clear that she is doing this to offer herself to the Other as the object of its desire, but concrete analysis has to discover who—which subject embodies for her the Other. Behind an extremely "feminine" imaginary figure, we can thus generally discover some kind of masculine paternal identification: she is enacting fragile femininity, but on the symbolic level she is in fact identified with the paternal gaze, to which she wants to appear likeable.[101]

There is no enactment of "fragile femininity" in Wolf's novel, only a gap between imaginary (feminine) and symbolic (masculine) identification. The political–ideological significance of this gap and of the hysterical performance will be found in a later novel by Wolf, *Kassandra/Cassandra,* on which the next chapter will focus. This story of the Trojan king's "favorite daughter," whose prophecies about the "true" state of the kingdom and its eventual fall are uttered in a "strange" voice from a body-out-of-control, will raise a question that has been hotly debated within feminist psychoanalysis: Is hysteria rebellion or defeat, the revolt of the repressed feminine against the paternal order or its utter failure? [102] Since the hysterical theater is part of a political fantasy in *Kassandra,* this question cannot be answered without analyzing the specific ideological parameters between which this psychosexual problematic is embedded, that is, the precise political content attributed to the feminine and masculine positions in Wolf's novel.

Der geteilte Himmel, however, not only produces the Oedipal problematic and this gap in identifications, but, together with *Moskauer Novelle,* links the problematic of the body, which becomes a symptom in the theater of hysteria, to the concepts of the sublime and the material body. In *Der geteilte Himmel,* the hysterical constellation is clearly linked to the question of the body: Rita/"she" becomes the sublime body, which is separated from the sexual body, whereas Rita/"he" incarnates the symbolic mandate. But as long as femininity is equated with the material, with the body in the larger *symbolic cultural universe* (the case in this Communist universe that defines women through their reproductive function, as we saw with

Seghers), Rita will always remain dangerously close to the body, even as the embodiment of the sublime body, in her symbolic identification. Only Wendland, the man, can be pure mind. As we have repeatedly seen, the presence of the voice, this "material support," [103] testifies to this continued presence. As my reading of this novel's prologue will demonstrate, the material body endures in its metaphor of maternal socialism.

Another Acoustic Mirror:

Mimesis of Narrative Voice/Fantasy of Purity

Like *Moskauer Novelle,* then, Wolf's novel features the figure of a daughter and her (somewhat skewed) insertion into the Oedipal order. And like the novella, *Der geteilte Himmel* links the fantasmatic production of the post-fascist body to a post-fascist voice born out of the split from a material body, a process accompanied by the realignment of voice with masculine symbolic identification. Yet, as we have seen, in the novel, the issue of the post-fascist voice is negotiated on a *different* level, that of *narration itself.* In this section, I will therefore trace an aspect of the narrative voice that goes beyond the production of the post-fascist body and the character's Oedipal problematic; this aspect pertains to the larger issue of the symbolic order and its aesthetic rules and regulations. My thesis is that the novel's split narrative voice is formed mimetically and that this mimesis involves the author Anna Seghers. Or, more precisely, it involves Wolf's construction of the author Seghers, which is opposed not only to the canonical author but to Seghers herself. As a sustained inquiry into her essays on Seghers will show, Wolf took over Seghers's literary–historical and political paradigm of an opposition between Goethe the classicist, on the one hand, and such authors of the Storm and Stress and Romantic period as Hölderlin, Lenz, Kleist, Büchner, and Günderrode, on the other. Wolf defined the Seghers of the pre-GDR era as a nonclassical author on the side of the "younger generation." *This* Seghers shared their experience of living in "transitional periods," [104] torn apart by the growing contradictions of their times, a problematic which marks their own works even on the level of form. It is this author with whom Wolf came to identify *against* what she constructed as Seghers the "classical national author." [105] Seghers's generational schema constituted the foundation upon which Wolf elaborated her notion of *subjective authenticity,* which, as I will demonstrate, involves *tone* as much as *attitude,* or *stance* (both terms from Wolf's essays on Seghers), a specific narrative voice, function, and form—*and* an ethico-political dimension. This voice emerged in the 1960s from a textual fabric to which *Moskauer Novelle* and *Der geteilte Himmel,* with their fantasy of the post-fascist body and its "pure" voice, made a crucial contribution. To strongly emphasize an important point, however: in contrast to the realism/modernism paradigm outlined in the introduction, and in contrast to feminist criticism with an equally teleological model—the idea of Wolf's gradually evolving "true" (i.e., feminine) voice—I see this mimetic voice, and the identification upon which it rests, as one that persists throughout Wolf's work; but it is only *one voice* within a fabric woven of the different, often contradictory, voices that constitute the author Christa Wolf. Ultimately, this study is directed against a line of criticism which mistakes an author's most obsessive desire, *to speak in a "pure" voice,* for a methodological premise, *to search for this author's "true" voice.* Wolf's desire for purity was most forcefully expressed in the famous lines from *Kassandra/Cassandra:* "To speak with my voice; the ultimate. I did not want anything more, anything different." [106] These lines are in vivid contrast to the passage in *Was bleibt* where Wolf meditates on the multiple being "of which 'I myself' consist." Yet, as we now know, the significance of these two statements does not lie in the temporal distance between them, nor is it the result of a different way of thinking; instead, as the previous readings demonstrated, this desire for a "pure" voice is belied by the actual complexity of voice that characterizes Wolf's literary texts. *Moskauer Novelle* and *Der geteilte Himmel* are works in which we never find a single voice but always a multiplicity of layered and conflicting voices. And Wolf's appropriation of Seghers's voice constituted yet another dimension of this layering of voices. Wolf thus wrote herself into the ideological narrative of the family both in her novels and in the definition of her own authorship, developing her "new" voice within a generational paradigm. Which position she will choose to occupy within this paradigm remains, for now, an open question.

As we have already seen, the prologue and epilogue of *Der geteilte Himmel* deploy Seghers's notion of the maternal in rather dramatic form, investing it with a powerful ideological significance. But it is not only the prologue's "life" that refers back to Seghers and her conception of maternal socialism. As palimpsest, the prologue also repeats Seghers's collective "we," from *Das siebte Kreuz,* this voice (already encountered in chapter 2) which thematized the threat that fascism posed to generational continuity.[107]

Wolf's intertextual network also incorporates whole books: the love story in Seghers's epic on Germany's division, *Die Entscheidung* (The Decision), informs the plot of *Der geteilte Himmel.* And, finally, of course, there is the similarly "scandalous" narrative voice and its logic of remembrance. *Der geteilte Himmel,* in other words, is woven with the voice of the author Anna Seghers *as Wolf constructs her in her essays.*[108]

Wolf's relationship to Seghers is well-known, acknowledged by both Wolf and her critics.[109] In the early 1960s, according to Wolf herself, she was engaged in writing Seghers's biography. This work was never completed, but the quite comprehensive section devoted to Seghers in Wolf's *Die Dimension des Autors,* consisting of several interviews, introductions to such works as the 1963 edition of *Das siebte Krauz,* and more general essays on the author from 1959 to 1985, can be seen as spinoffs of that project. Finally, in 1992, Wolf contributed an introductory piece to *Anna Seghers: Eine Biographie in Bildern* (Anna Seghers: A Biography in Pictures).[110] In her early interviews, Wolf questioned Seghers about the writing process itself, positioning herself as an aspiring writer and apprentice. These questions clearly characterize Seghers as a socialist realist writer, the author of a grand historical epic on the Cold War Germanies that could be reduced to one fundamental idea: "what leads some people to support socialism and others to obstruct it." [111] By 1976, when Adam Krzeminski interviewed Wolf, however, Seghers's significance for her had clearly changed:

When I studied German at the beginning of the fifties, for us Lukács was sacrosanct. Thus, in interpreting the argument between Anna Seghers and Lukács, we had respect for her but deferred to him, since it was Lukács who saw the future of the socialist novel as being to reproduce the achievements of the great bourgeois novel and German classicism, to reflect reality in its totality. My sympathy for Anna Seghers only developed later as a result of her undogmatic defense of those writers, like Lenz or Kleist, for whom reality with all its contradictions did not come together in an Olympian picture.[112]

By what process was Seghers transformed from a classical socialist realist author to a figure of aesthetic dissent for Wolf? Or did any such transformation really take place? To answer this question, we need to return to Wolf's 1968 "Glauben an Irdisches" (Faith in the Terrestrial), her afterword to Seghers's collection of stories with the same title. This piece demonstrates that Wolf's essay of the same year on her own poetics, "Lesen und Schreiben" (Reading and Writing), is intimately concerned with Seghers's poetics, indeed could not be understood without the foil of Seghers's own aesthetic writings from the 1930s.[113]

Right from the beginning, "Glauben an Irdisches" zeroes in on Wolf's main concern, the relationship between author and material, as *Seghers's* preoccupation: "This curious phenomenon, the way in which the meeting of outer reality and inner disposition produces a third thing: this curiosity has never ceased to occupy Anna Seghers." [114] In a strategic move, Wolf then immediately singles out "Der Ausflug der toten Mädchen," a story that will allow her to introduce the core categories and ideas on which her essay dwells: writing as the expression of *personal, biographical, psychical experience* and as the process of coming to terms with that experience, and the highly distinct *voice* that transmits it:

[Anna Seghers] will never talk about herself again, with a single exception. The exception is the story "Ausflug der toten Mädchen," which candidly reveals *personal, biographical, and psychic experiences* that could only be mastered through writing.

In this essay too, experience is being worked through. The *voice* which speaks here is the same. It reflects rather than asserts. Before trying to convince others, she comes to terms with herself.[115]

Tracing her life in exile, Wolf quotes from Seghers's speech to the 1935 Defense of Culture Congress in Paris. Seghers paid tribute there to the best among Germany's cultural elite—Hölderlin, Büchner, Günderrode, Kleist, Lenz, and Bürger—all of whom died young, writing hymns to a country "against whose social wall they banged their heads." [116] Wolf clearly equates Seghers at this point with these outsiders, drawing a parallel between her exile and Büchner's and claiming that Seghers never uttered a sentence that was not based on her own experience. The ensuing presentation of the Lukács-Seghers debate pursues the same strategy, situating the author on the side of Germany's outsiders. Like them, Seghers's own generation could not produce classical works of harmony and synthesis, but only those showing "the disintegration of the era reflected in the artist." [117] Wolf unequivocally aligns her own voice with that of the older author, indeed comes down squarely on her side against Lukács's "purely ideological critique" as a form of criticism which wrongly measures a work of art by its political-ideological content and adherence to a normative writing mode. She ultimately condenses the dispute between Seghers and Lukács into a conflict over the role of the author: "Anna Seghers foregrounds the active work of the author, who is not only a product of his time, but also a creative subject, in opposition to a theory that attempted to push the writer into the role of a passive mirror of objective reality." [118] Linking Seghers's three-level model of the creative process to Seghers's topos of the author as a "point of transformation," Wolf then further elaborates this phrase: "point of transformation: exchange, probably also transformation of intellectual goods, the clash of something of one's own and something foreign, point of tension, point of danger." [119]

A similar interpretative move is made with Wolf's appropriation of Seghers's famous phrase from Seghers's novel *Transit:* "What can be told has been overcome." According to Wolf, this *also* means: "What has to be overcome, should be told." Thus she legitimizes her own conception of writing as a process of working through experience, a process which changes both the subject and the object, the author/narrator and the experience to be told, by rephrasing Seghers's statement. Wolf comes back to this aspect, which is so central to her own conception of modern fiction, when she returns to "Ausflug der toten Mädchen," which "does not describe the decision to live, it *is* this decision; it does not portray recovery, but rather *is* recovery. . . . The narrator overcomes what can barely be overcome, by narrating. Writing, he pulls himself together." [120] She thus assimilates Seghers's dictum on the relationship between overcoming and narrating, as well as her definition of the novel ("to touch the innermost being of people" [121]) to her own conception of writing as a process that changes the author him/herself, all the while maintaining its didactic dimension, which she conceives of in terms of the author's "responsibility."

Leaping from the Seghers of the 1940s to the Seghers of the 1950s, the time of High Stalinism, Wolf draws a connection which will prove to be of central importance for her work: the connection between the therapeutic function of writing and the Party line; the writing process becomes a process of overcoming a personal crisis of "belief," while "overcoming through narrating" becomes equated with "pulling oneself together." Wolf first defines responsibility as the reaffirmation of the belief in literature's power to change people, but then elaborates by assigning literature the function of overcoming the author's doubt in this belief. Recalling Seghers's visits to the Dostoyevsky archives during the Stalinist 1950s, Wolf describes Seghers's understanding of Dostoevsky as a writer who lived the "conflict" between subordination and rebellion. She quotes Seghers's insight as she reads Dostoyevsky's manuscripts: "Everything that happened happened inside the person." Literature's function, Wolf concludes, is to inquire into the transformations and dangers of this interior.[122]

While "Glauben an Irdisches" shows Wolf openly engaged in an unconditional, identificatory appropriation of Seghers's aesthetic writings, the contemporaneous "Lesen und Schreiben" shows the same, if in a veiled manner. However, in her 1973 interview with Hans Kaufmann about her notion of subjective authenticity, Wolf emphasized the difference between herself and the older author. Responding to Kaufmann's question concerning her definition of the term "prose," Wolf clarified:

I am referring to Anna Seghers's statement: what has become narratable, has already been overcome. You see, I had learned—and I must say I learned to my surprise, and despite my own considerable unwillingness to accept it—what it really meant to have to tell the story of something in order to master it. I had found that storywriters—or perhaps I should say prose writers—can be compelled to abandon the strict sequence of first living through something, then digesting and "mastering" it, and lastly, writing about it. In order to achieve the inner authenticity for which they are striving, they can be forced to express the living and thinking processes they are embroiled in directly in their work process, in an almost unmitigated way.[123]

This passage exhibits three things: (1) that Seghers's connection between writing and "overcoming" is basic to Wolf's thinking about modern literature; (2) that Wolf has begun to take a stance in opposition to Seghers *while using Seghers's own concept;* and (3) that the author of *Christa T.* identifies with the author of "Der Ausflug der toten Mädchen" on the basis of their both having overcome "crises of belief" through writing.[124] The exact nature of Wolf's new position vis-à-vis Seghers, as well as her new construction of Seghers—from the pre-GDR writer identified with Hölderlin and the Romantics to the *classical national author*—becomes more visible in a 1974 essay entitled "Fortgesetzter Versuch" (Continued Attempt). This remarkable exercise in memory, recalling a visit to Seghers in August of that year, delves deeply into the question of Wolf's relationship with Seghers. After reporting on the circumstances of her visit as a journalist, Wolf recalls that, at some point during the afternoon, she began to think about telling Seghers "what would be lacking if I had not met her." But she immediately realizes that "it's not a question of talking about influences. Still, I can at any time reproduce the tone in which *Transit* is written, or the attitude of the first-person narrator in 'Der Ausflug der toten Mädchen,' without even opening the books." [125] She knows the power of suggestion of this *tone,* Wolf continued, and of this *stance,* for sentences and brief passages from Seghers's books, conversations, essays, and speeches sometimes light up inside of her "like signals." Yet there is another interruption in her stream of thought: "But any attempt to follow all the traces which her work and her life . . . left within me would be doomed to failure." [126] Then a series of memories follow, memories of all the trips she has taken in Seghers's steps, or rather in the steps of Seghers's stories: her trip to the Rhine to find the spot from which a character in *Das siebte Kreuz* looked across the plain; her trip to Mainz, following in Netty's footsteps; and her visit to the grave of Günderrode—the name she kept stumbling across in Seghers's essays. She had thought of Seghers, Wolf now remembered, upon walking past the Cafe de la Paix in Paris, and, upon landing in New York, had felt a "shadow of the same feeling of foreignness that she must have felt"—an identification she immediately qualifies, saying that nothing other than this feeling and the very fact of arrival was comparable. The same complex pattern of identification and dis-identification is repeated at the beginning of the next paragraph: "There are moments when my gaze is transformed through hers and —if one can put it this way—*into* hers. Her language becomes present, and I am fascinated by the stance of the individual who is able to speak in that way (a way of speaking, by the way, which forbids any mere parroting)." [127] Once again trying to define the exact nature of this relationship, Wolf rejects both "influence" and "model" as unsatisfactory terms. The latter would imply "empty admiration," "dependence," "submission"—attitudes that Seghers would not care for; and Wolf herself is sensitized because "too often, our generation was supposed to allow itself to be molded." Although Seghers's authority is strong, it is not "overwhelming." This passage not only expresses an authorial "anxiety of influence," focused on a way of speaking and its associated attitude, but also overlays that anxiety with an allusion to the fascist past. *And* it alludes as well to the "real existing socialist" present when Wolf points out that since Seghers respects authority, she might sometimes be duped by it—but never overwhelmed by it. Finally, Wolf concludes, "It is that rare stroke of luck in which a sustained and intense interest in another, fundamentally different, pattern of life has enabled me to get to know myself better"—thus allowing her to continue walking the tightrope of identity and difference by attributing to the other what actually defines the self: a "human being . . . whose own contradictions make her extremely sensitive to the contradiction of this time." However, this common sensitivity to the era's contradictions now becomes the very nodal point on which Wolf's construction of difference between Seghers and herself turns. And this difference is thematized in terms of the generation gap between them: "We are on opposite sides of the generational divide." [128]

What does this gap, this "pain of strangeness within the sway of a desired closeness," really signify? It has to be understood, Wolf argues, on the terrain of art. Here, Wolf deploys Seghers's own opposition between Goethe and the authors of the Storm and Stress and Romantic periods as the opposition between the "classical" author and those who, experiencing their era's disarray, cannot themselves produce complete and harmonious works of art. Seghers is "moderate," that is, has found her measure. Although Wolf emphasizes that this quality cannot be understood in the terms of German classicism, she nevertheless points out that Seghers's "moderate" attitude rests on unshaken foundations, "certainties that cannot be doubted and that are not doubted." And she adds that Seghers, the *classical* author, is opposed to the expression of "emotional upheaval," or shock; having pulled herself together, she likes neither "exaggerated feelings" nor "overflowing reactions." [129] Downplaying her own concerns, denying them and not conceding them to anyone younger than herself, Seghers is dismayed by the extent of the uncertainty among those "born after her." [130] Nevertheless, Wolf ends on a conciliatory note, invoking Seghers's understanding, even compassion:

But somehow she knows not only about the historical conditions in which a "classical national author" emerges, but also about the desperate, usually futile efforts of those generations who cannot make their times cohere into a convincing picture. And because she herself is alive, dynamic, and curious, she not only accepts whatever she sees as new talent, but knows how to defend it, when necessary. How significant the meeting of certain life stages with certain stages of history is—who should know that better than she herself? [131]

Of course, one can read this concluding passage as a legitimatory move on the part of a younger author, which it certainly is.[132] But there is another layer to be uncovered in this seemingly conciliatory ending, an almost aggressive assertion of difference that assigns the "classical national author" to a position of complicity and consent, the younger author to one of—if not rebellion—then an openness to the contradictions of her times, to suffering them, writing them. Using "aggressive" without any psychoanalytic undertones, I want merely to point out Wolf's desire to distinguish herself from the woman who dominated the East German literary field in order to establish herself—a strategy with aesthetic as well as political implications, obviously.[133] Later statements confirm this veiled aggression and the defiant stance that accompanied it.

In his 1979 interview with Wolf, Adam Krzeminski called Seghers the last man among women, one whose novels have a " 'male' feel to them" because they are full of "categorical statements, and definitive truths." [134] Wolf's novels, according to Krzeminski, differ significantly in "tone" from such socialist realist epics by Seghers as *Die Entscheidung* and *Das Vertrauen* (Trust). Although Wolf at first agrees with his assessment, she pulls back when Krzeminski asserts a blurring of differences between Seghers, on the one hand, and Willi Bredel and Hans Marchwitza, on the other. Wolf insists that the disparity runs deep, but she also sees similarities between them as a result of common generational experiences. Seghers's bourgeois family background and her early decision to join the Communist party, Wolf says, produced a certain "asceticism," that is, a tendency to "keep herself completely out of her literature": "Her objectivity almost reaches the point of self-suppression." Asked about Seghers's attitude toward her own writing, Wolf responds that she is loyal but not uncritical: "She did like *Nachdenken über Christa T.,* and always defended it, possibly because it depicts the life of a different generation. I think she is skeptical about my approach." [135] And then Wolf elaborates on this rather curious concept of asceticism, again distinguishing Seghers as "classical": "She does not like to expose herself, she prefers classical reserve. She would never have gone that far; what I mean is, she would never have fearlessly questioned certain phenomena that for her were beyond the realm of discussion." The interview then moves on to the 1950s and Wolf's shift of allegiance from Lukács to Seghers. When Krzeminski observes that in Seghers's 1930s work, she rehabilitated "those who had failed" and their literature of insanity, sickness, fever, but that this defense never really influenced her own writing, Wolf first contradicts him, citing Seghers's short stories, then says: "But basically, you are right. She did not want to expose herself to the same danger, but she understood what it meant for writers to be steeped in the conflicts of their age—Hölderlin, Dostoevsky." [136]

In my view, this 1976 interview, despite its determined claims of difference, did not constitute a real change in Wolf's view of Seghers but brought to light a contrast that Wolf had been gradually heightening between Seghers and herself as the classical versus the nonclassical author.

Wolf's construction of Seghers goes through several different stages: First, Seghers is celebrated—in an identificatory mode—as the author on the side of Germany's artistic outsiders; we might call this the *pre-GDR Seghers.* Then Wolf shifts emphasis, foregrounding the *classical national author*— East Germany's canonical socialist realist—with herself, the younger author, now occupying the position that she sees Seghers as having vacated. This authorial lineage rests upon a construction which is necessarily critical toward the older writer so as to enhance the effect of Wolf's "own" voice. Indeed, Wolf's writings exhibit a rather curious form of appropriation—an appropriation of the older author against herself, the nonclassical author of the GDR's pre-history *against* Seghers, the GDR's classical author.[137] But this appropriative reception was only made possible by the speaking position that Seghers constructed for herself after 1945, namely, the maternal one, as I argued in chapter 2. Moreover, as we shall see, Wolf created her own speaking position as, alternatively, the son or daughter to this maternal instance. Nor is it surprising, given the problematic of identity outlined in *Moskauer Novelle* (i.e., identity as merger and separation in the acoustic mirror stage), that the identity of the author Christa Wolf would be constructed around the concept of "voice"—the reflection of her own voice in that of an author imagined as mother.

What further conclusions can we draw from this inquiry into Wolf's essays on Seghers? First and foremost, they demonstrate beyond any doubt that Seghers's views on realism are absolutely central to Wolf's own poetics, constituting the very basis upon which she develops her notion of subjective authenticity and its peculiar mode of narration: the foregrounding of the narrator, who does not necessarily speak in the first-person voice (as we shall see again with *Kindheitsmuster/Patterns of Childhood*), and the irritating oscillation between narrator/author and narrator/character, which emerges with *Nachdenken über Christa T.* But whenever Wolf writes about Seghers's *tone* or *voice,* she also writes about what she calls Seghers's *stance.* The noncanonical author's first-person voice is not innocent; it carries a strong ethico-political dimension: to write is to work through a personal/political crisis, but also "to pull oneself together." Repeatedly, Wolf writes about Seghers in terms such as the following: "Anna Seghers never allowed herself to slip into negligent resignation." [138] Curiously, Seghers's "moral rigor," which Wolf returns to again and again, characterizes both classical and nonclassical author, the author Wolf repudiates and the author with whom she identifies. However, as the interview with Krzeminski demonstrates, Wolf's own attitude has changed. The writing of modern literature still serves to overcome a crisis, but the accent has shifted: while Wolf previously joined Seghers in stressing outcome, the affirmative resolution of the crisis, by 1973 she was emphasizing "exposure"—the "un-classical" gesture of publicly exhibiting the author's conflicts, doubts, and problems.

This *stance* of overcoming the temptations of resignation is more than obvious in *Der geteilte Himmel*. But what about the *tone?* How did Seghers's works and their narrative voices function as an acoustic mirror for Wolf's early novel? The connection is certainly complex. There is, on the one hand, a link to the classical realist through the topic of *Das siebte Kreuz* (daily life) and its prologue's collective voice, the "we" of the concentration camp survivor. But, on the other hand, there is also a first-person narrator. Does the novel's text then refer back to the noncanonical Seghers, the author of "Der Ausflug der toten Mädchen"? This thesis might be supported by the novel's overall structure, its structure of remembrance, but in fact we know (from "Reading and Writing" [139]) that Büchner was Wolf's source for this method that still provokes "a sense of strangeness" with the shift from first to third person, from "I" to "he." In terms of *Der geteilte Himmel,* I argued for a double reading of the split narrative voice: "I"/"she" and "I"/"he," or the female protagonist as woman and as man. This basic constellation recurs on the level of narration itself, as Wolf positioned herself toward Seghers as "son" with that novel. By elaborating Büchner's characteristic narrative mode, Wolf took up a particular position in Seghers's generational paradigm of German literary history, namely, that of the male author Georg Büchner. Writing her own speaking position as an East German author into yet another family-centered narrative, although in a rather unexpected way, made Wolf, like Büchner, the "son."

Two more aspects regarding Wolf's appropriation of Seghers need to be addressed: Seghers's Jewishness, and the status of romance. As we have seen, Wolf's works from the late 1950s to the 1970s form a fabric of concern with the question of voice—by this I mean *the speaking position Wolf elaborates,* which consists of the three following elements: (1) the increasing use of first-person narration; (2) the notion that modern prose should be a process of working through a crisis at once personal and political that yields a narrative exposure of what Wolf calls "being endangered"; and (3) the ethico-political dimension always present in this existential crisis—the struggle against resignation as an imperative sustaining all writing.

Wolf's early *literary* texts add a specific dimension to this whole complex of voice: the fantasy of a *pure voice* linked to a *purified body.* Throughout Wolf's essayistic reflections, the voice of the author Anna Seghers is drawn into this web through her story that mourns the Jewish mother. Wolf's privileging of this particular work signifies, I would argue, that the voice derived from Seghers the noncanonical author (albeit in a mediated form, via Büchner) carries yet another meaning—that of the *purity of the (Jewish) victim.* We thus find, on the level of aesthetic theory as well as on the level of narrative practice, an identification with the victim of National Socialism, a gesture which I am inclined to read as the indirect but nevertheless urgent mimesis of a "pure," or nonfascist voice. In Wolf's essays on Seghers, this aspect of the older writer's identity is present only as a lacuna—but a significant one, since it is repeatedly mentioned: Seghers's silence about her return to Mainz in 1947, the loss of her parents, the destruction of their home.

Earlier, I mentioned Wolf's 1992 biographical sketch in which she explicitly thematized the silence of Anna Seghers, "German Jew, Communist, female author, woman, mother"—a silence noted but not pursued in prior essays.[140] Indeed, Seghers's silence was an important factor in her role of official East German author. Her return to Germany, despite the Holocaust, and her embracing of the "German people" without resentment were of critical importance for Wolf and other authors of her generation.[141] "Gesichter der Anna Seghers" puts Wolf's 1993 statement (comparing herself to the exiles of 1933) into the context of her deep identification with Seghers. In the shadow of this complicitous silence, like Reimann in *Ankunft im Alltag,* Wolf engages in a politics of identification with the Jewish victim; but unlike Reimann, who has her protagonist identify with Rosa Luxemburg, Wolf's identification operates through the mimesis of an authorial voice, the "pure" voice of the victim, both in her fiction and in the speaking position she assumes in her essays on philosophy, history, and aesthetics.

How is this "pure" voice related to the trope of the body with respect to the work of Anna Seghers? Reviewing Gladkov's *Cement* in 1927, Seghers wrote: "There is still too much talk about love and not enough about cement." [142] In her own scathing 1973 self-criticism of *Moskauer Novelle,* Wolf focused on one specific element, the plot: "Apparently, my fear of dangerous explosives led to the use of controlling devices." [143] These potentially "dangerous explosives" are contained by the novella's pious politics, which proved successful, according to Wolf, in blocking any unwelcome political insights. The novella's plot, however, was also the only type of plot Wolf had used so far—the love story—and which she would employ only once more after *Moskauer Novelle,* in *Der geteilte Himmel.*[144] In this respect, Wolf's attitude is again very close to Seghers's, about whose novels she wrote in 1968:

Anna Seghers was born at the beginning of a century whose passions are not of a tender and lyrical nature. They are not private but public. . . . The novels devoted to that century deal only incidentally with the longing and fulfillment of love. Freedom is passionately desired, and not a woman; social justice is desperately missed, and not another's love; one does not believe in personal happiness, but in the daily happiness of human kind.[145]

In the context of Wolf's appropriation of a "pure" voice, eschewing the love story—centered as it is on the material, sexual body—seems only logical.

We now understand why the novel that was written contemporaneously with the essay "Reading and Writing," *Nachdenken über Christa T.,* treated the question of a new speaking position by concentrating on a fictional character whose very essence is expressed in a scream. And why *Moskauer Novelle,* far from being a deplorable early exercise in socialist realism and therefore a negligible text, is central to an understanding of the problematic of body and voice in Wolf's oeuvre. It was precisely in such early works that Wolf established the link between voice, this material support of language, and the body of the past. In her obsessive foregrounding of what Barthes called the "grain of the voice," [146] the problematic of the past as the problematic of the sexual body and its voice remains present throughout Wolf's work. In the next chapter, we will see how it is developed in *Kindheitsmuster* (1976) and *Kassandra* (1983).

This time my father also has the face of my mother, I never know exactly when he is my father, and when he is my mother; then the suspicion thickens and I know that he is neither, but some third thing. — Ingeborg Bachmann, *Malina* (1971)

5

The Paternal Family Narrative as Autobiography and as Parable: Christa Wolf's *Kindheitsmuster* and *Kassandra*

In an article which initiated the Christa Wolf controversy in the summer of 1990, Frank Schirrmacher, editor of the feuilleton section of the *Frankfurter Zeitung,* summarized *Der geteilte Himmel* in the following way: "Christa Wolf's first book . . . deals with the problem of escaping from the country, and with the fact that it is more strenuous and difficult but also more 'honorable and sweet' to hold out in the socialist fatherland." [1] Schirrmacher then connects Wolf's novel to her 1989 public statements, in particular "Für unser Land" (For Our Country). [2] This appeal, promising those who remained in East Germany everything that Rita had already been promised in the novel, also implied that those who left were only interested in an easy life, that they were cowards avoiding the harder but more honorable task of rebuilding socialism. Schirrmacher thus draws a single interpretative line through Wolf's work, without much concern for the specificity of literature or for the complex and contradictory nature of literary texts. In his reading of Wolf's work, Schirrmacher does not tell us anything we did not already know from *Kindheitsmuster,* Wolf's novel about the lasting effects of a Nazi childhood. In other words, his analysis remains on the level of the author's knowledge, while Wolf's fiction goes beyond that knowledge and requires a *symptomatic* reading, that is, one which focuses on each novel's symptomatic failures and traces them to its unresolved contradictions. Schirrmacher's understanding of *Der geteilte Himmel* is rather reductionist, missing the complex and conflicted ways in which it actually participates in the GDR's hegemonic project. Moreover, his other main charge — that Wolf cannot think the social except in terms of the family [3] — simply ignores the structuring significance of an ideology that Wolf took as her point of departure and elaborated in her writings, namely, East Germany's paternal narratives. Indeed, it is her relentless engagement with this central organizing discourse which has made Wolf's work so compelling.[4]

After writing *Der geteilte Himmel,* Wolf did not leave East Germany (the reproach on which the post-Unification debate over her work really centered), but instead began to consciously focus on this paternal narrative and its fantasies. With *Kindheitsmuster/Patterns of Childhood* (1976), Wolf took up the question: "How did we become what we are today?"[5] This novel explores the authoritarian patterns of behavior internalized by Nelly, the protagonist and the child who the narrator once was. Critics have called *Kindheitsmuster* the autobiography of a "victorious subject," a metaphor resonating with the novel's psychological *and* historical dimension. With respect to the former, the novel demonstrates the "victorious" emergence of the subject out of all those components that are repressed, denied, and split off in the course of this process;[6] with respect to its historical and ideological dimension, the novel plays with the SED's self-characterization as *victors of history,* with the assertion that the Party—its state and its population—represents those forces that resisted National Socialism. Wolf interrogates this "victorious subject"—the continuity of its psychological and social formation—and asserts the social, generational relevance of the individual case. But her novel becomes a Benjaminian "writing from the perspective of the loser," with its investment in retrieving the memory of what the autonomous subject needed to repress in order to emerge "victorious."[7] In *Kindheitsmuster,* Wolf thus approaches the paternal family from the discursive perspective of autobiography. In *Kassandra* (1983), the perspective changes; the novella represents a historicizing of myth and, through that process, an exploration of Western civilization and (according to both Wolf and the authors of *The Dialectic of Enlightenment*) its ultimately self-destructive repression of the "feminine."[8] In the accompanying lectures and the novella itself, Wolf hints at another layer of meaning, which she has since articulated explicitly: *Kassandra,* the story of the fall of the Trojan kingdom is a parable about the fate of East Germany.[9] In this chapter, I will concentrate on this level of meaning, reading *Kassandra* as a deliberate reflection on East Germany's paternal narrative, a conscious exploration into its power and its fantasies. My reading, however, will emphasize the extent to which this *conscious* project is itself caught up *unconsciously* within the very structures from which it tries to distance itself—a reading that pursues our inquiry into the topics of voice and body.

History, the Subject, and Voice: *Kindheitsmuster*

In *Kindheitsmuster,* Wolf again thematizes voice and body: the former both thematically and structurally in the oft-noted split between the narrating subject's "you" and the narrated subject's "she"; the latter as *a* site invaded by Nazism and as *the* site of resistance, but also as the body of memory. The novel's renowned opening problematizes autobiographical narration:

What is past is not dead; it is not even past. We cut ourselves off from it; we pretend to be strangers.

   People once remembered more readily; an assumption, a half truth at best. A re-newed attempt to barricade yourself. Gradually, as months went by, the dilemma crystallized: to remain speechless, or else to live in the third person. The first is im-possible, the second uncanny (TA).[10]

The passage rules out the customary autobiographical "I." The narrator resolves the impossibility of writing and remembering in the first-person voice by splitting the narration between the *narrated subject*—Nelly, the child, the past, for whom she uses the pronoun *she*—and the *narrating sub-ject,* herself in the present, reflecting on this past and on the process of writing and remembering, for whom she uses the pronoun *you.*[11] Wolf ini-tially attempted to write the novel in the first person, but then realized that it was impossible to overcome the fundamental nonidentity between nar-rating subject and narrated subject, a "strangeness" that she again attributed to her generation's specific experience:

I don't think that I ever hide the fact that the book is, so to speak, autobiographical. I admit this. But this "so to speak" is very important because I do not feel identity with my character. There is, and this is perhaps one of the peculiarities of my life story though others of my age may have the same experience, a sense of alienation from this period. From a definite moment, which one cannot trace to the exact day but certainly to the exact period, one is no longer the same person. I no longer feel that it was I who had thought, said or done those things. And that's what I wanted to express through the third person, or rather had to, because otherwise the material remained closed to me, as I learned from various attempts to make a start.[12]

In this "novel of memory," [13] the first person is thus historically precluded and exists only as the utopian end point of writing, to be reached only "when the second and the third person were to meet again in the first or, better still, were to meet with the first person" (*PC*/349; *KM*/453). With the use of "you," the process of writing—and remembering—becomes one of dialogue rather than monologue. Wolf thus shatters the contours of the autobiographical "I," proceeding from the nonidentity of child and adult, of narrator and author—that is, from different, potentially contradictory instances of the subject[14]—and hoping to unify them through the process of writing the subject's memory.

The narrator characterizes her solution as finding the appropriate "tone" (*PC*/22; *KM*/34). Wolf's memory project assigns a crucial role to the voice that speaks about the process of remembering:

> The present intrudes upon remembrance, today becomes the last day of the past. Yet we would suffer continuous estrangement from ourselves if it weren't for our memory of the things we have done, of the things that have happened to us. If it weren't for the memory of ourselves. And for the voice that assumes the task of telling it. (*PC*/4; *KM*/10)

Not to become estranged from oneself thus involves both *memory* and *voice*. But how is this "voice of memory"[15] to be accurately described? The narrative consists of three different, tightly interwoven time levels: (1) the narrated past between the 1930s and 1945; (2) the narrated past of 1971, covering a trip by the narrator and her family to the city (now in Poland) where she grew up; and (3) the present of the writing, from 1972 to 1975. As that part of the dialogic structure of the "you" concerned with the *representation of the past,* not with the narrative present or the more recent past of the trip to Poland, this voice belongs to the narrating subject, who meditates on Nelly and her past—a multiple, composite voice, one that recovers the voices of the characters it describes to the reader.[16] Thus, in chapter 2 ("How Does Memory Function? Family Pictures"), the narrator describes a weekend expedition with the family.[17] Here, a mixture of inner voices— some direct quotations of an identified character, others not attributed to anyone in particular—often interrupts the narrator's own reflections:

> These, then, are the voices that come streaming in. As if someone had opened the sluice gates, behind which the voices had been locked up. Always this to-do, said Whiskers Grandpa, always this fuss. (If you really think about it, he probably was a stranger in his own family.) They're all talking at once, some are even singing, as

they march straight through the woods toward Uncle Walter's car. . . . Uncle Alfons is singing in a loud voice: "Elmer is my son, tra la, 'cause it happened under an elm, tra la. . . .

Now that doesn't have to be sung in front of a three-year-old, who knows songs herself and loves to sing with her father, "We are the minstrels of Finsterwalde." . . . So that toward the end of the very successful outing Bruno Jordan's voice, too, will be heard, a voice perhaps kept silent for too long, as though it had nothing to say. But not so. Not that singing was his special strong point: not since they cut into his windpipe in earliest childhood. . . . *Sit down, Jordan. Music: F.* Everything else, incidentally, straight A's. . . .

Herewith a sample of Bruno Jordan's voice: "Ho, there he lies and yells no more, ho, there he lies and yells no more, the soldier boy is dead, the soldier boy is dead." (*PC*/32–33; *KM*/46–47)

Memory thus works, to answer the chapter title's question, not through images or pictures of the past but through the voices they evoke. We are touching here upon the topic of *medaillons,* those famous "prettily made craft items" that we take out, according to Wolf, when we speak of memory, but which are really nothing but the result of a "creeping, inevitable process of hardening, petrifaction, habit." [18] In "Reading and Writing," Wolf writes about her hope that language will help her enter the areas that people avoid with these *medaillons.* Language, we learn from *Kindheitsmuster,* is the collection of voices from the past.

In the passage quoted above, "voice" slides between its meaning as the voice that speaks and the voice that sings, as in the father's "Stimmprobe," referring at once to a sample of his voice and to his voice test. As it turns out, it is the mother who is the singer of the family, as the narrator remembers: "Charlotte prefers songs which bring out her still beautiful soprano" (*PC*/33; *KM*/48). On the discursive level of the narrator's *self-reflexive narration of the past,* her voice is often aligned with the mother's voice in particular. The narrator quotes her, often without quotation marks: "By then the Führer's picture in the parlor was already burning in the furnace (that felt good, let me tell you)" (*PC*/26; *KM*/38); these quotations are often clichés, or what the narrator calls "family jargon": "A windy business—the mother's term" (*PC*/9; *KM*/17).[19] The narrator also tells us what Charlotte Jordan would say: "If you could ask her, Charlotte would probably say: Do what you must" (*PC*/34; *KM*/48). It is the mother's voice that is most deeply involved in the narrator's earliest memory, the first time the child Nelly *says* "I":

Previous drafts had started differently: with the flight. When the child was almost sixteen. Or with the attempt to describe the working process of memory, a crab's walk, a painful backward motion, like falling into a time shaft, at the bottom of which the child sits on a stone step, in all her innocence, saying "I" to herself for the first time in her life. (*PC*/5; *KM*/11–12)

This experience, the narrator notes, has a specific effect: a child, who is thinking "I" for the first time in her life, will be slower to obey her mother's voice. In the self-conscious recreation of this scene, on whose status as an "original memory" the narrator insists, the mother's voice introduces the child's name into the narrative as she calls Nelly: "At this point, the mother would have to call the child in for supper. . . . For the first time, we hear the name by which the child will be called in these pages: Nelly!" (*PC*/6; *KM*/13). The narrator thus firmly establishes the child's identity with respect to the mother, reinforcing it with the "fictional baptism" by the mother's voice that the narrator "hears" and to which she acquiesces. For hearing the name in the mother's voice resolves that question, according to the narrator, "without dwelling on the tedious search for a suitable name." The question of just *how* difficult, *how* unbearably complex, this act of naming is and *why* the search for a "suitable" name is dropped from a narrative that otherwise seems to follow every possible connecting strand between past and present must be suspended for the moment.

Wolf's autobiographical novel is thus, like her earlier fiction, centrally concerned with voice as a phenomenon involving both unity with the mother *and* separation from her. In the scene explored above, the child's entry into language, played against the background of the acoustic mirror, roots the problematic of identity — in the imaginary *and* in the symbolic — in the mother's voice. Why, then, does this recovery of past voices occur? Precisely in order to explore them, I would argue, to trace their origins and their effects. But are there other reasons as well? Perhaps to preserve an experience that would otherwise be forgotten, or to save the protagonists from the lethal, debilitating "verbal impotence" that robs them of the possibility of knowing themselves, leaving them only with "[w]ordless pantomime" or their very bodies to express their conflicts — and, of course, to serve this elusive "authenticity," thematized in chapter 8 with respect to the outbreak of the Second World War. In this chapter, which opens with a quotation from Ingeborg Bachmann ("With my burned hand I write about the nature of fire"), the narrator remembers first a particular sentence from a radio speech by Goebbels, then Nelly subsequently looking at herself in the mirror, thinking "Nobody loves me." Pondering the difficulties of writing about the past in an "objective style," using factual material, the narrator advances her own project: "How can anybody be made to understand that these two completely unrelated sentences are, in your opinion, somehow connected? That, precisely, would be the kind of authenticity you're aiming for" (*PC*/165; *KM*/217). This attempt at authentic subjectivity produces two specific scenes, on whose reconstructed nature the narrator insists. Each scene of memory entails an act of opposition by the narrator's mother: the first a statement made by Charlotte Jordan in her store about the inevitable loss of the war, and the second her response to a mailman delivering draft orders: "The hell with your Führer" (*PC*/166; *KM*/219).

What these scenes point to is the role of the mother as a "Cassandra" under the Nazi regime.[20] The narrator herself—not without some irony—directs our attention to this figure at the center of her project when she recounts one of the dreams that accompany her writing:

Just then your mother comes in, even though she is dead, and sits down in the big room, something you had always secretly wanted. The whole family is gathered, the living and the dead. You alone are able to tell one from the other, but you have to go to the kitchen. . . .

Suddenly, a shock that penetrates even the roots of your hair: in the big room on the table lies the manuscript, with, on the first page, only one word, "MOTHER," in large letters. She'll read it, guess your purpose, and be hurt. (*PC*/10; *KM*/19)

As these segments demonstrate, the search for the mother is driven by a desire to find traces of resistance, of an "uneasy conscience." It is also driven by a late insight, again formulated with the help of the mother's voice, as the narrator recalls how her protest against her mother's exclamation "You're so much like me, if you only knew!" was stifled by the recollection of a photograph in which her mother wore an extravagant hat. "Although," she adds, "the daughter refuses to admit that the compulsion to use the mother's gestures, looks, and words grows stronger as she grows older" (*PC*/90; *KM*/122). This exploration, however oblique, of the narrator's relationship with her mother permits another reading of the text's *polyvocality:* in *Kindheitsmuster,* one voice, trying to recover repressed memories *and* repressed identifications and dis-identifications, resurrects lost voices and drags them through a narrative that becomes an ever denser "web." Among those lost voices, the mother's dominates.[21] So too does her part in the formation of the child's subjectivity become more visible. The mother is last mentioned when Nelly falls ill with tuberculosis in 1945, a physical and psychological breakdown that her mother experiences as yet another blow to herself: "Children as fate's weapons against mothers, Nelly knew this role and hated it" (*PC*/396; *KM*/515).

The Figure of the Mother, the Figure of the Father

In the archaeology of this crucial relationship, the narrator remains willfully opaque, leaving us to deduce its importance from the structural significance of the mother's voice as that which the narrator "carries" with her, in terms of both the narrated past and the narration of that past. It is striking how little use the narrator makes of Nelly's words, her stock phrases or clichés, in her writing, for instance. Moreover, it is the voice of her mother that admonishes her, demanding discipline in the act of writing: "One thing at a time, as Charlotte Jordan would say" (*PC*/290; *KM*/377). Despite this reticence, however, there are a few passages that evoke the relationship of mother and daughter more directly, and the narrator is clearly engaged in an effort to understand her mother better. She takes care to note the signs of her mother's physical and psychological deterioration during the last months of the war, her "transformation into an unrecognizable person" (*PC*/398; *KM*/519). And when she narrates her father's return from a prisoner-of-war camp, she does not hesitate to claim knowledge of her mother's experience at the moment of reunion: "With a single blow she had lost herself and her husband," for her husband did not recognize her and she did not recognize him.

Relieved that she might be able to finish the book in the fall of 1974, and using one of her mother's expressions to encourage herself to do so, the narrator remembers that this is the sixth autumn after Charlotte Jordan's death, again linking the project to her mother. Moreover, the entire sequence narrating the family's escape to the West begins with a traumatic experience: Charlotte Jordan's staying behind to take care of the house rather than leaving with her children. Although this abandonment of her children has become a family legend, the narrator thinks, it has never really been explored; thus the event reflects what most signally characterizes trauma: its lack of articulation. The image of the moment of separation, the *medaillon,* is evoked and recirculated again and again, but it is never examined. The scene, described from Nelly's perspective, is dramatic but undeveloped:

Now it's time to leave, hurry up, quick, it's getting late. Nelly, already inside the truck, holds out her hand to help her mother climb in. But she suddenly steps back, shakes her head: I can't. I'm staying here. I just can't abandon everything. (*PC*/284; *KM*/371)

Christel Zahlmann rightly understands this scene as the repetition of an earlier experience, the memory of which is preserved in Nelly's favorite fairy tale, the "Fundevogel." Nelly develops an intense interest in this tale after the birth of her little brother, and she identifies with the "Fundevogel." Full of self-pity, she imagines herself exchanged at birth, "an ugly duckling, homeless, unloved, despite all protests to the contrary" (*PC*/14; *KM*/24).[22] Her mother's desertion contributes to a state of numbness in which Nelly finds herself for months to come. When her mother finally rejoins the family, Nelly throws herself on the ground, crying. As in her reporting of the scene of separation, the narrator makes no further comment. But she is now close to recalling her mother's death in the autumn six years earlier—a memory that is accompanied by a seemingly unrelated outburst of tears on the narrator's part. In response to her own question, "What is it that you are crying for now?" (*PC*/301; *KM*/392; TA) the narrator answers, "You weep for everything that will one day sink into oblivion," then lists such losses as the shriveling of curiosity, the disappearance of the most urgent desires, the stifling of hope. What endows these effects with a certain coherence is the process of aging—"late-summer decline" (*PC*/302; *KM*/392)—but, given the context, the passage also mourns a loss—mourning for a mother who, the narrator notes, was as old at that time as she herself is now.

Pursuing voice in *Kindheitsmuster* thus leads to the mother, the dominant figure in this autobiographical family narrative. Nevertheless, two central episodes revolve around the figure of the father. The first is another reconstructed "authentic" scene: Nelly overhears a conversation between her father and his friend in which Bruno Jordan learns that the army unit from which he is on leave participated in the execution of Polish hostages. This sequence is strange because, unlike any other incident, it is told from Nelly's perspective and *as her memory,* with "Nelly" insisting on what she saw:

At this point, her father's ashen face appears. Nelly is sure she saw it in the mirror. A gray, sunken face. She insists: Her father reached for a sleeve of his battle-gray overcoat, to steady himself. He hurriedly ended the conversation with Leo Siegmann. (*PC*/178; *KM*/236)

This passage positions Nelly as the one who lives through the moment when "her father had missed becoming a murderer by a hair's breadth" (*PC*/181; *KM*/240). Moreover, her insistence on the authenticity of the memory ultimately makes it *her* desire to see the father shaken by the news. As Margarete Mitscherlich-Nielsen concludes: "There exists in Nelly . . . a deep longing for a father-ideal which cannot find any fulfillment in reality." [23] How fundamentally the reality of Nazi Germany belies this yearning becomes evident in the chapter that narrates her father's return from the prisoner-of-war camp. The man who appears is unrecognizable, greedy for food, a "stranger" (*PC*/398; *KM*/518). Unable to enjoy his return, Nelly is equally unable to accept her feelings of embarrassment, pity, and compassion as she measures this father (the narrator puts the word in quotation marks) against outdated standards: "Nelly doesn't understand that she no longer lives in that time and place where the poet rhymed 'finality' with 'personality' " (*PC*/399; *KM*/520).

The desire that propels Wolf's autobiographical family narrative surfaces in a scene at the beginning of the novel, the deep structure of which has been convincingly analyzed by Christel Zahlmann. The scene is a memory of the three-year-old Nelly, sitting at a table with her father and mother; they are happy, her mother's face radiant as her father counts the first week's income from their store. Zahlmann begins by pointing out an irregularity in the perspective introduced by the opening sentence, "The back room of our first store, the room where all three of us had to eat and sleep" (*PC*/35; *KM*/50): this is the only memory recounted in the first-person plural "we." Zahlmann explains this particularly intense identification as an expression of the original unity of the ego with itself, the parents, and the world: "*All three of us* signals that the memory of a we-feeling is inseparably linked to the constellation of three: Father, mother, child—the brother is missing." Emphasizing the timeless aura of the image, Zahlmann also traces this longing for unity further into the past, to a time before the separation from the mother. What is decisive about this scene is its speechlessness, since "the act of saying 'I' has not yet taken place." [24] The events covered by this particular chapter explain why this desire, this "we," is so problematic. As Nelly is lying in bed, her mother and father enter the room, the latter wearing the blue cap of a Nazi sports organization. "But who was it," asks the narrator, "that said to Nelly in a happy voice: See! Now your father is one of them, too?" (*PC*/42; *KM*/61). The very uncertainty about voice here—who welcomed the father's decision with excitement: one of them or both?—shows the multiple faultlines along which this unity breaks down,—destroyed not only by developmental necessity, but by a historical context whose violent impact on the present can still annihilate any previously constructed alignment of voices.

Yet despite history's devastating effects, *Kindheitsmuster* represents a reconciliation, even a reidentification, with the mother as the figure least implicated in the Nazi period. The narrator observes, for instance, that after meeting several concentration camp inmates on their flight, her mother speaks more but also becomes more despondent, that she physically deteriorates. Although she utters meaningless clichés ("Blessed be he who, free of guile, retains the pure soul of a child"), she is nevertheless the only family member with a conscience, capable of empathizing with people outside her own circle. After discussing with her brother whether she is entitled to write about their parents, the narrator comments on her tense and complicated relationship to this older generation:

> The sober present-day view with which you examine the past, and which would have been blurred with antipathy, not to say hate, a short time ago, contains its ample dose of unfairness. At least equal to its dose of fairness. Objects, helplessly imprisoned under glass, without any contact with us know-it-alls. (*PC*/184; *KM*/244)

Kindheitsmuster, ostensibly preoccupied with recovering the child "who was hidden in me" in order to answer the question "Who are you" (*PC*/406, 349; *KM*/530, 453), is also animated by the desire to remember and redeem the mother.

Voice and the Body: Site of Inscription and Resistance,
Symptom, and Memory

In contrast to the narrator's reticence elsewhere, her handling of the theme of voice in relation to National Socialism and to the body is more forthright. The Nazi songs are still present, the narrator notes, as she copies Heinrich Annacker's poem "FROM THE ME TO THE WE" (*PC*/191; *KM*/252). So are the verses that Nelly recited, such as the poem for the Führer's birthday. Stunned and unable to comprehend the collapse of the Hitler regime, Nelly keeps a diary in 1945 in which she swears eternal allegiance to the Führer and notes, together with a friend, the beginning lines of all the Nazi songs they can remember. On their trip back from Poland, the narrator and her family start singing songs from the Spanish civil war, which leads her to comment:

Throughout 1945 Nelly didn't learn a single one of these songs. She continued to write first lines of songs in her green imitation-leather notebook, but they were different songs. ("A drum can be heard in Germany," "When everyone deserts the cause . . .") Another two, three years and she'll sing . . . "Rebuild, rebuild." And she'll try to forget the songs in the green notebook. Which has been lost, incidentally. It never works, *overlapping eras of songs*. (*PC*/385; *KM*/499–500; my emphasis)

In a way, the Nazi past swirls around the narrator like a cacophony of voices—the screams at rallies, the songs of the Hitler Youth, her own songs, the ritual reciting of poems, among many other examples. There is one passage in particular, however, that strikingly shows the narrator connecting Nazi body and Nazi voice for the first time. In this scene, Nelly, at the age of five, is waiting with her parents for the Führer to come through town. For hours, they stand by the side of the road, listening to loudspeaker announcements of the Führer's approach, of every stop he makes on the way. In the middle of her description of this festive morning, the narrator states that it may be important to say how the five-year-old Nelly not only knew but also *felt* who the Führer was, a feeling located in her stomach and throat: "The Führer was a sweet pressure in the stomach area and a sweet lump in the throat, which she had to clear to call out for him, the Führer, in a loud voice in unison with all the others" (*PC*/45; *KM*/64). It is a very specific desire that the narrator discovers in Nelly, which, in being reproduced, is also explained:

Nelly could neither understand nor remember what was being talked about, but she took in the melody of the mighty chorus, whose many single shouts were building up toward the gigantic roar into which they were meant to break, finally, in a display of powerful unity. Although it frightened her a little, she was at the same time longing to hear the roar, to be a part of it. She longed to know how it felt to be at one with all, to see the Führer. (*PC*/45; *KM*/64)

209

Clearly, this description is not innocent, but rather informed by a Freudian subtext about the group's desire to merge with its Ego Ideal. What is foregrounded here is the mediation of this process through voice: the Führer is a feeling in the throat, and Nelly longs to hear her own voice reflected in the voices of the others. In this passage, Wolf has created the scenic equivalent of a metaphor she frequently uses to express compliance: *Hang zur Übereinstimmung,* or *Übereinstimmungssucht*—the process of attunement, the inclination, effort, and longing to make one's voice harmonize with the voices of others. And she has created a scenic representation of the acoustic mirror. The libidinal flavor with which this representation of "attunement" is laced becomes stronger in the next segment, concerned with voice and body.

The narrator begins the chapter "Memory Lacunae. Times of Peace. Training in Hatred" with a meditation on the reasons for her use of the pronoun "you" instead of "I." Forced to admit a certain feeling of embarrassment toward Nelly, the child, she realizes that she will never be her "ally" but always an "intruding stranger," pursuing the child and her "innermost secret that concerned no one else" (*PC*/119; *KM*/159). The secret she seeks is what specifically it means to Nelly to be a German girl.[25] (This chapter ends with the famous question "How did we become what we are today?" [*PC*/209; *KM*/276].) The narrator recalls Nelly learning in school that a German girl must be able to hate: Jews, Communists, and other enemies of the people. Because Nelly knows neither any Communists nor any Jews, however, she is unable to hate them. To make up for that, she writes a poem about the Jewish betrayal of the German people after World War I, earning the expected praise from her teacher. But, as the narrator then reminds herself, the issue is whether someone is capable of hate, and she now recalls an evening during which Nelly overheard her father's friend, an "old Party member," describe his hatred of Jews. Telling the story of the only Jewish boy in his school, whom every student struck once in the face as they filed into the classroom in the morning, Siegmann, the friend, concludes that it is a question of "instinct" (*PC*/133; *KM*/178). From this moment on, a film runs in Nelly's head which always takes her to the moment when she is about to slap the boy—and then the film snaps. As often as she repeats her "experiment," Nelly never finds out whether she would be able to do her "duty"; instead, she learns only about her flaw: she cannot hate anyone she knows as intimately as she knows this boy.

What the narrator remembers next is a seemingly unrelated incident in which a man exposes himself to Nelly, who then runs away from "a whitish, disgusting snake" (*PC*/134–35; *KM*/179). She does not understand what has happened, but she knows that she should not talk about it. And from now on she is unable to handle lizards or frogs. The narrator continues this series of associations:

It's a touchy matter to this day to inquire into the connection—it must have established itself at that time—between the nameless Jew boy, whom Nelly has come to know through Leo Siegmann, and the white snake. What does the pale, pimply boy have to do with toads, spiders, and lizards? What do they in turn have to do with the ardent, fanatic voice calling out from the flaming woodpile on that summer solstice night: "We pledge to stay pure and to consecrate ourselves to Flag, Führer, and Fatherland"? (*PC*/135; *KM*/180)

The narrator does not know how these associations came about—from "unchaste" to "vermin," to the "white snake," and finally to the "face of the Jew boy" (*PC*/136; *KM*/181). All she knows is that, without understanding them, we understand very little about National Socialism.[26]

What Nelly experiences when these images arise is not hatred or distaste but "awe," a feeling close to fear that leads her to avoid "das Unreine" and to join in—"perhaps too loudly"—a bloodthirsty anti-Semitic song that everyone, the narrator recalls, was singing at the time. In a familiar move, Wolf thus establishes sexuality as the ideological subject's innermost truth, Nelly's "secret." But in *Kindheitsmuster,* the relationship between sexuality and ideology is more ambiguous, or rather paradoxical. Of course, there is the anecdote about Nelly's involvement with Binder, the boy with the Hitler-style haircut, which associates fascism with sadomasochism, like so many movies of the 1970s (from Passolini to Caviani to Visconti).[27] Nelly is both repulsed and fascinated by Binder, until the day she surprises him in a basement where he is having himself whipped by the leader of a street gang. The expression in his eyes, which she finds unrecognizable, drives her away. But there are other passages which establish feminine sexuality as a more unequivocal site of resistance. Asking herself whether she loves Nelly, the narrator spontaneously exclaims: "Good God, no, would be the truthful answer" (*PC*/211; *KM*/278). She asks how one could love a child who steals, then presents Nelly in a situation of double transgression: eating chocolate stolen from her parents' store and reading the SS journal *Das Schwarze Korps*—strictly forbidden by her mother—from which she learns about *Lebensborn,* where "blond blue-eyed SS men are brought together with brides of similar background" (*PC*/223; *KM*/293). Having finished the article, Nelly drops the journal and thinks: "No, not that." The narrator then continues: "It was one of those rare, precious, and inexplicable instances when Nelly found herself in conscious opposition to the required convictions she would have liked to share. As so often, it was a feeling of guilt that engraved the incident in her memory" (*PC*/223; *KM*/294).

Nelly has the same reaction—"Not that!"—when she reads about a girl in the Thirty Years War who deliberately infected herself with the plague and then spread the disease in the enemy's camp. The narrator's comment that anything connected with her gender seemed unbearably complicated is correct with respect to Nelly's contradictory sense of being caught between "duty" and "feeling." But it does not accurately describe the stark but simple dichotomy which emerges with respect to the novel's most fundamental fantasy about the sexual body, the opposition between a *complicit, fascist male sexuality* and a *female sexuality linked to fascism through the utopia of chastity* (but also resisting that ideology by that very chastity). For Nelly's only moment of dis-identification with her revered model, the National Socialist women's leader and German teacher Julia Strauch, occurs with Nelly's sudden understanding that Julia Strauch hates being a woman. What differentiates the two is thus a concept of feminine sexuality as that terrain of subjectivity which remains potentially resistant to National Socialist inscription.

In *Kindheitsmuster,* the fantasy of the body works along several different registers: Nelly's sexual body functions both as the part of her which is drawn to this male universe and as the site of its spontaneous refusal. But her body also functions as "the site where psychic conflicts are worked out and as the field of symbolization of their significance."[28] Concerning her parents' life in a dictatorship that often requires them to deny their own spontaneous feelings and reactions, the narrator asks: "Why didn't they suffer? The question is wrong. They suffered without knowing it, they raged against their bodies, which were giving them signals: My head is splitting. I'm suffocating" (*PC*/156; *KM*/207). When confronted with a host of feelings she is not permitted to admit to herself, Nelly escapes into sickness. She reacts with a fever to the punishment of one of her friends in the Hitler Youth; in 1945, she again runs a high fever, which the narrator interprets in the following way: "It was Nelly's own body that ultimately signaled the fact that she actually knew without having been informed" (*PC*/280; *KM*/365). This "symptom-body"[29] also plays an important role in the writing process. Catherine Viollet quotes a sentence from one of Wolf's earlier drafts in which the body itself is referred to as a *locus* of memory, here the city of Wartberg, "whose web of streets lies well preserved not only in the depths of my memory, but in every cell of my body, subject to recall." [30] Toward the end of the book, the narrator herself falls ill, an instance when she is unable to decipher the body's language "because we are doggedly determined to separate the physical from the spiritual" (*PC*/349; *KM*/452).

The association between body and memory also links a chain of associations across the narrative in which the writing process is likened to torture. When the narrator is ruminating about the difficulty of making the child speak, for example, she notices that her heart is pounding and reflects upon the extent to which the twentieth century has restored the "old invention of torture, in order to make human beings talk" (*PC*/48; *KM*/66). The theme is further developed in the core image of a dream which threatens to disrupt the narrator's daily habit of writing:

In a whitewashed, incidentally rather primitive, room to which you withdrew, you were surprised to come upon a small, deformed man—the top of his head was egg-shaped—who left immediately, at your request. But minutes later, he was hurled back into the room in a most horrible way, through the splintering door, hanging upside down on a swinglike rope contraption, which torturers were pushing back and forth, while they beat the little man and yelled at him to disclose certain information. To your indescribable horror you realized that the little man was unable to speak, he had no mouth. . . . He could not obey his torturers' commands even if he had wanted to. In desperation you thought—a thought you immediately canceled in your mind—they ought to let him write if they want to find out something from him. (*PC*/170; *KM*/223–24)

When the torturers free the man, put him on the narrator's bed, and hand him pen and paper, he only utters sounds. The dreamer/narrator alone understands these sounds: the man knows nothing. And she ends her account of the dream by saying: "They continued to torture him on your bed" (*PC*/171; *KM*/224).

The experience and image that the narrator associates with the *Körper-gedächtnis* of the tortured body is that of an armored body, one rendered rigid through the sedimentations left by the ideological formation of the subject. The contrary, according to the narrator's dream, is a body that is alive: "You dream one single word: armor. With that you see, as you wake up, a statue whose golden surface is traversed by fissures. The living body beneath the armor and the face do not become visible" (*KM*/528).[31] But this "living" body is no longer available, as indicated by this strangely ambiguous last sentence that both asserts and denies the presence of another body inside the armor. What these different representations suggest is that the body is the "vantage point of an undeceitful language" which would tell us the truth if only we were able to listen to the "language of our organs" (*PC*/349; *KM*/452).[32]

Pure Body, Impure Voice

What we encounter once more, then, is the idea of a *pure body* beyond any ideological inscriptions and deformations, whether as Nelly's chaste body or as the elusive body inside the armor. In contrast to her earlier fiction, Wolf's autobiographical novel explicitly differentiates between male and female body, masculine and feminine sexuality. In *Kindheitsmuster,* masculine sexuality partakes of ideology, whereas the female body as a chaste one is both drawn into the imaginary of National Socialism and its celebration of purity and resistant to it. Yet while the construction of a pure body links *Kindheitsmuster* to Wolf's previous work, the novel does *not* establish the connection between pure body and pure voice that we saw before. On the contrary, this narrator's voice is thoroughly entangled in the past and its identifications, in those other voices it always carries with it, not unified into (or freed as) "I." Of course, the narrator does suddenly veer into first-person voice at the end, but the status of this I as a unity is provisional:

And the past, which can still split the first person into the second and the third—has its hegemony been broken? Will the voices be still?

I don't know.

At night I shall see—whether waking, whether dreaming—the outline of a human being who will change, through whom other persons, adults, children, will pass without hindrance. (*PC*406-7; *KM*/530)

My model of *Kindheitsmuster*'s narrative voice goes beyond the division into the "you" and "she" of Nelly's story, for what is important about this *you* is its polyvocality, the multiple voices of the past that become part of it. (It is only in Wolf's most celebrated work, *Kassandra,* that we find the unreserved use of first-person narration—and a pure voice again linked to a sublime body.) But another aspect of *Kindheitsmuster*'s narrative voice needs to be explored. Returning now to Nelly's "baptism," let us pursue a closer reading of the multiple textual strands converging in that passage.

Although the narrator explicitly left out what she called the "tedious search for a suitable name," we do know the following from Viollet's analysis:

In sketch 2, "Anna J." appears. Her father, "Bruno Jordan," will always have the same name in all outlines; the mother, however, is first called "Laura J., born Jabel" (sketch 2), then she becomes "Charlotte Jordan, born Menzel" (sketch 19). The doubt, the hesitation concerning the naming is thematized as the necessary transition to the story's universe: "And arranging these ever changing tables of names, where the familiar figures appear under the guise of a foreign name." (Sketch 18). The choice of a first name for the child—first "Anna" (sketch 2), then "Nelly" (starting with sketch 4)—becomes a reflection on the significance of the act of naming. At first it seems as if the child chose her own name—"Nelly always reappeared from the thicket of the fairy tales filled with glowing characters with her everyday name, which she had, however, chosen herself" (sketch 12)—a first name to which it [the child] would soon prefer a different one: ". . . one day she vehemently demanded to be called Joringel." (Sketch 13). But after that the child is called Nelly by the others: ". . . the child had been irrevocably baptized with a *false* name (which it would adopt, but only a little later). . . . (Sketch 22).[33]

What can we conclude from this extraordinary process? Finding the child's name was not only extremely difficult, but the name itself was highly unstable, even "false," and its very source kept changing.

Although Nelly's name is introduced through her mother's voice, whose voice *do* we hear at this moment? The appearance of "Anna," Seghers's name, above confirms a suspicion already raised by the similarity between "Nelly" and "Netty." Like an echo, Seghers's voice thus resonates in this baptismal scene, conjuring up "another" mother figure. But perhaps this reading proceeds too quickly, smoothing over the conflicts that arise at this particular textual moment. For example, why would Wolf, the quintessential writer of memory and its many "tricks," not include the search for one of the most crucial aspects of identity, the name? We might, on the contrary, be well advised to take Wolf at her word and dig deeper into this lacuna—one of those "areas which people avoid when they are making *medaillons*."[34] The name "Nelly" creates a link to "Der Ausflug der toten Mädchen," the Seghers story about which Wolf wrote: "Only once . . . is the persona bluntly and undisguisedly called 'I.' "[35] The similarities between Seghers's story and Wolf's novel are undeniable: a narrator reflecting on her childhood, the problematic of identity, even a search for the mother. "Nelly" thus creates a link to the young Jewish "Netty." But the very topic of *Kindheitsmuster* itself forced the vicissitudes of this identification with the Jewish victim of National Socialism into the foreground and contributed to the dilemma formulated at the beginning: to remain silent or *to write in the second person.* In this novel, Wolf looks back at the Nazi girl she was, at a childhood spent in the "shadow of the Auschwitz ovens" (*PC*/248; *KM*/326). This past makes it unbearable "to think the tiny word 'I' in connection with the word 'Auschwitz.' 'I' in the past conditional: I would have" (*PC*/230; *KM*/303).

It also makes it impossible to write in the same voice as the mentor, the victim, to echo the first-person voice of Seghers's "Der Ausflug." Thus Wolf was led to create the "fantasy" of a narrator speaking in the second person. Although Seghers's voice resonates loudly in *Kindheitsmuster,* it does so with all the complexity of a delving into the German past by someone "on the other side." As the child she once was, this someone now bears a "false" name, a doubly fractured and "damaged" name, perhaps because she knows that she never was the young Jewish Netty, that what underlies the desire to inherit the child's name from Seghers is a fantasy.

But perhaps Nelly's "baptism" tells us even more about these "sides" (or the fantasy about them). This ritual conferring her singularity—under a "false" name, as we have seen—weaves a densely tangled yet fragile web between women and their names, but it leaves out what ties the child to a social order and its dominant relations—the patronym. Viollet tells us that the patronym never undergoes any changes, a stability that can be read in conjunction with the wish to be called Nelly/Netty: by virtue of a "baptism" that leaves out the father's name, the child is positioned outside of her social order—and thereby outside of history—left to seek shelter in the damaged name, the impossible desire for identification with the Jewish victim. In this gesture, we recognize the doubling of a structure we encountered earlier: the identity, however precarious, outside of the father's history corresponds to the territory "outside" of ideology, the chaste body.

Conditions of a Narrative: *Kassandra*

In most of the critical literature on Wolf, *Kassandra* and the accompanying lectures are treated as a climactic work—the epitome of Wolf's feminist turn.[36] This view takes Wolf at her word when she states in the lectures that her very "lens on the world" changed in the course of her intense preoccupation with the myth and, more importantly, the figure of Cassandra: "My viewing lens . . . has undergone a decisive change. It is comparable to that decisive change that occurred more than thirty years ago, when I first became acquainted with Marxist theory and attitudes" (*C*/278; *V*/131). Wolf's feminist turn is often traced to her interest in Romantic writers such as Karoline von Günderrode (whose name she kept encountering in Seghers's essays) or Bettina von Arnim, Günderrode's correspondent.[37] The other markers on this path to feminism most often mentioned are Wolf's introduction to Maxie Wander's 1977 collection of interviews with East German women, *Guten Morgen, du Schöne. Frauen in der DDR: Protokolle* (Good Morning, My Lovely. Women in the GDR: Protocols), and her short story "Selbstversuch" (Self-Experiment), which narrates the (unsatisfying) transformation of a woman into a man.[38] The *Kassandra* lectures themselves, delivered in Frankfurt am Main in 1982, explore the possibility of a feminine aesthetic.

Wolf's feminism evolved within the context of the Frankfurt school and its understanding of Western civilization as a process of reification.[39] In particular, she was strongly influenced by Sylvia Bovenschen's feminist reading of *The Dialectics of Enlightenment,* which argues that the process of subject constitution throughout Western history traced by Adorno and Horkheimer rests on the exclusion of those qualities defined as "feminine," that is, qualities belonging to "nature," the object to be mastered.[40] This exclusionary logic ends in self-destruction, on the one hand, or in an idealization of nature and the feminine as what the autonomous male subject has lost, on the other. Like Adorno and Horkheimer's account, however, Wolf's feminism is both a critique and a defense of the Enlightenment. Her position stems from an understanding of fascism as a social movement that mobilizes deep, irrational fears and desires. Indeed, the entire theoretical thrust of her Cassandra project takes fascism as its ultimate reference point. Arguing against any form of feminism that abandons rationality altogether, Wolf espouses "the centering around the Logos, the word as fetish — perhaps the deepest superstition of the West, or at least the one of which I am a fervent devotee" (*C*/162; *V*/25). This feminist *grand récit* leads Wolf to privilege women because of their particular historical experience; replacing one universal subject of history with another, she claims that it is easier for women to say "I":

I look at history to explain why it should be that women in our society relate to one another more naturally, more closely and intimately and with a greater readiness to live out certain values than men. For more than a hundred and fifty years, men have been forced, both by the division of labour and by the patriarchal structure of bourgeois society, to conform and repress themselves. They have fully internalized the values which industrial society has impressed on them. The fact that women were not forced to do this to the same degree both oppressed them further in that they were driven further into the domestic sphere, and yet also reduced the pressure on them to accept these kinds of values completely.

It seems to me—and this is due not to biological but to historical factors—that women are now in a better position to take up new values which they feel to be "natural" and more human. They simply find this easier to do. And saying "I," although immensely difficult for the individual, is becoming easier for them collectively, too.[41]

A few years later, however, Wolf declared this faith in women's otherness and potential for change excessive and unjustified. Nevertheless, her embrace of this particular kind of feminism betrays the same desire we have encountered in Wolf's writings—for a position outside of history. As we saw in chapter 4, this longing runs like a thread through *Moskauer Novelle* and *Der geteilte Himmel,* with their constructions of the post-fascist body and its "pure" voice. It also runs through *Kindheitsmuster,* with its paradoxical constitution of Nelly's "chaste" body as both drawn and resistant to the fascist discourse on chastity, and it reappears in the notion of a feminine identity "untainted" by male history. What makes Wolf's literary work all the more intriguing then, is that it not only undermines this desire, but in doing so problematizes this particular kind of feminism—despite her own heavy investment in its idealization.

Wolf's growing interest in feminist theory in the late 1970s overlapped with a crisis, the expulsion of singer and writer Wolf Biermann from the GDR and the sanctions to which Wolf and many of her colleagues were subjected after signing a petition in his support.[42] This experience motivated Wolf's initial interest in the Romantics, whose outsider status in a postrevolutionary world she analogized to her own situation in a state that no longer cared about the critical cooperation of its intellectuals. *Kein Ort. Nirgends* (No Place on Earth), her 1979 story about a fictional meeting between Heinrich von Kleist and Karoline von Günderrode, revolves around an existential crisis caused by being "thrown back on literature alone." [43]

With the peace movement of the early 1980s, Wolf found a way out of this crisis state and back into the role of public intellectual. What was in hindsight the last major confrontation of the Cold War, the controversy around the installation of missiles in East and West Germany, accounts for her fascination with Cassandra and her role in the Trojan War. The lectures explore the possibility of "feminine" writing in opposition to the Western culture of war and its dominant art form, the heroic epic. This culture, based on the domination of inner and outer nature, and, as a result, the "colonization of woman by man" (*C*/263; *V*/118), finds its purest expression in the "blood-red thread" of the epic:

[T]he advent of property, hierarchy, and patriarchy extracts a blood-red thread from the fabric of human life . . . and this thread is amplified at the expense of the web as a whole, at the expense of its uniformity. The blood-red thread is the narrative of the struggle and victory of the heroes, or their doom. The plot is born. The epic, born of the struggles for patriarchy, becomes *by its structure* an instrument by which to elaborate and fortify the patriarchy. (*C*/296; *V*/147)

Again, we hear in this analysis of the Homeric epic a critique of Lukács's Aristotelian realism, a refusal of socialist realism's narratives of antifascism and its hero cult: "The hero is made to serve as model and still does so down to the present day" (ibid.). This culture is thus part of a system of masculine thought which, according to Wolf, characterizes all of Western civilization. Troy's fortress, that is, its culture of war, and the "steeled and armored" subject (*C*/276; *V*/129) are the inevitable results of abstract rationality's will to dominate nature and its tendencies toward an ever greater homogenization.

The feminine aesthetic that Wolf is seeking aims, on the contrary, to preserve the "precious everyday, the concrete" (*C*/270; *V*/125)—Seghers's familiar notion of daily life, now recast in a different theoretical framework. Such an aesthetic, Wolf argues, would subvert the patterns of masculine thought, this one-track-minded renunciation of both manifoldness for dualism and monism and of "subjectivity" for "a sealed 'objectivity' " (*C*/287; *V*/139). This system of thought cannot recognize that everything is fundamentally related, and its approach to both science and art, its "extraction of a single 'skein,' " destroys the entire fabric (*C*/302; *V*/139). Hesitantly, Wolf proposes another mode of writing, a "tissue formed of the most extraordinary, partly farfetched threads" (*C*/302; *V*/152). Wolf then links this idea of a "narrative network," as opposed to a "linear narrative," to a different mode of memory and, ultimately, a different mode of writing history. The reductive process that characterizes the Homeric epic and its historiography simplifies humans—reducing them to "ideal figures"—replaces the multiplicity of phenomena with a few symbolic acts, and fuses vast stretches of time, thus developing no memory for the "prosaic." The new writing renounces all forms of domination of the particular. It no longer wants to "create large-scale, vital, ideal figures; no longer wants to tell coherent stories held together by war and murder and homicide." Instead, this kind of narrative endorses a mode of memory no longer focused on "history as the story of heroes" (*C*/262; *V*/117).

The foundation of this new aesthetic is *everyday life as the world of women,* which in the traditional epic "shines through only in the gaps between the descriptions of battle" (*C*/233; *V*/92). This world, according to Wolf, produces a different experience and, therefore, a different, genuinely feminine writing:

To what extent is there really such a thing as "women's writing"? To the extent that women, for historical and biological reasons, experience a different reality than men. Experience a different reality than men and express it. To the extent that women belong not to the rulers but to the ruled, and have done so for centuries. To the extent that they are the objects of objects, frequently the objects of men who are themselves objects, and so, in terms of their social position, unqualified members of the subculture. To the extent that they stop wearing themselves out trying to integrate themselves into the prevailing delusional systems. To the extent that, writing and living, they aim at autonomy. (*C*/259; *V*/114–15)

Experimenting with "another kind of storytelling" (*C*/304; *V*/154) also means trying to turn women from objects into subjects of narration, in the hope of counteracting the "products of the alienation of our culture" (*C*/142; *V*/8). This culture reduces women to objects, to images without a voice of their own. *Kassandra,* Wolf writes, is the attempt to transform the woman-made-myth, and thereby object, into an autonomous subject with a voice. The project of a feminine aesthetic thus means, above all, the project of giving women the opportunity to say "I" (*C*/298; *V*/148). The effort of historicizing myth in fact becomes an unearthing of this lost feminine voice: "Now I have connected with the first voice that has been bequeathed to us, and I have tried to scrape off the entire masculine tradition, which had been superimposed upon this voice." [44]

Many critics have followed Wolf's suggestion, reading *Kassandra* as an exemplum of the rather problematic notion of feminine writing. Thus Cassandra's "alien" voice, expelled from her body in a series of outbursts that punctuate the narrative, is often conceptualized as the breakthrough of the semiotic into the symbolic order. Sonja Hilzinger, for instance, argues that "voice stands in for the female body, which is not realized but rather repressed in the act of speaking, or narrating—just like eroticism, sexuality, femininity in general." [45] This reading, which collapses the subject of enunciation with the subject of the enunciated—the Cassandra who remembers and thinks about her outbursts and the Cassandra who lives them—makes no sense structurally. As Sigrid Weigel has pointed out, far from being an avant-garde narrative in which the semiotic disrupts the symbolic order of language, *Kassandra* is "a closed work of art." Moreover, the speaking subject herself, Cassandra, does not constitute a different, "feminine" model of subjectivity. Instead, Wolf's story "describes in monologic form the inner development of a model heroine whose process of remembering is directed toward an unambiguous goal, her inner autonomy—being that has come to *a belief in itself.*" [46] Although Wolf has sought an alternative way of narrating—an "unheroic" literature which, taking the form of a narrative network, would no longer participate in the celebration of the hero— the text she finally produced differs radically from this project. According to Weigel, Wolf set out to critique the heroic model of subjectivity, the constitution of the self as autonomous subject,[47] but she ultimately resorted to that very model, that autonomous subject. *Kassandra* does not develop an alternative subjectivity, one which would avoid reducing the individual to a single instance, consciousness, based on the repression of everything "foreign" to it.[48] Weigel traces this discrepancy between the lectures and the narrative to the supplanting of one discursive mode by the other: the search for another kind of subjectivity by the story of "becoming a subject"— Cassandra's search for autonomy—"I lived on to experience the happiness of becoming myself and being more useful to others because of it" (*C*/12; *K*/15). As she explains to Aeneas at the end of her monologue, having achieved this inner autonomy, Cassandra chooses to die rather than submit to the law of the new masters. By means of this death, Cassandra comes to represent the ideal autonomous subject.[49]

The voice that results from the effort to make Cassandra speak—the "I" of the first-person narration—has to be distinguished from the voice that erupts out of Cassandra's body. Furthermore, rather than reading this "alien" voice as a genuine expression of femininity, or of the feminine body, a historically contextualized reading would understand it as part of the entire problematic of voice that unfolds in Wolf's work, that is, voice as connected to the post-fascist present and the fascist past, inextricably linked to the post-fascist body. It is only from a radically shifted perspective that we can make sense of this voice. Thus while *Kassandra* is almost exclusively concerned with voice and body, what it stages in Cassandra's outbursts is not some "true" voice of the feminine outside of the symbolic order but a highly idiosyncratic utopia, that of the *pure voice of the sexual body*— a counter-utopia to the post-fascist body, as a sublime, asexual body, and *its* "pure" voice. This voice is a symptom, the result of a conflict between feminine and masculine identifications, between the daughter's Oedipal identification with the mother's desire and her identification with the icon of antifascism, the sublime tortured body of the antifascist hero. Cassandra's "alien" voice is a hysterical voice, a symptom localized, like Nelly's, in the throat.[50] And as a symptom, it once more celebrates the *fantasy of a "pure" voice*—this time as the "truth" of experience expressed in the immediacy of a link between the sexual body's voice, *immune to any ideological inscription*. In a paradoxical move, yet one for which we have been prepared by *Kindheitsmuster,* Wolf makes feminine sexuality here the very locus of purity. And yet this "truth" can only be spoken because it rests on the identification with the antifascist hero. Cassandra's hysterical mise en scène thus involves a *masculine identity* as the antifascist hero and a *feminine identity* as the speaker of the body's truth. Like Rita, she is both *son* and *daughter.* And, as we shall see, the voice of the subject of enunciation, Cassandra's "I," partakes of a similar fantasy of purity—the radical, ultimately masochistic fantasy of a voice soon to be separated from its body. "With the story, I go to my death" (*C*/3; *K*/5; TA), Cassandra announces, beginning her testimony to the destruction of Troy. It is this fantasy which finally frees Wolf from the constraints that had prevented her from using "I." Here, for the first time, she fully appropriates the speaking position that she had ascribed to Seghers, creating a narrator who is in the process of overcoming the post-fascist body—this material support of the sublime body by which Wolf's other protagonists have been tied to their fascist past. (Which particular conditions allow this appropriation is a question that must be temporarily deferred.)

Unraveling the Fabric

The transition from *Kassandra*'s opening paragraph to the next one constitutes an ambiguous, undecidable zone in which an initially imperceptible, but all the more decisive, change of perspective takes place:

It was here. This is where she stood. These stone lions looked at her; now they no longer have heads. This fortress—once impregnable, now a pile of stone—was the last thing she saw. A long-forgotten enemy demolished it, so did the centuries, sun, rain, wind. The sky is still the same, a deep blue block, high, vast. Nearby, the giant fitted-stone walls which, today as in the past, point the way to the gate, where no trace of blood can be seen seeping out from beneath. Point the way into the darkness. Into the slaughterhouse. And alone.

With the story, I go to my death.

Here I end my days, helpless, and nothing, nothing I could have done or not done, willed or thought, could have led me to a different goal.[51]

In its repetitive use of *now* and *then,* the passage establishes this work as another narrative of remembrance, with someone—who? we don't know—*speaking* to the reader about a woman of the past, about a time centuries before our own. And the sentence fragments at the end of the first paragraph, their dramatic, breathless, escalating rhythm carrying the fear, but also the definitiveness, of these few minutes before death, enacting a moment of identification between the narrator and the woman going to her death. The same ambiguity characterizes the novel's last sentences:

The light went out. Is going out.
They are coming.

Here is the place. These stone lions looked at her.
They seem to move in the shifting light. (*C*/138; *K*/160)

In between these two liminal points, we follow Cassandra's monologue, or rather her stream of thought.[52]

The intricate nature of the opening passage demands that we take Wolf's notion of a "narrative network" seriously. Which discursive strands converge at the moment of Cassandra's arrival at the enemy's gate? Besides thematizing the entanglement of past with present, of protagonist with narrator, this opening also posits the connection between individual story and collective history, Cassandra's death and Troy's destruction, the necessary development of a character and the necessary end of an empire. These are the broad parameters of the narrative and its structure, a retrospective and teleological story told in the few remaining minutes before Cassandra, the prisoner, enters the city of the victors, Mycenae, where she will be killed by Clytemnestra, Agamemnon's wife.

But this is decidedly *not* a single story. For Cassandra's very first line—

"With the story, I go to my death"—subtly pulls in another, more familiar story: the one that Wolf created on the basis of Seghers's literary-historical reflections on the postclassical era. Let us recall that the authors of the younger generation, whom Wolf would later characterize as living in a post-revolutionary epoch, either committed suicide or "escaped" into insanity. Cassandra's reference to her story as her way into death introduces a specific literary–historical intertext—and thus the whole complex problematic that Wolf theorizes as the interrelation of tone and stance. On this level, *Kassandra* is, I would argue, a variation on the story of Büchner, Günderrode, Kleist, told as Cassandra's growing autonomy from the court's official language and the successful separation by the priestess of her office from her origin. Since it is also the story of the king's daughter, it adds another layer to the palimpsest of Wolf's story: the paternal order and its ideological narrative of the family. My reading of *Kassandra* thus works in reverse, against the grain of Wolf's classical narrative and against the "blood-red thread" of the heroine's story. *Kassandra* is a myth rewritten from a particular feminist perspective; a story from the realm of literary history; and a textual layer articulated to a legitimatory discourse. With respect to the latter, *Kassandra* is the story of the daughter, a parable or model of a specific ideological discourse.

King, Queen, and Daughter: Rewriting Myth as Paternal Narrative

Cassandra is determined to bear "witness" to the war, not to "relapse into creatureliness," not to split herself "for the sake of consciousness," even at the moment of death (*C*/22; *K*/28). She would like to ask Clytemnestra to find her another "voice" to transmit her tale, "a young slave woman with a keen memory and a powerful voice . . . that she may repeat to her daughter what she hears from me. . . . So that alongside the river of heroic songs this tiny rivulet, too, may reach those faraway, perhaps happier people who will live in times to come" (*C*/81; *K*/95–96). The associative, yet utterly determined work of memory that Cassandra undertakes is the history of the Trojan War from a woman's perspective, which leads her to follow the "thread of [her] life" (*C*/21; *K*/26) back in time in hopes of understanding herself. Quickly, the daughter's monologue arrives at the moment when her "ambivalent feelings" began, and this "strange voice which had stuck in my throat many times already" appeared (*C*/36, 39; *K*/44, 47). Cassandra is suddenly struck by the idea that she is "secretly" engaged in telling the story of her fear or rather, she corrects herself, of the "setting free" of her fear. Since fear can be set free, she thinks, it must therefore be connected "to everything and everyone who is oppressed." From then on, hers is a story of repression, a repression that forces a split between Cassandra the king's daughter and Cassandra the madwoman: "The king's daughter is not afraid, for fear is weakness and weakness can be amended by iron discipline. The madwoman is afraid, she is mad with fear" (*C*/35; *K*/42).

An early tableau captures the place of the king's daughter in minute detail. Reminding herself of her determination to remember even the things she would rather repress, Cassandra recalls the following scene:

I will not forget my confused, wayward father. But neither will I forget the father I loved more than anyone else when I was a child. Who was not too particular about reality. Who could live in fantasy worlds. . . . This made him less than the ideal king, but he was the husband of the ideal queen. . . . Night after night he used to go in to my often-pregnant mother, who sat in her megaron, in her wooden armchair, which closely resembled a throne, where the king, smiling amiably, drew up a stool. This is the earliest picture I remember, for I, Father's favorite and interested in politics like none of my numerous siblings, was allowed to sit with them and listen to what they were saying; often seated in Priam's lap, my hand in the crook of his shoulder (the place I love best on Aeneas). (*C*/13; *K*/17)

This scene lays the groundwork for telling Cassandra's story as the daughter's disillusionment with the idealized father. With the most essential elements of the daughter's story in place, the Oedipal triangle is cast in relief: the daughter on her father's lap, listening to her parents. *Kassandra*'s family tableau accentuates the daughter's love and her status as the father's favorite child, as well as her father's presence in her love for Aeneas, thus lightly touching on Cassandra's Oedipal desire.

Like Irmtraud Morgner in *Leben und Abenteuer der Trobadora Beatriz,* like Brigitte Reimann in *Ankunft im Alltag* and *Franziska Linkerhand*— like so many other authors of her generation—Wolf thematizes the loss of the Stalinist father. She tells of the daughter's growing disillusionment as a series of confrontations with this father/king, whereby the gap between real and symbolic father continues to widen. In *Kassandra,* the father/king represents the social order, yet at the end a wide chasm gapes between body and function—the father no longer embodies the king: "And most ghastly of all was the figure of the king at the head of the procession, his decayed body draped in purple, being carried by four strong young men" (*C*/135;

K/157). This image from Cassandra's memory highlights a body no longer able to hold power: the king's two bodies, the material and the sublime, are badly out of joint. Troy's declining power throws a merciless light on the "father"; Cassandra recalls that the king "crumbled" as the city turned into a "grave" (*C*/100, 135; *K*/118, 157). She understands her break with the new Troy, a once peaceful culture now unrecognizably transformed by war into a fortress, as the "loss of everything I had called 'father' " (*C*/129; *K*/150). Cassandra's allegiance to Troy, indeed her identity as part of a collective "we," is mediated through her relationship to her father: "Vacillating and fragile and amorphous was the 'we' I used, went on using as long as I possibly could. It included my father, but did it any longer include me? Yet for me there was no Troy without King Priam my father" (*C*/94; *K*/110–11). The daughter's relationship to Troy was a relationship to Priam the father, not the mere "mask" of Priam the king (*C*/48; *K*/57). When the order is given requiring all Trojans to refer to him as "our mighty king," Cassandra recollects that she never called him anything but father, at most "King Priam" (*C*/65; *K*/77). And she remembers their arguments about politics in a decidedly familial and intimate language, thus stressing her experience of Troy's social relations as familial. The first disagreement between father and daughter ends in an embrace, the father addressing her as "child." But when she rises up against him in the council and demands an end to the war, the king/father expels her, severing the familial bond: "She is no longer my child" (*C*/76; *K*/89). Cassandra, now realizing that at the time she had not understood that she no longer wanted the same thing "they" did, continues: "So what freedom it brought me the first time I said no, no, I want something different" (*C*/70; *K*/83). The unfolding events, in particular the king's acceptance of Eumelos's security measures which transform the very nature of the Trojan community, push Cassandra into an increasingly ambivalent stance toward her father. The decisive "No" is finally spoken in her last confrontation with him, over his plan to use Polyxena, her sister, to trap Achilles in the Apollonian temple. Again, Priam rejects her address, "father," and has her imprisoned until the plan is executed since she refuses to keep silent. Cassandra recalls being unable to act otherwise: "My life, my voice, my body would produce no other answer" (*C*/131; *K*/152).

Cassandra's conflict with the "father" and his world leads finally to her arrival in Troy's counter-world, the feminine universe of Mount Ida. Aeneas carries Cassandra to Mount Ida after the women there kill Panthous to avenge Penthesilea's death. Here Cassandra recovers under the care of

Arisbe, one of Mount Ida's mother figures, and discovers a new identity, a space into whose silence her voice fits perfectly: "Then there was a silence into which my voice fitted; now it had found exactly the space intended for it" (*C*/123; *K*/143). Her new identity is linked to a new community. Listening to Arisbe, Cassandra recalls: "There at last I had my 'we' " (*C*/124; *K*/144). Furthermore, in Cassandra's memory, her arrival at Mount Ida creates a fleeting moment of intimacy between mother and daughter. Cassandra recalls dreaming about "new patterns, which could be unbelievably beautiful" and about taking on new forms of identity, creatures neither human nor animal (*C*/124; *K*/145). Awaking from her dream, the first person she encounters is Hecuba, and the first word she pronounces is "Mother" (ibid.). This dream, with its images of a new identity, counters an earlier passage:

If I grope my way back along the thread of my life, which is rolled up inside me— I skip over the war, a black block; slowly, longingly backtrack to the prewar years; the time as a priestess, a white block; farther back: the girl—here I am caught by the very word "girl," and caught all the more by her form. By the beautiful image. (*C*/21; *K*/26)

Cassandra calls this girl she once was an "ideal image," an "image of longing." Her memory conjures up a powerfully nostalgic picture of a "bright young figure in the clear landscape, gay, candid, hopeful, trusting herself and others," and above all, "free" (*C*/23; *K*/28). Encountering this ideal image of herself for the second time, her thoughts permit a small but highly significant detail to slip into her account: it is Hecuba, the mother, who works behind the scenes to ensure that Cassandra becomes Troy's priestess, that Hecuba has designated the staff and the fillet for her. Cassandra now knows that she was never free but, on the contrary, "steered, guided, and driven to a goal others set" (ibid.). Here, Cassandra evokes a young woman dutifully following the path of the daughter, an image compellingly representing a (lost) imaginary identification, her ego ideal as the point from which she appears likeable to herself—and likeable to the superego embodied in the mother. Cassandra's dream upon her arrival at Mount Ida replaces the lost image of the "beautiful girl," Cassandra's lost ego ideal, the young woman who lived under the illusion of being free— "like a bird." And in the context of this dream, the mother figure functions as another point of origin, representing not the Trojan mother but the maternal world of Mount Ida.

This brief summary of Cassandra's entry into an alternative maternal universe already points to the feature of Mount Ida that precludes any interpretation of the story as celebrating its feminine counter-world. In *Kassandra,* the feminine realm is silent. Not only does Cassandra's voice fit into this silence, but the dream's core image, which metaphorically captures Cassandra's "new" identity and seems to express an identification with the mother as part of the universe of Mount Ida, is silent too. Despite the opposition between Troy and Mount Ida which seems to sustain the protagonist's narrative, making it climax in Cassandra's change of allegiance, *Kassandra* is not centrally concerned with this rather banal story. That reading would in fact ignore Cassandra the narrator. The real conflict of this narrative is, as I argued earlier, located elsewhere. We shall nevertheless return to this dream image, this new identity, but to read it from a different angle. We can avoid being drawn any further into the story's ostensible logic of a conflict between the masculine warrior world and the feminine realm of peace by focusing on Cassandra's outbursts.

The conflict between daughter and father/king is played out in Cassandra's moments of "madness" involving both body and voice. Under the new conditions of war and Eumelos's strategy of "mental armament," the city is now subject to numerous "linguistic regulations," including one requiring Troy's citizens not to speak of war but of a "surprise attack" (*C*/63, 71; *K*/95, 84). Living in a "palace of silence," Cassandra becomes obsessed with gaining knowledge, an obsession she experiences as an "alien being" eating its way into her (*C*/47, 48; *K*/57, 58). Finally, she breaks the "ring of silence" with her "new" voice.

A Body, and a Voice, out of Control

Cassandra's "alien" voice erupts for the first time into the silence imposed on Calchas, the seer, who has chosen not to return to Troy. A member of the delegation of the "SECOND SHIP" (*C*/36; *K*/45), he is afraid he will be punished for having wrongly predicted that the mission would succeed. Cassandra remembers the sudden emergence of the voice as follows:

"Not only that," I heard myself tell Aeneas, "I myself knew from the start." The voice that said this was a stranger's voice, and of course today I know—I have known for a long time—that it was no accident that this strange voice which had stuck in my throat many times already in the past should speak out of me for the first time in Aeneas' presence. I set it free deliberately so that it would not tear me apart; I had no control over what happened next. "I knew it, I knew it": over and over in this alien, high-pitched, moaning voice from which I had to get away to safety; so that I had to cling to Aeneas, who was shocked but held his ground. Held his ground, oh, Aeneas. Tottering, limbs shaking. I clung to him; each of my fingers followed its own inclinations, gripped and tore at his clothing; my mouth, as it expelled the cry, also produced a foam that settled on my lips and chin; and my legs, which were as much out of my control as all my other limbs, jerked and danced with a disreputable, unseemly delight that I myself did not feel in the least. They were out of control, everything in me was out of control, I was uncontrollable. Four men could scarcely hold me. (*C*/38–39; *K*/46–47)

This scene is made up of several, densely articulated layers of meaning. In terms of the voice itself, Cassandra later links it to "experience," and thus to Wolf's "subjective authenticity." Immediately before this passage, Cassandra recalls having always known that Marpessa, her servant, spoke the truth—the truth that no one wants her to know: Calchas has defected to the Greeks. Repeating "I knew it," Cassandra's "strange" new voice thus breaks through the officially imposed silence. In this instance, voice clearly does not function as a mirror—neither as the acoustic mirror of the imaginary nor as the mirror of the superego voice. On the contrary, the "mirroring effect" [53] inherent in the phenomenon of voice leads Cassandra *not* to recognize herself in this other voice. But neither does Cassandra's "alien" voice mirror any of the voices of Troy's intersubjective social order.

Then there is the erotic side of this act—the convulsions of a body out of control and the disreputable delight which Cassandra cannot even feel. The distortion of some key signifiers from *Kassandra*'s epigraph signals the existence of this second layer, with *limbs shaking* referring to the Sappho poem: "Once again limb-loosing love shakes me, / bitter-sweet, untamable, a dusky animal." [54] The theme of eros is introduced in a dream that immediately precedes this passage. Cassandra remembers having this dream after she had watched Aeneas join the crowd in calling "Hesione or death!" as the "SECOND SHIP" left (*C*/36; *K*/43). Shocked by Aeneas's calling for his own father's death (Anchises, Aeneas's father, was a member of the delegation), Cassandra dreams of being sexually aroused by Aeneas's threatening her. It is but a small step from this masochistic dream, in which Aeneas is named as the father's successor, to another one that unveils Cassandra's "madness" as an Oedipal fantasy, a scenario of performing an act both desired and resisted.[55] This is the dream which Polyxena tells Cassandra against her horrified resistance:

While she was sleeping with Andron, she began to dream about King Priam. Seldom at first but always the same thing; then more often, in the end every night. It was more than she could bear. In her distress, she came back to me again, after all. Her father violated her in her dream, she said. She was weeping. . . . I believe I was trembling with indignation. (*C*/98; *K*/115)

The constellation formed by the novel's depiction of the sisters' relationship confirms this reading.[56]

Polyxena: The Other Woman

Cassandra keeps herself from thinking of Polyxena, memories of whom provoke evasion and digression. But eventually, Cassandra gives in: "Yes. Yes. Yes. Now I will have a talk with myself about Polyxena" (*C*/95; *K*/97). The reason for this avoidance, as Cassandra finally admits to herself, is guilt. She feels responsible for Polyxena's dreadful end, which she is able to remember only at the end of her own story. Living in mortal fear of the Greeks after her willing participation in the murder of Achilles, Polyxena goes mad. Although Cassandra and Hecuba try to protect her, she is dragged away by the Greeks, screaming, when they finally enter Troy. "Yes. That is how it was" (*C*/137; *K*/159), Cassandra says, concluding her brief, precise, and therefore all the more chilling testimony. The sources of Cassandra's guilt feelings emerge bit by bit: Polyxena wanted to become Troy's priestess, but had to cede to Cassandra, the king's favorite daughter; Cassandra thinks that Polyxena wanted this office in order to escape her own desires and that, prevented from becoming priestess, she chose to "punish those she loved by ruining herself" (*C*/109; *K*/128). Then, against Cassandra's and her mother's wishes, Polyxena agrees to participate in a bargain between Achilles and the Trojans: Achilles will betray the Greeks' battle plans in exchange for Polyxena. Cassandra remembers how Polyxena displayed herself to Achilles:

In the evening before sunset she stood on the wall wearing that new, remote smile, and looked down on Achilles. He stared. He was almost drooling. Then my sister Polyxena slowly bared her breast, while at the same time—still with that faraway gaze—she looked at us: her lover, her brother, her sister. I answered her look imploringly. (*C*/109; *K*/127)

Feeling responsible for her sister's "voluptuousness of self-destruction" (*C*/113; *K*/131), Cassandra recalls Polyxena as "the woman I could not be," who had "everything I lacked" (*C*/95; *K*/111–12). (Polyxena had lovers, while Cassandra remained alone.) Cassandra also recalls a conversation with Panthous, the Greek priest, who agreed to anoint her rather than Polyxena, reminding her that she owed her position exclusively to her father's love, but then conceding that her "aversion to the approaches of mortal men" (*C*/26; *K*/32) had predestined her to become Troy's seer. Cassandra's "aversion" even extends to Apollo, the god of the seers, whose desires she refuses to satisfy. In a dream, Cassandra's fear of uniting with him causes the god to furiously spit into her mouth, thus cursing her forever: no one will ever believe her prophecies.

In Cassandra's memory, Polyxena thus emerges as her alter ego insofar as she allows herself to be drawn into the brutality of a masculine society, its war and its desires. For it is Achilles, above all, the man to whom Polyxena offers herself, who is the "brute," killing their brother in a sexual frenzy:

In what role was his enemy approaching my brother? As a murderer? As a seducer? Could such a thing be—the voluptuousness of the murderer and the lover in one? Was that allowed to exist among human beings? The fixed gaze of the victim. The capering approach of the pursuer, whom I now saw from behind, a lewd beast. (*C*/74; *K*/87)

For Cassandra, Achilles represents "naked hideous male lust," but it is Polyxena who is deeply drawn into the warrior culture Achilles represents through her own sadomasochistic desires.[57] As Sonja Hilzinger observes, Polyxena exemplifies "deformed femininity." [58] But, as her dream of Aeneas shows, Cassandra's desires are not so different from Polyxena's; as she herself admits, "I could not help despising Polyxena because I did not want to despise myself" (*C*/97; *K*/114). What emerges, then, is a constellation in which Polyxena, acting out the desires that Cassandra denies, is the Oedipal daughter and, as such, is a deeply ambivalent figure. At the end, Polyxena actually does cross the boundary into insanity, acquiring an "alien" voice of her own: as the Greeks approached, Polyxena "screamed and sang" (*C*/137; *K*/159). She is brutally dragged away by the Greeks, while Hecuba is forced to watch Cassandra being raped by Aias. This scene makes Polyxena the ultimate victim of her own desires, whereas Cassandra, even though she "lives" her/Polyxena's rape fantasy, survives sane. That very constellation allows us to read Polyxena's incestuous dream into Cassandra's "madness," rendering it an instance of hysterical theater, an incestuous fantasy. We should not, however, accept the logic of denial implicit in this constellation, with its ambivalence toward feminine sexuality. Rather, the tremendous anxiety about sexuality deployed in this text can be more productively traced to the conflict at the core of the hysterical scene—the conflict between masculine and feminine identifications.

Hysteria and Multiple Identification

From a classically Freudian view, the "nucleus of hysteria" is the conversion of psychic conflict into bodily symptoms.[59] Freud also emphasized the reenactment of a repressed fantasy in hysteria: "a complex structure characterized by a particular mode of expressing repressed fantasies, these fantasies being essentially oedipal in content." The body is the "locus for a communication, which is potential, implicit, veiled and fixed." Emphasizing the communicative side of hysteria, Laplanche proposes that hysteria be understood as a "mise-en-scène" or fantasy scenario.[60] Also relevant to our context here is Freud's belated insight into the bisexuality of the hysterical scene; the conflicting desire for both father and mother, entailing both feminine and masculine identification, results in an inevitable unfaithfulness to one parent with the choice of the other as object.[61]

We have already encountered the latter aspect in the context of *Der geteilte Himmel,* with Kohon's notion of the "hysterical stage" as both a fantasy scenario *and* a developmental stage at which the subject becomes "fixed" or paralyzed by his/her inability to shift from the mother to the father as primary object. The hysterical scene, then, both enacts the conflict and seeks to resolve it. Another factor here is Žižek's imaginary versus symbolic identification, a problematic linked to the gaze to which the hysterical subject wants to appear likeable and with which she may identify on the symbolic level.

The way in which Cassandra remembers her outburst enacts what Žižek calls the hysteric's "excessive femininity": staging, *as Polyxena,* a feminine body performing "disreputable, unseemly lust"—a body in the thrall of desire. This desire is Oedipal, with Aeneas, the man whose clothing Cassandra's "uncontrollable" fingers tear at, standing in for the father. Cassandra's moment of madness stages an Oedipal fantasy—the hysterical enactment of Polyxena's dream (the daughter's seduction) in the arms of Aeneas, the father's substitute.

Once More: Another Body, Another Voice

The most basic story which this first scene tells us through the mediation of Polyxena's dream is that of the daughter's desire for the father—accompanied by the eruption of an "alien" voice. Recalling this fantasy scenario as a loss of control, Cassandra observes that the voice's erupting in Aeneas's presence was no accident, given their sexual relationship—how their bodies had gone "mad" before. And she also reveals that she had never known until then "what a voice my throat had at its command" (*C*/88; *K*/104). Like this memory fragment, the hysterical outburst links feminine sexuality and voice in a scenario of immediacy, involving the father/Aeneas. In this mise en scène of hysteria, we can read a utopian moment in which body and voice are intimately connected—the *fantasy of the voice of the sexual body*. This utopia of immediacy briefly evades the threat that Wolf associates with the sexual body in all of her work: the body's determination by the fascist past. In offering herself as an object of desire to the father, Cassandra is Polyxena, the daughter who fantasizes taking the mother's place and identifies with the mother's desire. This identificatory process with the sister/the mother—with feminine sexuality—produces a spectacle of truly utopian dimensions. Its foundation lies in *Kindheitsmuster,* in Nelly's protest against the demands of fascist ideology on her body; there, the *chaste* feminine body represents the site of resistance. But the utopian moment of the sexual body and its voice is utopian precisely *because* it celebrates heterosexual desire and its authentic voice, even if this celebration is thickly laced with fear.

Cassandra's hysterical performance releases an overwhelming anxiety, for the voice that erupts unimpeded from the sexual body is a "voice of death" (*C*/60; *K*/71). This level of pain, even terror, is even more pronounced in her second outburst, during Menelaos's visit to Troy. Cassandra remembers it beginning as an inner vibration triggered by the trembling voice of Oinone behind the "hoarse, piercing voice of Eumelos" (*C*/58; *K*/69), a signal given by her body. When Paris demands Helena, Menelaos's wife, during the ceremonies honoring the guest, his demand is followed by absolute silence. Then Cassandra remembers:

But I, I alone saw. Or did I really "see"? What was it, then? I felt. Experienced—
yes, that's the word. For it was, it is, an experience when I "see," when I "saw."
Saw that the outcome of this hour was our destruction. Time stood still. I would
not wish that on anyone. And the cold of the grave. The ultimate estrangement from
myself and from everyone. That is how it seemed. Until finally the dreadful torment
took the form of a voice; forced its way out of me, through me, dismembering me as
it went; and set itself free. A whistling little voice, whistling at the end of its rope,
that makes my blood run cold and my hair stand on end. Which as it swells, grows
louder and more hideous, sets all my members to wriggling and rattling and hurl-
ing about. But the voice does not care. It floats above me, free, and shrieks, shrieks,
shrieks. "Woe," it shrieked. "Woe, woe. Do not let the ship depart!" (*C*/59; *K*/70)

Cassandra faints and is carried out of the hall. When she awakens, she refuses to eat, not wanting to nourish this "criminal body, where the voice
of death had its seat" (*C*/60; *K*/71). She retreats into "madness," which
she calls "black milk, bitter water, sour bread," to protect herself from
the "intolerable pain which these two would otherwise have inflicted on
me" (ibid.).

In order to understand the superimposition of several iconographic cultural images on this scene of fear and pain, we must explore these different
yet related affects: first the shadow cast by the fear of sexuality over the
entire narrative, then the pain. This exploration will show that Cassandra's
hysterical body constitutes an immensely powerful representation of the
body as memory, simultaneously embodying the past *and* a dramatic move
to escape its stranglehold.

Mount Ida's Symptomatic Structures

The anxiety deployed around the structural identification with the mother's
desire and its "product," the utopian voice of the sexual body, permeates
the entire narrative, even determining the depiction of Mount Ida. Representing a feminine alternative to Troy's sadomasochistic warrior fortress,
this world of women closely resembles the utopia of everyday life sketched
in the epilogue to *Der geteilte Himmel:*

Who would believe us, Marpessa, if we told them that in the middle of war we used
to meet regularly outside the fortress on paths known to no one but us initiates?
That we, far better informed than any other group in Troy, used to discuss the situa-

tion, confer about measures (and carry them out, too); but also to cook, eat, drink, laugh together, sing, play games, learn? (*C*/52; *K*/62)

The community revolves around the worship of Cybele, the ancient goddess who testifies to a matriarchal culture superseded by Troy, and its depiction is reminiscent of the maternally coded socialism in Wolf's earlier fiction. What this realm excludes is sexuality, an exclusion most obviously reflected in Anchises, a maternal father figure. He teaches Cassandra his way of seeing Troy, of making sense of Troy's official historiography and the transformations within the palace. For him, the utopia of Mount Ida acquires a Blochian quality: "Anchises, I believe, loved our life in the caves wholeheartedly, loved it without reservation, sadness, and scruple. He was fulfilling a dream of his and was teaching us younger ones how to dream with both feet on the ground" (*C*/135; *K*/156). Anchises gives the universe of Mount Ida its political and utopian meaning. When Cassandra formulates its philosophical underpinnings—the celebration of this third thing, "the smiling vital force," crushed between the sharp distinctions of Troy's male culture (*C*/106; *K*/125)—she uses the concept most intimately associated with Anchises: empathy. Anchises thus emerges as the advocate of a maternal philosophy, but he is also represented as being maternal himself. Cassandra longs for his comforting presence in the moments before her death: "Anchises. If only Anchises were here. If he were with me I could bear anything" (*C*/91; *K*/106). Remembering that he treated her like a "very dear and respected daughter" (*C*/92; *K*/108), she describes his main characteristics as "serenity" and "delicacy of feeling." This maternal father figure could be understood as the projection onto an idealized father figure of qualities lacking in the mother figures here. For Cassandra recalls her mother's lack of empathy and her own ambivalence early on: "Hecuba, my mother, knew me when I was young and ceased to concern herself with me. 'This child does not need me,' she said. I admired and hated her for it" (*C*/12; *K*/15). Yet in view of the tremendous fear surrounding sexuality, Anchises can be read as the perfect compromise solution to a deep ambivalence felt toward the mother and her sexuality. Paradoxically, Anchises, not being a woman, can better incarnate the maternal as separate from sexuality. In fact, he is the symptom of the maternal's separation from sexuality. The side of the mother involved in sexuality—her reproductive body, her desire for the father—is succinctly expressed in the tableau of the Trojan triangle: recalling her father sitting at her mother's feet, Cassandra characterizes the queen with a single formula: "often-pregnant" (*C*/13; *K*/17).

Yet sexuality is not entirely absent from Mount Ida. On the contrary, this is a universe split between potentially destructive sexuality and maternal emotions depicted (as is often the case in Wolf's work) in a way that verges on kitsch. For example, Cassandra recalls a "touch-fest" at Mount Ida, where we spontaneously touched each other and got acquainted" (*C*/133; *K*/154). As in *Kindheitsmuster,* the "chaste" feminine body can thus become a territory outside of the dominant order. But, ultimately, feminine sexuality is always threatened by "contagion": Mount Ida is also the realm of Sapphian abandon, of "limb-loosing Eros." To honor the goddess Cybele, the women dance, as Cassandra vividly recalls:

Marpessa slid into the circle, which did not even notice my arrival—a new and actually painful experience for me. They gradually increased their tempo, intensified their rhythm, moved faster, more demandingly, more turbulently; hurled individual dancers out of the circle, among them Marpessa, my reserved Marpessa!; drove them to gestures which offended my modesty; until, beside themselves, they shook, went into howling contortions, sank into an ecstasy in which they saw things invisible to the rest of us, and finally one after another sagged and collapsed in exhaustion. (*C*/19–20; *K*/24–25)

And this sexual frenzy eventually turns into murderous lust in the killing of Panthous by a mob of women out of control, seeking revenge for Penthesilea's death at the hands of Achilles.

The utopia of the sexual body and its voice, associated with the Oedipal daughter and thus with the mother whose place she desires to usurp, therefore leads from the opposition Polyxena/Cassandra to the split realm of Mount Ida—dangerously sexual and maternally nonsexual. These structures are the products of fear. What then are the products of pain, or rather with what is pain associated?

The Body in Pain: Hysteria as Identification with the Symbolic Father

On the level of incestuous fantasy, Cassandra's mise en scène involves the "real" father, but there is also an identificatory process involving the symbolic father. To begin with, a string of masculine identifications runs through Cassandra's tale.[62] King Priam himself sketches his favorite daughter's fantasy of assuming his place on the throne "dressed in his clothes"

(*C*/44; *K*/52). Furthermore, just as Cassandra's femininity is defined by her sister Polyxena, she fantasizes her masculinity with respect to her twin brother, Helenos:

Oh Helenus, identical in appearance, different in kind. The image of me—if I had been a man. If only I were! I thought in despair when they made you the oracle—not me! not me! . . . If only I were he. If only I could exchange my sex for his. If only I could deny it. Yes, really, that is how I felt. (*C*/28–29; *K*/35)

Like Rita in *Der geteilte Himmel,* Cassandra's masculine identification is a symbolic identification since, in its focus on both brother and father, it involves their positions within the symbolic order, their symbolic mandates: to be Troy's king and Troy's highest priest, the "oracle" (ibid.).

But this is not exactly what I mean by Cassandra's masculine identification; rather, these images are aftereffects of the one involved in Cassandra's fantasy scenarios. In order to better grasp this image, we have to explore the difference between the first and second scenes: the scene caused by the silence surrounding Calchas, and the scene causing the silence during Menelaos's visit. In the latter, Cassandra's voice tears her apart. Obviously, unlike the first scene, this second outburst foregrounds not pleasure but pain, inflicted by a voice that tortures her limbs instead of making them dance. In this image of *the body in pain,* we reencounter the iconic image of Gotsche's antifascist hero in *Die Fahne von Kriwoj Rog*—the body of Brosowski:

They turned Brosowski like a spindle around himself, so that his joints cracked and blood spilled from his mouth. He remained silent. Did he weaken once? —No. He could say that with a good conscience. His body might fail, his arms, legs, hearing—*he* did not fail.

He was hanging like a ball of tangled ropes on the wall, he moaned, drawn-out and dangling from the window frame, his dislocated joints swollen and red, *he no longer possessed a body.*

What remained of it was the Communist Brosowski. Ribs, bones, sinews—they no longer belonged to him. They could take it and trample it, they could burn it and break it and hang it. Only the brain was still there, and the thoughts—they belonged to the Communist Brosowski. And he remained silent. (*DF*/369–70; my emphasis)

In her painful spectacle, Cassandra enacts the identification with the antifascist father, an identification not with any particular father figure, but with a symbolic father who presents himself in the image of the antifascist resistance fighter. This is the moment when the lost father whom Cassandra mourns is restored by an act of identification.

To insert the image of the antifascist father into Cassandra's madness is not farfetched; it is not only justified by our knowledge of Wolf's previous works—and by our recognition of a central cultural icon—but *Kassandra* itself signals this historical inscription through a striking textual allusion, namely, to Celan's metaphor in Cassandra's description of her madness after her second outburst as "black milk." This allusion cannot be anything but deliberate.[63] But the master image of the antifascist hero has radically changed; it has acquired a heavy patina, overlapping layers of meaning specific to Wolf's work and the problematic that informs it.[64] *Now* it is the voice that tortures the body. How does Wolf rewrite East Germany's founding image in *Kassandra?* The hysterical scene, with its utopian spectacle of an authentic voice bursting forth from a sexual body, is a radical reworking of the original antifascist fantasy—but a reworking that preserves the fantasy's essential dimensions. First, while Gotsche's novel represses the libidinal dimension of the icon—its feminine masochism tied to the negative Oedipal complex—Wolf's foregrounds the Oedipal foundation of East Germany's antifascist narrative by sexualizing the image, by bringing its sexual dimension to the surface. The transformation of the original image then proceeds along the lines of the body/mind dichotomy which underpins the sublime Communist body. That is, the fantasy of a body divided into its transcendent part, which incorporates the Laws of History and binds the Communist to his historical mission, and its material support, symbolized by sexuality. Second, whereas Gotsche imagines the Communist hero as mind, not body, Wolf imagines the reverse with her utopian link between sexual body and voice. While the antifascist hero remains silent, able to control his voice because he has overcome his body, Cassandra's voice breaks out of an ecstatic sexual moment. But she speaks with a voice that tortures the body.[65] Reading *Kassandra* in terms of hysteria renders Cassandra's "madness" a conflict between masculine and feminine identifications—between Cassandra/Polyxena, the Oedipal daughter, and Cassandra/the antifascist hero and son. Her outburst is a moment of "hysterical resistance," the "effect and testimony of a failed interpellation into the symbolic order," [66] produced by *a conflictual identification* with both *the maternal,* as Oedipal daughter, and *the paternal,* as antifascist hero.

Resistance to what? First, on an individual level, resistance to her interpellation as daughter. But Cassandra's hysterical theater represents an exceedingly complex articulation with several layers of meaning. Wolf reads and stages East Germany's Oedipal drama of antifascism around its founding icon, the antifascist body in pain, but Cassandra's hysterical act establishes numerous links between the individual and social levels of this reading. The association of *sexual body* and *voice of experience* constitutes an act of resistance by the Oedipal daughter to that other icon of the antifascist fantasy, the daughter who represents the post-fascist body and its "purified" voice. Yet it is crucially important to recognize that the utopian image of a sexual body linked to an authentic voice does *not cancel* the image of the antifascist hero *as a layer of identification.* On the contrary, this identification persists for the very reason that the utopia of another body/another voice can only be deployed safely *against the backdrop* of the identification with the antifascist father. If we keep in mind the exact articulation of the different images in these scenes, Cassandra's *alien, torturing frightened voice* can be understood as the *symptom* of these articulations, a "malfunctioning" produced by the clash of the icon of antifascism—the silent hero with the sublime body—and the Oedipal daughter's sexual body—a body-out-of-control, and a voice-out-of-control.

From this vantage point, Cassandra's moments of "madness" become understandable as explosions of meaning around that particular element which all of Wolf's works make dangerous and threatening—the sexual body as the part of subjectivity linked to the National Socialist past. But does Cassandra's hysteria truly enact a moment of resistance? I called the free association of the sexual body with the voice of experience a utopian moment. And yet the hysterical daughter written into the antifascist narrative and its utopian fantasy—a "pure" connection of sexual body and voice—expresses the same longing for purity that characterizes Wolf's entire oeuvre and its imaginary, centered on the body and its voice. The utopian moment in *Kassandra* longs for expression outside of history, where neither the sexual body nor its voice are within ideology.

Who Is Speaking?

In shifting the focus of analysis from Cassandra as *character* to Cassandra as *speaker* we move from the subject of the enunciated (statement) to the subject of enunciation. What characterizes Cassandra the speaker is the suppression of feeling in order to achieve one ultimate end: "I will continue a witness even if there is no longer a single human being left to demand my testimony" (*C*/22; *K*/27). Early in her reflections, touched by "mortal fear," Cassandra thinks: "What will it be like? Will I be overcome by weakness? Will my body take control of my thinking? Will the mortal fear . . . successfully sweep away even the resolution I sought and formulated on the way here: that I will not lose consciousness until the end?" (*C*/21; *K*/26–27). She then wonders whether this resolve to remain conscious in order to bear witness does not signify an even greater "malady": "that I, divided inside myself, observe myself" (*C*/22; *K*/28). Speaking in a controlled manner up to this point, Cassandra now begins to use language marked by her mounting terror:

Will I split myself in two until the end before the ax splits me, for the sake of consciousness? In order not to writhe with fear, not to bellow like an animal — and who should know better than I how animals bellow when they are sacrificed! Will I, until the end, until that ax — Will I still, when my head, my neck is already — Will I — ? (*C*/22; *K*/28)

What is involved in this act and this skill which she has practiced her entire life: "to conquer my feelings by thought" (*C*/8; *K*/11)? In the past it was love she had to conquer; now it is fear. But what Cassandra ultimately chooses is the final, definitive separation from her body in death.

What characterizes the position from which Cassandra speaks is, first and last, her separation from Aeneas. The man she loves is the leader of a group which leaves Troy in order to survive its demise and to found a new Troy "somewhere else." Cassandra refuses to accompany him, and, on the last page of the novel, explains why: "You had to snatch a few hundred people from death. You were their leader. Soon, very soon, you will have to become a hero. . . . I cannot love a hero. I do not want to see you transformed into a statue" (*C*/138; *K*/160). Her entire account is addressed to him, and their separation is one more step in the desexualization of their relationship. In a sober, determined tone, Cassandra recalls at the beginning of her narrative their final separation: "Aeneas and I did not touch each other anymore" (*C*/6; *K*/8). Their love has been destroyed: "He touched me. Nothing stirred. I wept. Aeneas wept. They had finished us" (*C*/115; *K*/135). Cassandra as *subject of enunciation* again speaks from the position of *the sublime post-fascist body,* the body bound to a higher mission, "purified" of its materiality. But even that body is ultimately overcome in death. Cassandra's higher mission is the testimony she considers her duty.

As we have seen, Wolf herself calls this subject position the "steeled" and "armored" subject in her lectures. Comparing this position to the autonomous subject Wolf criticizes in those lectures, Weigel argues that the latter reemerges from the superimposition of one story line upon another, the psychologizing narrative of Cassandra's process of becoming autonomous from the court overlaid upon the project of historicizing myth. The first story line, Weigel argues, is the effect of the author's identification with her character: "Christa Wolf *is* Cassandra." [67] What ultimately results from the double approach to the myth of Cassandra—a historicizing one and a psychologizing one—is both a metanarrative of the dialectic of enlightenment and a contemporary problematic: Cassandra's (and Wolf's) struggle against fixed patterns of perception and expression—in short, the problematic of a discourse distinct from the "official" one. What are the precise points along which this identification proceeds? Weigel draws attention to the beginning of the lectures, where Wolf describes her first encounter with the Cassandra material in passages such as the following, with its double mirroring, both specular and auditory:

Cassandra. I saw her at once. She, the captive, took me captive; herself made an object by others, she took possession of me. Later I would ask when, where, and by whom the pacts were joined that made this magic. It worked at once. I believed every word she said. (*C*/144–45; *V*/10)

In Wolf's readings here (as so often in her writing), the identification thus works through her "voice" and through a particular *existential problematic* similar to her own situation after 1979. Wolf understands Cassandra's death as a decision resulting from the "collapse of all her alternatives" (*C*/150; *V*/15) and characterizes her condition as one in which everything that linked her to Troy has vanished, while no threads have yet been woven into a new net. Moreover, in Wolf's story about her, Cassandra loses her homeland "because the Troy she wanted to save did not exist" (*C*/162; *V*26). Ultimately, it is due to her sense of Cassandra's increasing independence from Troy and what it represents, her "struggle for autonomy," that Wolf identifies most deeply with this woman in a "man's profession" (*C*/264, 153; *V*/118, 17): "So, is pain the point at which I assimilate her, a particular kind of pain, the pain of becoming a knowing subject [*Schmerz der Subjektwerdung*]?" (*C*/230; *V*/89).

In Wolf's lectures, a strong parallel emerges between Cassandra's bearing witness to the destruction of Troy and Wolf's own duty to bear witness to the threatened destruction of Europe. And with respect to this duty, an even stronger parallel is drawn between the heating up of the Cold War in the 1980s and the rise of National Socialism in the 1930s. In her third lecture, Wolf mentions conversations with friends about emigrating to Australia before the entire European continent was destroyed, a catastrophic scenario that leads her to say, "For the first time I think the line: Hitler has caught up with us" (C/251; V/107). Part of this lecture is devoted to listing all those things that will have made "us" collaborators in the annihilation, the "total finishing off of Europe," if the Cold War continues. Wolf names the habits that "enable me, enable us, to resist" (C/253; V/109).[68] The signifier of resistance, so highly charged in the German context, is taken up in a later passage in which Wolf draws a line of self-destruction from Troy to Dachau, ending with a question that reinforces the analogy between then and now: "Isn't it inevitable that a dearth of action such as that imposed on progressive forces over vast stretches of German history will lead to atrocities?" (C/258; V/114). In this role of a Cassandra who wants to prevent her society's destruction, Wolf fully identifies with her character: "At night the madness goes for my throat" (C/240; V/97).

That Wolf thus identifies with Cassandra, however, is no reason to identify Cassandra with her author. Instead, I understand Cassandra, the narrator of her story, as a variation on the writers Seghers discusses in her own lecture, "Vaterlandsliebe":

Think about the astonishing number of young German authors who dropped out after a few excessive [or inordinate] efforts . . . the very best: Hölderlin, who died insane, Georg Büchner, who died . . . in exile, Karoline Günderrode, who died by suicide, Kleist by suicide, Lenz and Bürger insane. Here in France that was the time of Stendhal, and later Balzac. These German authors wrote hymns celebrating their country, against whose social wall they banged their heads.[69]

Although the historical framework has changed, the basic premise has not: German reality—the restoration period that followed the upheavals caused by the French Revolution, the crackdown that followed Biermann's expulsion, the intensification of the Cold War, which could lead to another sort of holocaust—drives its intellectuals to their deaths. Cassandra, as the Oedipal daughter in an ideological narrative who chooses death, speaks from within Seghers's literary-historical framework, and from a *remembering* position developed on the basis of Seghers's work, Cassandra speaks in what Wolf called Seghers's *tone*. But the *stance* involved in this subjective authenticity, the ethico-political dimension, has changed: Cassandra is resigned—like

Günderrode, she decides to die. In her mimetic approach to her protagonist, Wolf situates herself again as a daughter vis-à-vis Seghers. But what allows her to finally speak in the first person, the "I" so anxiously avoided in her previous novels? Significant here is the equation between Cold War and National Socialism, East Germany and Troy: Cassandra's account is testimony to a catastrophe like that of the last war or, more precisely, like the Holocaust. In Western legal, philosophical, and epistemological terms, being a witness is formally defined as "first-hand seeing." And eyewitness testimony draws its power from the "uniqueness of the voice," the testifying power of the particular, distinctive voice of the witness.[70] In my view, the use of first-person narrative here is overdetermined, with Cassandra's going to her death a gesture of identification with the Jewish victim on her way to the "slaughterhouse" (*C*/4; *K*/5). This last aspect makes *Kassandra* the most densely layered literary text on the GDR legitimatory discourse—the discourse of antifascism.

The Harmonization of Voices: Übereinstimmung in *Kassandra*

Cassandra's speaking position differs significantly from the speaking position that Wolf ascribed to the early Seghers—a narrator speaking in the first person about an existential, a personal, *and* a political crisis, who was also, in Wolf's analysis, "reserved." While Seghers's first-person narrator was reluctant to engage in any "act of exposure," this cannot be said of Cassandra, the subject of the enunciated; the Cassandra of the hysterical theater is decidedly "unrestrained." This brings us to a question that is crucial for our understanding of the mise en scène: Who embodies the Other—the symbolic order—for the hysterical subject?[71] For whom does she act? To whose gaze does she want to appear likeable? Cassandra herself asks a similar question:

What is holding me back? Who is there left to see me? Do I, the unbeliever, still see myself as the focus of a god's gazes, as I did when a child, a girl, a priestess? Will that never pass?

Wherever I look or cast my thoughts, there is no god, no judgment, only myself. Who is it that makes my self-judgment so severe, into death and beyond? (*C*/22–23; *K*/28)

Another passage may shed some light on the problem: immediately before she recalls her first hysterical outburst, Cassandra thinks back to the time when she burst into tears as the second ship returned without Calchas and Hecuba had reprimanded her: "[The] rulers had to control themselves. I rebelled against my mother's rules. In retrospect I see she took me seriously. My father only looked to me for consolation" (*C*/37; *K*/45). Cassandra then tells us that she never again wept publicly. The superego, which Cassandra locates in relation to the Trojan mother, formulates a specific prohibition against the public display of emotions. During her attacks, Cassandra is "uncontrollable," her body vocally erupting in protest not only against the court's discursive regulations but also against the "mother's rules." But Cassandra tells her story under the gaze of the mother and according to her rules—to show restraint, not to expose herself. Those are the discursive rules that Wolf discovers in her construction of the author Anna Seghers, so *Kassandra* can thus be read as both in opposition to and in agreement/attunement (*Übereinstimmung*) with the author who functioned as a mother figure for Wolf. Moreover, *Kassandra,* together with *Der geteilte Himmel,* suggests that Seghers also embodied for Wolf the socio-symbolic order of the GDR, its discursive "regulations." Wolf's "feminist" novel, currently held by many critics to be the "farthest from Moscow,"[72] is thus actually mired in the GDR's defining discourse of the paternal family, its fantasies about the body, and that body's voice.

Surely, we need to know more about the mechanisms involved in these operations. From the analysis of the hysterical scene as a clash of two identifications—Oedipal daughter and antifascist hero—we can deduce the following: Wolf has inverted the Law under which the antifascist hero operates (not to speak, to remain silent) into a mandate to speak the truth. But she does so on the basis of the same image: the National Socialist victim as a body-in-pain. And while the antifascist hero's obedience to the Law rested on the splitting of mind from body, on a sublime body that overcomes the weakness of its mere material support, Cassandra/Polyxena's obedience to the imperative to speak the truth requires her sexual body. From this perspective, Cassandra the narrator becomes *a compromise formation:* the daughter's "reserved" voice in a post-fascist body-in-control, a body soon to be overcome. *Kassandra* thus relies on a construction which equates *masculine* identification with *silence, feminine* identification with *voice.* Furthermore, *voice* itself is connected, relative to the subject of both the enunciated and the enunciation, with the *mother:* relative to the former through the daughter's identification with the mother's desire—and the voice of that desire, which erupts from the Oedipal body; relative to the latter through voice's connection to Seghers, the author who occupies the position of mother figure. We thus again encounter the *zone of voice,* this quite undefined area spread across the realms of the imaginary and the symbolic. Voice at once touches upon the imaginary synthesis with the pre-Oedipal mother, her body, and the subject's own body. It reaches into a stage during which no clear difference exists between the subject and the other; yet voice also acts a first mirror, establishing in the mimesis of voices the first contours of a bodily ego; and finally, voice is also connected to the symbolic, the realm of the superego, of a separate identity—under the gaze of the Other.

Inscribing the Daughter in the Paternal Narrative
of Antifascism

In a 1992 work, Wolf created yet another image of the sublime body. "Nagelprobe" (Nail Test) ends with the following poem:

Principle Hope
Nailed
to the cross past

Every movement
drives
the nails
into the flesh.[73]

This stream-of-consciousness narrative again interweaves the speaker's individual history with her country's past. The narrator's meditation opens with a dream (told to "someone whom I do not know yet") about standing in a lecture hall with nail-studded walls that slowly close in on her. It thus alludes thematically and structurally to a public speech, yet quickly veers into an inner monologue or imagined dialogue. The narrator's voice may be silent or she may be speaking aloud; she does speak in the first person, either to herself or to someone else. And her meditation proceeds along two parallel tracks: "the child thinks, I am remembering" (N/161). While "Nagelprobe" revolves obsessively around the central themes of Wolf's work—guilt, pleasure, and pain—what it casts in relief is the Christian subtext of the antifascist discourse and its fantasies. It does so with a critical impetus, but what it demonstrates once again is the extent to which the speaker is entangled with the imaginary world of antifascism—and her own, very individual fantasies constructed within that world. For here again we encounter the image of the tortured, interrogated body, as the speaker moves from the auditorium to the world of fairy tales to the world of the Inquisition. She tells us about an iron contraption that penetrates someone with "nail-sharp spikes" as its lid is being closed. The narrator dwells on the moment when these spikes pierce "soft, twitching flesh" and the tortured victim is finally "willing to confess or testify," declaring himself guilty (N/156). The victim becomes a writer with the invocation of Karoline (von Günderrode), whose works the narrator is currently reading. She connects Günderrode and the writer in the auditorium by referring to the Romantic author as privileged, in having been able to select her own method of death.

The fragments of the narrator's individual history, a series of precisely circumscribed scenes centered on mother and child, culminate in an apocalyptic image inspired by Cranach's *Melancholia*. The undertones of this image encourage us to read it as a commentary on the GDR's demise: then a group of hunters "descends upon us already, with spikes and sticks, and we hear the hunting call urging them on, and the warm breath strikes the back of our neck, and when we look back into their faces we are frightened by our own likeness" (N/168). "Nagelprobe" acquires a certain coherence by sliding from one mother/daughter image to another. The bridge between Günderrode and the first scene is the first line of a song the narrator remembers: "S/t/u/d/d/e/d/with/nails." She calls this song, which her mother used to sing to her, the "regular evening threat" (N/157). Her mother's song leads her back to an image in which the nexus of disobedience, guilt, fear— the nexus of body and voice—is captured as "pleasure in pain": "Covered with roses, studded with nails, my mother is singing, I am remembering, a child in her bed covered with numerous tiny nails, a child in her bed larded with nails so to speak, tomorrow morning, if God is willing, threatens my singing mother" (N/160). Tortured by the thought that God might not be willing to wake up a child who offends him every day with her "misdemeanors," the child/narrator imagines herself in her coffin, "stiff and rigid and dead" (ibid).

From here, the narrative leaps to a wooden sculpture from the Congo which is covered, front to back, with nails, its mouth open in a silent scream. Shifting from this "fetish" to the Isenheimer Altar, the narrative moves from the topic of "acts of pain and sacrifice" (N/164) back to the girl, whose idea of expiation is to sleep with a nail under the covers. But, as the narrator tells us with some irony, this attempt at atonement failed due to the "weakness of the flesh" (N/165): in the morning, the nail is lying on the floor. From the child's failed effort to expiate her sins, after many digressions, the narrator's thoughts move to Cranach's *Melancholia*. Focusing first on the picture's main figure, a very young girl, the narrator notices that she is doing something rather surprising: sharpening the end of a stick. Her gaze then shifts to the upper left corner of the painting and its representation of the Apocalypse, fixing on the female figures: two naked old women, followed by a girl whom she interprets as the other side of the young Melancholia. This girl is "stark naked," and "devilishly" resembles Melancholia, who, although demure, wears a red dress and is busy sharpening her little rod, albeit "innocently" (N/166). The narrator comments immediately on this division into good and bad: "All our good behavior and wanting-to-remain-innocent is in vain, isn't it, the dark bold militia is coming across the country, possibly in our guise" (N/167–68).

These "scenes and nightmares" produce a meaningful articulation of individual and political history, a form of totalizing knowledge which provides the narrator with a sense of coherence. It is this knowledge that permits a particular speaking position, the split unity of the narrator's mnemonic "I" paired with the voice of the child or the mother: "the child is thinking, I am remembering" (N/161); "my mother is singing, I am remembering" (N/160). This split voice is contained by that of a narrating subject, who, although groping for a mode of expression, nevertheless speaks in the first person: "I was sitting in a room, I am thinking, or I am telling" (N/156). The interest of this piece does not lie in its thematics; as we have seen, writing the subject's personal history into the country's history from the vantage point of the past has been accomplished in far more complex ways, conscious and unconscious, in Wolf's previous literary texts. What is crucial is the fact that the link between past and present, which the narrator establishes through her stream-of-consciousness, leads once more to an embodiment of the socialist project through the iconography of antifascism. Wolf's closing gesture powerfully indicates that the discourse of antifascism represents the vantage point from which meaning is possible, from which totalizing knowledge can be translated into "I."

In discussing Wolf's particular speaking position, subjective authenticity in chapter 4, I emphasized that my goal has not been to uncover *Wolf's voice*. On the contrary, my assumption is that there is no such single, unified voice—and that there never will be such a voice. What I have traced is that speaking position, that peculiar narrative mode, which combines a specific structure (a narrator remembering the story of a protagonist), a specific story (of an existential and political crisis), a specific set of narrative voices, and, finally, a specific ethico-political dimension. It is a particular relationship among those elements that enables the narrator of *Kassandra* to say "I." Disentangling the elements of a speaking position which aims to blur the boundaries among author, narrator, and character has uncovered a crucial overdetermination of this possibility of saying "I" (as Cassandra says, "To speak in my own voice, the ultimate"): the overdetermination of Cassandra's (the narrator's) voice based in a post-fascist body and on an identification with the victims of the Holocaust. *Kassandra* has taken the logic of the fantasy of the post-fascist body and its post-fascist voice to the extreme: for a post-fascist voice to be possible, that body has to die. And like Brosowski, Cassandra is finally silent. What Cassandra enacts is the Law of the (antifascist) Father, the *identification unto death* analyzed in chapter I. I thus understand Wolf's "feminist" novel, with its purportedly "feminine" voice, as profoundly enmeshed in the GDR's legitimatory discourse of antifascism in all its key dimensions: the identification with the father as antifascist son, the sublime body, and its pure voice.[74] *Kassandra* remains obsessively caught in its post-fascist fantasies of purity.

This reading then sheds an entirely new light on Wolf's own self-description, for instance, in her 1993 interview with Günter Gaus:

In my case, things always developed through crises, often existential crises. . . . I always went through crises realizing, I absolutely do not want this, and through that I also realized what I really wanted. . . . My life does not proceed in a regular manner, is not taking a regular course. There are very clear breaks where I can say "before" and "after." And every time "after" I had come to myself a little more, and I have been able to show that in my books.[75]

This teleological model of an incremental series of sudden shifts away from the GDR's dominant ideology — "my inner liberation," Wolf called it in 1990 — sustains most of the criticism on Wolf.[76] One recent example is a reading of Wolf's work as a form of romantic anticapitalism by Robert Sayre and Michael Löwy, according to whom Wolf's cultural critique is inspired by premodern values and reinterpreted in feminist terms. It equates the alienating forms of modern scientific and technical rationality with patriarchy and its hierarchy of values. They trace Wolf's *Zivilisationskritik* (cultural critique) and its "Marxist/feminist utopia" through her work, from

Moskauer Novelle to *Was bleibt.* Sayre and Löwy certainly capture an important dimension of Wolf's work, one of her voices, but their teleological reading of her as slowly but steadily articulating a genuine alternative discourse, "indissolubly feminist and Romantic," and their reduction of Wolf's entire oeuvre to this particular discourse, is as problematic as the thesis they set out to criticize.[77] Moreover, they argue that Wolf's feminist approach is an integral part of her Marxist—or rather, Frankfurt school—critique of modernity, not a "qualitatively new and autonomous" departure from Marxism.[78] Thus, rather than tracing Wolf's path from Marxism to feminism, Sayre and Löwy trace Wolf's *Marxist feminism* back to her earliest work. There is no doubt that this feminist Zivilisationskritik runs through *Kassandra* and the lectures, but the literary text is ultimately marked by post-fascist fantasies of purity.[79] It is also beyond doubt that Wolf's political thought evolved from orthodox Marxism to a form of Western Marxism inspired by Ernst Bloch and the early Lukács before embracing the feminist critique of modernity outlined by Sayre and Löwy. But by concentrating on the development of her *political thought,* Wolf's critics miss another crucial dimension of her work: its imbrication *on the level of fantasy* in the discourse of antifascism. In fact, Sayre and Löwy are not that different from the feminist scholars they criticize, for they too assert a teleological development away from the official ideology and a unified, oppositional voice. The question that we as (feminist) critics have to ask ourselves is what we are looking for when we posit a voice that finally frees itself. Do we not want this voice to act as an acoustic mirror, that is, to reflect our own voice, which we assume to be expressing the truth? But the critique of ideology must resist this desire for a mirror if it is to understand the conditions that produce such a voice. For feminism especially, self-reflective criticism means *not* ignoring what Wolf's narratives "know"—their author and her critics notwithstanding: feminine subjectivity does not exist outside of the structures of the symbolic—"you can't change the way the unconscious works." [80]

Wolf did indeed write a novel saturated with romantic rhetoric on the artist as an outsider to the ever-increasing division of labor in modern societies. What distinguishes this work from *Kassandra* is its radically destabilized speaking position. As I argued at the beginning of this chapter, the peace movement of the 1980s offered Wolf a way out of an existential crisis, another occasion to occupy the role of *preceptor nationis.* The novel written in direct response to that crisis, *Kein Ort. Nirgends* (No Place on Earth), represents the most radical exploration of voice in Wolf's work. In

Kein Ort. Nirgends, unlike *Kassandra,* there is no possibility of saying "I," no identity centered in a "new" antifascist stance, no identity centered in *a pure body.* Imagining a meeting between Heinrich von Kleist and Karoline von Günderrode, the novel opens with a passage which, thematizing voice and the possibility of speaking in an existential crisis, radically undermines any coherent speaking position.[81] Here, we do not know who is speaking because the voices of the narrator, of Kleist, and of Günderrode overlap. Voice in *Kein Ort. Nirgends* traverses a different register and emerges through a mimetic interaction with various voices, including the "voice" of Ingeborg Bachmann.

Thus there are many voices rather than *a voice* in the work of Christa Wolf. In this chapter and the preceding one, I have traced the voice that emerged from Wolf's engagement with antifascism. But in the process, I hope to have shown that Wolf's work demonstrates voice's entanglement in layers upon layers of history: in short, voice and body—that is, identity—do not exist outside of the subject's history. And this entanglement results from, among other things, a constant slippage between different vocal registers—voices that serve as points of identification. While this insight may be rather banal, what makes Wolf's work so compelling, often despite her own stated beliefs and intentions, is the sheer complexity of these entanglements *and* the highly idiosyncratic connection made between antifascism's fantasies about the sublime Communist body and its voice. As I showed in chapter 3, the metaphor of the post-fascist body is not unique to Wolf's work. Her specific contribution, starting with *Moskauer Novelle,* has been her exploration of the post-fascist body's voice, an exploration which has significant repercussions on the process of narration itself. Ultimately, in Wolf's novels voice becomes the symptom of the body's relationship to the past, often developing into a "malfunctioning" of the vocal apparatus within a specific system of discursive regulations. As a symptom, voice reorganizes the conventions of this aesthetic system through "subjective authenticity"; *the symptom voice* introduces the narrator and her body into the regulatory system of (socialist) realism, but as a symptom, it also remains part of that system.

Our memory repeats to us what we haven't understood. Repetition is addressed to incomprehension. — Paul Valéry, "Commentaires de Charmes"

We have come to recognize that our present will inevitably have an impact on what and how we remember. It is important to understand that process, not to regret it in the mistaken belief that some ultimately pure, complete, and transcendent memory is possible. — Andreas Huyssen, *Twilight Memories* (1995)

History as Trauma

Sometime during the night of November 9, 1989, at a moment which cannot be pinpointed with any accuracy, the Berlin Wall collapsed, and the East German state began to wither away. Sudden and unexpected, yet steady and inexorable, this implosion was completed on October 3, 1990. Now, several years after the "event," political observers and cultural critics are discovering an unsettling phenomenon: the rise of nostalgia for the German Democratic Republic, or *Ostalgie*. Symptoms of Ostalgie were observed earlier among former East Germans: a longing for a system that had guaranteed a basic level of social security,[1] endless, yet understandable complaints about the radical transformation of the most mundane aspects of everyday life. But now the phenomenon has materialized in shops with names like "Back to the Future," which sell goods made exclusively in the territory of the former GDR and packaged just as they were before 1989; bestselling reprints of socialist realist classics long considered "cultural corpses" and reissued recordings by East German rock bands;[2] regular meetings of Trabi owners; exhibits about life in the GDR with everything from the socialist realist art of High Stalinism to the furniture in Honecker's office. These exhibitions and their representation of the GDR range from "real existing *Horrorkabinett*" to ironic display of a form of everyday life that suddenly disappeared. One recent exhibit was entitled "Rarities, Kitsch, and Curiosities from the GDR." [3]

According to Michael Rutschky, we are witnessing the coming-into-being of an *imaginary* GDR.[4] What seems to be reflected in this phenomenon is the experience of a still barely known and uncertain present, of rapid, massive change in all realms of life, and of a turn toward a past whose meaning has been equally disrupted, as evinced by the title of the exhibit on GDR curiosa: "There's No Time Left to Bid Farewell." Barbara Köhler, an East German author, has formulated this loss of the past as "the country's contours" vanishing "in the rearview mirror": "Before us a plain, the past, which is our past. DO YOU KNOW THE COUNTRY WHERE—where did we live. Did we live." [5]

To understand the aftereffects of this tremendous change, and the transformation itself, it is apparently necessary to first recreate the past. History, so it seems, is once again trauma. What I mean by *history as trauma* is the need to comprehend what has happened as the result of a specific structure of experience in which an overwhelming event has not been assimilated or fully experienced at the time of its occurrence but only belatedly, as it repeatedly "possesses" those who lived through it. Trauma, as we recall, is characterized by a "delay or incompletion in knowing." History as trauma means that those who have lived through momentous changes "carry an impossible history within them," a history which they cannot assimilate.[6] It is as if an unassimilable historical moment, in this case the recent past of the GDR's dissolution, is now approached from the vantage point of the not-so-recent past because that past, although it too has lost its contours, is still more familiar than the present.

There is an alternative reading of 1989 as an experience of "sublime enthusiasm" about a unique moment of openness—the brief moment in which the symbolic order itself collapsed. Writing in 1993 about the transformation of Eastern Europe as a whole, Slavoj Žižek observed:

The most sublime image that emerged in the political upheavals of the last years—and the term "sublime" is to be conceived here in the strictest Kantian sense—was undoubtedly the unique picture from the time of the violent overthrow of Ceausescu in Romania: the rebels waving the national flag with the red star, the Communist symbol, cut out, so that instead of the symbol standing for the organizing principle of the national life, there was nothing but a hole in its center. It is difficult to imagine a more salient index of the "open" character of a historical situation "in its becoming" . . . of that intermediate phase when the former Master-Signifier, although it has already lost the hegemonical power, has not yet been replaced by the new one. . . . [T]he masses who poured into the streets of Bucharest "experienced" the situation as "open," . . . they participated in the unique intermediate state of passage from one discourse (social link) to another, when, for a brief, passing moment, the hole in the big Other, the symbolic order, became visible.[7]

The events of the fall of 1989, especially the mass rallies in East Germany's major cities, certainly expressed this euphoria over the "hole" in the social-symbolic order. But these events also constituted an experience of trauma, if we understand trauma in this sense of being overwhelmed by an event that can only be understood belatedly. Nothing conveyed this striking inability to comprehend what was happening better than the word "nonsense," that terrifyingly meaningless utterance articulated over and over again as thousands of East Germans poured through the hastily opened breaches in the Berlin Wall during the night of November 9th.[8]

In certain respects, the historical moment of 1989 resembled the situation after 1945, when Germans experienced the utter destruction of Nazi Germany and its social disorganization as a loss of social structures and social identity: "We do not have a society anymore." [9] In one of the dominant genres of the immediate postwar years, journalism, this experience was captured in a series of metaphors, such as "vacuum," "waiting room," and "no-man's-land." [10] But in claiming that the experience of 1989 was, like that of the end of the Third Reich, traumatic, I am not equating the GDR and Nazi Germany along the lines of the totalitarianism theories of the 1950s; neither do I want to diminish the suffering of the Nazi regime's victims by comparing their traumatization to the decidedly less traumatic experiences of collaborators, perpetrators, and bystanders.[11] Rather, I am using "trauma" in its most abstract sense, without qualifying the sources, the extent, or the moral implications of the events which produce this particular effect of noncomprehension. Undoubtedly, the revelations about the criminal nature of the Nazi regime in 1945 produced a level of shock against which the post-1989 revelations pale in comparison. As Christa Wolf put it, "For me the postwar period was a shock, when I learned and had to accept as factual what *we* had done, we Germans. I was in a state of deep despair for months, even years, and I did not know how to continue living with this knowledge." [12] Such deep feelings of horror and guilt resulting from the traumatic collapse of the symbolic system of National Socialism and the discovery of its crimes were certainly not universal but confined to a small, influential minority. For the majority of Germans, who continued to believe in an eventual victory right up to the very end of the war, the experience of a transitional moment outside of history probably had very little of the euphoria described by Žižek.

There was, however, as we have seen, a certain enthusiasm on the part of the returning members of the KPD, who quickly set out to fill—and hegemonize—the "hole" left by the disappearance of National Socialism.[13] As in 1989, the attempt to construct a new national identity in the face of a situation that even the Communists experienced as traumatic—as the result of a defeat in the face of National Socialism—involved a turn toward the past. In this book, I have traced the enduring power of one of East Germany's master-signifiers, the antifascist hero constructed to "fill" this "hole." In its different incarnations—as a variation on the figure of Thälmann heroically fighting the Nazis or as Brosowski, the Communist under torture—the image of the antifascist father functioned as the most visible icon of the GDR's legitimatory discourse of antifascism. There is no question that this was the last of the founding Communist discourses to lose its hegemonic power. Thus, for instance, in the aforementioned petition "Für unser Land" (For Our Country) signed by Wolf and other leading East German intellectuals in the fall of 1989, the GDR's antifascist tradition was again invoked as a basis for a "socialist alternative to the Federal Republic": "We still have time to recover the antifascist and humanist ideals from which we once started." [14] This should not be too surprising since the Federal Republic's identity also rested on its opposition to Nazi Germany. Significantly, the continuing process of constructing German national identity after 1989 has come to rely more heavily on ceremonies to commemorate the Holocaust and on grandiose monuments to its victims.[15] Yet what my study has uncovered is both the enduring power and effectivity *and* the fundamental instability of this discourse and its central image, for in the GDR's foundational narratives, the place of the father ultimately remained empty. And the Red Flag, which in these narratives was passed from father to son/daughter and which stood metonymically for the Communist Party, proved to be a fetish, a signifier of defeat. In the second generation, the Red Flag bore the dark shadow of the swastika. The work of Wolf, the author who chose to explore this founding past through a focus on individual history, is characterized by the tensions surrounding the fantasies of purity that developed against the backdrop of this dark shadow.[16] Without an approach that combined traditional strategies of ideology critique with a psychoanalytic reading of the fantasies that operate within history, it would have been impossible to uncover the instabilities and blank spots in the founding discourse of the GDR's post-fascist hegemonic formation. And more importantly, it would have been impossible to detect the very depth of influence this founding discourse had on the post-fascist fantasies of a sizable and influential minority.

What this study of the production of ideology in the realm of literature

254

ultimately shows is that the notion of totalitarianism is misleading if we use it in the sense of an externally imposed system of thought beneath which we find an untouched identity ready to emerge as soon as that system collapses. The foundations of the East German socialist project had a strong moral appeal.[17] But most importantly, these foundational narratives were cast in a form which bridged the histories of subject and country. Antifascism is more than a political discourse of legitimation in these narratives; it is the presence of the past in the psyche of the post-fascist subject. And the body is the object around which unconscious fantasies about the past crystallize. As Žižek's writings on the sublime Communist body demonstrate, this ideological fantasy is not limited to the GDR. Being a Communist means having a Communist body, a body which is more than a material support (or, recalling Erik Neutsch, a body which harbors the Party inside). Yet in the context of East Germany's history, this shared fantasy took on a specific form: the material part of the Communist's transcendent body was fantasized as nonsexual. The post-fascist body was based on a dichotomy involving sexuality, not on an opposition between sickness and health.

As we saw in chapter I, the armored body of the antifascist fighter—this iconic figure incarnating the military vanguard and precariously occupying the place of the Stalinist father—was created in an effort to establish firm boundaries against feminine sexuality (representing castration, i.e., weakness). The emergence of the post-fascist body with the GDR's *Aufbau-generation* introduced that generation's own problematic: the sexual body, no longer a signifier of weakness, now signifies an "impure" past, with the dichotomy of strength versus weakness replaced by that of purity versus impurity. Modeled on the father's armored body, the nonsexual body of fantasy represents that generation's desire to break with its National Socialist past; yet it also reveals the deep fascination with the ideal of purity that characterized its Nazi upbringing. In the case of Christa Wolf, we uncovered an intricate network of fantasies woven around this notion of purity involving not only the post-fascist body but also its "pure" post-fascist voice. Enlisted as a method for reading unconscious fantasies, psychoanalysis helped to reconceptualize Wolf's notion of "authentic subjectivity." More broadly, it helped to highlight a specific level of historical continuity between the National Socialist past and the post-fascist present, a continuity on the level of the body and the fantasies formed around it. For the body is indeed more than a material support; it is the site of fantasies, of a whole fantasmatic history that is both social and individual.[18] And it is that specific power of ideology—to draw on those fantasies, to mobilize them for a political project—that was involved in the Communists' attempt to occupy the empty locus of power.

Notes

Unless otherwise stated, all translations from German and French in this volume are mine. TA at the end of a quote indicates that I modified an existing translation.

Critical Orthodoxies

1 Anton Ackermann, "Gibt es einen besonderen deutschen Weg zum Sozialismus?" *Einheit* 1 (1946): 22–32. Ackermann's theses were briefly advocated by the Socialist Unity Party in 1948; see Dietrich Staritz, "Ein 'besonderer deutscher Weg' zum Sozialismus?" in his *Was war: Historische Studien zu Geschichte und Politik der DDR* (Berlin: Metropol, 1994), 55–84. The Socialist Unity Party (SED) was founded in 1946, uniting the Social Democratic Party of Germany (SPD) and the Communist Party (KPD). This party conference is known as the *Einheitsparteitag* (unity conference). The most recent research reconfirms the tensions between voluntary unification and *Zwangsvereinigung* (forced unification) experienced by most founding members, both Social Democrats *and* Communists.

2 This was part of a widespread popular consensus that found expression even in the so-called Ahlener Programm of the new Christian Democratic Party, which advocated such measures as the nationalization of core industries; see Sigrid Meuschel, *Legitimation und Parteiherrschaft: Zum Paradox von Stabilität und Revolution in der DDR 1945–1989* (Frankfurt a.M.: Suhrkamp, 1992), 32ff.

3 See Wolfgang Fritz Haug, "The Surrender of the Fortress: Did the East German People Vote for the Restoration?" *Rethinking Marxism* 4 (1991): 26.

4 See, for instance, Robert Darnton's account of his euphoric investment in a third way in his *Berlin Journal 1989–1990* (New York and London: Norton, 1991), 15; cf. "Aufruf für eine eigenständige DDR" (November 26, 1989), in *"Wir sind das Volk"*, ed. Charles Schüddekopf (Reinbek: Rowohlt Taschenbuch Verlag,

1990), 240ff. A collection which foregrounds the hopes for an alternative German Democratic Republic is Dirk Philipsen, *We Were the People* (Durham: Duke University Press, 1993).

5   The protagonist of Irina Liebmann's autobiographical novel expresses this very feeling: "Out of here" (*Raus hier*) is the phrase she keeps repeating; *In Berlin* (Cologne: Kiepenheuer and Witsch, 1994), 27. The best-known case of the S E D's resistance to Gorbachev's reform politics was its suppression of the Soviet magazine *Sputnik;* see *Der Spiegel,* No. 48 (1988): 26ff. However, the late 1980s was also when oppositional groups started to form around the issues of disarmament and ecology, finding a semipublic sphere in the churches. The government reacted with what one might call repressive tolerance, that is, a mixture of surveillance and overt repression. For instance, the so-called Umweltbibliothek (a library collecting data on environmental pollution) was raided; dissidents were allowed to participate in the annual demonstration commemorating Rosa Luxemburg in January 1988, but then several participants were expelled from the country (among them the film director Freya Klier). See Mary Fulbrook, "The Growth of Political Activism," in her *Anatomy of a Dictatorship: Inside the GDR 1949-1989* (Oxford: Oxford University Press, 1995), 201-42. On the concept of the public sphere in the GDR, see David Bathrick, *The Powers of Speech* (Lincoln and London: University of Nebraska Press, 1996).

6   A few months earlier, Egon Krenz, a high-level functionary, had congratulated the Chinese government for Tiananmen Square.

7   And probably also because the leadership realized that, unlike in 1953, they would not have the support of the Soviet army.

8   Darnton's account of the "accidental" opening of the wall (*Berlin Journal,* 11-12) is still valid.

9   *Die Geschichte ist offen: DDR 1990—Hoffnung auf eine neue Republik,* ed. Michael Naumann (Reinbek bei Hamburg: Rowohlt Taschenbuch Verlag, 1990). Another telling title was *Aufbruch in eine andere DDR* (Awakening of/Departure to Another GDR), ed. Hubertus Knabe (Reinbek bei Hamburg: Rowohlt Taschenbuch Verlag, 1990).

10 Haug, "The Surrender of the Fortress," 26.

11 At both historical conjunctures, women's organizations were the first casualties in the ensuing rollback of the radical democratic structures that had developed throughout the transformation. For a discussion of the fate of the autonomous women's organizations after 1989, see Barbara Einhorn, *Cinderella Goes to Market: Citizenship, Gender, and the Women's Movements in East Central Europe* (London: Verso, 1993).

12 For a critique of this approach and its relationship to the "Historians' Debate" of the 1980s, see Jürgen Habermas, "Bemerkungen zu einer verworrenen Diskussion: Was bedeutet 'Aufarbeitung der Vergangenheit' heute?" *Die Zeit,* No. 15 (April 10, 1992): 17-19.

13 The term "verstaatlichte Gesellschaft" translates literally as "governmentalized" or "nationalized" society; see Sigrid Meuschel, "Überlegungen zu einer

Herrschafts- und Gesellschaftsgeschichte der DDR," *Geschichte und Gesell-schaft* 19 (1993): 5–14.

14 Meuschel, *Legitimation und Parteiherrschaft,* 10.

15 Ralph Jessen, "Die Gesellschaft im Staatssozialismus," *Geschichte und Gesell-schaft* 21 (1995): 100. For another excellent discussion of Meuschel's analysis and a first attempt to adumbrate the limits of *Durchherrschung* (a term denoting the total penetration of society by state power) in a modern dictatorship, see Thomas Lindenberger, "Projektvorstellung: Herrschaft und Eigen-Sinn in der Diktatur—Studien zur Gesellschaftsgeschichte in Berlin-Brandenburg 1945–1990," *Potsdamer Bulletin für zeithistorische Studien,* No. 5 (December 1995): 37–52. Much of the research on the Third Reich has moved away from totali-tarianism as successful penetration of the entire society and toward approaches which inquire into its peculiar mixture of ordinary life and terror, foreground-ing the often chaotic organization of Nazi Germany and its various modes of nonconformity and resistance to domination. For a recent theoretical discussion, see Ian Kershaw, *The Nazi Dictatorship* (London: Arnold, 1993).

16 The actual core of this argument, that East Germany was economically and technologically less developed, does not necessarily translate into the view that it was a premodern, undifferentiated system. On the contrary, Meuschel's model—and the more popularized versions of totalitarianism theory—under-estimate the degree of social differentiation in the East, where, one could argue, the different spheres were not less differentiated but differently articulated. For an alternative discussion of the GDR in terms of regulation theory, see George Steinmetz, "Die (un-)moralische Ökonomie rechtsextremer Gewalt im Über-gang zum Postfordismus," *Das Argument* 203 (Jan./Feb. 1994): 23–40. Like the somewhat older discussion on Germany's *Sonderweg,* Meuschel's analysis is also flawed by its contrasting the East to an idealized model of the West. On this problematic, see George Steinmetz, "German Exceptionalism and the Ori-gins of Nazism: The Career of a Concept," in *Dictators Unleashed: Historical Approaches to Nazism and Stalinism,* ed. Ian Kershaw and Moshe Lewin (Cam-bridge: Cambridge University Press, forthcoming).

17 Claude Lefort, "The Logic of Totalitarianism," in his *Political Forms of Modern Society,* ed. John B. Thompson (Cambridge, Mass.: MIT Press, 1986), 286–87. (In chapter 1, I shall discuss Lefort's theory in more detail.)

18 State repression was, of course, a reality in the GDR, as was the Wall, the fre-quent Party purges, etc. By insisting that the concept cannot explain the actual complexity of the GDR, I do not intend to blur the boundaries between democ-racy and what Haug calls Soviet-style "barracks socialism" ("Surrender of the Fortress," 26). Lefort himself is not clear on whether he intends his theory as the description of an ideal type or of an actually existing system. I will use it in the former sense.

19 See Mary Fulbrook, *Anatomy of a Dictatorship,* 15. I will deal in more detail with one of the periods characterized by significant intra-party dissent, the early 1960s, in a later chapter.

20 Ulrich Greiner, "Die deutsche Gesinnungsästhetik," *Die Zeit* 45 (Nov. 2, 1990): 15.

21 See, for instance, Andreas Hyussen, "After the Wall: The Failure of German Intellectuals," *New German Critique* 52 (Winter 1991): 109–43; and in *Twilight Memories* (New York and London: Routledge, 1995), 37–66; see also *Der deutsch-deutsche Literaturstreit oder "Freunde, es spricht sich schlecht mit gebundener Zunge",* ed. Karl Deiritz and Hannes Krauss (Hamburg: Luchterhand Literatur Verlag, 1991); *"Es geht nicht um Christa Wolf": Der Literaturstreit im vereinten Deutschland,* ed. Thomas Anz (Munich: Spangenberg, 1991); Stephen Brockmann, "Introduction: The Unification Debate," *New German Critique* 52 (Winter 1991): 3–30 (special issue on German unification). For a reading of the debates in terms of their gendered politics, see Anna S. Kuhn, " 'Eine Königin köpfen ist effektiver als einen König köpfen': The Gender Politics of the Christa Wolf Controversy," in *Women and the Wende: Social Effects and Cultural Reflections of the German Unification Process,* ed. Elizabeth Boa and Janet Wharton (Amsterdam and Atlanta, Ga.: Rodopi, 1994), 200–215. For a reading of the controversy which questions its guiding categories and argues for a proper historicizing approach to the concept of socialist realism, see Julia Hell, Loren Kruger, and Katie Trumpener, "Dossier: Socialist Realism and East German Modernism—Another Historians' Debate," in *Rethinking Marxism,* 7 (Fall 1994): 36–44, as well as my discussion of Christa Wolf's *Divided Heaven* in the same issue: "Christa Wolf's 'Divided Heaven' and the Collapse of (Socialist) Realism," 62–74.

22 In the wake of singer Wolf Biermann's expulsion in 1976, many authors who had supported his return and protested his expatriation were put under surveillance. In 1979, several of them were expelled from the writers' union and subsequently decided to leave for the West.

23 Ulrich Greiner, "Mangel an Feingefühl," *Die Zeit,* June 1, 1990; repr. in Anz, ed., *"Es geht nicht um Christa Wolf",* 66.

24 Ulrich Greiner, "Keiner ist frei von Schuld," *Die Zeit,* July 27, 1990; repr. in Anz, *"Es geht nicht um Christa Wolf",* 179.

25 Karl-Heinz Bohrer, "Kulturschutzgebiet DDR?" *Merkur* 500 (Oct./Nov. 1990): 1015–18. This argument was directed as much against Wolf as against the entire postwar generation of East and West German authors whose main focus has been the Nazi past. Bohrer, Greiner, and Frank Schirrmacher all pursued this topic in articles on postwar West German literature; see, for instance, Frank Schirrmacher, "Abschied von der Literatur der Bundesrepublik," *Frankfurter Allgemeine Zeitung,* Oct. 2, 1990, L1–2.

26 The name refers to a group of young authors under the leadership of Hans Werner Richter who began meeting in 1947. At times, the group also included Ingeborg Bachmann, Alfred Andersch, Paul Celan, and Peter Weiss, among many other West German, Austrian, and Swiss authors.

27 I will return to this controversy in chapter 2.

28 On the background of this controversy, see Klaus Michael, "Feindbild Literatur:

Die Biermann-Affäre, Staatssicherheit und die Herausbildung einer literarischen Alternativkultur in der DDR," *Aus Politik und Zeitgeschehen,* May 28, 1993, 23–31.

29 Prenzlauer Berg, a one-time working-class district in East Berlin, evolved into an alternative lifestyle area in the 1980s, the site of semipublic poetry readings, exhibits, performances, and punk rock played in private apartments. For a detailed discussion of whether it really had any oppositional potential, see *Macht-Spiele: Literatur und Staatssicherheit im Fokus Prenzlauer Berg,* ed. Peter Böthig and Klaus Michael (Leipzig: Reclam Verlag, 1993).

30 The term *Klandestinität* was first introduced by the writer Gerd Neumann to characterize the production of this new group outside the official channels of the GDR's cultural institutions. Gert Neumann, *Die Klandestinität der Kesselreiniger* (Frankfurt a.M.: 1989). On *Klandestinität,* see Antonia Grunenberg, "In den Räumen der Sprache: Gedankenbilder zur Literatur Gert Neumanns," in *Die andere Sprache,* ed. Heinz Ludwig Arnold (Munich: Text und Kritik, 1990), 210. For discussions among its members, see the collection of essays from the underground magazine *Ariadnefabrik,* in *Abriss der Ariadnefabrik,* ed. Andreas Koziol and Rainer Schedlinski (Berlin: Galrev, 1990).

The Stasi now appeared in an entirely new light, namely, as the sponsor of a subculture, argued Lutz Rathenow, in " 'Schreiben Sie doch für uns': Was sich die Staatssicherheit einfallen liess, um die Literatur zu bändigen," *Frankfurter Allgemeine Zeitung,* November 27, 1991, 36. Although intriguing, this thesis seems less convincing than its alternative, that the Stasi's cultural officers tried to keep abreast of what from their perspective (the established categories of "avant-garde elitism") seemed a rather circumscribed, and therefore ultimately harmless, phenomenon. In my view, the term "repressive tolerance" would be highly appropriate here. Brockmann points to another rather curious angle of the entire Stasi activity: after having read his own Stasi file, the East German author Klaus Schlesinger observed, "I added that the structure of this novel was borrowed from European modernism, where the characters take shape through the gaze of the other characters"; quoted in Stephen Brockmann, "Preservation and Change in Christa Wolf's *Was bleibt,*" *The German Quarterly* 67 (Winter 1994): 81.

31 Rainer Schedlinski, "Dem Druck, immer mehr sagen zu sollen, hielt ich nicht stand," *Frankfurter Allgemeine Zeitung,* January 14, 1992, 25. Another East German author, Wolfgang Hilbig, explores the psyche of a Stasi informer-turned-writer in his recent novel *Ich* (Frankfurt a.M.: Fischer Verlag, 1993).

32 Her decision was prompted, she wrote, by the accusations against Heiner Müller for his routine conversations with Stasi officers; see Christa Wolf, "Eine Auskunft," *Berliner Zeitung,* January 21, 1993; repr. in *Akteneinsicht Christa Wolf: Zerrspiegel und Dialog,* ed. Hermann Vinke (Hamburg: Luchterhand Literaturverlag, 1993), 143–44.

33 This was after she had posed for years as the GDR's only genuine dissident, attacking—rather viciously—other East German intellectuals, in particular Wolf

and Müller. Maron's conversations with the Stasi concerned her Western acquaintances; see her interview by Frank Schirrmacher, " 'Meine Mutter hat für Mielke Schmalzstullen geschmiert': Ein Gespräch mit Monika Maron über ihre Kontakte zur 'Hauptverwaltung Aufklärung' des Staatssicherheitsdienstes der DDR," *Frankfurter Allgemeine Zeitung,* August 7, 1995.

34 Some members of the West German P E N who had emigrated from the GDR in the late 1970s and early 1980s opposed this unification, arguing that the Eastern P E N chapter had not sufficiently "purged" its ranks of authors affiliated with the Stasi or the s e d; see Gunter Hofmann, "Schmerzen einer deutschen Familie: Die neue Unversöhnlichkeit unter den Schriftstellern ist eine Chiffre für den Zustand der Republik," *Die Zeit,* Oct. 6, 1995, 3.

35 But this criticism did not constitute a form of witch hunt, as some East German critics argued. This misunderstanding resulted from the East Germans' familiarity with a different context in which rebuttals were only rarely published.

36 Fritz J. Raddatz, "Von der Beschädigung der Literatur durch ihre Urheber," *Die Zeit,* February 5, 1993, 17.

37 Ibid., 18.

38 Wolfgang J. Mommsen, "Die DDR in der deutschen Geschichte," *Aus Politik und Zeitgeschehen,* July 16, 1993, 23, 29; Bernd Hüppauf, "Moral oder Sprache: DDR-Literatur vor der Moderne," in *Literatur in der DDR: Rückblicke,* special issue of *Text + Kritik* (Munich: Text + Kritik, 1991), 223.

39 Hüppauf, "Moral oder Sprache," 223, 222, 223.

40 Ibid., 225.

41 Bohrer, "Kulturschutzgebiet DDR," 1015, 1016.

42 Hüppauf, "Moral oder Sprache," 228; his emphasis.

43 Peter Geist, "Nachwort," in *Ein Molotowcocktail auf fremder Bettkante* (Leipzig: Reclam-Verlag, 1991), 76ff.

44 Fredric Jameson, "Beyond the Cave: Demystifying the Ideology of Modernism," in *The Ideologies of Theory: Essays 1971–1986* (Minneapolis: University of Minnesota Press, 1988), 2: 115–32.

45 As Jonathan Arac observed, "Since Lukács was identified with representation, with realism, with humanism, and also with Stalinism . . . antirepresentationalism became not only a defense of modernism, but also a declaration of anti-Stalinism"; see his "Introduction" to *Postmodernism and Politics,* ed. Jonathan Arac (Minneapolis: University of Minnesota Press, 1986), xxii.

46 As Patricia Herminghouse points out, another consequence of this binary logic was to classify successful authors such as Wolf and Müller as "German" or even "European" writers; see "Whose German Literature? GDR Literature, German Literature, and the Question of National Identity," *GDR Bulletin* 16 (Fall 1990): 9.

47 For a thorough critique of such unhistorical transfers of the literary–historical categories of nineteenth-century realism/twentieth-century modernism, see Sibylle Maria Fischer, "Representation and the Ends of Realism" (Ph.D. dissertation, Columbia University, 1995).

48 For a critique of this type of criticism, see Bernhard Greiner's review article "DDR-Literatur als Problem der Literaturwissenschaft," *Jahrbuch zur Literatur der DDR* 3 (1983): 233–54. Greiner correctly points out that much of the literary criticism written outside the GDR reproduced the latter's basic paradigm, namely, literature conceptualized in terms of reflection theory. This often led to a simplified model of literary works as reflecting social reality in a one-to-one relation. (See also Herminghouse, "Whose German Literature?" 8.) Greiner's argument leads to two conclusions: first, that literature itself is implicated in the construction of social reality; and second, that because of the polyvalent and often contradictory nature of the literary text, literature cannot be reduced to a single, unambiguous political text, a "message." Although banal, this is still worth arguing in the context of GDR studies. Peter V. Zima offered a similar argument in "Der Mythos der Monosemie: Parteilichkeit und künstlerischer Standpunkt," in *Literaturwissenschaft und Sozialwissenschaften 6: Einführung in Theorie, Geschichte und Funktion der DDR-Literatur,* ed. Hans-Jürgen Schmitt (Stuttgart: Metzler Verlag, 1975), 77–108: reflection theory operates with a concept of the literary text which denies the polysemic value of literature itself. The problem with Zima's argument is that he himself conceives of socialist realism in those terms, yet the socialist realist text is just as unstable and conflicted as any other literary work (a point to which I shall return). For a more detailed discussion of the issue of form in the reading of GDR literature, see my "Crisis Strategies: Family, Gender, and German History" (Ph.D. diss., University of Wisconsin–Madison, 1989). My current work differs from the paradigm developed in my dissertation, however, in that I no longer conceive of socialist realism as an aesthetic system that succeeds in formally organizing a coherent, nonconflictual text (an issue to which I shall also return).

49 Hüppauf, "Moral oder Sprache," 228.

50 For a reading of Schirrmacher's, Greiner's, and Bohrer's interventions as a "preventive" marginalization of a new oppositional literature in the postunification period that could become a version of the GDR's engaged literature, potentially replacing the critical but now historically obsolete *Nachkriegsliteratur* (postwar literature) of the Gruppe 47, see Jochen Vogt, "Langer Abschied von der Nachkriegsliteratur? Ein Kommentar zur letzten westdeutschen Literaturdebatte," in Deiritz and Krauss, eds., *Der deutsch-deutsche Literaturstreit,* 61–62. This view makes sense, given the dogmatic exclusion of this kind of political literature from the realm of the "aesthetic."

51 This premise might seem paradoxical because Hüppauf himself advocates exactly that division. But what he means in this context is that since GDR aesthetics were based on this connection, to deny it now in discussing this literature would make no sense. Hüppauf directs his critique against those who defended Christa Wolf by underlining her courage and outspokenness outside of her writing. I agree with Hüppauf that this defense is problematic, as is the other strategy often used to "defend" a GDR author, namely, foregrounding the "aesthetic quality" of the work, with the implicit or explicit intention of separating art

from politics; see, for example, Ute Brandes, *Anna Seghers* (Berlin: Colloquium Verlag, 1992).

52 Wolfgang Emmerich, "Gleichzeitigkeit: Vormoderne, Moderne und Post-moderne in der Literatur aus der DDR," in his *Die andere deutsche Literatur: Aufsätze zur Literatur aus der DDR* (Opladen: Westdeutscher Verlag, 1994), 129–50; Genia Schulz, "Kein Chorgesang: Neue Schreibweisen bei Autorinnen (aus) der DDR," in *Text & Kritik,* ed. Heinz Ludwig Arnold (Munich: Text & Kritik, 1988), 212–25.

53 Of course, Emmerich focuses on such authors as Christa Wolf, Volker Braun, Heiner Müller, Irmtraud Morgner, and Franz Fühmann, that is, those canonized by Emmerich himself and by his Western colleagues, leaving "party writers," such as Helmut Baierl, Helmut Sakowski, Harry Thürk, Hedda Zinner, and Eva Strittmatter, out of his story.

54 Emmerich, "Gleichzeitigkeit," 136, 138. He discusses Brecht as an exception, the playwright who does not fit into the cultural landscape, with Uwe Johnson similarly exceptional among fiction writers (137, 138).

55 Ibid., 145, quoting Wolf's tribute to the East German author Thomas Brasch on the occasion of his receiving the prestigious West German Kleist-Preis in 1987, after he left the GDR.

56 "Aesthetic modernity is . . . the appropriation of modernity with artistic means *at a moment of crisis,* in the phase of its consciousness of its immanent pathology" (ibid., 132). Nevertheless, Emmerich argues, this particular form of aesthetic modernism maintains its hold on a concept of utopia (133). For a discussion of the concept of modernism by East Germany's leading critics, see Jost Hermand, "Das Gute-Neue und das Schlechte-Neue: Wandlungen der Modernismus-Debatte in der DDR seit 1956," in *Literatur und Literaturtheorie in der DDR,* ed. Patricia Herminghouse and Peter Uwe Hohendahl (Frankfurt a.M.: Suhrkamp, 1981), 73–99.

57 Schulz, "Kein Chorgesang," 214. In contrast to many other critics, Schulz thought that a theory of this feminine writing still remained to be formu-lated (*ebenda*). For a discussion of the relationship between GDR literature and American feminism, see Angelika Bammer, "The American Feminist Recep-tion of GDR Literature (with a Glance at West Germany)," *GDR Bulletin* 16 (Fall 1990): 18–24.

58 Dorothea Böck, " 'Ich schreibe, um herauszufinden, warum ich schreiben muss': Frauenliteratur in der DDR zwischen Selbsterfahrung und ästhetischem Experi-ment," *Feministische Studien* 1 (1990): 64.

59 Love argued that realism and modernism are both modes of writing in which "an essentially patriarchal quality of authorship" is figured "as authority"; see her "Christa Wolf and Feminism: Breaking the Patriarchal Connection," *New German Critique* 16 (Winter 1979): 44. See also Sara Lennox's discussion of the relationship between Wolf's critique of the traditional novel and Silvia Boven-schen's concept of a feminine aesthetic in " 'Der Versuch, man selbst zu sein':

Christa Wolf und der Feminismus," in *Die Frau als Heldin und Autorin,* ed. Wolfgang Paulsen (Bern and Munich: Francke Verlag, 1979), 217–22.

60 See also, more recently, Allison Lewis on the "bourgeoning of women's literature" in the 1970s: "These writers [Christa Wolf and Irmtraud Morgner] provide instructive examples of the ways women's literature is able to subvert the dominant aesthetic paradigm; their works experiment with numerous ways of resisting the normative effects of socialist realism, its containment of female desire, and its neutralization of feminine difference"; see her " 'Foiling the Censor': Reading and Transference as Feminist Strategies in the Works of Christa Wolf, Irmtraud Morgner, and Christa Moog," *The German Quarterly* 66 (Summer 1993): 372.

61 As developed in Christa Wolf, "Reading and Writing" (1968), in *The Author's Dimension: Selected Essays,* ed. Alexander Stephen, trans. Grace Paley (New York: Farrar, Straus and Giroux, 1993), 20–48; and in "Subjective Authenticity: A Conversation with Hans Kaufmann" (1973), in *The Fourth Dimension: Interviews with Christa Wolf,* trans. Hilary Pilkington (London and New York: Verso, 1988), 17–38. I will discuss this notion in more detail in chapters 4 and 5.

62 Axel Goodbody, Dennis Tate, and Ian Wallace, "The Failed Socialist Experiment: Culture in the GDR," in *German Cultural Studies: An Introduction,* ed. Rob Burns (Oxford: Oxford University Press, 1995), 200, 167, 164. For a similar account, see Ursula Heukenkamp, "Soll das Vergessen verabredet werden? Eigenständigkeit und Eigenart der DDR-Literatur," *Aus Politik und Zeitgeschichte,* October 4, 1991, 3–12. Arguing against the subsumption of forty years of GDR literature under the heading of "regional literature, child of the provinces, in the middle of modernity," Heukenkamp concludes her discussion with a celebration of East Germany's women's literature. She dismisses the early GDR literature as responding exclusively to the expectations of East Germany's cultural politics. Pragmatic, moralizing, and didactic, it is, she writes, rightfully forgotten. But she wants to rescue the literature of the 1960s from the accusation of conformism, arguing that it sketched a new democratic model of communication. Its fundamental flaw was its utopian impetus, which women's literature, developing in the 1970s, overcame by being *pragmatic.*

63 Wolfgang Emmerich, "Affirmation–Utopie–Melancholie: Versuch einer Bilanz von vierzig Jahren DDR-Literatur," *German Studies Review* 14 (May 1991): 339. "Sinngebungsliteratur" denotes literature that provides a totalizing meaning.

64 Ibid., 335–36. In this essay, Emmerich alludes to Lyotard, Gorz, and Enzensberger and their postmodernist critique of "totalitarian utopias" (336ff.).

65 Ibid., 181, 180.

66 The terms are from a petition which was signed by many members of East Germany's intelligentsia.

67 This is the subtitle of Anna S. Kuhn's influential study, *Christa Wolf's Utopian Vision* (Cambridge: Cambridge University Press, 1988), which is also informed by the narrative of the progression from socialist realism to modernism. In this

respect, Kuhn's study is similar to the standard East German work on Wolf, Therese Hörnigk's *Christa Wolf* (Berlin: Aufbau-Verlag, 1989).

68 That Morgner was one of the few prominent authors who wholeheartedly supported the SED's decision to prevent Wolf Biermann from returning to East Germany in 1979 should give us pause.

69 In contrast to the established view of socialist realism as a traditional, closed literary system, Antoine Baudin, Leonid Heller, and Thomas Lahusen understand it as an "open" system, consisting of works continually rewritten, continually revised; see their "Le réalisme socialiste sovietique de l'ère Jdanov: Compte rendu d'une enquête en cours," *Etudes de Lettres* 10 (1988): 69–103. As Leonid Heller argues, socialist realism was not a system characterized by "stability and stasis" but by "shock therapy and chronic destabilization." Socialist realist works, continually being revised, could never attain the rigidity that both Soviet theorists and Western critics claimed to be the essential characteristic of that system; see Leonid Heller, "A World of Prettiness: Socialist Realism and Its Aesthetic Categories," *South Atlantic Quarterly* 94 (1995): 687–714. These works were the result, I would add, of particular *modern* pressures. For a discussion of the rewriting of so-called socialist realist classics such as Fyodor Gladkov's *Cement* and Gorky's *The Mother,* see Thomas Lahusen, "Socialist Realism in Search of Its Shores: Some Historical Remarks on the 'Historically Open Aesthetic System of the Truthful Representation of Life,'" *South Atlantic Quarterly* 94 (1995): 673ff.

70 As we shall see in chapter 2, Seghers herself defended modernist techniques in her correspondence with Lukács.

71 Including Georg Büchner's *Lenz,* which Wolf herself identified as her model, a point to which I will return in chapter 4.

72 The important contribution of Emmerich's "Gleichzeitigkeit" *at the time* lay precisely in his project of historicizing East German literature "internally" instead of ignoring it as an "un-German" literature or forcing it into the straitjacket of an "all-German literature" (129).

73 See Julia Hell, "At the Center an Absence: Foundationalist Narratives of the GDR and the Legitimatory Discourse of Antifascism," *Monatshefte* 84 (Spring 1992): 23–45.

74 In chapter 2, I will trace the ways in which Seghers's novel diverges from this structure and point out the reasons for this divergence.

75 Ironically, the characterization of East Germany as an essentially transparent social order (Hüppauf) thus corresponds more to the SED's presentation of its own rule than to the actual complexities of the GDR's social system.

76 Adopted by the SED in the early 1960s to counter a growing tendency to compare actual socialism with its ideals, "real existing socialism" was a term purporting to orient politics away from "utopian," idealist thinking that did not take into account the material conditions under which East German socialism had to develop. Part of that discussion instantiated an opposition between the contradictions said to stem from the capitalist past, holdovers that were expected to

disappear with time, versus those contradictions that were inherent to the new order.

77 Thomas Lahusen, "Thousand and One Nights in Stalinist Culture: *Far from Moscow,*" *Discourse* 17 (Spring 1995): 58.

78 In its focus on the body, this book also partakes in the project outlined by Leslie Adelson, namely, to "rethink the role played by bodies in the constitution of social subjects"; see *Making Bodies. Making History: Feminism and German Identity* (Lincoln and London: University of Nebraska Press, 1993), 3. However, in contrast to Adelson's approach, my framework is psychoanalytic, one that enables us to understand the precise mechanisms through which we think and fantasize—in short, live our bodies. But my book is decidedly *not* a contribution to the currently fashionable psychohistory of "the East German," in which wildly speculative generalizations are made about the psychological structures of East Germans, with psychoanalytic categories applied not only to an entire population but to an entire state. See, for instance, Hans-Joachim Maaz, *Der Gefühlsstau: Ein Psychogramm der DDR* (Munich: Knaur, 1992): "In the language of psychotherapy (we could argue that) the development of the GDR was arrested at the oral stage" (86). Maaz's book also fights on another ideological front since it ultimately blames East German *women* for what he calls a *Mangelsyndrom* (syndrome of lack) afflicting East Germans, the consequence of a majority of East German women working outside the home. This pathologizing move, I would argue, is part of a crude attempt to "subordinate" the new Eastern states and their populations to the West German way of life as the only alternative.

79 Quoting from Ruth Rehmann, *Unterwegs in fremden Träumen* (Munich: Hauser, 1993), 30; and Jacqueline Rose, "Introduction: Feminism and the Psychic," in her *Sexuality in the Field of Vision* (London and New York: Verso, 1991), 5.

80 See Jean Laplanche and Jean-Bertrand Pontalis, "Fantasy and the Origins of Sexuality," in *Formations of Fantasy,* ed. Victor Burgin, James Donald, and Cora Kaplan (London and New York: Methuen, 1986), 8.

81 My approach here also intends to break finally with the tendency among critics—both Eastern and Western—to observe the Communist Party's taboo on psychoanalysis. The first text by Freud, *Trauer und Melancholie: Essays,* appeared only as recently as 1982; see Antal Borbely and John Erpenbeck, "Vorschläge zu Freud," *Deutsche Zeitschrift für Philosophie* 35 (1987): 1021. By 1989, his complete works had still not been published.

82 Slavoj Žižek, *For They Know Not What They Do: Enjoyment as a Political Factor* (London: Verso, 1991), 255. I will discuss this notion in more detail in chapter 1.

83 These novels of arrival are better understood within the framework of popular literature. The introduction of the topic of sexuality and desire has to do with the fact that these authors were called upon to write popular literature, literature capable of replacing the love stories that were still widely read. And popular literature, as we know from studies such as Janice Radway's *Reading the Romance* (Chapel Hill: University of North Carolina Press, 1984), draws precisely upon

the domain of desire. On this topic, see my "Soft-Porn, Kitsch, and Post-Fascist Bodies: The East German Novel of Arrival," *South Atlantic Quarterly* 94 (Summer 1995): 747–72.

84 The argument is often made specifically with respect to the GDR's emerging women's literature; see, for instance, Einhorn, *Cinderella Goes to Market,* 236ff. I will deal with this controversy in more detail in the chapters devoted to Wolf.

85 See, for instance, Wolfgang Emmerich, *Kleine Literaturgeschichte der DDR,* rev. ed. (Frankfurt a.M.: Luchterhand Literaturverlag, 1989), 62ff.

86 Emmerich's term is difficult to translate. It oscillates between the denotation of the author's commitment to socialism and a voluntary, self-imposed bondage.

1 Specters of Stalin, or Constructing Communist Fathers

1 Joseph V. Femia, *Gramsci's Political Thought* (Oxford: Oxford University Press, 1988), 24.

2 "Ulbricht group" refers to one of the three groups of high-ranking Party members brought in by the Soviets to administer the Soviet Occupied Zone. While Ulbricht headed the group assigned to the Berlin region, Anton Ackermann was assigned to Saxony and Gustav Sobottka to Mecklenburg–Pommern. The structural changes initiated under the program of "antifascist-democratic transformation" (Hermann Weber, *Die DDR 1945–1986* [Munich: R. Oldenbourg Verlag, 1988], 2), an attempt to belatedly realize the failed popular front of the 1930s, slowly laid the foundations for a Soviet-style system, with the SED (Socialist Unity Party) as the "leading party." Wolfgang Leonhard attributes this transformation to the dominance of the Moscow exiles over the so-called Western exiles. Many members of the latter group advocated a reconstruction based on democratic consensus. Equally crucial, of course, was the presence of the Soviets. Leonhard's *Die Revolution entlässt ihre Kinder* (Cologne and Berlin: Kiepenheuer and Witsch, 1955) is still one of the most reliable accounts of this period. In its founding manifesto (June 11, 1945), the KPD declared that its goal was not a "Soviet Germany." Instead, the authors of the new program argued that Germany's situation demanded the completion of the failed democratic revolution of 1848. Their goal was the "establishment of an antifascist-democratic regime, a parliamentary-democratic republic with all the rights and freedoms for the people" (Weber, *Die DDR,* 4). In January 1949 (the GDR was founded on October 7), the SED's first Party conference introduced democratic centralism, Party discipline, and the nomenclatura. During the previous year, the Party had purged most of its dissenting Social Democratic members and abolished the principle of parity of Social Democratic and Communist representation on Party committees. In the context of Stalin's conflict with Tito, the idea of a special German path to socialism, formulated by Anton Ackermann in the Party press in 1946, was abandoned, and, at the second SED Party confer-

ence in 1952, Ulbricht informed the delegates that the S E D had decided to build socialism "according to plan" (Weber, *Die DDR,* 32).

3   Edward Shils, "Center and Periphery," in his *Constitution of Society* (Chicago: University of Chicago Press, 1982), 93.

4   Emmerich (*Kleine Literaturgeschichte,* 66) calls these novels "Epochenbilanzen in Romanform" (epochal surveys in epic form). David Bathrick also discusses them as part of a—failed—attempt to come to grips with the immediate past, in "Geschichtsbewusstsein als Selbstbewusstsein: Die Literatur der DDR," in *Neues Handbuch der Literaturwissenschaft,* ed. Klaus von See (Wiesbaden: Athenaion, 1979), 21: 280. For an East German reading of this literature, "the artistic discovery of the 'ancestors' of today's socialists," see Herta Herting, *Geschichte für die Gegenwart* (Berlin: Dietz Verlag, 1979), esp. intro. and 70–88.

Anna Seghers, *Die Toten bleiben jung* (Neuwied and Darmstadt: Luchterhand, 1981 [1949]); *The Dead Stay Young* (London: Eyre and Spottiswoode, 1950). References to the English text will be cited as *DS*/page number; those to the German text as *DT*/page number. Hans Marchwitza, *Die Kumiaks* (Berlin and Weimar: Aufbau-Verlag, 1965 [1934]); *Die Heimkehr der Kumiaks* (Berlin and Weimar: Aufbau-Verlag, 1964); and *Die Kumiaks und ihre Kinder* (Berlin: Verlag Tribüne, [1959]). Willi Bredel, *Die Väter* (Dortmund: Weltkreis Verlag, 1981 [1941]); *Die Söhne* (Dortmund: Weltkreis Verlag, 1981 [1949, rev. eds. 1952, 1960]); *Die Enkel,* Vol. 1 (Dortmund: Weltkreis Verlag, 1981), Vol. 2 (Dortmund: Weltkreis Verlag, 1981 [1953]). References to these novels will be cited as follows: *VB1*/; *VB2*/; *VB3a*/; and *VB3b*/page number. Otto Gotsche, *Die Fahne von Kriwoj Rog* (Halle: Mitteldeutscher Verlag, 1959), will be cited as *DF*/page number.

5   Bredel started work on the novel in 1939 while he was in exile in Moscow (he returned to Germany on August 31, 1946), it was first published in 1940. For a discussion of Bredel's role in the literary debates of the 1920s and 1930s about the proletarian novel, see Fritz J. Raddatz, "Von der Arbeiterkorrespondenz zur Literatur: Willi Bredel, F. C. Weiskopf," in his *Traditionen und Tendenzen: Materialien zur Literatur der DDR* (Frankfurt a.M.: Suhrkamp Verlag, 1972), 254–78.

6   Ironically, it was Otto Grotewohl, the Social Democratic leader of the newly unified party (Wilhelm Pieck represented the Communist wing), who proposed "The Fathers" for the title of the 1948 edition; see Rutger Booss, "Nachwort," *Die Väter,* 479.

7   Ibid., 477.

8   Maxie Wander, *Guten Morgen, du Schöne. Frauen in der DDR: Protokolle* (Darmstadt and Neuwied: Luchterhand Verlag, 1978), 87.

9   Intent on portraying his state as the apogee of German literary as well as political history, Abusch contrasts Mann's novelistic treatment of the *decline of the bourgeoisie* with Bredel's celebration of the *rise of the proletariat;* see his "Willi Bredels Roman-Trilogie einer proletarischen Familie," in *Willi Bredel: Dokumente seines Lebens* (Berlin: Aufbau-Verlag, 1961), 34. In his autobiography, the former director of the Aufbau-Verlag, Walter Janka, reports that Willi Bredel

was in charge of reediting *Buddenbrooks* in East Germany; see his *Spuren eines Lebens* (Reinbek bei Hamburg: Rowohlt Taschenbuch Verlag, 1992), 229. See Annemarie Auer, "Proletarischer Familienroman und Nationalliteratur," in *Kritik in der Zeit,* ed. Klaus Jarmatz (Halle/Saale: Mitteldeutscher Verlag, 1969), 308.

10 See Martin Schulz, "Arbeiterdichter aus dem Kohlenpott," in Jarmatz, ed., *Kritik in der Zeit,* 140.

11 Gotsche was Ulbricht's private secretary. During his tenure, he organized the conferences of the Bitterfelder Weg (Bitterfelder Path), a cultural-political initiative to which I will return. Gotsche was also in charge of the Mitteldeutscher Verlag, the publishing house of the Bitterfelder Weg. That his novel was published by Aufbau means that it was considered a classic since, at the time, Aufbau published the works of Thomas and Heinrich Mann, Arnold Zweig, and other "humanists," or "critical realists."

12 See Wolfgang Brekle, *Schriftsteller im antifaschistischen Widerstand 1933–1945 in Deutschland* (Berlin and Weimar: Aufbau-Verlag, 1985), 70–71, 75–77.

13 See Otto Gotsche, "Literatur und Geschichtsbewusstsein: Interview mit Otto Gotsche," in *Auskünfte: Werkstattgespräche mit DDR-Autoren* (Berlin and Weimar: Aufbau-Verlag, 1974), 66–67. Here, Gotsche identifies the "revolutionary literature" of Gladkov, Fadeev, Fedin, and, most importantly, Gorky, as his model (68).

14 Christa Wolf, "Sozialistische Literatur der Gegenwart," *Neue deutsche Literatur* 7 (May 1959): 3–7.

15 Wolfgang Jacobsen informs us that the film was regularly shown in schools; see *Babelsberg: Ein Filmstudio, 1912–1992,* ed. Wolfgang Jacobsen (Berlin: Argon, 1992), 290. For more details, see Kurt Maetzig, *Filmarbeit* (Berlin: Henschelverlag Kunst und Gesellschaft, 1987).

16 The script for the latter was written by Christa Wolf, and the film released in 1968. In *Babelsberg,* Georg Leopold mentions that Bredel's trilogy was the basis for a television series as late as 1971. In *Filmarbeit,* Maetzig details his collaboration with Bredel on his *Thälmann* films (1952/53), in which the actor Michel Piccoli appeared. (Ernst Thälmann was the leader of the Communist Party during the Weimar Republic. Arrested in 1933, he was executed in 1944 at Buchenwald. Thälmann's bust became one of the central exhibits of the camp under the SED; see James E. Young, *The Texture of Memory* [New Haven and London: Yale University Press, 1993], 78.) These films constituted a major Cold War event, with their scripts discussed by the Politbureau. Maetzig, calling himself and his team "creators of a monument" (257), adds that an entire generation grew up with this "image of Thälmann" (78). The film scripts introduced by Wilhelm Pieck and Walter Ulbricht were published; see Willi Bredel and Michael Tschesno-Hell, *Ernst Thälmann: Sohn seiner Klasse—Literarisches Szenarium von Willi Bredel und Michael Tschesno-Hell* (Berlin: Henschelverlag, 1954); and *Ernst Thälmann: Führer seiner Klasse—Literarisches Szenarium von Willi Bredel und Michael Tschesno-Hell* (Berlin: Henschelverlag, 1955).

17 This might be viewed as an exaggeration of the importance of these novels by Bredel, Marchwitza, and Gotsche, since many literary historians in the West viewed the former members of the Bund Proletarisch-Revolutionärer Schrift-steller (Union of Proletarian Revolutionary Writers [BPRS]) as marginal, rela-tive to the supposedly dominant strand of "bourgeois humanist" literature. But these critics vastly underestimated the importance of the BPRS authors. The role played by their novels may be better understood in the context of what Alexan-der Stephan calls the *Zweigleisigkeit* of KPD, and later SED, cultural politics, that is, the permanent *coexistence* of tendencies toward a cultural popular front—privileging "bourgeois humanist" literature—and tendencies toward a social-ist cultural revolution, which foregrounded the tradition of socialist literature; see his "Pläne für ein neues Deutschland: Die Kulturpolitik der Exil-KPD vor 1945," *Basis: Jahrbuch für deutsche Gegenwartsliteratur,* ed. Reinhold Grimm and Jost Hermand (1977): 62. For a discussion of GDR cultural politics with re-spect to the socialist movement, see Frank Trommler, "Die Kulturpolitik der DDR und die kulturelle Tradition des deutschen Sozialismus," in *Literatur und Literaturtheorie in der DDR,* ed. Peter Uwe Hohendahl and Patricia Herming-house (Frankfurt a.M.: Suhrkamp, 1981), 13–72.

18 Claude Lefort, "The Image of the Body and Totalitarianism," in *The Political Forms of Modern Society,* 297.

19 See John B. Thompson, "Editor's Introduction," in ibid., 25; see also 291.

20 Lefort employs the term "democratic revolution" ("Image of the Body," 302) to emphasize the process active since 1789, not the historical event itself. The king's body, according to Lefort, was "underpinned by that of Christ" (306). (Lefort relies heavily on Ernst Kantorowicz's seminal study *The King's Two Bodies: A Study in Medieval Political Theology* [Princeton: Princeton Univer-sity Press, 1957], especially the section on "Christ-Centered Kingship." For an excellent analysis of the body of Christ as an organizing metaphor for the pro-duction of social and individual identity, see Sarah Beckwith, *Christ's Body: Identity, Culture, and Society in Late Medieval Writings* (London and New York: Routledge, 1993).

21 See Lefort, "Image of the Body," 302. See also Beckwith's argument about the body of Christ as both the image of social unity and the site of contestation, in particular "Christ's Body and the Imaging of Social Order," in *Christ's Body,* 22–44.

22 As Lefort argues, those who exercise power now do so as mere mortals; see "Image of the Body," 303, 305.

23 The best-known study of the National Socialist imaginary and its relation to Hitler is Alexander Mitscherlich and Margarete Mitscherlich, *Die Unfähigkeit zu trauern* (Munich: Piper Verlag, 1987 [1967]). For a psychoanalytically oriented study of Hitler in the context of literature, see Alice Yaeger Kaplan, *Reproduc-tions of Banality* (Minneapolis: University of Minnesota Press, 1986). A satiri-cal account of the centrality of Hitler's body is the West German film *Schtonk,* a comedy about the scandal surrounding the forged Hitler diaries that begins

in 1945 with the desperate attempt to burn Hitler's body and the exasperated cry: "He won't burn!" A somewhat less satirical representation of the Führer's body can be found in Goebbels's novel of formation from 1923 (*Michael: Ein deutsches Schicksal in Tagebuchblättern* [Munich: Zentralverlag der NSDAP, 1929], 101). The protagonist, who styles himself after Wilhelm Meister, experiences a veritable epiphany as he hears—and sees—Hitler, "a prophet," for the first time. Indeed, much of the National Socialist literature, film, and drama generates sublime representations of the leader (sublime in the sense of the limitlessness of power and the Führer's connection to some higher mission): see, for instance, the sublime portrait of Göring in Gudrun Streiter's "Diary of an SA Man's Bride," in *Nazi Culture,* ed. George Mosse (New York: Schocken Books, 1985), 125; the queen's body in the Nazi film *Kolberg* (Veit Harlan, dir., 1945); and, finally, the leader's suffering, Christlike body in a number of the *Thingspiele* (a form of Nazi mass theater which merged expressionism with the ritual structures of the passion play), for example, Richard Euringer's *Deutsche Passion 1933* (Oldenburg i.O. and Berlin: Stalling, 1933).

24 On the notion of symbolic forms, see Clifford Geertz, "Ideology as a Cultural System," in his *Interpretation of Culture* (New York: Basic Books, 1973), 213; and "Centers, Kings, and Charisma," in his *Local Knowledge: Further Essays in Interpretive Anthropology* (Basic Books: New York, 1983), 124.

25 *DDR-Lesebuch: Stalinisierung 1949–1955,* ed. Ilse Spittmann and Gisela Helwig (n.p.: Edition Deutschland Archiv, 1989), 30–31.

26 On Becher's relationship to Stalinist politics, see Matias Mieth, " 'Der Mensch, der nicht geschunden wird, wird nicht erzogen': Johannes R. Becher und die Gewalt des Stalinismus," *Weimarer Beiträge* 5 (1991): 764–72.

27 Anna Seghers, "Das Unsterbliche der Völker war in ihm verkörpert," *Neue deutsche Literatur* 4 (1953): 5–6. See Manfred Jäger, *Kultur und Politik in der DDR* (Cologne: Deutschlandarchiv, 1982), 66, for Johannes R. Becher's poem "Danksagung" (Expression of Thanks), which ends with the following lines:

And no mountains set him any limit,
No enemy is strong enough to resist
To the man whose name is Stalin, because his thought
Becomes deed, and Stalin's will becomes reality.

28 Stephan Heym's article, which appeared in the West German weekly *Die Zeit* in 1965, was originally delivered as a speech at an international writers' colloquium in 1964. It could not be published in the GDR; see Jäger, *Kultur und Politik,* 111. Hein's text elaborates on a Komar and Melamid painting called *I Saw Stalin Once When I Was a Child;* see his *Die fünfte Grundrechenart: Aufsätze und Reden* (Frankfurt: Luchterhand, 1990), 155–59.

29 Dieter Segert, "Fahnen, Umzüge, Rituale: Die Macht der Rituale und Symbole," in *DDR—Ein Staat vergeht,* ed. Thomas Blanke and Rainer Erd (Frankfurt a.M.: Fischer Taschenbuch Verlag, 1991), 27. Recent studies of East Germany's symbolic politics have focused on the meaning of the *Tribüne* (on the first of May,

for instance, everyone would march past the Party and State functionaries assembled on a platform). Monika Gibas and Rainer Gries understand this specific
ritual as a "symbolic 'paternalist' exchange," where the leadership guaranteed
"law and order, social security and a relatively undisturbed existence in toler-
ated private niches," in exchange for work discipline and other "classical German secondary virtues"; see their "Vorschlag für den ersten Mai: Die Führung
zieht am Volk vorbei!' Überlegungen zur Geschichte der Tribüne in der DDR,"
Deutschlandarchiv 5 (1995): 488. Jürgen Danyel writes about the adaptation of
Soviet (ritual) practices as a history of "failures, bad luck, and mishaps," citing
Birgit Sauer's work on May Day: the construction of the Palace of the Republic
was intended to provide the GDR leadership with a platform equal to that of the
Lenin Mausoleum. But when the Palace was finished in 1976, the demonstrations had to be relocated to the Karl-Marx-Allee because the distance between
the platform and "the people" was so great that individual functionaries could
no longer be recognized; see his "Politische Rituale als Sowjetimporte," ms., 5.

30 This official narrative of the GDR as the culmination of the working-class
struggle is most clearly stated in *Grundriss der Geschichte der deutschen Arbeiterbewegung* (Précis of the History of the German Workers' Movement): "The
world historical victory of the Soviet Union and of the peoples of the anti-Hitler
coalition over fascist Germany liberated the German people from the fascist
yoke. The bloody struggle of the German Communists and of all antifascists had
decisively contributed to the possibility of a new democratic life"; special issue
of *Einheit* (August 1962): 143. The *Grundriss* was used in the Party schools of the
SED. Its publication in 1962 as a special issue of the Party's theoretical journal
Einheit (Unity) was a major event. Written by a special commission of the SED
Central Committee, the *Grundriss* defines its historical field as reaching from
the *Communist Manifesto* (1848) to the present (1962). This story of victory is
embedded within a larger narrative spanning all of German history, establishing
the working class as heir to Germany's progressive tendencies. Historical discourse was not homogeneous. Alexander Abusch's *Der Irrweg einer Nation* (A
Nation's Erroneous Path) (Berlin: Aufbau-Verlag, 1946), a different version of
the German past, portrays German history as history gone astray. (I will return
to this text in chapter 2.) On the GDR's legitimatory discourse of antifascism,
see Eve Rosenhaft, "The Uses of Remembrance: The Legacy of the Communist
Resistance in the German Democratic Republic," in *Germans against Nazism:
Essays in Honor of Peter Hoffmann,* ed. Francis R. Nicosia and Lawrence D.
Stokes (New York and Oxford: Berg, 1990), 369–88; and Meuschel, *Legitimation und Parteiherrschaft,* 29–81. For a detailed comparison of the four phases
of historiography concerned with the Nazi past in East and West, see Ines
Reich, "Geteilter Widerstand: Die Tradierung des deutschen Widerstands in der
Bundesrepublik und der DDR," *Zeitschrift für Geschichtswissenschaft* 42 (1994):
635–43; for a highly controversial reading of antifascism as participating in the
antimodern tendencies of the Weimar Republic, see Antonia Grunenberg, *Antifaschismus — ein deutscher Mythos* (Reinbek bei Hamburg: Rowohlt, 1993); for

an insightful critique of Grunenberg, see Wolfgang Fritz Haug, "Liberalität, die sich selbst aufhebt," *Freitag,* May 6, 1994.

31   The Bund Proletarisch-Revolutionärer Schriftsteller (BPRS), the writers' organization of the German Communist Party, was disbanded in 1933. Bredel, Marchwitza, and Gotsche had been founding members, and Seghers joined in 1928. Helga Gallas's *Marxistische Literaturtheorie: Kontroversen im Bund proletarisch-revolutionärer Schriftsteller* (Darmstadt and Neuwied: Luchterhand, 1971) is still the best book on the BPRS.

The following definition of the antifascist imperative is typical: "The antifascist resistance struggle was essentially a class struggle between the working class, and other working people, and monopoly capital" (K. Mammach, *Die deutsche antifaschistische Widerstandsbewegung 1933–1939: Geschichte der deutschen Widerstandsbewegung im Inland und in der Emigration* [Berlin: Dietz, 1974], 255). On the gradual transformation of East German historiography since the mid-1970s, see Reich, "Geteilter Widerstand."

32   Bernhard Greiner, "Das Dilemma der 'Nachgeborenen': Paradoxien des Brecht-Gedichts und seiner literarischen Antworten in der DDR," in *Frühe DDR-Literatur,* ed. Klaus R. Scherpe and Lutz Winkler (Hamburg: Argument-Verlag, 1988), 179.

33   Georg Lukács, "Schicksalswende," in *Schicksalswende: Beiträge zu einer neuen deutschen Ideologie* (Berlin: Aufbau-Verlag, 1956), 145. On this discourse of the relationship to the past as a relationship to the fathers, see also the extended discussion at the Seventh Writers' Conference in 1973, especially "Arbeitsgruppe II: Literatur und Geschichtsbewusstsein" (Workshop II: Literature and Historical Consciousness), where the East German literary critic Hans Jürgen Geerdts compares the novels by Bredel, Seghers, and Gotsche with the "petty bourgeois" *Ahnen* (Ancestors) by Gustav Freytag (*VII. Schriftstellerkongress der Deutschen Demokratischen Republik: Protokoll* [Berlin and Weimar: Aufbau-Verlag, 1974], 110–11). This extremely interesting discussion turns on the definition of "fathers" as the GDR's "founding fathers" versus the "real fathers," those German men who did not join the resistance movement. The author Herrmann Kant is most explicit: "What constitutes the tragedy in which an entire generation finds itself because of fascism and war? It consists among other things in the fact that this declaration of loyalty to the fathers has become impossible, because the fathers screwed them" (102). Christa Wolf, already working on *Kindheitsmuster,* argues, "Of course, one can adopt spiritual fathers . . . but one cannot adopt a biological father, never, although an entire generation might not have been disinclined to do so" (150). (We will return to this crucial issue later.)

34   Vladimir Mayakovsky, "Toi storone," in *Collected Works in Twelve Volumes* (Moscow: Pravda, 1978), 183 (quoted lines translated by Thomas Lahusen and Evgeny Dobrenko). In the 1926 film version of Gorky's novel by Vsevolod Pudovkin, the father is a strikebreaker who dies during a strike. As in many other

texts and films of the postrevolutionary period, the breaking off of family ties is accentuated. The typical revolutionary cuts these ties, sacrificing father and mother (or daughter, as in *Cement*) for the sake of the revolution; Soviet revolutionaries even take on new names (Stalin, Trotsky, Lenin, etc.). The father/son theme had been a central trope of Russian literature since Turgenev's *Fathers and Sons* (1862).

35 The German Communist Party was utterly traumatized by what it understood as the Left's *unexpected* defeat in 1933: the KPD leadership continued to speak of an immanent German revolution until 1935. But it was even more traumatized by the mass defection of young, unemployed men to the NSDAP. The Communists' reeducation program was explicitly designed to win back the minds of those who, they hoped, were not entirely committed to the Nazi ideology. This reeducation took several different forms: the school curricula included not only the reading of these foundational novels but also regular visits by former concentration camp inmates and members of the anti-Nazi resistance; streets and buildings were named after those whom the SED deemed true representatives of the resistance movement (see Maoz Azaryahu, *Vom Wilhelmplatz zu Thälmannplatz: Politische Symbole im öffentlichen Leben der DDR* [Gerlingen: Bleicher Verlag, 1991]); finally, the Party leadership themselves assumed the habitus and self-presentation of founding fathers and mothers, as did authors such as Bredel, Seghers, and Gotsche.

36 Danyel argues ("Politische Rituale," 10, 13) that the "mise-en-scene of the GDR state" was influenced by Soviet-style politics, an influence evident not only in the monumentalism of Stalinist architecture but also in the monuments' use as backdrop for ritualized mass events (e.g., Buchenwald's use for military ceremonies, specifically, the swearing in of East German officers). The most obvious example is the gigantic Treptow monument erected in honor of the Red Army. Danyel makes the important point, however, that these ritual forms should be understood as "effects of a symbiosis between (East) German and Soviet phenomena," which in this case raises the question of a psychological disposition toward mass rituals in a population accustomed to their enactment under National Socialism.

37 Katerina Clark, *The Soviet Novel: History as Ritual* (Chicago: University of Chicago Press, 1985), 114–15.

38 Heller, "World of Prettiness," 709.

39 Ibid.

40 Žižek, *For They Know Not What They Do,* 258.

41 Ibid.

42 Erik Neutsch, *Spur der Steine* (Munich: Damnitz Verlag, 1975 [1964]), 291–92.

43 The "objet petit a" functions here as the object of *the Other's* desire.

44 Žižek, *For They Know Not What They Do,* 260. With respect to Aleksandr Fadeev's *Young Guard* (1945, 1951) and its "death-and-transfiguration situation," Clark notes the distinction between "earthly bodies," subject to torture, and the

protagonist's "spirit," which "wafted at an immeasurable height, wafted as only man's creative spirit can" (*Soviet Novel,* 181). We will reencounter this image of the soul or spirit hovering over the tortured body in Gotsche's novel. He may have been inspired by Fadeev's novel about young Soviets fighting Nazi soldiers, which went through numerous editions in the GDR.

45 The significance of the mausoleum as an organizing cultural metaphor is further underscored by its frequent mention in Soviet literature; see Thomas Lahusen, "L'Homme nouveau, la femme nouvelle et le héros positif ou de la semiotique des sexes dans le réalisme socialiste," *Revue des Etudes Slaves* 50 (1988): 851.

46 Alexander Kluge and Oskar Negt, *Öffentlichkeit und Erfahrung: Zur Organisationsanalyse von bürgerlicher und proletarischer Öffentlichkeit* (Frankfurt a.M.: Suhrkamp, 1972), 404. This self-image was, of course, especially cultivated in the Party's military organizations, such as the RFB, the Communist militia. The RFB leadership referred to itself as "General Staff of the Socialist Liberation Army of Germany" (see Rosenhaft, *Beating the Fascists?,* 107, and, for her analysis of the militarization of the Party, 73). In his autobiographical account, Georg K. Glaser, a former member of the Communist Party, writes about becoming a "loyal soldier of the coming times," proud to be called a "young officer of the future Red Army of Germany"; see his *Geheimnis und Gewalt: Ein Bericht* (Stuttgart and Hamburg: Scherz and Coverts, 1953), 73.

47 In contrast to Žižek, who thematizes the material body within the health/sickness dichotomy, Kantorowicz pointed to reproduction as the signifier of the material in *The King's Two Bodies.*

48 On the religious images and metaphors that emerged during the Hungarian uprising, see Anna Szemere, "Bandits, Heroes, the Honest and the Misled: Exploring the Politics of Representation in the Hungarian Uprising of 1956," in *Cultural Studies Reader,* ed. Lawrence Grossberg, Cary Nelson, and Paula A. Treichler (New York: Routledge, 1992), 637. See also Christian Semler, "Gestrenge Ansichten der Henker Christi," *TAZ,* December 8, 1993, on the analogous structure of Soviet socialist realist paintings of Party meetings and canonical representations of the Last Supper (12). The most dramatic version of the Communist martyr is the portrayal of Pavel Korchagin in Ostrovsky's 1932 fetish novel *How the Steel Was Tempered:* the protagonist loses one body part after another in the service of building socialism, finally having to give up the struggle because of a terminal disease. At the 1973 Writers' Conference, the East German author Gabriele Eckart spoke about the teaching of literature. One of the essay questions she mentioned was "Which positive characteristics does Pavel Korchagin have, and what can I learn from them as a member of the Free German Youth?" (in *VII. Schriftstellerkongress,* 128). Clark analyzes the martyr plot as one of the main subplots of Soviet socialist realism (*Soviet Novel,* 178ff.).

49 Clark, *Soviet Novel,* 119, 129.

50 Jacques Lacan, quoted in Juliet Mitchell, *Psychoanalysis and Feminism* (New York: Vintage Books, 1975), 394.

51 Sigmund Freud, "The Ego and the Id" (1923), in *The Standard Edition of the*

Complete Psychological Works of Sigmund Freud, ed. James Strachey (London: Hogarth Press and the Institute of Psycho-Analysis, 1961), 19: 33ff.

52 Mitchell, *Psychoanalysis and Feminism,* 392, 391.

53 Jacqueline Rose, *The Haunting of Sylvia Plath* (Cambridge, Mass.: Harvard University Press, 1993), 232. Rose correctly singles out fascism as "in fact one of the few historical moments which historians have generally recognized as needing psychoanalytic concepts of desire and identification in order for it to be fully understood" (7). (The best-known example of this type of research is Klaus Theweleit's *Male Fantasies,* to which I will return.)

54 Ibid., 7.

55 Before the purges of the late 1940s and early 1950s, the S E D was far from homogeneous. For the most succinct overview of the GDR's oppositional groups, see Christoph Klessmann, "Opposition und Dissidenz in der Geschichte der DDR," *Aus Politik und Zeitgeschehen,* Jan. 25, 1991, 52–62.

56 Although Gotsche's novel was written after 1945, it clearly participates in the same basic pattern.

57 See Janet L. Beizer, *Family Plots: Balzac's Narrative Generations* (New Haven and London: Yale University Press, 1986), 6.

58 This dimension of the family narrative is certainly not new. In nineteenth-century France, the ubiquitous issue of legitimacy was worked out in narratives about fathers and sons; see Peter Brooks, *Reading for the Plot: Design and Intention in Narrative* (New York: Vintage Books, 1985), 62ff. *Buddenbrooks* (1910) also thematizes the issue: "We are not free, separate, and independent entities, but like the links in a chain, and we could not by any means be what we are without those who went before us and showed us the way" (Thomas Mann, *Buddenbrooks: The Decline of a Family,* trans. H. T. Lowe-Porter [New York: Knopf, 1964], 120).

59 On different cultural frames, see Clifford Geertz, "Centers, Kings, and Charisma: Reflections on the Symbolics of Power," 121–46. In *The Family Romance of the French Revolution* (Berkeley: University of California Press, 1992), Lynn Hunt argues that family narratives are central to "the constitution of all forms of authority" (8). This claim seems overstated and curiously ahistorical. However, it is striking that the family narrative is a discourse used by both Communist and National Socialist authors starting in the 1930s. The most famous example from Nazi culture is probably the 1933 film *Hitlerjunge Quex* (Hitler Youth Quex), directed by Steinhoff. The story revolves around a conflict between fathers and sons, with the former representing the old republic (Social Democrats or Communists), the latter the new Third Reich; see *Geschichte des deutschen Films,* ed. Wolfgang Jacobsen, Anton Kaes, and Hans Helmut Prinzler (Stuttgart: Verlag J. B. Metzler, 1993), 123ff. The most famous counter-narrative is Brecht's 1932 poem "Deutschland," in which Germany is allegorically represented by a mother figure whose skirt is covered with blood from the murder of one son by the others (*Die Gedichte von Bertolt Brecht in einem Band* [Frankfurt a.M.: Suhrkamp Verlag, 1981], 487).

60 Joan Wallach Scott, "Gender: A Useful Category of Historical Analysis," in her *Gender and the Politics of History* (New York: Columbia University Press, 1988), 42, 45.

61 See Ursula Heukenkamp, "Das Frauenbild in der antifaschistischen Erneuerung der SBZ," in *"Wen kümmert's, wer spricht": Zur Literatur und Kulturgeschichte von Frauen aus Ost und West,* ed. Inge Stephan, Sigrid Weigel, and Kerstin Wilhelms (Cologne and Vienna: Böhlau Verlag, 1991), 10. For a discussion of this often allegorical use of images of women in several Eastern European countries and of the further evolution of this discourse after the transformations in the late 1980s, see Einhorn, "Gendered Symbolism: The Nation as Woman," in *Cinderella Goes to Market,* 221ff.

62 Michael Rohrwasser uses this phrase to characterize the KPD's serial novels, in *Saubere Mädel, starke Genossen: Proletarische Massenliteratur?* (Berlin: Verlag Roter Stern, 1975), 102.

63 Although he essentially defends East German censorship, Alfred Klein's discussion of "self-motivated" rewritings nevertheless provides an interesting insight into the mechanisms of what Baudin, Heller, and Lahusen ("Le réalisme socialiste sovietique") call the "openness" of socialist realism; see Klein's "Werkstattcharakter oder ideologische Repression?" *Sinn und Form* 42 (1990): 467–78.

64 Ilja Fradkin, "Lehren der Geschichte," special issue of *Sinn und Form* on Willi Bredel (Berlin: Rütten und Loening, 1965), 228ff.

65 See Booss, "Nachwort," in *Die Söhne,* 564–65.

66 These events include the 1923 Kapp-Putsch, a right-wing attempt to overthrow the Weimar Republic, which started in Munich, and the so-called Bloody Sunday of May 1, 1929, in Berlin, when a May Day demonstration was broken up by the city's Social Democratic chief of police.

67 Bowing to the criticism leveled at his main character, Peter Kumiak (the father), Marchwitza rewrote him as class-conscious worker, erasing the naiveté which had characterized Kumiak in the first edition. On the reception of the trilogy, see Beate Messerschmidt, "Neue Wege, von Arbeitern zu erzählen: Hans Marchwitza, *Die Kumiaks,*" in *Erfahrung Exil: Antifaschistische Romane 1933–1945,* ed. Sigrid Bock and Manfred Hahn (Berlin: Aufbau-Verlag, 1979), 73–93; and "Sozialistische Literatur im Exil: Das Beispiel Hans Marchwitza," *Internationales Archiv für Sozialgeschichte der deutschen Literatur* 12 (1987): 213–36.

68 "Die Freunde" was the East German term used to refer to the Soviets.

69 The categories of "ideological" and "aesthetic" project are borrowed from Pierre Macherey, *Pour une théorie de la production littéraire* (Paris: Seuil, 1966).

70 With respect to narrative voice, these texts engage in writing about authority with authority, that is, they typically use an omniscient narrator, who, as Peter Brooks writes apropos of the nineteenth-century novel of paternity, assumes a "paternalist" attitude toward his characters (Brooks, *Reading for the Plot,* 75).

71 See Patricia Drexel Tobin, *Time and the Novel: The Genealogical Imperative* (Princeton: Princeton University Press, 1978), 54ff.

72 Within the version of Marxist historiography inscribed in Bredel's trilogy, the Paris Commune figures as the first, but failed, Socialist attempt to seize state power. Moreover, the standard Communist reading argues that the Commune's failure demonstrated the inevitability of a proletarian dictatorship.

73 Until the so-called Brussels Conference in 1935, the leadership of the Communist Party opposed a popular front with the Social Democratic Party, arguing that the latter's politics were "social-fascist." Before 1933, this judgment often led the Party press to denounce social democracy as the "real" enemy, neglecting the danger posed by the N S D A P. Although this tendency proved fatal, it was abandoned only reluctantly and retained a strong following within the Party, especially among the cadres who remained in Germany.

74 "He started to undress . . . and stood there stark naked, with only a pair of socks on his feet. Proud and satisfied, he gazed at his belly. In his view, belly and beard were the most necessary attributes of masculinity. And he was satisfied."

75 On Thälmann, see note 16.

76 This "disposition" is due to the "constitutional bisexuality of each individual" (Freud, "Ego and the Id," 31).

77 Ibid., 34.

78 Mitchell, *Psychoanalysis and Feminism,* 71.

79 It is, of course, problematic to use the term "symbolic father" for this image of the ideal father which the substitute represents, since, as I mentioned before, within Lacan's theory (from which the term is derived) no actual person ever embodies the symbolic father. However, for the Oedipal crisis to be resolved, the actual father has to be identified with the Name-of-the-Father (i.e., the symbolic father), who represents the Law of the Symbolic order. It is this identification of the Communist father figure with the symbolic father that these texts insist upon, denying the gap. Lacan describes the composite nature of the paternal function as follows: "Even when in fact it is represented by a single person, the paternal function concentrates in itself both imaginary and real relations, always more or less inadequate to the symbolic relation that essentially constitutes it"; Jacques Lacan, "The Function and Field of Speech and Language in Psychoanalysis," in *Écrits: A Selection* (New York and London: Norton, 1977), 67.

80 Theweleit analyzes this armored body in his *Male Fantasies,* 2 vols. (Minneapolis: University of Minnesota Press, 1987, 1989). Although my approach is similar to Theweleit's in attempting to account for the structures of fantasy deployed in texts, my material, with its emphasis on the figure of the father, demands a different explanation.

81 For this narrative of the *test,* see also Bredel's *Die Prüfung* (The Test) (Dortmund: Weltkreis Verlag, 1981 [1934]), an autobiographical novel about a Communist journalist in Hamburg who is interrogated and imprisoned by the Gestapo for his clandestine activities.

82 In *Cement,* the classic socialist realist text about the construction of communism after the civil war, Gladkov created a scene which dramatically stages this armored body. Gleb, the protagonist, who has recently returned from the

civil war to the ruined cement factory, participates in a meeting of the factory's Party cell. Accused of having survived the war, he rips off his shirt, asking his comrades to touch his body by pointing to the scars that cover his torso. The exhibition of the Bolshevik soldier's wounded body suffices; it does not require phallic proof: still angry, Gleb asks the assembled Party members if they want him to pull down his pants so that they can see more scars. Eyes riveted on his naked, scar-covered body, his audience falls silent; Fjodor Gladkow and Heiner Müller, *Zement,* ed. Fritz Mierau, trans. Olga Halpern (Leipzig: Verlag Philipp Reclam, Jr., 1975), 91–92.

83 See Thomas Lahusen, "Between Engineers: *Far from Moscow,* the Pearl of Creation, and Homosocialist Desire," in his *Life Writes the Book: Real Socialism and Socialist Realism in Stalin's Russia* (Ithaca, N.Y.: Cornell University Press, 1997).

84 Both Juliet Mitchell and Teresa Brennan remind us that, for Freud, femininity and masculinity were not biological concepts but modes present in both sexes; see Mitchell, *Psychoanalysis and Feminism,* 50ff; Teresa Brennan, *The Interpretation of the Flesh: Freud and Femininity* (London: Routledge, 1992), 6ff.

85 Hell, "At the Center an Absence."

86 This distinguishes them from the literature of the Freikorps, the authors of which engage in the elimination of women, whom they perceive as castrating (see Theweleit, *Male Fantasies,* I: 74, 89ff.).

87 Rose, *Haunting of Sylvia Plath,* 231.

88 Such flag-burnings did actually occur in several German cities in the spring of 1933.

89 See Sigmund Freud, "The Economic Problem in Masochism," in *Standard Edition,* 19: 169.

90 The phrase is from Walter Benjamin's review of *Die Mutter,* "Ein Familiendrama auf dem epischen Theater," in *Materialien zu Bertolt Brechts "Die Mutter",* ed. Werner Hecht (Frankfurt a.M.: Suhrkamp Verlag, 1969), 22–26.

91 Freud, "Economic Problem in Masochism," 162; my emphasis.

92 These were the very scenes which *NDL* published in its 1959 issue, thus marking them as the novel's most significant contribution to the antifascist legacy.

93 Freud, "Economic Problem in Masochism," 169.

94 Ibid.

95 Ibid.

96 Kaja Silverman, *Male Subjectivity at the Margins* (London: Routledge, 1992), 197.

97 Elaine Scarry has analyzed torture as a spectacle of power in which the body is transformed into voice: the body acts as an agent of power, trying to coerce the tortured prisoner's voice to mimic that of the torturer; see *The Body in Pain* (New York and Oxford: Oxford University Press, 1985), 45. In Gotsche's scenario, the body is being punished, but it is *not* transformed into voice (an aspect that will turn out to be crucial in Christa Wolf's reworking of the image of the antifascist's body-in-pain).

98 Freud, "Economic Problem in Masochism," 165.

99 Sigmund Freud, "Fetishism," *Standard Edition,* 21: 152–53.

100 Ibid., 157.

101 In 1964, with a little help from "the friends," Gotsche would publish another story of resistance revolving around the preservation of an object: a statue of "father Lenin," as it is repeatedly called. The bronze monument, transported by the German Army from the Soviet Union to the German town of Eisleben, is saved by a group of Communists, who erect it in the middle of the marketplace and cover it with Red Flags to welcome the Red Army in 1945: "Lenin stood in the heart of Germany, erect." Again, the connotations are interesting, such as in the reaction of one of the Communists as he touches the statue for the first time: "He stroked the warm metal, it warmed not only his hand"; Otto Gotsche, *Zwischen Nacht und Morgen* (Halle/Saale: Mitteldeutscher Verlag, 1964), 724, 725.

102 Frank Trommler, *Sozialistische Literatur in Deutschland: Ein historischer Überblick* (Stuttgart: Metzler, 1976), 704.

103 Freud, "Fetishism," 154.

104 Gotsche's Communist subject might be read as the epitome of Žižek's "totalitarian leader." According to Žižek, this totalitarian "subject" constitutes itself as object, the *objet petit a* of Stalinism's Other, which are the Laws of History. The Stalinist leader is thus one who, through the structure of perversion (that is, by making himself the object which is working for the enjoyment of the Other, not itself), avoids the division which constitutes the subject, projecting it onto the enemy ("bourgeois subjectivity"). The totalitarian leader thus represents a "radical objectivization–instrumentalization of his own subjective position" (Žižek, *For They Know Not What They Do,* 235).

105 This section ends with the following lines: "When the flag of Kriwoj Rog was flying over the land / Lenin marched in with his sons with iron steps"; Stephan Hermlin, *Mansfelder Oratorium,* 2d ed. (Leipzig: Verlag C. F. Peters, 1953), 19.

106 In this three-volume socialist realist dinosaur, Neutsch rewrites once more the GDR's story, focusing on the younger generation's transformation from HJ to FDJ-members. The Red Flag plays a central role in the story of Achim: first, he faces the decision whether to carry the flag at an FDJ parade, and later on, we witness with him the raising of the Red Flag on the Brandenburg Gate during the FDJ's first *Deutschlandtreffen*—a dramatic moment of triumph over the old Germany, "Prussia's glory." *Der Friede im Osten* (Halle: Mitteldeutscher Verlag, 1974), 1:465–66. One of the songs of the Young Pioneers takes up the theme:

I am carrying a flag,
and this flag is red.
It is the workers' flag
that my father carried through misery.
The flag never fell
however often its carrier fell.
It is flying over our heads today, too,
and it can already see the goal of our longing.

(Eberhard Görner, "Ich trage eine Fahne . . . Nachdenken über eine untergegangene Partei und ihre Lieder," *Deutschland Archiv* 3 [March 1992]: 264).

107 Annette Simon, "Ich und sie: Versuch, mir und anderen meine ostdeutsche Moral zu erklären," *Kursbuch* (February 1993): 27.

108 The FDJ (Free German Youth) was the East German Communist Party's youth organization. Wolf describes the generational nexus as follows: "We were then presented with an attractive offer: you can rid yourself of your potential but not yet realized guilt by actively participating in the construction of the new society"; Christa Wolf, "Unerledigte Widersprüche: Gespräch mit Therese Hörnigk," in her *Im Dialog* (Darmstadt and Neuwied: Luchterhand Verlag, 1990),29.

109 Wolf goes on to praise *Die Fahne* for bringing back to life a family whose exemplary story created the "foundations of the Socialist ethic which we are today trying to develop as a general norm" (Wolf, "Sozialistischen Literatur der Gegenwart," 5–6).

110 Wolf has spoken of the strong emotional investment of one generation in the other: "The interest of the older people in transmitting their ideals to us was really considerable — also because one's own life was justified when the younger generation understood itself as a succeeding generation" ("Unerledigte Widersprüche," 44).

111 Brigitte Reimann, *Franziska Linkerhand* (Munich: Deutscher Taschenbuch Verlag, 1984 [1974]), 380. Sigrid Meuschel thus correctly claims that the discourse of antifascism contributed to a repression of the GDR's Stalinist past (*Legitimation und Parteiherrschaft,* 40). Nevertheless, as many of these texts demonstrate, Stalinism was covertly thematized as *loss.* Curiously enough, this phenomenon has never attracted the attention of critics; see, on this topic, Patricia Herminghouse, "Confronting the 'Blank Spots of History': GDR Culture and the Legacy of 'Stalinism,' " *German Studies Review* 2 (May 1991): 345–65.

112 Irmtraud Morgner, *Leben und Abenteuer der Trobadora Beatriz* (Darmstadt and Neuwied: Luchterhand, 1976), 310–11.

113 Ibid., 185.

114 Samuel Weber, *Return to Freud: Jacques Lacan's Dislocation of Psychoanalysis* (Cambridge: Cambridge University Press, 1991), 137.

115 Stefan Schütz, "Kekse und Totenschädel: Ein Gespräch mit Stefan Schütz von Axel Schnell," *Die Zeit,* April 13, 1990, 26. In his *Hinze-Kunze-Roman,* Volker Braun visualizes the participation of the dead in the yearly rally commemorating the deaths of Rosa Luxembourg and Karl Liebknecht. Among these *Novembertoten,* the protagonist recognizes his proletarian grandfather. In this riotous tableau, those who died fighting in the *Novemberrevolution* — the "immature, impatient, the bloody amateurs of the beginning, the theoreticians of spontaneity" — are the ones who are truly alive, a "provocation" to regulated and petrified state socialism; Volker Braun, *Hinze-Kunze-Roman* (Leipzig: Reclam-Verlag, 1990 [1985]), 37–38.

2 Stalinist Motherhood, or the Hollow Spaces of Emotion

1 Anna Seghers is a pseudonym. Born Netty Reiling in 1900, in 1925, on her marriage to Hungarian Communist and philosopher Laszlo Radvanyi, she became Netty Radvanyi, but she had already published her first story in 1924 under the pseudonym Antje Seghers. She joined the German Communist Party in 1928, and, although Laszlo Radvanyi took a Party name (Johann-Lorenz Schmidt), we do not know whether Netty took one. According to Steffie Spira, her friends called her "Tchibi" (Hungarian for owl).

2 Ursula Heukenkamp argues that the Nazi past had produced a crisis in the concept of motherhood, whereas masculinity continued to function as an unequivocally positive attribute ("Das Frauenbild in der antifaschistischen Erneuerung," 9–10). Yet since the central component of the East German hegemonic project, the paternal narrative, is essentially unstable, masculinity must be in crisis. On dismantling the myth of masculinity, see Annemarie Tröger, "Between Rape and Prostitution: Survival Strategies and Chances of Emancipation for Berlin Women after World War II," in *Women in Culture and Politics: A Century of Change,* ed. Judith Freidländer and Carroll Smith-Rosenberg (Bloomington: Indiana University Press, 1986), 97–118.

3 Toril Moi, *Simone de Beauvoir: The Making of an Intellectual Woman* (Oxford and Cambridge: Blackwell, 1994), 6, 5. What makes Moi's contribution so unique is her insistence on not theorizing subjectivity exclusively as interiority but also, from a Bourdievian perspective, as a social event—hence the chapters on Beauvoir's education and on her standing in the literary field as a female author, then and now. See also Toril Moi, "Appropriating Bourdieu: Feminist Theory and Pierre Bourdieu's Sociology of Culture," *New Literary History* 22 (Autumn 1991): 1017–49.

4 She began the novel in 1944, according to Ute Brandes, *Anna Seghers,* 58.

5 According to the Seghers archive, the manuscript has disappeared, so it is now impossible to trace her changes.

6 J. Knipowitsch, "Lehren der Geschichte," quoted by Inge Diersen, "Jason 1948—Problematische Heimkehr," in *Unerwünschte Erfahrung: Kriegsliteratur und Zensur in der DDR,* ed. Ursula Heukenkamp (Berlin and Weimar: Aufbau-Verlag, 1990), 317; *Literatur der DDR,* Vol. 11 of *Geschichte der deutschen Literatur* (Berlin: Volk und Wissen Volkseigener Verlag, 1977), 173.

7 Anna Seghers, "Aufgaben der Kunst," in *Glauben an Irdisches: Essays,* ed. Christa Wolf (Leipzig: Reclam, 1974), 170.

8 Anna Seghers, *The Seventh Cross,* trans. James A. Galston (New York: Monthly Review Press, 1987), 146; see also *Das siebte Kreuz* (Frankfurt a.M.: Luchterhand Literaturverlag, 1988 [1942]), 182–83.

9 As indicated in chapter 1, note 4, quotations from *The Dead Stay Young* will be cited in the text as *DS*/page number, followed by the corresponding page number in *Die Toten bleiben jung* (*DT*/page).

10 Given the patrilinear logic of this metaphorical narrative, it is not surprising

that most critics assume the child to be a son; see, for instance, Lutz Winkler, " 'An der Zerstörung des Faschismus mitschreiben': Anna Seghers' Romane *Das siebte Kreuz* und *Die Toten bleiben jung,*" in *Antifaschistische Literatur,* ed. Lutz Winckler (Königstein/Ts.: Athenäum Verlag, 1979), 3:181.

11 See, for instance, Emmerich, *Kleine Literaturgeschichte,* 68.

12 Anna Seghers, "Volk und Schriftsteller," in her *Die Macht der Worte: Reden-Schriften-Briefe* (Leipzig and Weimar: Gustav Kiepenheuer Verlag, 1979), 48. On motherhood and National Socialism, see Claudia Koonz, *Mothers in the Fatherland* (New York: St. Martin's Press, 1987).

13 On Seghers's aesthetics, see Werner Roggausch, *Das Exilwerk von Anna Seghers 1933–1939* (Munich: Minerva Publikation, 1979), 299–326; for an "official" East German reading, see Kurt Batt, "Der Dialog zwischen Anna Seghers und Georg Lukács," *Weimarer Beiträge* 5 (1975): 105–39. For a strong defense of the "early" experimental versus the later "socialist realist" Seghers, see Brandes, *Anna Seghers,* 6–10, 63ff. As I mentioned earlier, I find the binary categories guiding Brandes's study (private vs. public, aesthetic vs. political) highly problematic.

14 "A Correspondence with Anna Seghers," in Georg Lukács, *Essays on Realism,* ed. Rodney Livingston, trans. David Fernbach (Cambridge, Mass.: MIT Press, 1981), 171, 186.

15 Winckler, " 'An der Zerstörung des Faschismus mitschreiben,' " 172.

16 Sigrid Bock, "Erziehungsfunktion und Romanexperiment: Anna Seghers, 'Die Toten bleiben jung,' " in *Erfahrung Exil. Antifaschistische Romane 1933–1945: Analysen,* ed. Sigrid Bock and Manfred Hahn (Berlin and Weimar: Aufbau-Verlag, 1979), 406. What Winckler, a West German critic, defends becomes a matter of nervous concern among some East German critics, but not Kurt Batt, who arrives at the same conclusion as Winckler; see his *Anna Seghers: Versuch über Entwicklung und Werke* (Leipzig: Verlag Philipp Reclam, 1973), 210. Inge Diersen, however, avers that the experiment fails because the connection between the five narrative threads of the novel tends to gradually loosen; see her "Kompositionsfragen in Anna Seghers' Romanen," in *Kritik in der Zeit: Der Sozialismus-seine Literatur-ihre Entwicklung,* ed. Klaus Jarmatz (Halle/Saale: Mitteldeutscher Verlag, 1969), 465.

17 See Bock, "Erziehungsfunktion und Romanexperiment," 419.

18 Linearity also results from Erwin's curse: one by one, all those who took part in his execution will die, first Klemm and Becker, then Nadler, Lieven, and finally Wenzlow. Repetition is another part of this rigid prestructuring. While some characters mention Erwin's murder periodically, for Wenzlow it becomes a disturbing memory which erupts at various points in his story. Like Wenzlow, Marie will always remember the evening when she waited for Erwin in vain, thus keeping the initial episode alive.

19 Beizer, *Family Plots,* 2.

20 See, for instance, Ernst Bloch, *Erbschaft dieser Zeit* (Frankfurt a.M.: Suhrkamp Verlag, 1985 [1935]).

21 Anna Seghers, "Aufgaben der Kunst," in *Glauben an Irdisches,* 170. See Winckler, " 'An der Zerstörung des Faschismus mitschreiben,' " 174ff., for a good presentation of Seghers's thoughts on the subject.

22 On the transformation of the figure of Dasha, especially her de-eroticization and reemphasized maternal qualities, see Leonid Heller and Thomas Lahusen, "Palimpsexes: Les metamorphoses de la thématique sexuelle dans le roman de F. Gladkov 'Le Ciment,' " *Wiener Slavistischer Almanach* 15 (1985): 211–54. (Heller and Lahusen argue that the many revisions of *Cement* exemplify the destruction of the formal coherence of a work that was initially close to the Soviet avant-garde. Their structuralist analysis remains, however, on the level of description, with no conclusions drawn from the changes they observe.) In *The Women's Liberation Movement in Russia* (Princeton: Princeton University Press, 1990), Richard Stites traces the disappearance of the iconic image of the female commissar from Soviet culture in the late 1920s (322ff.). A similar figure, the woman as revolutionary soldier, appears in the novel *Far from Moscow* by Vassili Ashaev (*Fern von Moskau* [Berlin: Verlag Kultur und Fortschritt, 1951], 771–72). This figure is rare in East German literature, making only a brief appearance in Heiner Müller's 1972 adaptation of *Cement.*

23 Anna Seghers, "Maerz 1933—Verhaftung Thälmanns," *Freies Deutschland* 2 (1943): 12.

24 On *Nadja,* see Robin Suleiman, *Subversive Intent: Gender, Politics, and the Avantgarde* (Cambridge, Mass.: Harvard University Press, 1990), 88ff.

25 On feminine allegory as the representation of "pure" idea linked to "pure" body, see Sigrid Weigel, " 'Das Theater der weissen Revolution': Körper und Verkörperung im Revolutions-Theater von Heiner Müller und Georg Büchner," in *Die Marseillaise der Weiber,* ed. Inge Stephan and Sigrid Weigel (Berlin: Argument Verlag, 1989), 163. For a historical reading of the shift from Delacroix's *Liberty,* the sexualized feminine icon of the people, to the suffering mother figures of the working-class movement, representing "spirit, not body," see Eric Hobsbawm, "Man and Woman: Images on the Left," in his *Workers: Worlds of Labor* (New York: Pantheon Books, 1984), 89. On the woman figure as an allegory for which men fight, see Gertraud Gutzmann, "Zum Stellenwert des Spanischen Bürgerkriegs in Anna Seghers' Romanen 'Die Entscheidung' und 'Das Vertrauen,' " in *Wen kümmert's, wer spricht? Zur Literatur und Kulturgeschichte von Frauen aus Ost und West,* ed. Inge Stephan (Cologne: Bohlan, 1991), 201, 205.

26 And it fit the official image of women that the S E D propagated in the 1950s. Ina Merkel traces the coexistence of traditional images of women with the new ideal of the liberated woman; see "Charme, Zement und Schwefelsäure: Frauenbilder in der D D R der 5oer," in *Alltäglicher Stalinismus,* ed. Ostberliner Geschichtswerkstatt (Hamburg: Ergebnisseverlag, 1992), 48; see also Merkel's extended study, . . . *und du, Frau an der Werkbank: Die DDR in den 5oer Jahren* (Berlin: Elefantenpress, 1990). According to Steffi Spira, Seghers herself felt very ambivalent about working mothers, expressing concerns about the disappearance

of housewives and mothers; see Spira's *Rote Fahne mit Trauerflor* (Freiburg: Kore, 1990), 16.

27   Cettina Rapisarda, "Women and Peace in Literature and Politics: The Example of Anna Seghers," in *German Writers and the Cold War 1945–61,* ed. Rhys W. Williams, Stephen Parker, and Colin Riordan (Manchester and New York: Manchester University Press, 1992), 162. Rapisarda quotes Seghers's "Offener Antwortbrief an eine sowjetische Mutter" (Open Letter to a Soviet Mother), in which she argues that women are a force for peace since life originates with them.

28   Anna Seghers, "Frauen und Kinder in der Emigration," *Argonautenschiff* 2 (1993): 320.

29   "Vierzig Jahre der Margarete Wolf" (1958; in *Frauen in der DDR,* ed. Lutz-W. Wolff [Munich: Deutscher Taschenbuch Verlag, 1990], 46–57) merges aspects of *Das siebte Kreuz* with *Die Toten bleiben jung,* recounting the GDR's "prehistory" from the perspective of Margarete Wolf, the sister of Ernst Wallau, one of the seven escapees and the voice of the Communist Party in *Das siebte Kreuz.* The novels are linked by the story when we learn that Ernst Wallau married Hilde Berger, a member of the Communist Berger family in *Die Toten bleiben jung.* "Agathe Schweigert" (1965; in her *Kraft der Schwachen* [Neuwied and Berlin: Luchterhand Verlag, 1966], 7–31) is the story of a mother who, upon learning that her son has left Germany to fight in the International Brigades, decides to follow him to Spain.

30   The stories were published together with a third one, "Das Ende" (The End), by Wieland Herzfelde's Aurora-Verlag, an exile publishing house in New York.

31   Anna Seghers, "Post ins gelobte Land," in her *Erzählungen* (Darmstadt and Neuwied: Luchterhand Verlag, 1977), 1:161. Quotations will be cited as P/page number.

32   Kathleen LaBahn, *Anna Seghers' Exile Literature* (New York: Peter Lang, 1986), 22ff.

33   The most detailed study of Seghers's family background and her religious upbringing is Friedrich Schütz, "Die Familie Seghers-Reiling und das jüdische Mainz," *Argonautenschiff* 2 (1993): 151–73. Jörg Bilke quotes a letter from Elisabeth Stimbert, a friend of Seghers, on the latter's orthodox upbringing, in "Auf der Suche nach Netty Reiling," *Blätter der Carl-Zuckmayer Gesellschaft* 6 (1980): 189.

34   Seghers was struck by a car in Mexico City in 1943 and spent several months hospitalized, in a coma. There has always been speculation about the accident. Some friends of Seghers maintain that it was a deliberate attempt on her life (the car hit her at full speed and drove away), ordered by either the Nazis or Stalin; see, for example, Sigrid Bock, "Die Farbe der Sonne und der Nacht: Gespräch mit Lenka Reinerova," *Argonautenschiff* 3 (1994): 129.

Seghers's mother was deported on March 20, 1942 to Piaski, a camp in the Auschwitz complex, according to Ute Brandes (*Anna Seghers,* 135); see also

Frank Wagner, "Deportation nach Piaski: Letzte Stationen der Passion von Hedwig Reiling," *Argonautenschiff* 3 (1994): 117–26.

35 See Christa Wolf's recent comment about Seghers's silence, in "Gesichter der Anna Seghers—zu einem Bildband," in her *Auf dem Weg nach Tabou: Texte 1990–1994* (Cologne: Kiepenheuer and Witsch, 1994), 225.

36 Quoted in Alexander Stephan, " 'Ich habe das Gefühl, ich bin in die Eiszeit versetzt': Zur Rückkehr von Anna Seghers aus dem Exil," *Germanic Review* 12 (1987): 145.

37 Ibid., 151, 152. According to another letter quoted by Stephan, Seghers still hoped to save her mother (169).

38 Ibid., 157. In 1992, Seghers's daughter, Ruth Radvanyi, recalled her earliest memories of her grandmother, particularly a day she spent with her at the age of four. The memory was accompanied by an "uncanny" feeling; Radvanyi added that every time she thought of this day, another string of images would follow: her grandmother and other people walking through Mainz, suitcases in their hands; her grandmother getting into a cargo car; the train driving through the night. She concluded by saying that her mother "certainly" was "pursued" by the same images throughout the last half of her life. And that she never talked with her about it; see *Anna Seghers: Eine Biographie in Bildern,* ed. Frank Wagner, Ursula Emmerich, and Ruth Radvanyi (Berlin: Aufbau-Verlag, 1994), 30. This memory alerts us again to the issue of the generational transmission of trauma and about the centrality of the journey metaphor in Seghers's writing.

39 Cathy Caruth, "Introduction," in *Trauma: Explorations in Memory,* ed. Cathy Caruth (Baltimore and London: Johns Hopkins University Press, 1995), 5.

40 Eric Santner quotes this definition of the survivor in "History Beyond the Pleasure Principle: Some Thoughts on the Representation of Trauma," in *Probing the Limits of Representation,* ed. Saul Friedlander (Cambridge, Mass.: Harvard University Press, 1992), 364.

41 F.-W. Eickhoff, "Identification and Its Vicissitudes in the Context of the Nazi Phenomenon," *International Journal of Psycho-Analysis* 67 (1986): 33–44; see also David Rosenfeld, "Identification and Its Vicissitudes in Relation to the Nazi Phenomenon," *International Journal of Psycho-Analysis* 67 (1986): 53–64.

42 Eickhoff, "Identification and Its Vicissitudes," 34.

43 I use "identifying with" in the sense defined by Mervin Glasser: "Identification is the process in which the subject modifies his self-representation in such a way as to be the same as one or more representations of the object. . . . Identification can be regarded as the changing of the 'shape' of one's self-representation by the incorporation of an object-representation, or a part of it. There is a significant difference between the processes involved when we talk of 'identifying with' as distinct from 'making an identification with.' 'Identifying with' is a temporary, reversible, putting oneself in the place of the object, or vice versa: it implies the recognition of something in common. . . . 'To make an identification with' means . . . to incorporate permanently an aspect of the external world into

the self. Difference—something in the environment which the subject does not have—is here the essential condition"; see his "Identification and Its Vicissitudes as Observed in the Perversions," *International Journal of Psycho-Analysis* 67 (1986): 9, 12.

44 In contrast to Christiane Zehl Romero, I focus on the figure of the mother in "Post ins gelobte Land"; see her reading of the story in *Anna Seghers* (Reinbek and Hamburg: Rowohlt Verlag, 1993), 91ff. See also Erika Haas, " 'Post ins gelobte Land' —Ein Requiem," *Argonautenschiff* 4 (1995): 146; she reads the story as a "break with . . . Zionism . . . [and] orthodox Jewry" —a reading that clearly misses an important dimension of the text, although it does pinpoint Seghers's conflicted position.

45 Anna Seghers, "The Outing of the Dead Girls," in *Three German Stories,* ed. and trans. Michael Bullock (London: Oasis Books, 1984), 42; see also the German text in Anna Seghers, *Der Ausflug der toten Mädchen: Erzählungen* (Darmstadt and Neuwied: Luchterhand Verlag, 1989), 80. (English text: O/page, German text: A/page.)

46 Santner, "History Beyond the Pleasure Principle," 144. According to Santner, narrative fetishism releases one from the burden of reconstituting identity *after the loss.*

47 Letter of September 4, 1944 (addressee unknown), cited in Alexander Stephan, *Anna Seghers im Exil: Essays, Texte, Dokumente* (Bonn: Bouvier, 1993), 160.

48 In a 1943 essay, Seghers argued against the fascist concept of *Volksgemeinschaft,* claiming that the true "inner unity of the people" was tragically expressed in the massive number of German victims. She demanded a "united front of the dead against Hitler, after the living did not manage to create this front in time"; see her *Aufsätze, Ansprachen, Essays: 1927–1953* (Berlin: Aufbau-Verlag, 1980), 132.

49 Letter to Wolf, in Stephan, " 'Ich habe das Gefühl,' " 145.

50 In "Volk und Schriftsteller" (1942), Seghers argued that writers are bound to the people by social ties, not by any "mystical blood ties" or a vague and "mysterious racial belonging" (52).

51 Alexander Abusch, *Der Irrweg einer Nation* (Berlin: Aufbau-Verlag, 1946).

52 For instance, in a post-script to his own article "Hitlers Antisemitismus und wir" (Hitler's Anti-Semitism and Us), Merker argued that there was an important difference between Jewish and political persecution. Like Abusch, he thought the Jews, an "unprotected, national, religious, and caste-like minority," were used as a convenient scapegoat. They were the victims of an "outrageous unjustice" that had to be righted— "as far as that is even possible"; see his "Das Echo: Diskussion über 'Hitlers Antisemitismus und wir,' " *Freies Deutschland* 2 (1943): 33.

53 Olaf Groehler, "Juden erkennen wir nicht an," *Konkret* 3 (1993): 51. On the trials, see H. Weber, *Die DDR 1945–1986,* 30ff. On the Merker trial in particular, see Jeffrey Herf, "German Communism, the Discourse of 'Antifascist Resistance' and the Jewish Catastrophe," in *Resistance Against the Third Reich 1933–*

1990, ed. Michael Geyer and John W. Boyer (Chicago: University of Chicago Press, 1992), 257–94; and "East German Communists and the Jewish Question: Fourth Alois Mertes Memorial Lecture," Occasional Paper No. 11 (Washington, D.C.: German Historical Institute, 1994). For the effects of this period on East Germany's Jewish population, see Robin Ostow, *Jews in Contemporary Germany: The Children of Moses in the Land of Marx* (New York: St. Martin's, 1989).

54 Groehler ("Juden erkennen wir nicht an," 53–54) emphasizes that the majority of the participants voted for such recognition "partly out of party discipline, partly out of open outrage against the ignorant narrowmindedness," which he attributes to the "astonishing indifference of German antifascists and Communists toward the survivors of the Holocaust." According to Groehler, speeches by Julius Meyer and Leon Löwenkopf were crucial to the outcome of the vote. Löwenkopf expressed his shock at the behavior of some of his "comrades" in the following terms: "I am a Jew and I find it actually embarrassing and strange that I have to speak as a Jew today. Until 1920, I did not know that I was a Jew. Only then, when anti-Semitism began, was I told: you are a Jew, and then I started thinking of myself as a Jew. And now I thought that that would no longer be necessary today, (but) suddenly I realize I have once again become a Jew. . . . Did these men in the meantime fly around as angels somewhere in the sky, were they not on earth, did they not see what happened everywhere in Germany, and were they not in the camps, the KZs, and did they not see there how the Jew was not only beaten by the SS and by the peasants, but also by people who are now wearing the Red Triangle. . . . When people now say that those who were affected by the Nuremberg laws are not victims of fascism, then I do not understand that."

55 See Robin Ostow, "Being Jewish in the Other Germany: An Interview with Thomas Eckert," *New German Critique* 38 (Spring/Summer 1986): 74, 79. For an East German historian's account, see Helmut Eschwegge, *Fremd unter meinesgleichen: Erinnerungen eines Dresdner Juden* (Berlin: Links, 1991).

56 Quoted in Groehler, "Juden erkennen wir nicht an," 54. What Hermlin does not mention here is the issue of class, from which he did not shy away on other occasions, provocatively calling himself a "spätbürgerlicher Schriftsteller" (late-bourgeois author). Hermlin recently recounted a confrontation with Otto Gotsche as an example of anti-Semitic tendencies in the SED, although it should be noted that Gotsche was disciplined at the highest level — by the Politbureau; see Petra Boden, "Ornamente und Tabus: Antifaschismus als Herrschaftsdiskurs," *Weimarer Beiträge* 41 (1995): 108–9.

57 See, for instance, the 1953 "Aufruf zum Aufbau nationaler Mahn-und Gedenkstätten" (Appeal for the Construction of National Memorials) drafted by a committee consisting of Grotewohl, Becher, Brecht, Bredel, Cremer, Havemann, Hermlin, Seghers, and Zweig, among others. The appeal praised "the heroes of the antifascist resistance," mentioning Thälmann (KPD) and Breitscheid (SPD), the Christian Paul Schneider, the "working-class functionaries" Ernst Schneller and Matthias Thesen, and the "unforgotten young heroine" Katja Niederkirch-

ner (*Ravensbrücker Ballade oder Faschismusbewältigung in der DDR,* ed. Klaus Jarmatz [Berlin: Aufbau-Verlag, 1992], 49).

It should be kept in mind, however, that the Communist movement was not the only source of silence on the catastrophe of the Holocaust. Claude Lanzmann recalled in an interview that Sartre's *Réflexions sur la question juive,* published in 1946, never mentions the Holocaust: "There is not a word in it about the Holocaust, because the Holocaust is an event that no one at the time could grasp in its full scope"; quoted in Shoshana Felman, "The Return of the Voice," in *Testimony,* ed. Shoshana Felman and Dorri Laub (London: Routledge, 1992), 244.

58 Anna Seghers, "Der Schriftsteller und die geistige Freiheit: Rede auf dem 1. Schriftstellerkongress 1947," quoted in Dieter Schlenstedt, *Die neuere DDR-Literatur und ihre Leser: Wirkungsästhetische Analysen* (Munich: Damnitz Verlag, 1980), 58.

59 Anna Seghers, "Deutschland und wir" (1941), in her *Glauben an Irdisches: Essays,* ed. Christa Wolf (Leipzig: Reclam, 1974), 18.

60 Seghers, *Aufsätze, Ansprachen, Essays,* 206. Seghers was certainly not unique in this regard. Ursula Heukenkamp, writing on the cultural reconstruction in the Soviet Occupied Zone, notes that the founding members of the Kulturbund had to "renounce their rage and their consciousness to be historically in the right," and, to do so, they had "to repress a part of themselves"; see "Ein Erbe für die Friedenswissenschaft: Das Konzept der kulturellen Erneuerung in der SBZ (1945–1949)," in her *Unerwünschte Erfahrung: Kriegsliteratur und Zensur in der DDR* (Berlin and Weimar: Aufbau-Verlag, 1990), 38.

61 Quoted in Stephan, " 'Ich habe das Gefühl,' " 145.

62 Ibid., 147. Stephan also mentions Seghers's letters to Brecht, expressing confusion and hesitation over whether to live in the East or the West. For an extended study of the conflicting attitudes of Jews returning to Germany, see John Bornemann and Jeffrey M. Peck, *Sojourners: The Return of German Jews and the Question of Identity* (Lincoln: University of Nebraska Press, 1995).

63 Quoted in Schlenstedt, *Die neuere DDR-Literatur,* 59.

64 Quoted in Stephan, *Anna Seghers im Exil,* 150. For more details on the accident, see the account by Seghers's son, Pierre Radvanyi, "Einige Erinnerungen," *Argonautenschiff* 3 (1994): 188.

65 Bernhard Greiner makes a similar observation in " 'Kolonien liebt, und tapfer Vergessen, der Geist': Anna Seghers' zyklisches Erzählen," *Argonautenschiff* 3 (1994): 171.

66 Christa Wolf, "Glauben an Irdisches" (1968), in her *Die Dimension des Autors* (Frankfurt a.M.: Luchterhand Literaturverlag, 1990), 1: 309, 319, 320.

67 Alexander Abusch, "Drei Briefe an Anna Seghers," *Sinn und Form* 5 (1975): 886–89.

68 Frank Benseler, "Anna Seghers Treffen," in *Anna Seghers Materialienbuch,* ed. Peter Roos and Friderike J. Hassauer-Roos (Darmstadt and Neuwied: Luchterhand, 1977), 33.

69 Andreas Schrade mentions that Seghers had hoped to become more actively involved in education, in "Der Schriftsteller als Propagandist des sozialistischen Aufbaus: Standortbestimmung nach der Rückkehr aus dem Exil," *Argonautenschiff* 2 (1993): 58.

70 One can understand this move as her reaction to the attempt to separate Jewish from Communist emigrants. According to Antonia Grunenberg (*Antifaschismus*, 193–94), all Communists were under orders to organize themselves according to nations during the exile in Mexico. This meant that the Jewish Communists were expected to organize themselves separately. Walter Janka (*Spuren eines Lebens*, 194, 198ff.) describes the relationship between Communist emigrants and Menorah in Mexico as positive. He also discusses the difference between the so-called Moscow and West emigrations with respect to the Jewish question, a difference that apparently concerned the issue of reparations. See also Gertrud Koch, "Vom Verschwinden der Toten unter den Lebenden: Holocaust und Identitätskonfusion in den Filmen von Konrad Wolf," *Babylon* 12 (1993): 97–112.

71 For a reading that emphasizes Seghers's modernism, see Katie Trumpener, "On the Way to Socialist Realism: Teleology, Subject Formation, and Anna Seghers' 'On the Way to the American Embassy,' " *Rethinking Marxism* 7 (1994): 45–52.

72 In 1944, Goebbels financed a film called *Der Führer schenkt den Juden eine Stadt* (The Führer Gives the Jews a City), directed by Kurt Gerron, which was shown to representatives of the International Red Cross. Briefly transforming the camp into a film studio, as soon as *Der Führer* was finished its director and actors were gassed; see Karsten Witte, "Film im Nationalsozialismus: Blendung und Überblendung," in Jacobsen, Kaes, and Prinzler, eds., *Geschichte des deutschen Films*, 152. See also Gitta Sereny (*Into That Darkness* [New York: Vintage, 1983]), who was told by the Kommandant of Treblinka, Franz Stangl, about his efforts to disguise the arrival ramp of the camp as a quaint-looking German train station: "It is difficult to describe it adequately now, but it became really beautiful" (166).

73 In her reading of "Der Ausflug der toten Mädchen," Christa Wolf calls this narrative habitus the simple sense of justice of the fairy tale—"simple" meaning "positive" because it allows the narrator to distinguish clearly between good and bad (see "Zeitschichten," in Wolf, *Die Dimension des Autors*, 1: 360). In an interview with Wolf in 1959, Seghers described her idea of the author's function in a way which foregrounded its maternal qualities: "I believe that the author is never allowed to abandon people. Reading, everyone should feel: look, this (author) understands me, even when my own husband, my best friend, my mother no longer understand me. He knows about my worries and takes me by my hand, he knows something about me" (see "Fragen an Anna Seghers," in ibid., 1: 258).

74 Achim Roscher, "Wirkung des Geschriebenen: Gespräche mit Anna Seghers," *Neue Deutsche Literatur* 10 (1983): 61.

75 Ibid., 62, 70.

76 "Christa Wolf spricht mit Anna Seghers," in Wolf, *Die Dimension des Autors*, 1: 280.

77 Ibid., 286.

78 "Anna Seghers, die Trägerin des Kleistpreises," cited in Bilke, "Auf der Suche nach Netty Reiling," 18.

79 Roscher, "Wirkung des Geschriebenen," 66–67, 70.

80 Ibid., 69.

81 Ibid., 62.

82 Seghers wrote her dissertation on Rembrandt, now available as Netty Reiling (Anna Seghers), *Jude und Judentum im Werke Rembrandts,* intro. Christa Wolf (Leipzig: Reclam-Verlag, 1990).

83 Roscher, "Wirkung des Geschriebenen," 68.

84 Christa Wolf, "Bei Anna Seghers," in her *Die Dimension des Autors,* 1: 332–33.

85 Anna Seghers, "Die Toten auf der Insel Djal," in her *Über Kunstwerk und Wirklichkeit: IV Ergänzungsband,* ed. Sigrid Bock (Berlin: Akademie Verlag, 1979), 205; henceforth I/page.

86 Bernhard Greiner, "Der Bann der Zeichen: Anna Seghers's Entwürfe der Identitätsfindung," *Jahrbuch zur Literatur in der DDR* 3 (1993): 132. See also Brandes, *Anna Seghers,* 31.

87 Greiner, "Der Bann der Zeichen," 132.

88 Sandra M. Gilbert and Susan Gubar, *Madwoman in the Attic* (New Haven: Yale University Press, 1984), 59.

89 Roscher, "Wirkung des Geschriebenen," 68.

90 This mystery surrounded the author until she received a prestigious literary prize, the Kleistpreis, in 1928 for *Aufstand der Fischer von St. Barbara.* The reporter for the newspaper *Mainzer Warte* expressed surprise at learning, as did "the world," that Seghers was the name of a young woman. Nobody could tell from reading the book that it had been written by a woman: "If something like masculine writing exists, then this novella is written in it" ("Wofür eine Mainzerin den Kleistpreis erhielt," *Mainzer Warte,* Jan. 19, 1929). This "mystery" has to be seen in the context of a discussion in the 1920s concerning "feminine" and "masculine" literature. In 1929, Kurt Pinthus published an article entitled "Männliche Literatur" (Masculine Literature) in which he calls expressionism a literature characterized by "feminist femininity." "Neue Sachlichkeit" (New Sobriety), on the other hand, "is without bathos, without any sentimentality. . . . It is sober, masculine; it is the form of expression of man, if one understands by man not the . . . *volkish* notion of masculinity, which is sentimental in its mendacious heroization, exaggerated, thus not masculine." The domain of this "masculine" literature is work, as opposed to the feminine realm of love. A good example of this "sober, merciless" literature, says Pinthus, is the work of Seghers. Like the anonymous reporter, he expresses surprise at the fact that Seghers turned out to be a woman; see *Weimarer Republik: Manifeste und Dokumente zur deutschen Literatur 1918–1933,* ed. Anton Kaes (Stuttgart: Metzler, 1983), 328, 330, 331–32.

91 Marianne Hirsch, *The Mother/Daughter Plot: Narrative, Psychoanalysis, Feminism* (Bloomington: Indiana University Press, 1989), 57.

92 This discussion of Seghers's authorship is, of course, far from complete. An exhaustive study would include her early stories "Grubetsch" (1927) and "Die Fischer von St. Barbara" (1928). "Grubetsch," a story about the destructive force of desire, might be particularly important: Anna, the victim of her own desire to escape the misery of a poverty-ridden tenement, eventually disappears from the text, but this story is where the transition from Antje to Anna Seghers occurs. A comprehensive study would also have to include the recently discovered story "Der sogenannte Rendel" (The So-called Rendel). Published in 1940, but probably written in 1930, the story was based on a newspaper article (which also served as a source for Brecht) about a woman who lived as a man in order to work and to protect a friend with an illegitimate child. Obviously, I would address the issue of gender here in terms of Seghers's authorship, but differently from Margret Iversen, who argues that Seghers was a "male" author since she did not focus on women's oppression; see her "Das Frauenbild bei Anna Seghers. Und dann ihr: Eure kalten Augen," *Spuren* 3 (1979): 39.

93 Christa Wolf, "Das siebte Kreuz," in *"Das siebte Kreuz" von Anna Seghers: Texte, Daten, Bilder,* ed. Sonja Hilzinger (Darmstadt and Neuwied: Luchterhand, 1990), 148. Kurt Batt (*Anna Seghers,* 187) commends Seghers for never having fallen prey to the so-called *Miseretheorie* of German history as a series of failures and catastrophes (obviously referring to Abusch's book).

94 This may be the moment to address the question of Seghers's implication in the SED's Stalinism, to answer the question raised by Walter Janka's *Spuren eines Lebens:* Why didn't Seghers speak up during his trial, since she herself had asked Janka to travel to Hungary? Marcel Reich-Ranicki, recalling the early 1950s in a recent interview, pointed out that the West German state was governed by people involved in Nazi Germany, the East German state by former concentration camp inmates and emigrants. Thinking of the GDR as the "better" Germany, he also believed that communism would protect him from anti-Semitism; see his "Ja, ich habe dran geglaubt," *Die Zeit,* June 17, 1994, 14, 13. Ranicki spoke critically of Seghers's behavior during the Janka affair, yet added: "But that changes nothing about the quality of 'Das siebte Kreuz' " (14). I am not interested in saving Seghers as the "good" artist, but rather in identifying the tensions that run through her texts, literary and nonliterary. My reading of her work from this particular period demonstrates that her investment in the "new" Germany was enormous—and enormously conflicted. This investment obviously did not allow her to voice any criticism beyond what emerges in her story "Der gerechte Richter," which she did not dare publish (see Anna Seghers, *Der gerechte Richter* [Berlin: Aufbau-Verlag, 1990]).

95 Anna Seghers, *Die Entscheidung* (Neuwied and Darmstadt: Luchterhand Literaturverlag, 1985), 26, 65.

3 The Past in the Present

1   Interview with Bert Papenfuss-Gorek (February 14, 1991), in *Literary Intellectuals and the Dissolution of the State: Professionalism and Conformity in the GDR,* ed. Robert von Halberg (Chicago: University of Chicago Press, 1996), 279–80.

2   This discourse on fathers and sons, fathers and daughters, also exists in the West, of course, but in the GDR it remained dominant throughout its forty-year existence. On generational discourse in the Federal Republic, see Thomas Elsaesser, *New German Cinema: A History* (New Brunswick, N.J.: Rutgers University Press, 1989), 239ff; Manfred Schneider, "Väter und Söhne, posthum: Das beschädigte Verhältnis zweier Generationen," in his *Den Kopf verkehrt aufgesetzt oder Die melancholische Linke* (Darmstadt and Neuwied: Luchterhand, 1981), 8–64 (on the West German "Väterliteratur" of the 1970s); and Sigrid Weigel, "Väterbücher—Töchterschriften," in her *Die Stimme der Medusa* (Dülmen: Tende, 1987), 154–59 (on West German "daughter's" literature). It also constitutes part of the political discourse. Antje Vollmer, one of the leaders of the Green Party, wrote about the acceptance of Willy Brandt by the May '68 generation as connected to his role of "grandfather" to a "fatherless" generation; see her "Die SPD nach dem Tod Willi Brandts," *Tageszeitung,* October 17, 1992, 10.

3   I am paraphrasing Jameson on the continuing effect of the master-narratives pronounced dead by Lyotard; see Fredric Jameson, "Foreword" to Jean-Francois Lyotard, *The Postmodern Condition* (Minneapolis: University of Minnesota Press, 1984), xii.

4   Monika Maron, *Stille Zeile Sechs* (Frankfurt a.M.: Fischer Verlag, 1991); see also her "Ich war ein antifaschistisches Kind," in *"Die Geschichte ist offen",* ed. Michael Naumann (Frankfurt a.M.: Fischer Verlag, 1991), 117–36; Kerstin Hensel, *Im Schlauch* (Frankfurt a.M.: Suhrkamp Verlag, 1993); Klaus Drawert, *Spiegelland: Ein deutscher Monolog* (Frankfurt a.M.: Suhrkamp Verlag, 1992). For an earlier text on the father–daughter problematic, see Angela Krauss, *Der Dienst,* (Frankfurt a.M.: Suhrkamp, 1990 [1988]). Wolfgang Hilbig, in his "Stasi novel," *Eine Übertragung* (Frankfurt a.M.: Fischer Taschenbuch Verlag, 1992), weaves the father-son plot into his protagonist's story of writing and betrayal. (And then there are the unofficially circulated letters of Gabriele Eckart, "Briefe an meinen Vater" [Letters to My Father]—accusatory tirades against a Stasi father.) For a discussion of the later literature in relation to the paternal narrative, see Katharina von Ankum, "Sibirien liegt (nicht) bei Ravensbrück: Gender and the Deconstruction of the Anti-Fascist National Narrative in the GDR," in *History and Memory* 7 (Fall/Winter 1996): 41–69.

5   Emmerich, *Kleine Literaturgeschichte der DDR,* 107.

6   Roland Barthes, *The Pleasure of the Text,* trans. Richard Miller (New York: Hill and Wang, 1994), 47.

7   For a discussion of the formal constraints of genre in the East German context, see my "Christa Wolf's *Divided Heaven.*"

8   Rose, "Introduction," *Sexuality,* 5.

9 Kaja Silverman (*Male Subjectivity*, 15, 30) theorizes the paternal family and its structure of subject constitution, the Oedipal crisis, as "dominant fiction," that is, a "reserve of images and manipulator of stories" through which a society represents the core elements of its consensus and which serves to establish an imaginary relationship to the society's ruling Law. I use Silverman's notion with some hesitation because of the ahistoricity of her model. First, the Oedipal crisis does not always and everywhere function as dominant fiction; and second, when it does come into play as a model, it need not always and everywhere be the dominant one. I understand the East German narratives as a historically specific case.

10 According to Juliet Mitchell, these scenarios involve a "range of excitations and activities that produce pleasure beyond the satisfaction of any basic physiological need"; see her "Introduction—I," in *Feminine Sexuality*, ed. Juliet Mitchell and Jacqueline Rose (New York and London: W. W. Norton, 1985), 2.

11 Žižek, *For They Know Not What They Do*, 258.

12 Silverman, *Male Subjectivity*, 24.

13 Elisabeth Cowie, "Fantasia," in *The Woman in Question*, ed. Parveen Adams and Elizabeth Cowie (Cambridge, Mass.: MIT Press, 1990), 159.

14 Wilhelm Reich, *Die sexuelle Revolution* (Frankfurt a.M.: Fischer Taschenbuch Verlag, 1973), 167.

15 Of course, the SED deployed a strong puritanical discourse in the 1950s and again during the early 1960s. See, for instance, Walter Ulbricht, "Sozialistische Ethik und Moral" (1958), in *Kurzwort: Ewig blühe: Erinnerungen an die Republik der Lobetrotter* (catalogue), ed. Tobias Böhm (Berlin: Westermann, 1992), 20; Kristine von Soden, who quotes Honecker in "Sexualität als Produktionskraft," in her *Irmtraud Morgners hexische Weltfahrt* (Berlin: Elefantenpress, 1991), 101–8; and Lutz Niethammer's interviews in his and Dorothee Wierling's *Die volkseigene Erfahrung* (Berlin: Rowohlt, 1990), esp. 488, 494 on repression of sexuality in the FDJ. But this discourse should be seen as the background to these fantasies—another strand woven into the scenarios—not as their determining cause.

16 Mitchell, "Introduction—I," in Mitchell and Rose, eds., *Feminine Sexuality*, 22. See also Elizabeth Cowie, "Representations," in Adams and Cowie, eds., *Woman in Question*, 115.

17 I agree with Rose ("Introduction," *Sexuality*, 10ff.) that an uncritical celebration of the unconscious as an essentially nonviolent life force that is merely distorted by the social (as in Reich, for instance) should be avoided.

18 Heiner Müller, "Der Vater," in his *Germania Tod in Berlin* (Berlin: Rotbuch Verlag, 1977), 20–26, henceforth cited as V/page. In 1958, Karl Mickel had published a similarly titled poem, "Bericht über meinen Vater" (Report about My Father), *Neue Deutsche Literatur* 7 (1958): 45:

I am born in thirty
My father was born in 1906.

From a photograph I know
How he looked when he left.

With my mother I visited him.
He was lying in the dirt of the barracks.
Where before his face had been
There now was but a white stain.

A postcard was all
We received from Russia.
There was a cross
After his name.

19 Heiner Müller, "Bericht vom Grossvater," in his *Geschichten aus der Produktion* (Berlin: Rotbuch Verlag, 1974), 7–9; quote from p. 7.

20 See Genia Schulz, *Heiner Müller* (Stuttgart: Metzlersche Verlagsbuchhandlung, 1980), 175. Frank Hörnigk's study of Müller's *Geschichtsbegriff* touches upon the trauma recounted in "Der Vater," yet does not view the latter from the perspective of continuity versus discontinuity; see his " 'Texte, die auf Geschichte warten . . . ': Zum Geschichtsbegriff bei Heiner Müller," in *Heiner Müller Material: Texte und Kommentare,* ed. Frank Hörnigk (Leipzig: Verlag Philipp Reclam, 1989), 132.

21 In his recent "autobiographical interviews," Müller talked about both stories in detail. He described the narrative stance of "Bericht vom Grossvater" as one grounded in his identification with the new order, which depended for its functioning on an ascetic attitude and sacrifices: "Actually, I wrote this story about the grandfather with the attitude of a functionary." He saw himself among the victors at the time because of his father's position. He also explained his decision to remain in the East—with Brecht—after his family left for the Federal Republic: Brecht was the legitimation which made it possible to "be for the GDR"; see *Krieg ohne Schlacht: Leben in zwei Diktaturen* (Cologne: Kiepenheuer and Witsch, 1992), 16, 52, 112.

22 This opens up what Müller called the "continuum of history" on a *structural* level, allowing for a representation of history which does not force the past into a single story, but instead enables a multiplicity of stories to unfold. "Der Vater" realizes in the short story what Müller theorized with respect to his early plays as the necessity of the fragment; see "Geschichte und Drama: Ein Gespräch mit Heiner Müller," *Basis: Jahrbuch für deutsche Gegenwartsliteratur* 6 (1976): 49ff.

23 Schulz, *Heiner Müller,* 176.

24 The fantasy of the "other origin" also plays a role in Uwe Saeger's novel *Nöhr,* which traces the slow breakdown of Johannes Nöhr, a thirty-year-old leading cadre. Nöhr is the illegitimate child of a Red Army soldier, raised by a father whom Saeger portrays as weak and cowardly, decidedly not an antifascist hero. Nöhr, after having staged his own death, expresses his selfdoubts in a long, rambling monologue. What he cannot understand about himself is his own cow-

ardice and fear of authority, since, after all, he is the offspring of a "Helden-vater" (hero-father). With such a father, he should have been one of those "healthy, beaming faces in the newspapers." Instead, he has come to realize that he actually resembles his stepfather, "der Kakerlak" (The Cockroach is the West German title). His friend tells him that his colleagues and comrades, believing him to be dead, eulogized him as a hero at the official ceremony; see *Nöhr* (Ros-tock: Hinsdorff Verlag, 1980); *Der Kakerlak.* (Munich and Zurich: Piper, 1990).

25 Isidore Ducasse Comte de Lautreamont, *Les Chants de Maldoror* (Paris: Gal-limard, 1943 [1869–74]). Lautreamont's prose poem has been interpreted as rebellion against the "fathers" and their value system; see Maurice Blanchot, *Lautreamont et Sade* (Paris: Minuit, 1963). Maldoror is at once the incarnation of evil, the purest expression of God's creation, and a rebel. The poem con-sists of a number of blasphemous, violent scenes, some desecrating the notion of a benevolent God, others attacking the "sacred" ties of the family (such as the segment that tells of the boy tortured by his father, mother, and brother). These "dramatic episodes" introduce the narrative within the poem, which is about the destruction of a family: Maldoror's seduction of the son culminates in the melodramatic death of the mother and father. In "Reflections on Post-Modernism" (*New German Critique* 16 [Winter 1979]: 198–200), Müller men-tions Lautreamont's work as one of the "outstanding literary products of the century": "Lautreamont, the anonymous catastrophe" (57).

26 Lautreamont, *Chants de Maldoror,* 25.

27 Antonin Artaud, *Antonin Artaud: Selected Writings,* ed. Susan Sontag (New York: Farrar, Straus and Giroux, 1976), 540.

28 Taking the father's place already hints at a problematic that Arlene Teraoka traces in Müller's later plays, namely, "the act of betrayal," which is "primarily the act of the son becoming the father"; see her *Silence of Entropy or Universal Discourse: The Postmodernist Poetics of Heiner Müller* (New York: Peter Lang, 1985), 175.

29 Heiner Müller, "The Walls of History," *Semiotext: The German Issue* (ed. Syl-vere Lotringer) 4 (1982): 54.

30 Ibid., 56.

31 Sigmund Freud, "On the Universal Tendency to Debasement in the Sphere of Love," in *The Standard Edition,* 11: 183ff.

32 Schulz, *Heiner Müller,* 177.

33 In the last scene of the play, Hilse dreams of the young prostitute as "red Rosa," and the young worker's desperate monologue images the Party as whore, saint, and holy virgin; see Müller, *Germania: Tod in Berlin,* 76ff. Schulz's connection seems legitimate since Müller had already started working on *Germania* in 1956.

34 As Schulz has argued so convincingly elsewhere, other women figures connote hope, production, and the future of communism in Müller's early work; indeed, certain constellations of problems are linked in Müller's work to the image of woman. Schulz observes a definite split between an early phase, dominated by the constellation of life/love/silence, and a later phase, dominated by that of

death/sexuality/speaking, with Müller's adaptation of *Zement* and the figure of Dasha representing the thematic and formal caesura; see her "Abschied von Morgen: Zu den Frauengestalten im Werk Heiner Müllers," *Text und Kritik: Sonderband Heiner Müller,* ed. Heinz Ludwig Arnold (Munich: Edition Text und Kritik, 1982), 68–69.

35 Müller takes up the topic once more in *Die Hamletmaschine;* see *Die Hamletmaschine: Heiner Müllers Endspiel,* ed. Theo Girshausen (Cologne: Prometh Verlag, 1978 [1977]), 11–23.

36 Dieter Noll, *Die Abenteuer des Werner Holt: Roman einer Heimkehr* (Berlin and Weimar: Aufbau-Verlag, 1983 [1963]), 14 (henceforth cited as *WH*/page). This is actually volume two in what was intended to be a trilogy: the first volume, *Die Abenteuer des Werner Holt: Roman einer Jugend,* was published in 1960; the third volume was never finished. On the first volume, see Martina Langermann, "Dieter Nolls 'Die Abenteuer des Werner Holt I': Entstehung und wirkungsästhetische Aspekte des Romans," *Weimarer Beiträge* 35 (1989): 1640–54. Noll's later novel *Kippenberg* (Berlin and Weimar: Aufbau-Verlag, 1979) deals with the existential crisis of a former worker turned director of a research institute.

On the genre of the GDR novel of formation, see Frank Trommler, "Von Hölderlin zu Stalin: Über den Entwicklungsroman in der DDR," in *Zum Roman in der DDR,* ed. Marc Silberman (Stuttgart: Klett Verlag, 1980), 23–39; see also his "DDR-Erzählung und Bitterfelder Weg," *Basis* 3 (1972): 61–97.

37 Julia Kristeva, *Powers of Horror: An Essay on Abjection,* trans. Leon S. Roudiez (New York: Columbia University Press, 1982 [1980]), 16.

38 Holt's reservations emerge as he watches a demonstration. Although he notes that none of the marchers seems able to keep in step with the others, Holt nevertheless feels a growing revulsion against any form of marching (*WH*/312).

39 Peter Brooks, *Body Work: Objects of Desire in Modern Narrative* (Cambridge, Mass.: Harvard University Press, 1993), 5.

40 Ravensbrück was a Nazi concentration camp for women near Berlin.

41 Judith is not the only maternal figure. For instance, Holt's reliving his father's life also positions Gundel once again as the mother, not as her counterpart whose love will redeem Holt but now as the object which has been lost.

42 Kristeva, *Powers of Horror,* 1, 15.

43 Ibid., 1, 10, 15, 16.

44 Ibid., 8.

45 Barthes, *The Pleasure of the Text,* p. 47.

46 After publishing *Kippenberg,* Noll fell silent. He would have one highly publicized moment when he denounced the authors who left the country in 1979, following the forced expatriation of singer Wolf Biermann in 1976 and their own exclusion from the Writers' Union, as well as their supporters. Noll's open letter to Honecker, expressing his support of the official cultural policy and viciously attacking Seyppel, Heym, and Rolf Schneider, was published in *Neues Deutschland* (reprinted in *Protokoll eines Tribunals: Die Ausschlüsse aus dem*

DDR-Schriftstellerverband, ed. Joachim Walther, Wolf Biermann, and Günter de Bruyn et al. [Reinbek bei Hamburg: Rowohlt Verlag, 1991], 97–98). Ironically, his own son, Hans/Chaim Noll, would rebel against what he described in his autobiography as an authoritarian Communist father figure—in the name of Judaism; see Hans Noll, *Der Abschied: Journal meiner Abreise aus der DDR* (Hamburg: Hoffmann und Campe, 1985); and Hans (Chaim) Noll, *Nachtgedanken über Deutschland* (Reinbek bei Hamburg: Rowohlt, 1992).

47 Sigmund Freud, "Family Romances," in *The Standard Edition,* 9: 238–39.

48 Reimann died of cancer in 1973 at the age of forty. The novel for which she received the most official praise was *Ankunft im Alltag* (1961), which she wrote in Hoyerswerda in close contact with the industrial construction site "Schwarze Pumpe." Shorter pieces include the 1962 story "Die Frau am Pranger" (The Woman in the Pillory) and the 1963 novella *Die Geschwister* (The Siblings), the story of a "sister" whose friend succeeds in preventing her brother from leaving for the West. (Reimann's own brother left for Hamburg in the 1960s.) Reimann was a member of various organizations, such as the Writers' Union and the youth commission of the s e d's Central Committee, but never of the Party itself. Her unfinished novel *Franziska Linkerhand,* posthumously published in 1974, became something of a "cult book of the seventies," according to Freya Klier, quoted in *Brigitte Reimann Hermann Henselmann Briefwechsel,* ed. Ingrid Kirschey-Feix (Berlin: Verlag Neues Leben), 124. Her correspondence with both Hermann Henselmann, the GDR's star architect, and Christa Wolf testifies to her difficulties in writing this book within the given ideological and aesthetic parameters. As she wrote to Henselmann in 1969: "It seems to me that my relationship to the party is at times like that of an adolescent and his strict father, against whom one lives in continuous rebellion, who always knows better— what is most bothersome is that he is most often right, but, please, you would like to make your own experiences; you play pranks . . . but you wait all the time for him . . . to say: you did that well" (88). The person who represented "the Party" to Reimann was Annemarie Auer, the editor with whom she worked on *Franziska Linkerhand* and whose Party-line criticism seems to have been responsible for Reimann's problems; see, for instance, *Sei gegrüsst und lebe: Eine Freundschaft in Briefen, 1964–1973,* ed. Angela Drescher (Berlin: Aufbau-Verlag, 1993), 17. For a reading of *Franziska Linkerhand* which emphasizes its embeddedness in the GDR's paternalistic order, see Kornelia Hauser, *Patriarchat als Sozialismus* (Hamburg: Argument-Verlag, 1994), 245ff. With the publication of Reimann's correspondence from 1947 to 1972 in *Aber wir schaffen es, verlass Dich drauf! Briefe an eine Freundin im Westen,* ed. Ingrid Krüger (Berlin: Elefantenpress, 1995), Reimann acquired the aura of a "rebel" among the GDR's women writers. See, for instance, the "fictional" biography by Barbara Krause, *Gefesselte Rebellin: Brigitte Reimann* (Berlin: Verlag Neues Leben, 1994), in which Reimann's "enemy" Christa Wolf, editor of *NDL,* rejected a story by the young author (110). Reimann worked for the Stasi from 1957 to 1958 under the name "Caterine." Joachim Walther discusses her with Wolf as another young

idealist who soon found ways to stop the collaboration. Noll, on the other hand, worked for the Stasi since 1957 with, it seems, much fervor. Joachim Walther, *Sicherungsbereich Literatur: Schriftsteller und Staatssicherheit in der Deutschen Demokratischen Republik* (Berlin: CH. Links Verlag, 1996), 478, 486, 572, 670.

49 The term is borrowed from Andreas Huyssen, "The Politics of Identification: 'Holocaust' and West German Drama," in his *After the Great Divide: Modernism, Mass Culture, Postmodernism* (Bloomington and Indianapolis: Indiana University Press, 1986), 94–114.

50 The slogan was defensive: if we discuss our past mistakes, we will weaken our position in the Cold War.

51 Reimann, *Ankunft im Alltag*, 6, 5, 10 (henceforth cited as *AA*/page). The "red fortress" is what Recha calls the school she attended, suggesting that she has come to "Schwarze Pumpe" an already committed Communist. Part of what she has to learn is how to translate the "idealism" with which her teachers imbued her into practice.

52 Nikolaus has passed his own test by finally understanding that socialist reality has little to do with the romantic images he had in mind when he arrived: "And what astonishes me most . . . is the everydayness of the whole thing" (*AA*/228). He concludes that the idea of heroism has to be redefined.

53 Given this particular construction, it is not surprising that the depiction of the relationship between Nikolaus and Recha avoids any erotic moments, indeed has to exclude them from the diegesis. Unlike Curt, Nikolaus berates himself as "primitive" (*AA*/131) for merely thinking about kissing Recha.

54 On the advice of Hamann, the central father figure, Recha plans to study architecture, already imagining the outlines of the socialist "dream cities" (*AA*/174) that she will help to build. What resulted from these idealistic plans for model socialist cities is known to readers of Reimann's third, unfinished novel, *Franziska Linkerhand*—and to those who have seen the concrete deserts of Hoyerswerda, the former Stalinstadt, and Eisenhüttenstadt, among others.

55 Stites, *Women's Liberation Movement in Russia*, 380. The connection between "morality" and the "work ethic" is drawn in a long discussion about Recha's colleague Friedel, who flirts too much and works too little (*AA*/150).

56 In one of their many arguments, Preuss explains to Curt that "discipline" in their private life ("to keep private life clean" [*AA*/259]) is crucial for their discipline at the workplace.

57 The NVA was the East German army (National People's Army).

58 Recha mainly understands those statements as Curt's trying on the role of the troubled young man—an interpretation with which the narrator complies. But at one point, she starts to take him seriously, "and this time Recha found herself on the side of her contemporary, against his parents" (*AA*/177)—as does the narrator and, therefore, the reader.

59 Reimann, *Franziska Linkerhand*, 380. The passage, a conversation between Franziska and her lover, a victim of Stalinist repression, continues: " 'Strange,'

Franziska said. 'What?' She shrugged her shoulders. The herb of forgetting grows on the graves."

60 In the aftermath of the Twentieth Congress, Stalin monuments were taken down and street names changed. Other novels about the period mention in passing the disappearance of these statues; see, for instance, Renate Feyl, *Bau mir eine Brücke* (Build Me a Bridge) (Berlin: Verlag Neues Leben, 1972), 146, 196. Her protagonist, Klara, briefly reflects on the fact that the empty pedestal which she passes on her way to work once was occupied by Bismarck, then by the "Generalissimo," whose statue was dismantled in 1956. Feyl also describes the unremarked removal of all portraits, statues, and photographs of Stalin from the mayor's office—to the great, but silent, dismay of his followers.

61 The GDR slogan "No Discussion of Mistakes" was accompanied by a denial that any such cult of personality was ever practiced in East Germany; see Janka, *Spuren eines Lebens,* 249: as head of the Aufbau-Verlag, he was asked to publish numerous monographs on Ulbricht, Pieck, and Becher, among others.

62 Both the uprising in Hungary and the revelations of the Twentieth Party Congress occurred in 1956.

63 Hans Marchwitza, *Roheisen* (Berlin: Verlag der Tribüne, 1955). Like other production novels, or *Aufbauliteratur,* such as Eduard Claudius's *Menschen an unserer Seite* (1951), Maria Langner's *Stahl* (1952), and Karl Mundstock's *Helle Nächte* (1952), *Roheisen* is modeled on Gladkov's *Cement.* While Gladkov's novel succeeds in conveying the revolutionary enthusiasm of these massive undertakings—the revolutionizing not only of work but also gender relations—Marchwitza's novel drowns in its extraordinarily flat, functionary prose, despite making the still engaging topic of women's liberation through work one of its main strands. This topos of the "atmosphere of an industrial Wild East" and pride in the achievements of the "work of reconstruction" still resonates in the interviews conducted by Lutz Niethammer in the 1980s (see Niethammer, Plato, and Wierling, eds., *Die volkseigene Erfahrung,* 396). Reimann herself has one of the protagonists of her 1963 novel *Die Geschwister* (Munich: Deutscher Taschenbuch Verlag, 1988) reminisce nostalgically about their participation in the GDR's "Aufbaujahre," the "wonderful pathos" and "beautiful fervor" on the construction sites, "the whole questionable romanticism of our provisional life" (70, 71, 76).

64 Both *Franziska Linkerhand* and her letters indicate the extent of Reimann's disillusionment with this romanticized era and its landscape; see, for example, her January 29, 1969, letter to Christa Wolf, in Brigitte Reimann and Christa Wolf, *Sei gegrüsst und lebe: Eine Freundschaft in Briefen 1964–1973* (Berlin: Aufbau Taschenbuch Verlag, 1995), 13–14.

65 Wolfgang Hilbig, *Die Weiber* (Frankfurt a.M.: Fischer Verlag, 1987), 67–68. In the original, this passage is one continuous sentence. "Reconstruction" was the Aufbau term for the postwar period.

66 Papenfuss-Gorek, Kerstin Hensel, and Klaus Drawert were all born in the 1950s.

Although Hilbig was born in 1941, his work is in many ways closer to that of their generation than to the work of Wolf, Braun, and Müller.

67 And with the post-fascist body. This fantasy was not unique to the novel of arrival, however; it also appeared in such production novels of the 1950s as Karl Mundstock's *Helle Nächte* (Halle/Saale: Mitteldeutscher Verlag, 1952). Like *Ankunft im Alltag,* this novel focuses on a group of young people committed to the construction of a new factory, which at this stage resembles one of "Jack London's gold digger camps." Gerda, a member of the women's brigade "Red October," has a past: she was involved in black market activities and let herself be used as a "decoy." Since she is still rumored to have an active sex life, one of her comrades, Christa, wants her excluded from the brigade. In justifying Gerda's exclusion, Christa thematizes the issue of the *new man* through the discourse of sexuality: "I would like to tell you a few things. . . . I learned this from books: from Gorky, Sholokov, Ashaev, Sionushkin. The old human being with his lowly instincts is like an animal inside of us. We have to fight it so that the new human being can emerge. Capitalism fills us with this animal nature through its trashy novels, trashy pictures, shameless movies because it needs us that way for its war against humanity. But our good, moral world order, the socialist order of welfare and eternal peace, demands that we be free of the dominance of this animal nature" (28, 26, 139). Again, it is Gerda's link to the *past* which makes her the bearer of sexuality.

68 Wolf, "Unerledigte Widersprüche," in *Im Dialog,* 29–30.

69 Developed in analogy to Fredric Jameson's theses on nineteenth-century realism as "the production of a whole new world—on the level of the symbolic and the imaginary." "The Realist Floor-Plan," in *On Signs,* ed. Marshall Blonsky (Baltimore: Johns Hopkins University Press, 1986), 373–74.

70 Barbara Köhler, "A la recherche de la révolution perdue," *German Monitor* (1994): 2.

4 Post-Fascist Body/Post-Fascist Voice

1 Wolf, "Sozialistische Literatur der Gegenwart," 6.

2 This was first published as an excerpt from a diary commissioned by the Soviet journal *Iswestija,* then reprinted in the journal of the East German Writers' Union for which Wolf had worked as an editor in the 1950s: Christa Wolf, "Dienstag, der 27. September 1960," *Neue Deutsche Literatur* 22 (1974): 11–22. See also the English translation, "Tuesday, September 27," in *What Remains and Other Stories,* trans. Heike Schwarzbauer and Rick Takvorian (Chicago: University of Chicago Press, 1995), 23–39.

3 Christa Wolf, *Moskauer Novelle,* in *An den Tag gebracht: Prosa junger Menschen,* ed. Heinz Sachs (Halle: Mitteldeutscher Verlag, 1961), 145–222 (henceforth cited as *MN*/page). According to Therese Hörnigk (*Christa Wolf,* 84, 271),

the novella was read on East German radio in 1960, then published in various women's journals and newspapers.

4   Therese Hörnigk, "Das 11. Plenum und die Folgen: Christa Wolf im politischen Diskurs der 60er," *Neue Deutsche Literatur* 38 (1990): 239. On the period before 1965 as one of limited reforms, see Joachim Bischoff and Christoph Lieber, "Woran der Staatssozialismus scheiterte," *Sozialismus* 3 (1993): 15–19; and various contributions in *Kahlschlag. Das 11: Plenum des ZK der SED 1965,* ed. Günther Agde (Berlin: Aufbau-Verlag, 1991).

5   Wolf described how she tried to remember the events between 1959 and 1962 after discovering in May 1992, while reading her own "victim" file covering 1968 to 1980, that she had acted as an "IM" (informal contributor): "Naturally, I then began to search my memory and despite all my efforts I only discovered the image of two men who came to see me and with whom I met several times; I remembered a feeling of threat although these men were friendly. I do not remember the fact that I had a cover name, or that I had produced a handwritten report, and I did not know anything about the content of our conversations." She called this a "classic act of repression"; see "Margarete in Santa Monica" (the interview with Fritz-Jochen Kopka) (Wochenpost, 28.1.93)," in *Akteneinsicht Christa Wolf: Zerrspiegel und Dialog,* ed. Hermann Vinke (Hamburg: Luchterhand Literaturverlag, 1993), 165.

6   Christa Wolf, " 'Auf mir bestehen': Christa Wolf im Gespräch mit Günther Gaus," in Vinke, ed., *Akteneinsicht Christa Wolf,* 254.

7   Ibid., 256.

8   Quoted from "Margarete in Santa Monica," 166.

9   See Wolf, " 'Auf mir bestehen,' " 254; but also Alexander Stephan, *Christa Wolf* (Munich: Edition Text and Kritik, 1976), 177.

10 Christa Wolf, "Ein Deutscher auf Widerspruch: Rede für Hans Mayer," in her *Auf dem Weg Nach Tabou* (Cologne: Kiepenheuer and Witsch, 1994), 25.

11 Christa Wolf, "Erinnerung an Friedrich Schlotterbeck," in *Die Dimension des Autors,* 244. In an interview with Hörnigk, Wolf called the 1950s "a time of intense discussions"; see her *Im Dialog: Aktuelle Texte* (Frankfurt a.M.: Luchterhand Literaturverlag, 1990), 41.

12 Christa Wolf, "Erinnerungsbericht," in Agde, ed., *Kahlschlag,* 269. The person who was apparently instrumental in supporting her commitment for change *within* the SED was the director Konrad Wolf (266–67). On Konrad Wolf's own work on antifascism, see Marc Silberman, "Remembering History: The Filmmaker Konrad Wolf," *New German Critique* 49 (Winter 1990): 163–85.

13 In 1965, Wolf was already reading her own biography as both harmoniously and critically linked to the rise of "her" state: "Since we learned to move around freely and securely in this society, to identify with it and at the same time stay critical . . . since that time . . . our books have become more vivid, more truthful, and filled with reality"; Christa Wolf, "A Few Notes about My Work as a Writer," in *The Author's Dimension: Selected Essays,* ed. Alexander

Stephan, trans. Grace Paley (New York: Farrar, Straus and Giroux, 1993), 12. Wolf seems to have felt most comfortable then in the stance of the "critical" intellectual (a position modeled on the antifascist intellectual/émigré), which balanced two moral pressures: a commitment to the new, antifascist society, and a critical distance necessary for the intellectual—a "lesson" learned from those who had lived through the Nazi period. It was thus not surprising that Wolf reactivated this pattern in 1993, comparing herself to the "German emigrants," "mostly Jewish" but also "Communist," who were forced to leave Nazi Germany ("Äusserungen Christa Wolfs in der Sendung 'Kulturreport,' January 24, 1993," quoted in Vinke, ed., *Akteneinsicht Christa Wolf,* 170). This statement reveals how deeply anchored Wolf's thought remains in the problematic of that period (i.e., the possibility of a popular front against National Socialism) and how strong her identification with those who left Nazi Germany remains.

14 In *Christa T.,* an unidentified narrator pieces together the story of her friend, Christa T., from fragments of letters and stories that she finds in her personal papers. Initially attracted to the ideals of the new state, Christa T. gradually moves toward a marginal existence as the gap between her utopian ideals and the reality of this socialism continues to widen. About to gain her greatest desire— her own house, which obliquely stands for the realization of a Blochian *Heimat* (see Andreas Huyssen, "Auf den Spuren Ernst Blochs: Nachdenken über Christa Wolf," *Basis* 5 [1975]: 107)—Christa T. dies of cancer before the house is even finished. The narrator describes the relationship between narrator and character as one between reality and utopia—Christa T.'s life is "a promise that is unrepeatable and unfulfilled"; Christa Wolf, *The Quest for Christa T.,* trans. Christopher Middleton (New York: Farrar, Straus and Giroux, 1970), 15 (henceforth cited as *QT*/page); *Nachdenken über Christa T.* (Hamburg and Zurich: Luchterhand Literaturverlag, 1991 [1968]), 23 (henceforth cited as *CT*/page). The attack on the book as "pure subjectivism"—Hans Koch, "Referat auf der Vorstandssitzung des Deutschen Schriftstellerverbandes am 30. 10. 1969," quoted in *Dokumentation zu Christa Wolf "Nachdenken über Christa T.,"* ed. Angela Drescher (Hamburg: Luchterhand Literaturverlag, 1991), 158—reached a climax when the novel was praised in the West as a veiled critique of the GDR; see Marcel Reich-Ranicki, "Christa Wolf's unruhige Elegie," in Drescher, ed., *Dokumentation zu Christa Wolf,* 104–7. Wolf defended herself against this Western reading and insisted that the novel represented neither the failure of a utopian project nor its author's resignation, but rather a process of "Selbstverständigung," or self-understanding, the goal of which was to reappropriate the original utopian impulse; Christa Wolf, "Notwendige Feststellung," December 22, 1969, in Drescher, ed., *Dokumentation zu Christa Wolf,* 186. This debate exemplifies the pressures on GDR writers to assume what Foucault called the "author function." Hans Koch's major problem consisted of not being able to pin down the author and her opinion (quoted in Drescher, ed., *Dokumentation zu Christa Wolf,* 154). And, in "Das Neue und das Bleibende in Unserer Literatur," Max Walter Schulz, another influential East German critic, complained that Wolf's "subjec-

tively honest" intention (which, he granted, followed the Party's line) was of no use, for her novel "provoked" the "ambiguity of its overall message" and thus led to a situation where the "other side" could choose what it liked, to decipher what it preferred to decipher (quoted in Drescher, ed., *Dokumentation zu Christa Wolf,* 113).

15 Reimann and Wolf, *Sei gegrüsst und lebe,* 20. Hörnigk ("Das 11," 239) quotes Wolf as using the word "Verlierergefühl" (i.e., a feeling of having been defeated) after the Eleventh Plenary. For a more detailed account of the controversy surrounding the publication of *Christa T.,* see Wolf's diary excerpts, in Drescher's *Dokumentation zu Christa Wolf,* which also include a detailed account of her conversation with Otto Gotsche, who called her book "ideologically miserable," but wanted to bring her back to the right path (208ff.).

16 Christa Wolf, "Ein Brief," in Drescher, ed., *Dokumentation zu Christa Wolf,* 190. The letter is dated August 21, 1991.

17 Wolf, "Christa Wolf im Gespräch mit Günther Gaus," in Vinke, ed., *Akteneinsicht Christa Wolf,* 248.

18 In his review of *Was bleibt* (Frankfurt a.M.: Luchterhand Literaturverlag, 1990), Kurt Wenzel makes the simple but crucial point "that the voices of a life speak impurely"; see his "Die Stasi-Debatte als Vorgang," *Neue deutsche Literatur* 6 (1993): 170.

19 Christa Wolf, *Was bleibt,* 57; *What Remains,* 262.

20 Christa Wolf, "The Fourth Dimension: A Conversation with Joachim Walther," in her *Fourth Dimension: Interviews with Christa Wolf,* trans. Hilary Pilkington (London and New York: Verso, 1988), 6.

21 For an excellent discussion of this blurring of boundaries as an aspect of "epic prose," a conscious appropriation of Brecht's estrangement strategies that aims to direct the reader's attention to the process of writing itself, see Kuhn, *Christa Wolf's Utopian Vision,* 58ff.

22 Christa Wolf, "Reading and Writing," in *The Author's Dimension,* ed. Stephan, 46. ("Lesen und Schreiben" [1972], in *Die Dimension des Autors,* 2: 463–503.)

23 Bernhard Greiner, "Die Schwierigkeit, 'ich' zu sagen: Christa Wolfs psychologische Orientierung des Erzählens," *Deutsche Vierteljahresschrift für Literaturwissenschaft und Geistesgeschichte* 55 (1981): 327.

24 At the Sixth Writers' Conference (1969), the main task of which was to draw the boundaries of the permissible using *Christa T.,* Klaus Gysi, the cultural minister, defined the omniscient narrator's role as equipping the reader with an "unwavering confidence in victory, a vast historical consciousness, the great ideal of unbroken heroes, great love for the people, and sharp hatred of its enemies" (quoted in Klaus-Michael Bogdal, "Wer darf sprechen? Schriftsteller als moralische Instanz—Überlegungen zu einem Ende und einem Anfang," *Weimarer Beiträge* 37 [1991]: 601). The other genre in which this topic of a "new" voice developed was lyric poetry; see Volker Braun's concept of "working subjectivity," in Emmerich, *Kleine Literaturgeschichte,* 387ff.

25 Wolfgang Emmerich, "Der verlorene Faden: Probleme des Erzählens in den siebziger Jahren," in his *Die andere deutsche Literatur: Aufsätze zur Literatur aus der DDR* (Opladen: Westdeutscher Verlag, 1994), 52, 53; my emphasis. Wolf's own defense of *Christa T.* from 1966 reflects this debate about subjectivity. Defending herself against the charge of retreating into "inwardness," she argued that the GDR had reached a stage where the "practical foundations for the individual to realize himself" were laid. Now, "the individual" could live "an ever more sovereign existence within his society"; see her "Interview with Myself," in *The Author's Dimension,* ed. Stephan, 18–19. For a book-length study of East German literature working with the paradigm of subjectivization, see Friedrich H. Schlegel, *Die Romanliteratur der DDR: Erzähltechniken, Leserlenkung, Kulturpolitik* (Opladen: Westdeutscher Verlag, 1991).

26 Emmerich, "Der verlorene Faden," 54. See also Katharina von Ankum, "Christa Wolfs Poetik des Alltags: Von *Juninachmittag* bis *Was bleibt,*" in *Zwischen gestern und morgen: Schriftstellerinnen der DDR aus amerikanischer Sicht,* ed. Ute Brandes (Berlin and New York: Peter Lang, 1992), 183–98.

27 Emmerich, "Der verlorene Faden," 54. For a similar reading that emphasizes new forms of narration, see Rainer Nägele, "Trauer, Tropen, und Phantasmen: Ver-rückte Geschichten aus der DDR," in *Literatur der DDR in den siebziger Jahren,* eds. Peter Uwe Hohendahl and Patricia Herminghouse (Frankfurt a.M.: Suhrkamp Verlag, 1983), 193–222. For a similar assessment of *Nachdenken über Christa T.,* see Kuhn, *Christa Wolf's Utopian Vision,* 52.

28 The essay's origins reach into the period adumbrated above. According to Angela Drescher's introduction to *Dokumentation zu Christa Wolf "Nachdenken über Christa T."* (14), permission to publish the essay was already sought in 1968. Wolf's correspondence with Reimann makes it clear that the essay was written as a reaction to Annemarie Auer's critique of Reimann's *Franziska Linkerhand* as lacking in plot. Writing about experiences that were "possible or necessary or significant," Wolf declared, is more important than any plot (Reimann and Wolf, *Sei gegrüsst und lebe,* 21).

29 Wolf, "Reading and Writing," in Stephan, ed., *The Author's Dimension,* 44.

30 Ibid., 37.

31 Ibid., 46, 37.

32 Wolf, "Subjective Authenticity," in *The Fourth Dimension,* trans. Pilkington, 23–24; "Subjektive Authentizität," in *Die Dimension des Autors,* 2: 773–805.

33 The same argument was put forward by Franz Fühmann, after his encounter with Bitterfeld, in *Briefe 1950–1984,* ed. Hans-Jürgen Schmitt (Rostock: Hinsdorff Verlag, 1994), 33–40.

34 The concept which links her Lukácsian period to her later poetics is clearly that of responsibility; see, for instance, her essay on censorship, "Kann man über alles schreiben?" *Neue Deutsche Literatur* 6 (1958): 15.

35 Wolf, "Interview with Myself," in Stephan, ed., *The Author's Dimension,* 18. Wolf's notion of "experience" is clearly meant to exceed the biographical: "It seems to me it would be ideal if writers were sensitive to other peoples' ex-

periences as if they were their own, and to their own almost as if they were a stranger's" (Wolf, "The Fourth Dimension," 2). For the specifically feminine dimension of this notion of experience as amalgam of emotion and ratio, see Lennox, " 'Der Versuch, man selbst zu sein.' " Lennox also points to the potential trap represented by this fundamental dichotomy of female emotionality and male rationality (221).

36 Schulz, "Kein Chorgesang," 213. Schulz correctly points out that radical forms of modernist prose such as Uwe Johnson's *Mutmassungen über Jakob* (1956) were always excluded from the East German literary field. In a context with Johnson and Fritz Rudolf Fries, her assessment of Wolf makes sense: "Christa Wolf adopted the gesture of doubt and questioning, but the tendency to provide an answer always remained inscribed in her prose" (213).

Bogdal ("Wer darf sprechen?") contrasts the opposition between the socialist realist concept of the author and Wolf's notion of subjective authenticity as the "truth of the collective" versus the "experienced truth of the individual" (602). Wolf's foregrounding of the narrator and the construction of a dialogic situation that this implies should also be seen as part of the attempt by East German authors to propose alternative, "democratic" forms of communication. Thus, for instance, in his poetry lectures, Uwe Johnson argued against the omniscient narrator's authoritarian stance: "He listened to his people speak. There was a tone that rebelled against this certainty which was so irrevocable . . . things were said clearly, and he obediently wrote them down. . . . But he had given up any claim to omniscience; he only spoke up when the others were silent . . . they invited him to help. . . . He was working with them"; see his *Begleitumstände: Frankfurter Vorlesungen* (Frankfurt a.M.: Suhrkamp Verlag, 1992), 133, 139. On this topic, see also my discussion of Christoph Hein's alternative model of narration: "Christoph Hein's *Der fremde Freund/Drachenblut* and the Antinomies of Writing under 'Real Existing Socialism,' " *Colloquia Germanica* 25 (1992): 307–37. In the context of the literature of the Prenzlauer Berg, this conception of the narrator/author as "speaking for others" was severely attacked; see Manfred Jäger, "Wem schreibe ich?," in *Die andere Sprache: Neue DDR-Literatur der 80er Jahre,* special issue of *Text und Kritik,* ed. Heinz Ludwig Arnold (Munich: Text und Kritik, 1990), 68–69. Hilbig attacked the function of the author in the GDR as an instance that destroys the dialogic character of language, in "Literatur als Dialog," in his *Zwischen den Paradiesen* (Leipzig: Reclam Verlag, 1992), 198. Wolf herself declared in 1990 that the epoch when authors were asked to speak for others was over; see her "Heine, die Zensur und wir: Rede auf dem ausserordentlichen Schriftstellerkongress der DDR," in her *Im Dialog,* 166.

37 Bernhard Greiner, " 'Mit der Erzählung geh ich in den Tod': Kontinuität und Wandel des Erzählens im Schaffen von Christa Wolf," in *Christa Wolf: Ein Arbeitsbuch,* ed. Angela Drescher (Berlin and Weimar: Aufbau-Verlag, 1989), 342.

38 Greiner (ibid., 333–34, 343) correctly argues that Wolf writes against both the illusion that the self constitutes a unity *and* against a form of modernist writing that accepted the dissolution of the subject. He understands Wolf's oeuvre

as an inquiry into the history of this self on different levels: the constitution of the subject in a socialist state (*The Divided Heaven* and *Quest for Christa T.*); the constitution of the subject in the fascist era (*Patterns of Childhood*); the constitution of the subject within the horizon of bourgeois enlightenment (*No Place on Earth*); and, finally, the constitution of the subject within the horizon of Western history (*Cassandra*). Although Greiner's psychoanalytic perspective sheds new light on Wolf's texts, his paradigm again involves a covert teleology in which the author moves progressively away from her orthodox beginnings.

39 Kuhn, *Christa Wolf's Utopian Vision*, 61.

40 Love, "Christa Wolf and Feminism," 45.

41 Ibid., 34. For a critical assessment of Love's reading as ahistorical (an assessment I share), see Kuhn, *Christa Wolf's Utopian Vision*, 93–94.

42 Sonja Hilzinger, "Weibliches Schreiben als eine Ästhetik des Widerstands: Über Wolf's 'Kassandra'-Projekt," in *Christa Wolf: Ein Arbeitsbuch,* ed. Angela Drescher (Berlin and Weimar: Aufbau-Verlag, 1989), 222; and *Kassandra: Über Christa Wolf* (Frankfurt a.M.: Haag and Herchen, 1984), 75. Hilzinger understands Wolf's concept of subjective authenticity as writing in which the author guarantees with her personality the truth/authenticity of what she narrates. In terms of Wolf's novel *Kassandra,* Hilzinger defines this presence of the female author, with Kristeva, as a dialectical process, in which "the subject . . . takes on its entire (unconscious) structure and brings it into the act of symbolization" ("Weibliches Schreiben als eine Ästhetik des Widerstands," 222). I will discuss the problems with this approach in chapter 5.

43 Dorothea Böck, "Ich schreibe um herauszufinden warum ich schreiben muss: Frauenliteratur in der DDR zwischen Selbsterfahrung und ästhetischem Experiment," *Feministische Studien* 1 (1990): 61–74.

Other critics who locate the beginnings of an emancipatory women's literature in the publication of *Christa T.* are Patricia Herminghouse, "Wunschbild oder Portrait? Zur Darstellung der Frau im Roman der DDR," in *Literatur und Literaturtheorie in der DDR,* ed. Patricia Herminghouse and Peter Uwe Hohendahl (Frankfurt a.M.: Suhrkamp, 1981), 281–334; Helen Fehervary, "Die erzählerische Kolonisierug des weiblichen Schweigens: Frau und Arbeit in der DDR-Literatur," in *Arbeit als Thema in der deutschen Literatur vom Mittelalter bis zur Gegenwart,* ed. Reinhold Grimm and Jost Hermand (Königstein/Ts: Athenäum, 1979), 171–95.

44 Böck, "Ich schreibe um herauszufinden warum ich schreiben muss," 64, 65.

45 Helen Fehervary makes this point by contrasting Wolf and Müller. She understands Wolf's writing as the attempt to constitute a feminine authorship, while Müller moves toward the destruction of authorship in projecting his utopian desires onto "woman." This other, Fehervary writes, is not available to the woman author, whose inquiry thus turns into a reflection on authorship itself; see "The Gender of Authorship: Heiner Müller and Christa Wolf," in *Studies in Twentieth Century Literature,* special issue on Modernism and Postmodernism in Contemporary German Literature, ed. Rainer Nägele 5 (Fall 1980): 41–58.

46 See, for instance, Hörnigk's chapter on *Der geteilte Himmel,* "The Discovery of One's Own Voice," in *Christa Wolf,* 48–105. See also Kuhn's "Beginnings: Experimentation with Socialist Realist Paradigms. *Moscow Novella* and *Divided Heaven,*" in *Christa Wolf's Utopian Vision:* "Yet this authorial subjectivity remains anomalous in the text [*Moscow Novella*]. The author immediately reasserts her 'objective' stance. . . . We will have to wait until the *Quest for Christa T.* for the full development of that narrative style" (24). Fehervary discusses *Moscow Novella* from a similar perspective, linking it to nineteenth-century women's literature, in "Christa Wolf's Prose: A Landscape of Masks," *New German Critique* 27 (1982): 170.

47 Christa Wolf, "The Sense and Non-Sense of Being Naive," in *The Author's Dimension,* ed. Stephan, 49–57.

48 See Angela Drescher's reductionist reading of *Der geteilte Himmel* as the book of a daughter (she equates Rita with the author) who rebels against the conditions of life established by her parents' generation; "In der blauen Höhle: Mutter-Tochter-Beziehungen in Büchern von Christa Wolf," in *Christa Wolf in feministischer Sicht,* ed. Michel Vanhelleputte (Frankfurt a.M.: Peter Lang, 1992), 139.

49 Žižek, *For They Know Not What They Do,* 260.

50 I have benefited greatly from Kaja Silverman's study *The Acoustic Mirror: The Female Voice in Psychoanalysis and Cinema* (Bloomington and Indianapolis: Indiana University Press, 1988). However, since I am dealing with literary texts, my approach necessarily differs from hers.

51 Didier Anzieu, "L'Enveloppe sonore du Soi," *Nouvelle Revue de Psychanalyse* 13 (Spring 1976): 175.

52 Ibid., 173. This very first experience of bodily unity, however undefined, and this first link to the mother are preconditions for the mirror stage.

53 Guy Rosolato, "La voix: Entre corps et language," *Revue Française de Psychanalyse* 38 (1974): 79. According to Rosolato, imitating the mother's voice is the first step in the process of corporeal identification, the first stage of those (partial) introjections that prepare the identifications at stake in the subject's Oedipal structuration.

54 Rosolato argues that the auditory sense, like the other sensory registers, plays an important role in the early structuration of the child's body.

55 Paul-Laurent Assoun, *Leçons psychanalytiques sur le Regard et la Voix* (Paris: Anthropos, 1995), 1: 50.

56 Freud, "The Ego and the Id," 19: 26.

57 Sigmund Freud, "Lecture XXXI: The Dissection of the Psychical Personality," in *New Introductory Lectures on Psychoanalysis,* ed. James Strachey (New York: Norton, 1965), 63.

58 This applies to partial objects, such as the breast.

59 Mitchell, *Psycho-Analysis and Feminism,* 71.

60 Assoun, *Le Regard et la Voix,* 2: 75. Freud is concerned with the relations among ego, id, and superego, their permeable boundaries, and their relations to the systems of the unconscious, the preconscious, and consciousness in "The Ego and

the Id." See also his "Lecture XXXI" (58, 60, 61), for Freud's discussion of the agency of the superego as an instance in the ego, an observing and judging instance which sets itself over and against the ego and whose relations to the ego may change (e.g., in melancholia, when the subject experiences some periods during which the superego is extremely severe and others when it seems to melt into the ego).

61 Freud, "The Ego and the Id," 25.

62 Assoun, *Le Regard et la Voix,* I: 51.

63 Indeed, Freud goes on to say that the superego is not constructed on the model of the parents but on the "parents' super-ego; the contents which fill it are the same and it becomes the vehicle of tradition" (Freud, "Lecture XXXI," 67, 64).

64 Freud, "The Ego and the Id," 34.

65 Assoun, *Le Regard et la Voix,* I: 52.

66 Ibid., I: 50.

67 The anonymous voice(s) of the subject's ego ideal—the conscience that regulates the subject—translates the split of superego from ego (ibid., I: 49).

68 Freud, "The Ego and The Id," 36.

69 Assoun, *Le Regard et la Voix,* I: 54.

70 Ibid., I: 55, 78.

71 This connection to *jouissance* means that the sound of the singing voice is linked to the memory of complete and total satisfaction, a desire once entirely fulfilled in the union with the other, the pre-Oedipal mother. It is the memory of this total pleasure, rendered impossible once and for all by the child's renunciation of unity with the mother after its entry into the symbolic order, which generates the *object a,* the forever unattainable object of desire. (It is important to keep in mind that this pre-Oedipal mother is not a woman, since sexual difference is only introduced with the Oedipal crisis.) For a discussion of the utopian potential of voice, see Rosolato on music, in particular opera ("La Voix," 88).

72 Assoun, *Le Regard et la Voix,* I: 79, 80.

73 Sigmund Freud, quoted in Elizabeth Cowie, "Representations," in *The Woman in Question,* ed. Parveen Adams and Elizabeth Cowie (Cambridge, Mass.: MIT Press, 1990), 116.

74 Jean Laplanche and Jean-Bertrand Pontalis, "Fantasy and the Origins of Sexuality," in Burgin, Donald, and Kaplan, eds., *Formations of Fantasy,* 25; my emphasis. In this reading of Freud, drive becomes autoerotic only after the loss of the object: "If it can be said of auto-eroticism that it is object-less, it is in no sense because it may appear before any object relationship, nor because on its arrival no object will remain in the search for satisfaction, but simply because the natural method of apprehending an object is split in two: the sexual drive separated from the non-sexual functions, such as feeding, which are its support (*Anlehnung*) and which indicate its aim and object" (ibid.).

75 Mitchell, *Psycho-Analysis and Feminism,* 110.

76 "Übereinstimmung" is a central term in Wolf's own discussions of her involvement in East German politics. Besides the idea of agreement, the word carries

the notion of voices harmonizing with each other, of being in attunement. (I will come back to this notion.)

77 Rosolato, "La voix," 82–83.

78 Fredric Jameson, *The Political Unconscious: Narrative as a Socially Symbolic Act* (Ithaca: Cornell University Press, 1981), 180.

79 As Wolf acknowledged in "Dienstag, der 27. September 1960," her "diary excerpt" published in a 1974 issue of *Neue deutsche Literatur.* As a chronicle of her daily activities as a mother, an author, and a participant in the Bitterfelder movement, "Dienstag" became something of a minor feminist classic of GDR literature. What is more interesting in the present context are its descriptions of literary-theoretical discussions between Wolf and her husband, who was then editing Lenin's letters to Gorky for publication; "Dienstag" contains an implicit condemnation of any dogmatic interference in the process of literary production. The party leadership and cultural functionaries are clearly being criticized by contrasting their methods with Lenin's, a strategy that Wolf called "dialogue" and employed throughout her career. On the different genres of the Bitterfelder Weg, from the production diary to the novel, see Ingeborg Gerlach, *Bitterfeld: Arbeiterliteratur und Literatur der Arbeitswelt in der DDR* (Kronberg/ Ts.: Scriptor-Verlag, 1974); Bernhard Greiner, *Von der Allegorie zur Idylle: Die Literatur der Arbeitswelt in der DDR* (Heidelberg: Quelle und Meyer, 1974); and Marc D. Silberman, *Literature of the Working World: A Study of the Industrial Novel in East Germany* (Bern/Frankfurt: H. Lang, 1976).

80 Wolf, "Dienstag," 22.

81 See Hörnigk, *Christa Wolf,* 87ff.

82 Christa Wolf, *The Divided Heaven,* trans. Joan Becker (New York: Adler's Foreign Books, 1983), 5 (henceforth cited as *DH*/page); Christa Wolf, *Der geteilte Himmel* (Munich: Deutscher Taschenbuchverlag, 1973), 11 (henceforth cited as *gH*/page).

83 What also betrays the ideological character of this resolution is that this portrait of the simple life seems like something conjured up from Germany's long tradition of idyllic literature. This image in the epilogue strongly contrasts with the prologue's image of "the city" as a site not of premodern community but of industrial production. On this topic, see Richard Herzinger and Heinz-Peter Preusser, "Vom Äussersten zum Ersten: DDR-Literatur in der Tradition deutscher Zivilisationskritik," in *Literatur in der DDR: Rückblicke,* ed. Heinz-Ludwig Arnold (Munich: Edition Text und Kritik, 1991), 195–209.

84 On *Moskauer Novelle,* see, for instance, Gerda Schultz's review in *Neue deutsche Literatur.* Performing a kind of genre policing, Schultz charges the work with failing to be either a story or a novella and notes other "transgression" as well, such as violating the main character's perspective with authorial intrusions in the descriptions of Moscow (Gerda Schulz, "Ein überraschender Erstling," *Neue deutsche Literatur* 9 (1961): 130, 131).

On *Der geteilte Himmel,* see *"Der geteilte Himmel" und seine Kritiker,* ed. Martin Reso (Halle: Mitteldeutscher Verlag, 1965). One attempt to defend the novel by containing its meaning through a focus on the issue of its "subjective" narrative voice was Dieter Schlenstedt's "Motive und Symbole in Christa Wolf's Erzählung 'Der geteilte Himmel,' " *Weimarer Beiträge* 10 (1964): 77–104. Many critics addressed the ubiquitous problem of an optimistic versus a pessimistic theme, an issue made all the more burning by the novel's comparison with Uwe Johnson's *Mutmassungen über Jakob* (Speculations about Jacob), a 1959 novel about a suicide. For a concise summary of the plot similarities between *Der geteilte Himmel* and Johnson's novel, see Hans Bunge, "Im politischen Drehpunkt," in *Christa Wolf: Ein Arbeitsbuch,* ed. Angela Drescher (Berlin and Weimar: Aufbau-Verlag, 1989), 13–17.

85 On Lukács's role in the GDR before and after 1956, see Bernhard Spies, "Georg Lukács und der sozialistische Realismus in der DDR," in *Literatur in der DDR: Rückblicke,* ed. Heinz-Ludwig Arnold (Munich: Edition Text und Kritik, 1992), 34–44.

86 In 1965, Inge von Wangenheim published a novel called *Das Zimmer mit den offenen Augen* (The Room with the Open Eyes) (Halle: Mitteldeutscher Verlag, 1965), which was reissued in 1977 with an afterword proclaiming it one of Bitterfeld's wrongly forgotten novels. It is the story of Gudrun Retha's development from a fanatical BDM girl to an equally "committed" SED member. The narrator tells us that Gudrun's generation cannot find a goal worthy of its idealism because its "energy" and "fire" were abused. Once Gudrun joins the SED, she refers to herself as a "warrior" (383). Obsessively aiming for the most totalizing genre, Wangenheim ends up drawing upon so many different ones—novel of formation, family novel, romance, and adventure story—that the work ultimately creates the impression of a ruin (in the Benjaminian sense). Moreover, it applies Lukácsian realism so literally that each character is made to stand at the window of the castle on the hill for the widest possible panoramic view, which often leads to historical reflections on the country and its people. In a later essay, Wangenheim pushed this *Totalitätswahn* to its limits, demanding that the socialist author aim for the perspective of the *Kosmonaut;* see Inge von Wangenheim, "Die Geschichte und unsere Geschichten: Gedanken eines Schriftstellers auf der Suche nach den Fabeln seiner Zeit," in her *Von Zeit zu Zeit: Essays* (Halle: Mitteldeutscher Verlag, 1975), 95.

Why do I mention this rather minor novel? Because in its last scene, Wangenheim constructs a tableau which merges this omniscient perspective with the family narrative, thus generating the clearest example of the *textual structures* of East Germany's hegemonic project. The novel concludes with a double wedding on the hill, at the end of which Gudrun's father addresses the guests, intertwining the metaphor of the "view from above" with the topic of history as genealogy: "You are the youth of our present, and the oldest man in your circle, who has looked upon this world from his window for more than six decades, only wants to say one thing: see the world with open eyes. . . . In this hour we are standing up here and a whole new world lies at our feet. Before us many generations have worked this cultural landscape for thousands of years, and many generations after us will continue our work" (*Das Zimmer,* 561). The father, a minor character, now stands at the center, legitimating the new order by lending it his authority. It is this authority, invested in the narrative structure of (socialist) realism—specifically, in its voice—that is at stake in Wolf's second novel, which poses a fundamental question: Who has the authority to speak? In the production novels of the 1950s, the realist imperative took on a different guise. For instance, in Karl Mundstock's *Helle Nächte* (Bright Nights) of 1952, one of the protagonists dreams that she climbs a crane, from the top of which she can see the entire country. This totalizing perspective coincides with the climax of her own development, for she has reached her goal and learned how to operate a crane (35). The same totalizing metaphor, encompassing subjective development, the history of the GDR's construction, *and* the narrative perspective, appears in Erik Neutsch's 1964 *Spur der Steine* (The Trace of the Stones), when Balla, the worker and former "anarchist," mentally surveys his construction site from his "scaffold high above the earth" and imagines that he is making history (823).

87 See Joseph Pischel, "Gewebe der Gesittung—Gewebe des Erzählens: Christa Wolfs Verhältnis zu Anna Seghers," in *Christa Wolf: Ein Arbeitsbuch,* ed. Angela Drescher (Berlin and Weimar: Aufbau-Verlag, 1989), 383.

88 Wolf, "Das siebte Kreuz," in *Die Dimension des Autors,* 1: 269. Wolf considers Seghers's novel to be about the "network of the people's daily life," a life which, she continues in a Segherian tone, consists of "banality and poetry," the "taste of daily bread and the people's daily struggle for bread," the "hardship of their struggle and the greatness of the people" (264). Wolf mentions in this review that Seghers once planned to write an essay on the topic of a life at once "ordinary" and "dangerous" (269).

89 Rita's father is remembered as a gentle man who died in the war, but who had no connection to National Socialism.

90 On the importance of the *other's* gaze in the mirror stage, see Samuel Weber, *Return to Freud,* 12ff.

91 On these so-called rabbit films, see Barton Byg, "What Might Have Been: DEFA Films of the Past and the Future of German Cinema," *Cineaste* 17 (1992): 9.

92 Hörnigk, "Das 11," 56.

93 See E. Friedman, "Where Are the Missing Contents? (Post)Modernism, Gender, and the Canon," *PMLA* 2 (1993): 240–53. In contradistinction to the male perspective of these films, in which feminine utopian power is textualized as the transgressive power of the feminine erotic, the bearer of this utopian potential in Wolf's novel is the "pure" body.

94 Slavoj Žižek, *The Sublime Object of Ideology* (London and New York: Verso, 1992), 104.

95 Ibid., 106ff., 110.

96 Ibid., 106.

97 Rose, "Introduction," in *Sexuality,* 15–16.

98 Quoted in Hörnigk, *Christa Wolf,* 97.

99 Gregorio Kohon, "Reflections on Dora: The Case of Hysteria," in *The British School of Psychoanalysis: The Independent Tradition,* ed. Gregorio Kohon (New Haven and London: Yale University Press, 1986), 363. For a reading of Beauvoir in terms of Kohon, see Moi, *Simone de Beauvoir,* 122ff.

100 Kohon, "Reflections on Dora," 378.

101 Žižek, *Sublime Object of Ideology,* 106.

102 On this question, see the "Exchange" between Hélène Cixous and Catherine Clément in Hélène Cixous and Catherine Clément, *The Newly Born Woman* (Minneapolis: University of Minnesota Press, 1991), 135–60. See also Toril Moi's more recent interview of Juliet Mitchell, "Psychoanalysis, Feminism, and Politics: A Conversation with Juliet Mitchell," *South Atlantic Quarterly* 93 (1994): 925–49.

103 Julia Kristeva, *The Kristeva Reader,* ed. Toril Moi (New York: Columbia University Press, 1986), 113.

104 Christa Wolf, "The Shadow of a Dream: A Sketch of Karoline von Günderrode," in Stephan, ed., *The Author's Dimension,* 133.

105 Christa Wolf, "Fortgesetzter Versuch" (Continued Attempt), in *Die Dimension des Autors,* 1: 345.

106 Christa Wolf, *Cassandra: A Novel and Four Essays,* trans. Jan Van Heuck (New York: Farrar, Straus and Giroux, 1984), 4 (henceforth cited as *C*/page); *Kassandra: Erzählung* (Darmstadt: Luchterhand Literaturverlag, 1986 [1983]), 6 (henceforth cited as *K*/page).

107 Wolf's review of *Das siebte Kreuz* begins with its famous lines: "We have now arrived. What happens now is happening to us"—thus deploying the same urgent collective voice (Wolf, "Das siebte Kreuz," in *Die Dimension des Autors,* 1: 263).

108 In a letter to Wolf, Brigitte Reimann observed in 1966: "It seems to me that your language in 'The Divided Heaven' was indebted to Anna Seghers, even on the level of the rhythm of its sentences, of its choice of images; but this was more than mere influence, it was agreement/attunement [*Übereinstimmung*]" (Reimann and Wolf, *Sei gegrüsst und lebe,* 8). Reimann commented more critically on *Christa T.,* in which she claimed not to recognize her friend's style anymore, calling it "borrowed."

109 Lowell A. Bangerter reads *Nachdenken über Christa T.* as an intertextual reworking of "Der Ausflug der toten Mädchen," in "Anna Seghers and Christa Wolf," *Germanic Review* 58 (Summer 1993): 127–32; Pischel, "Gewebe der Gesittung—Gewebe des Erzählens," in Drescher, ed., *Christa Wolf: Ein Arbeitsbuch.* Indeed, this collection covering Wolf's entire oeuvre opens with a letter from Seghers ("Ein Brief," 11–12) about *Der geteilte Himmel,* which she criticizes for being too simplistic in its portrayal of the West. See also Peter Beicken, "Nachfolge nicht Nachahmung: Zur Beziehung Anna Seghers–Christa Wolf," in *Deutsche Exilliteratur,* ed. Wolfgang Elfe et al. (Bern, Frankfurt, Las Vegas: Peter Lang, 1981), 114–32. For an explicitly feminist reading of their relationship, see Christiane Zehl Romero, " 'Remembrance of Things Future': On Establish-

ing a Female Tradition," in *Responses to Christa Wolf,* ed. Marilyn Sibley Fries (Detroit: Wayne State University Press, 1989), 108–27.

110 Reimann and Wolf, *Sei gegrüsst und lebe,* 5; Christa Wolf, "Gesichter der Anna Seghers" (The Faces of Anna Seghers), in *Anna Seghers: Eine Biographie in Bildern,* ed. Frank Wagner, Ursula Emmerich, and Ruth Radvanyi (Berlin and Weimar: Aufbau-Verlag, 1994), 6–9. Wolf's essay originally appeared in *Neue deutsche Literatur* 12 (1992), and was reprinted in Christa Wolf, *Auf dem Weg nach Tabou: Texte 1990–1994* (Cologne: Kiepenheuer and Witsch, 1994).

111 In her review of *Die Entscheidung,* Wolf calls it a novel about "the great transformation of a people" (Christa Wolf, "Land, in dem wir leben," *Neue deutsche Literatur* 5 [1961]: 59). In "Fragen an Anna Seghers" (*Die Dimension des Autors,* 1: 279–92), Wolf asks, "What do you consider the basic idea of your book?" Seghers's answer adumbrates the concerns of Wolf's novel as well: "The book is called 'The Decision.' I primarily wanted to show how the division which separates the world into two parts affects all parts of our lives, even the most private ones: like politics and economy, love, marriage, profession are part of the great decision. No one can escape, everybody is confronted by the question: For whom, against whom are you?" (256).

112 Christa Wolf, "The Sand and Pines of Brandenburg: A Conversation with Adam Krzeminski," in *The Fourth Dimension,* trans. Pilkington, 68–69.

113 The term *authenticity,* however, stems from Ingeborg Bachmann's "Frankfurter Vorlesungen" (lectures on poetics held in Frankfurt), as Wolf's 1966 essay, "The Truth You Can Expect: The Prose of Ingeborg Bachmann" (in *The Author's Dimension,* ed. Stephan, 99–109), indicates. In these lectures, we find the central topics that Wolf's work revolves around: "authenticity," the "I" as "representative of the human voice," the concern with a "history inside the subject" (Geschichte im Ich), and the utopia of a "language other than this bad one" (Ingeborg Bachmann, "Frankfurter Vorlesungen," *Gesammelte Werke* [Munich: Piper Verlag, 1978], 4: 193, 237, 230, and 270–71). Bachmann's voice will become another crucial point of identification for Wolf, especially on the latter topic. However, at this point I want to stress that, in Wolf's "Reading and Writing" (1968), Bachmann's topics are inscribed into the framework derived from Seghers: Bachmann will become a possible position for the writing daughter. The 1966 essay on Bachmann starts with the familiar concept of "subjective authenticity" developed in the later essays: "You will hear a voice: daring and lamenting. A voice that suits the truth, that is: talking about what is certain and uncertain, on the basis of personal experience" (99). Despite Bachmann's influence, it is not surprising that Wolf concludes this piece with the idea that prose "supports the process by which man becomes a free individual," that prose is "revolutionary" ("Reading and Writing," 48). Pointing out the discrepancy between this "unproblematic synthesis of subject, revolution, and realism" and Bachmann's poetics, Sigrid Weigel argues that Wolf reduces the latter to fit her own program. Obviously, the essay is an attempt to inscribe Bachmann into an aesthetic project whose major outlines are defined by Wolf's reception

of Seghers. See Sigrid Weigel, "Vom Sehen zur Seherin: Christa Wolfs Um-deutung des Mythos und die Spur der Bachmann-Rezeption in ihrer Literatur," in *Christa Wolf—Ein Arbeitsbuch,* ed. Angela Drescher (Berlin and Weimar: Aufbau-Verlag, 1989), 196.

114 Wolf, "Glauben an Irdisches," in *Die Dimension des Autors,* 1: 294.

115 Ibid., 295; my emphases.

116 Ibid., 298.

117 Ibid., 302.

118 Ibid., 303.

119 Ibid., 303–4.

120 Ibid., 309; her emphasis.

121 See Seghers's 1973 defense of the novel in "Wird der Roman überflüssig?" (Will the Novel Become Superfluous?), in *Die Macht der Worte: Reden–Schriften–Briefe* (Leipzig and Weimar: Kiepenheuer Verlag, 1979): "No cosmonaut can fly as high and no cyclotron can accelerate particles the way a true writer can set his characters in motion and uncover in their soul the most minute components." And she claims that plot "can transform [the reader] from the inside" (116). See also Seghers's 1947 "Vorwort zum Roman 'Die Rettung' " (Preface to the Novel "The Rescue"), in *Die Macht der Worte,* where she states that the novel reveals the actions and emotions of people under different social conditions, "often ac-tions that were little noticed and intended, often secret and hidden emotions" (15). While the former essay attempts to rescue the novel in a scientific age, the latter defends it against the primacy of politics: "A novel is not a lead article."

122 Seghers said something similar when Wolf asked her about the meaning of "mastering," or "overcoming": speaking about Tolstoy, Seghers described his novels as always aimed at an intense moment of crisis involving "something powerful in both the private and the social realm" (Wolf, "Ein Gespräch mit Anna Seghers," 291).

123 Wolf, "Subjective Authenticity," in Pilkington, trans., *The Fourth Dimension,* 20; TA.

124 The argument is resonant with Wolf's defensive insistence on the writing of *Christa T.* as a process of overcoming an existential and political crisis in ward-ing off the "dangers" of resignation. (See especially Wolf's correspondence with Reimann on the topic of resignation.) It was indeed *Christa T.* which earned Wolf Seghers's praise. In an open letter to Wolf, Seghers wrote: "I think I really liked *The Quest for Christa T.* because this book searches for the truth about a dead woman, who was not able to cope with life"; see her "Für Christa Wolf," *Sinn und Form* 31 (1979): 282. But this novel was also the source of their first disagreement. When Wolf told Seghers that *Christa T.* would not be published, the latter offered to read it and find a way to change "one or two sentences" to make it publishable. Wolf laughed and quoted Seghers as saying, "Listen, one can represent everything, if one has the ability." Seghers, said Wolf, had come to the conclusion that ultimately the Party was always right, adding, "But that is exactly the conclusion I can no longer draw" (nor, she admitted, would she have

rebelled against Seghers in this way earlier); see Drescher, ed., *Dokumentation zu Christa Wolf,* 193–94, 207.

125 Wolf, "Forgesetzter Versuch," in *Die Dimension des Autors,* I: 341. With respect to *Transit,* Wolf makes a similar observation: "No one will ever be able to separate the author's most personal experience from the experience of the narrator of *Transit,* an intentionally and artfully iridescent figure"; see her "Transit: Ortschaften" (1985), in *Die Dimension des Autors,* I: 370.

126 Wolf, "Forgesetzter Versuch," I: 341–42.

127 Ibid., 343.

128 Ibid.

129 Ibid., 344.

130 Ibid., 344–45. Wolf uses the Brechtian term *Nachgeborene* (i.e., those born after National Socialism).

131 Ibid., 345. Wolf would often draw an analogy between the historical context of the authors Seghers mentioned in her essay (Kleist, Büchner, Lenz, Günderrode) and that of her own generation. For the earlier generation, as for her own, the "basic formative experience" was the inability to translate the lofty expectations of a revolution (in their case, the French Revolution) into actual politics. Theirs was the first generation to have experienced this gap between their political potential and their ability to intervene politically; see her "Romanticism in Perspektive," in Pilkington, trans., *The Fourth Dimension,* 95ff. Scholars have tended to accentuate influence and continuity, not adversarial antagonism, in the relationship of these two women/authors. For instance, Pischel ("Gewebe der Gesittung—Gewebe des Erzählens," 395) writes about Wolf's development as a growth from "succession" to "acquiring her own profile" in the 1980s, that is, with *Kassandra.* My thesis is that the relationship was both identificatory and antagonistic from the very beginning.

132 See Harold Bloom, *The Anxiety of Influence* (New York: Oxford University Press, 1973).

133 In "Gesichter der Anna Seghers" (*Auf dem Weg nach Tabou,* 228), written after the brief debate about Seghers's complicity in Stalinist politics, Wolf again makes the point that although Seghers was well aware of the GDR's "contradictions," she never transgressed the increasingly tight boundaries within which she worked.

134 Wolf, "Sand and Pines of Brandenburg," in *The Fourth Dimension,* trans. Pilkington, 67.

135 Ibid., 68.

136 Ibid., 69.

137 My reading thus differs sharply from Heidi Gidion's, who argues that Wolf lends her voice to those authors who have not been sufficiently heard. With respect to Seghers "the teacher," Wolf defended her against Lukács; with respect to Bachmann "the sister," Wolf made her voice be heard, allowing Bachmann to speak, "as if her sister's writing were a part of her," in her lectures on Kassandra; see Heidi Gidion, "Wer spricht? Beobachtungen zum Zitieren und zum Sprechen

mit der eigenen Stimme an Christa Wolfs Günderrode- und Kassandra-Projekt," in Drescher, ed., *Christa Wolf,* 205. Gidion thus misses the ways in which Wolf, rather than sympathetically lending her voice to others in an attempted "reparation," appropriates their projects/voices for her own theory.

138 Christa Wolf, "Anmerkungen zu Geschichten" (1970), in *Die Dimension des Autors,* 1: 330. See also Wolf, "Glauben an Irdisches," 322.

139 See Wolf, "Reading and Writing," 37.

140 Wolf, "Gesichter der Anna Seghers," in *Auf dem Weg nach Tabou,* 224. Cf., e.g., "Glauben an Irdisches," 318, or "Anmerkungen zu Geschichten," 324, both in her *Die Dimension des Autors,* vol. 1.

141 In later essays, such as "Zeitschichten" (Layers of Time), of May 1983, and "Transit: Ortschaften" (Transit: Places), of September 1985, Wolf would elaborate on Seghers's Jewish origins and experiences. The former recounts how Wolf once followed "Netty" home, using the last pages of "Der Ausflug der toten Mädchen" as her guide (see *Die Dimension des Autors,* 1: 357ff.). In the latter, Seghers's novel *Transit* serves as Wolf's travel guide to the South of France, eventually leading her to the ruins of the camp where Seghers's husband was interned before going to Mexico. This strange meditation, so symbiotic in quality as to leave little distance between Wolf and the narrator of *Transit,* gains its particular quality from another intertextual link—to Peter Weiss's 1963 "Meine Ortschaft" (My Place), written after his visit to Auschwitz.

142 Seghers, *Aufsätze, Ansprachen, Essays,* 6.

143 Wolf, "Sense and Non-Sense of Being Naive," in Stephan, ed., *The Author's Dimension,* 53.

144 In "Sense and Non-Sense" a curious displacement occurs, with the "explosive forces" of this particular plot, a story of forbidden love, displaced to the erotic investment of transgression. Coming close to the limits of what can be said and transgressing this boundary "at an unforeseeable point, only to discover that he [the author] cannot do it after all, that he is not allowed to because he is unable to violate a self-imposed taboo," constitutes a moment of the highest tension— and the very fascination of writing and reading (ibid., 54).

145 Wolf, "Glauben an Irdisches," 320–21. In 1989, when Aafke Steenhuis asked Wolf why she did not write about sexuality, she replied that writing is generated by tensions, and "in our country social tensions were in the foreground"; Christa Wolf, "Schreiben im Zeitbezug: Gespräch mit Aafke Steenhuis," in *Im Dialog,* 155.

146 Roland Barthes, *Image–Music–Text* (New York: Hill and Wang, 1985), 179.

5 The Paternal Family Narrative as Autobiography and as Parable

1 Frank Schirrmacher, "Dem Druck des härteren, strengeren Lebens standhalten: Auch eine Studie zum autoritären Charakter," in *"Es geht nicht um Christa Wolf": Der Literaturstreit im vereinten Deutschland,* ed. Thomas Auz (Munich:

Spangenberg, 1991), 78. See also Anna Kuhn, who has pointed out that Wolf herself, in *Patterns of Childhood,* explored the formation of an authoritarian personality under National Socialism as her own and her generation's most fundamental problem, in "*Was bleibt.* (Re)Assessing Christa Wolf Scholarship after the *Wende:* A Review Essay," *Germanic Review* (1992): 173–80.

2 Christa Wolf, "Für unser Land," in *Im Dialog,* 170–71. Here, Wolf called on citizens of the GDR to stay in East Germany and to participate in the construction of a "socialist alternative to the Federal Republic"; she also reaffirmed antifascism as a founding value of this new GDR. Signed by a large number of East German intellectuals, the petition was thoroughly discredited as soon as Egon Krenz, Erich Honnecker's successor, added his signature, but its signers had also underestimated GDR interest in joining the West. In referring to Wolf calling on East Germans to choose "not an easy life but one that is useful and interesting . . . not quick prosperity, but participation in great transformations," Schirrmacher actually quoted from two different texts, the second of which Wolf read on East German television in November 1989; Christa Wolf, "Dokumente," in *Im Dialog,* 169–70. While Schirrmacher's critique of both appeals to asceticism—their denigration of "easy prosperity" in favor of a "useful life" ("Dokumente," 169)—was justified, we should not forget that these were signed by many East German intellectuals and such citizens' groups as the New Forum, the Social Democratic Party, and Democracy Now.

3 Schirrmacher, "Dem Druck des härteren, strengeren Lebens standhalten," 81.

4 For a more nuanced assessment of Wolf's position in the GDR, see Huyssen, "After the Wall," 124.

5 Wolf, *Patterns of Childhood,* 209 (henceforth cited as *PC*/page); and *Kindheitsmuster,* 276 (henceforth cited as *KM*/page). The book's relationship to the S E D's official antifascism has been thoroughly discussed; see, for instance, Patricia Herminghouse, "Vergangenheit als Problem der Gegenwart: Zur Darstellung des Faschismus in der neueren DDR-Literatur," in *Literatur der DDR in den siebziger Jahren,* ed. Peter Uwe Hohendahl and Patricia Herminghouse (Frankfurt a.M.: Suhrkamp Verlag, 1983), 259–94. Wolf's own discussion of this relationship can be found in "Subjective Authenticity," in Pilkington, trans., *The Fourth Dimension,* 24ff. Of interest here is the justification by the narrator of *Kindheitsmuster* of her self-censorship, which clearly demonstrates the trap of Cold War thought: "Today you know that the honest word doesn't exist in the age of suspicion because the honest speaker depends on an honest listener." At the same time, the narrator knows that this self-imposed silence is damaging not only to her writing but to her very experience: "We can no longer tell what we have experienced" (*PC*/362; *KM*/468). In October 1989, Wolf expressed a desire to write about the "patterns of childhood of Stalinism"; see her "Leben oder gelebt werden," in *Im Dialog,* 113.

6 Christel Zahlmann, "*Kindheitsmuster:* Schreiben an der Grenze des Bewusstseins," in *Erinnerte Zukunft,* ed. Wolfram Mauser (Würzburg: Verlag Königshausen und Neumann, 1985), 141–42.

7   Zahlmann (ibid., 142) connects this notion of the victorious subject with Benjamin's thesis that history should be written from the perspective of the vanquished, not the victor; see also Greiner, "Mit der Erzählung geh ich in den Tod," 115; and Ortrud Gutjahr, " 'Erinnerte Zukunft': Gedächtnisrekonstruktion und Subjektkonstitution im Werk Christa Wolfs," in Mauser, ed., *Erinnerte Zukunft,* 71ff.

8   For a reading of the "feminine" as "nature" in *The Dialectic of Enlightenment,* see Silvia Bovenschen, *Die imaginierte Weiblichkeit* (Frankfurt a.M.: Suhrkamp Verlag, 1979).

Wolf lists the *Dialectic* in her bibliography to the lectures. The novella was actually the last of the lectures given in Frankfurt in 1982, but it was published separately from the lectures in the West; see Christa Wolf, *Voraussetzungen einer Erzählung: Kassandra. Frankfurter Poetik Vorlesungen* (Darmstadt and Neuwied: Luchterhand Verlag, 1984 [1983]), henceforth cited as *V*/page; with *C*/page referring to Van Heuck's translation, *Cassandra: A Novel and Four Essays* (New York: Farrar, 1984). The invitation to give the prestigious Frankfurter Poetik Vorlesungen was a sign of Wolf's enormous cultural capital in the West; see Katharina von Ankum, *Die Rezeption von Christa Wolf in Ost und West: Von "Moskauer Novelle" bis "Selbstversuch"* (Amsterdam: Rodopi, 1992).

9   In her lectures, Wolf parallels the conflict between the Greeks and Trojans and the contemporary tensions between East and West (e.g., the controversy over the installation of U.S. and Soviet missiles in Europe), as well as using a series of code words to refer to the Stasi. (Her 1990 claim that, with *Kassandra,* she had foretold the events of 1989 aroused some indignation.) Furthermore, her lectures include theoretical reflections on the possibility of another language that can be related to the king's daughter's difficulties with speaking the "truth."

10 The translation of the last sentence poses a problem: in the original, it is clear that "the first" and "the second" do not refer to (first- or second-person) voice but to the two sides of the dilemma facing the speaking subject: "Das eine unmöglich, unheimlich das andere" (KM/9).

11 See Catherine Viollet, "Nachdenken über Pronomina: Zur Enstehung von Christa Wolfs 'Kindheitsmuster,' " in Drescher, ed., *Christa Wolf: Ein Arbeitsbuch,* 101, on Wolf's initial version, in which she used the autobiographical "I." Zahlmann (*"Kindheitsmuster,"* 144) correctly emphasizes the nonidentity of author and narrator, arguing that the author establishes a certain distance from her own biography by fantasizing a narrator separate from herself.

12 Christa Wolf, "A Model of Experience: A Discussion on *A Model Childhood,"* in Pilkington, trans., *The Fourth Dimension,* 45.

13 Viollet, "Nachdenken über Pronomina," 102.

14 Ibid., 111.

15 Zahlmann, *"Kindheitsmuster,"* 142.

16 On this novel's relationship to autobiographical writing, see Sandra Frieden, "A Guarded Iconoclasm: The Self as Deconstructing Counterpoint to Documenta-

tion," in *Responses to Christa Wolf,* ed. Marilyn Sibley Fries (Detroit: Wayne State University Press, 1989), 266–78; and " 'Falls es strafbar ist, die Grenzen zu verwischen': Autobiographie, Biographie, und Christa Wolf," in Drescher, ed., *Christa Wolf: Ein Arbeitsbuch,* 121–39; Heinz-Dieter Weber, " 'Phantastische Genauigkeit': Der historische Sinn der Schreibart Christa Wolfs," in Mauser, ed., *Erinnerte Zukunft,* 97ff.; and Marie-Luise Linn, "Doppelte Kindheit: Zur Interpretation von Christa Wolfs *Kindheitsmuster,*" *Der Deutschunterricht* 30 (1978): 52–66.

17 The chapter titles were unfortunately not included in the English translation. In the original, they are not part of the text itself, but are printed together at the end as a table of contents.

18 Wolf, "Reading and Writing," in Stephan, ed., *The Author's Dimension,* 31.

19 The narrator also calls these language fragments "memory aids": "Lists of names, scraps of paper with sayings, typical family expressions, proverbs the mother or the grandmother were fond of using, first lines of songs" (*PC*/8; *KM*/15).

20 On the importance of the mother, see also Margarete Mitscherlich-Nielsen, "Gratwanderung zwischen Anspruch und Verstrickung," in Drescher, ed., *Christa Wolf: Ein Arbeitsbuch,* 114–20. Mischerlich-Nielsen argues that the mother is Nelly's "ambivalently loved ideal" (117), later replaced by Julia Strauch, the Nazi teacher, a substitute for the lost "mother ideal." Surprisingly, Marianne Hirsch focuses exclusively on the relationship between the narrator and Lenka, her daughter (see *The Mother/Daughter Plot,* 154–61).

21 Given the narrator's report of her mother's desire to write about a dream that keeps waking her up, one might read the daughter's autobiographical novel as the book the mother never wrote down (see *PC*/51; *KM*/71).

22 Zahlmann, *"Kindheitsmuster,"* 152ff.

23 Mitscherlich-Nielsen, "Gratwanderung zwischen Anspruch und Verstrickung," 118.

24 Zahlmann, *"Kindheitsmuster,"* 148.

25 The narrator links this question to the East German present when she remembers what Nelly and her friends strove to be: perfect, "new humans" (*PC*/128; *KM*/172)—a term from the 1950s, invoking the New Communist Man (*sic*).

26 The connection between anti-Semitism and chastity has been made clearer by the recent work of historians such as Detlev Peukert on National Socialism as a utopia of racialist purity; see, for instance, his chapter "National Comrades and 'Community Aliens'," in *Inside Nazi Germany: Conformity, Opposition, and Racism in Everyday Life* (New Haven and London: Yale University Press, 1987).

27 See Saul Friedlaender, *Kitsch und Tod: Der Widerschein des Faschismus* (Munich: Karl Hanser Verlag, 1984).

28 Sigrid Weigel, " 'Blut im Schuh'—Körper-Gedächtnis und Körper-Sprache in Christa Wolfs Prosa," in her *Bilder des kulturellen Gedächtnisses* (Dülmen: Tende, 1994), 67.

29 Sigrid Weigel, "Die im Stand der Ähnlichkeit entstellte Welt: Vorbemerkung," in *Bilder des kulturellen Gedächtnisses,* 16. See also Eric Santner, who uses a similar concept, that of the body "as a sort of writing tablet and mnemonic device of the unconscious," in *Stranded Objects: Mourning, Memory, and Film in Postwar Germany* (Ithaca and London: Cornell University Press, 1990), 157. Karen Remmler discusses the body and memory with respect to *Nachdenken über Christa T.* in "Decipering the Body of Memory: Writing by Former East German Women Writers," in *Postcommunism and the Body Politic,* ed. Ellen E. Berry (New York and London: New York University Press, 1995), 148ff.

30 Wolf, *Entwurf 18* (draft 18), in Viollet, "Nachdenken über Pronomina," 105.

31 This passage was left out of the English version.

32 Weigel, "Blut im Schuh," 70.

33 Viollet, "Nachdenken über Pronomina," 107; my emphasis.

34 Wolf, "Reading and Writing," 32.

35 Christa Wolf, "Zeitschichten," 357.

36 In one recent collection, *Christa Wolf aus feministischer Sicht,* ed. Michel Vanhelleputte (Frankfurt a.M.: Peter Lang, 1992), most of the articles are devoted to *Kassandra.*

37 Wolf's essay on Günderrode, "Der Schatten eines Traumes: Karoline von Günderrode—ein Entwurf" (in *Die Dimension des Autors,* 2: 511–71), dates from October 1978; her piece on Bettina von Arnim, "Nun ja! Das nächste Leben geht aber heute an: Ein Brief über die Bettine" (in *Die Dimension des Autors,* 2: 572–610), from December 1979.

38 Christa Wolf, "Berührung: Maxie Wander," in *Die Dimension des Autors,* 1: 196–209; and "Selbstversuch: Traktat zu einem Protokoll," *Sinn und Form* 2 (1973): 301–23.

39 In foregrounding the destructive effects of the division of labor, Wolf's feminist theorizing remains within the Marxist tradition, specifically that of the early Lukács (*History and Class Consciousness*). On this tradition within Marxism, see Martin Jay, *Marxism and Totality: The Adventures of a Concept from Lukács to Habermas* (Berkeley and Los Angeles: University of California Press, 1984).

40 Bovenschen, *Die imaginierte Weiblichkeit,* 37.

41 Christa Wolf, "I Admire a Certain Lack of Restraint: A Conversation with Wilfried F. Schoeller" (1979), in Pilkington, trans., *The Fourth Dimension,* 88; TA. See also her interview with Richard A. Zipser, "Literary Work in the GDR," in ibid., 75. This analysis is predicated on an understanding of the GDR as not essentially different from other modern industrial societies that are, according to Wolf, patriarchal and hierarchically organized. Wolf establishes a parallel between the exclusions of the "intellectual" and the "feminine" element. Both exclusions are the result of an increasing division of labor that results in a division of both society *and* the subject: "At what point did the division of labour take hold of people to such a degree [that] literature came to be expelled

from . . . society. . . ? At the same time, the feminine element was also being expelled"; see Wolf, "Romanticism in Perspective," 91.

42 See Walther, Biermann, and de Bruyn et al., eds., *Protokoll eines Tribunals,* for a report on the discussions within the Writers' Union during which the decision to expel nine authors was reached, as well as Wolf's letter of June 10, 1979, justifying her vote against their expulsion (116–17). As a result of signing the petition, her husband was expelled from the SED. Wolf hoped to be expelled, too, rather than quitting the Party, but that did not happen. Wolf left the SED in the summer of 1989.

43 Wolf, "Romanticism in Perspective," 90. *Kein Ort. Nirgends* is engaged in an even more radical questioning of the narrating subject, accompanied by a fundamental problematizing of masculinity and femininity. Voice, gender, identity all become "impure." As Sigrid Weigel argues ("Blut im Schuh," 70), Wolf's crisis provided the conditions for this "impurity."

44 Christa Wolf, "From a Discussion at Ohio State University: A Conversation with Christa and Gerhard Wolf" (1983), in *The Fourth Dimension,* trans. Pilkington, 109, TA. Historicizing myth means first, of course, reestablishing its social and historical coordinates, which Wolf does by situating Cassandra's story at the point of transition from matriarchy to patriarchy (*K*/256ff; *C*/195ff.).

45 Hilzinger, "Weibliches Schreiben als eine Ästhetik des Widerstands," 223. Interestingly, Hilzinger has to abandon her own thesis in the course of her article since Wolf's negative representation of sexuality in Cassandra makes the appropriation of "sexuality as a productive force" impossible. Hilzinger borrows this phrase from Morgner and equates it (I think, erroneously) with Cixous's concept of feminine voice (229). Both moves—to find Cixous in Wolf and to read Morgner's concept in the same way—are rather ahistorical, despite Hilzinger's stated intention to historicize her theoretical concepts. Sabine Wilke approaches *Kassandra* from a similar angle and likewise concludes that this feminine body does not acquire the positivity it gains in Cixous or Irigaray because desire remains bound to pain; see her " 'Wenn ich die Zeit noch habe, sollte ich von meinem Körper sprechen': Der Status des Körpers als Schauplatz der Inszenierung der Weiblichkeit," in her *"Ausgraben und Erinnern": Zur Funktion von Geschichte, Subjekt und geschlechtlicher Identität in den Texten Christa Wolfs* (Würzburg: Königshausen und Neumann, 1993), 163. For other essays that argue for reading *Kassandra* in terms of feminine writing, see Christiane Zehl Romero, " 'Weibliches Schreiben'—Christa Wolfs *Kassandra," Studies in GDR Culture and Society* 4 (1984): 15–27; Michel Vanhelleputte, "Christa Wolf und der Bankrott des patriarchalischen Prinzips, oder die Voraussetzungen ihres Entwurfs eines weltverändernden Feminismus," in *Christa Wolf in feministischer Sicht,* ed. Michel Vanhelleputte (Frankfurt a.M.: Peter Lang, 1992), 13–22; Madeline Lutjeharms, " 'Doch schreiben wir weiter in den Formen, an die wir gewöhnt sind': Überlegungen zum 'weiblichen Schreiben' aus sprachwissenschaftlicher Sicht am Beispiel der *Kassandra* von Christa Wolf," in Van-

helleputte, ed., *Christa Wolf in feministischer Sicht,* 115–26; Gerhard Neumann, "Christa Wolfs *Kassandra:* Die Archäologie der weiblichen Stimme," in *Erinnerte Zukunft,* ed. Wolfram Mauser (Würzburg: Königshausen und Neumann, 1985), 233–64; and Heidi Gilpin, "*Cassandra:* Creating a Female Voice," in *Responses to Christa Wolf,* ed. Marilyn Sibley Fries (Detroit: Wayne State University Press, 1989), 349–77.

46 Sigrid Weigel, "Vom Sehen zur Seherin: Christa Wolfs Umdeutung des Mythos und die Spur der Bachmann-Rezeption in ihrer Literatur," in Drescher, ed., *Christa Wolf: Ein Arbeitsbuch,* 171. See also Jacqueline Grenz's remarks in Christa Wolf, "Ursprünge des Erzählens: Gespräch mit Jacqueline Grenz," in *Die Dimension des Autors,* 2: 914; and Sibylle Cramer, "Eine unendliche Geschichte des Widerstands: Zu Christa Wolfs Erzählungen 'Kein Ort. Nirgends' und 'Kassandra,'" in *Christa Wolf: Materialienbuch,* ed. Klaus Sauer (Darmstadt and Neuwied: Luchterhand Verlag, 1983), 121–42.

47 Wolf argues, along with Adorno and Horkheimer, that the repressive development of the autonomous (male) subject ultimately destroys subjectivity; see Theodor W. Adorno and Max Horkheimer, *Dialektik der Aufklärung* (Frankfurt a.M.: Fischer Taschenbuch Verlag, 1984 [1947]), 179.

48 Weigel does not define feminine subjectivity, but merely argues that it has to be different from this dominant subjectivity which has proven (self-)destructive ("Vom Sehen zur Seherin," 179).

49 Ibid., 182.

50 Wolf's most recent collection of essays includes "Befund" (Diagnosis), a first-person inner monologue about the "proliferation of a thicket" in the narrator's throat. This growth hampers her breathing and robs her voice of its full force, such that "it can only push through the thicket as a little voice, as a thin sound" (*Auf dem Weg nach Tabou,* 189).

51 Christa Wolf, *Kassandra: Erzählung* (Frankfurt a.M.: Luchterhand Literaturverlag, 1988), 5 (henceforth cited as *K*/page); *C*/5; TA.

52 For her own view of the narrative voice in *Kassandra,* see Christa Wolf, "The Origins of Narration: A Conversation with Jacqueline Grenz," in Pilkington, trans., *The Fourth Dimension,* 118. Cassandra's thoughts are periodically interrupted by her "present," that is, her knowledge of her impending death and her awareness of the people around her on her way to the castle.

53 What Paul-Laurent Assoun means by this is our either recognizing or not recognizing ourselves in our own voice (*Le Regard et la Voix,* 1: 36).

54 In the German, the adjective "gliederschüttelnd" is used in the main text, a condensation of the poem's terms: "Schon wieder *schüttelt* mich der *glieder / -lösende* Eros."

55 See Jean Laplanche, "Panel on 'Hysteria Today,'" *International Journal of Psycho-Analysis* 55 (1974): 466.

56 Wolfram Mauser stresses the importance of this dream as one of the "rough spots" allowing entry into the narrative at a level that lies beyond the author's intention; see his "Das 'dunkle Tier' und die Seherin: Zu Christa Wolfs

Kassandra-Phantasie," in *Freiburger literaturpsychologische Gespräche* (Frankfurt a.M.: Peter Lang, 1985), 142, 141. Mauser also views the figure of Polyxena as crucial to an understanding of Cassandra.

57 Polyxena is also the woman from the Thirty Years War whom Nelly, in *Kindheitsmuster,* reads about: infecting herself with the plague, she uses her body to destroy the enemy.

58 Hilzinger, "Weibliches Schreiben als eine Ästhetik des Widerstands," 229.

59 Laplanche ("Panel on 'Hysteria Today,' " 466, 467) argues for the centrality of conversion.

60 Ibid., 466, 468.

61 Ibid., 466. In "Hysterical Phantasies and Their Relation to Bisexuality" (1908), Freud wrote: "Hysterical symptoms are the expression on the one hand of a masculine unconscious sexual phantasy, and on the other hand of a feminine one" (165). In "Some General Remarks on Hysterical Attacks" (1909), he elaborated on the issue of identification: "The attack becomes obscured through the fact that the patient attempts to carry out the activities of both the figures who appear in the phantasy, that is to say, through *multiple identification.* Compare, for instance, the example I mentioned . . . in which a patient tore off her dress with one hand (as the man) while she pressed it to her body with the other (as the woman)" (230); both quotes from *The Standard Edition,* vol. 9.

62 Cassandra identifies with Aeneas so strongly that she says she knows him as if "I were he" (*C*/5; *K*/7).

63 As we shall see in the discussion of Cassandra the speaker, in Wolf's lectures she draws an explicit analogy between the onset of the Nazi period and the early 1980s (when a nuclear war seemed possible), thereby situating *Kassandra* within the problematic of National Socialism.

64 Wolfram Mauser interprets Cassandra's "contradictory structures of experience" (by which he means the "emotional synthesis of pain and pleasure") as an expression of her sadomasochism ("Das 'dunkle Tier' und die Seherin," 149, 151). I would stress, moreover, that this disposition, which constitutes one of the axes along which the constellation Polyxena/Cassandra works, is clearly overdetermined by Cassandra's identification with the master trope of the antifascist hero.

65 As I mentioned in chapter 1, Elaine Scarry argues that the torture victim's unconscious splits the subject into self and body, resulting in an adversarial relation between body and voice: "The goal of the torturer is to make the one, the body, emphatically and crushingly *present* by destroying it, and to make the other, the voice, *absent* by destroying it." This adversarial split turns the subject's own body into the torturer's weapon (Scarry, *Body in Pain,* 48). In her introduction to Gotsche's novel, Wolf refers to the often oppressive "mute impenetrability" of the antifascist hero. In fact, the core scene of Gotsche's novel stages the *mute* body-in-pain whose thoughts are conveyed by the omniscient narrator. In this scene, we do not have a transformation of body into voice. However, the voice of the prisoner is "restored" to him by the narrator, thus warding off the threat

of "corporeal engulfment," according to Scarry. Wolf, however, restores the voice to the victim without using an omniscient narrator, by having her reclaim her voice, thus turning "mute impenetrability" into a scream. What she risks by this move is Cassandra's "corporeal engulfment."

66 Žižek, *Sublime Object of Ideology,* 114, 113.

67 Weigel, "Vom Sehen zur Seherin," 187.

68 And she elaborates on the National Socialism parallel by quoting from a television program in which a woman tells a reporter: "I would not like it if later on my children had to ask me—the way we asked our parents and grandparents—Why didn't you speak up at the time?" (*C*/256; *V*/112).

69 Anna Seghers, "Vaterlandsliebe: Rede auf dem I. Internationalen Schriftstellerkongress zur Verteidigung der Kultur 1935," in *Die Macht der Worte: Reden-Schriften-Briefe* (Leipzig and Weimar: Kiepenheuer Verlag, 1979), 33.

70 Felman, "Return of the Voice," 207, 277.

71 Žižek, *Sublime Object of Ideology,* 106.

72 *Far from Moscow,* by the Soviet novelist Ashaev, was canonized in the GDR in the 1950s as a model of socialist realism (see Lahusen, *Life Writes the Book*).

73 Christa Wolf, "Nagelprobe," in *Auf dem Weg nach Tabou,* 169 (henceforth cited as N/page). "Nagelprobe" was occasioned by an exhibit of the work of Günther Uecker, an artist who left East Germany in the 1950s.

74 Wolfgang Emmerich concludes his recent reassessment of GDR studies with a sympathetic reading of Schirrmacher's articles on Wolf and West German literature since 1945. Emmerich welcomes in particular the argument that West German literature rested on a "foundational myth," an antifascist and didactic conscience seeking to reeducate the Federal Republic's population. This myth bestowed the role of *preceptor* on authors such as Grass, Bachmann, Böll, Andersch, Weiss, and others. With that era now over, that role is no longer available. This change, Emmerich argues correctly, is not fundamentally different from the changes experienced by GDR authors. Like the production of their Western counterparts, GDR literature functioned as a "belated act of resistance"—and 1989 put an end to that particular organization of the literary field around the Nazi past; Wolfgang Emmerich, "Für eine andere Wahrnehmung der DDR-Literatur," in his *Die andere deutsche Literatur: Aufsätze zur Literatur aus der DDR* (Opladen: Westdeutscher Verlag, 1994), 204. As I mentioned in the introduction, Emmerich analyzes the failure of East German authors as their having been caught in a specific oppositional gesture: holding up the utopian ideal to make visible the shortcomings of "real existing socialism." We can now understand this strategy as motivated yet again by the desire for purity.

75 Wolf, "Auf mir bestehen," 257.

76 Wolf, "Schreiben im Zeitbezug," 148.

77 Robert Sayre and Michael Löwy, "Romanticism as a Feminist Vision: The Quest of Christa Wolf," *New German Critique* 64 (Winter 1995): 105–34.

78 Ibid., 118; quoting Helen Fehervary and Sara Lennox's introduction to the first English translation of Wolf's "Selbstversuch."

79 Sayre and Löwy understand *Kassandra* as a climactic moment in Wolf's work, the result of a "whole process of maturation of the combined feminist and utopian Romantic worldview" (ibid., 125). Their assertion that it was only during the period of *Moskauer Novelle* and her contacts with the Stasi that Wolf was "still strongly swayed by an inferiority complex in relation to the anti-fascist aura of the regime's leaders" is simply wrong (ibid., 133).

80 Moi, "Psychoanalysis, Feminism, and Politics," 936. What a psychoanalytically oriented feminism can contribute is precisely a demonstration of the ways in which feminine subjectivity resists *and* complies with the structures of the symbolic. Any denial of that complicity—of the unconscious and its fantasies—has disastrously simplifying results. On this issue, see "An Interview with Jacqueline Rose," in Jacqueline Rose, *Why War?* (Oxford and Cambridge: Blackwell, 1993), 238ff.

81 Christa Wolf, *Kein Ort, nirgends* (Darmstadt and Neuwied: Luchterhand Verlag, 1981 [1979]), 5-6.

History as Trauma

1 An extensive, well-researched literature has accumulated on the effects of Unification, especially its devastating impact on the economic conditions of women. See, for instance, Barbara Einhorn's *Cinderella Goes to Market;* and "Women in the Federal States after the *Wende:* The Impact of Unification on Women's Employment Opportunities," in *Women and the Wende: Social Effects and Cultural Reflections of the German Unification Process,* ed. Elizabeth Boa and Janet Wharton (Amsterdam and Atlanta, Ga.: Rodopi, 1994), 18-29. See also Frigga Haug, "Ökonomie der Zeit, darin löst sich schliesslich alle Ökonomie auf. Neue Herausforderungen an einen sozialistischen Feminismus," *Das Argument* 184 (1990): 879-94; and Irene Dölling, "Between Hope and Helplessness: Women in the GDR after the Turning Point," *Feminist Review* 39 (1991): 3-15.

2 For instance, Harry Thürk's antiwar novel *Die Stunde der toten Augen* (The Hour of the Dead Eyes) has been reissued, and the third volume of Erwin Strittmatter's *Der Wundertäter* (The Miracle Worker) trilogy, *Der Laden* (The Store), was published in 1992. On East German rock bands, see Anke Westphal, "Mein wunderbarer Plattenbau. Hoppla, wir leben noch: Ob Puhdys, Oktoberclub, Ernst Busch, Franke-Echo-Quintett oder Theo Schumann-Combo—das Ostlied wird wieder nachgefragt. Alles nur gestaut? Oder kommen jetzt die Liebhaber und Historiker?" *Die Tageszeitung,* August 25, 1995, 15-16.

3 *Der Spiegel* 27 (1995): 56. In 1993, plans were discussed to turn Eisenhüttenstadt (formerly, Stalinstadt) into an outdoor museum of socialism (see *Die Tageszeitung,* August 31, 1993). The Museum Berliner Arbeiterleben organized an exhibit called "Ewig blühe: Erinnerungen an die Republik der Lobetrotter" (May It Bloom Forever: Memories of the Republic of the Lobetrotter), subtitled "Requisiten aus einem Stück deutscher Geschichte zwischen 1946 und 1989" (Props

from a Play on German History between 1946 and 1989); see *Kurzwort: Ewig blühe: Erinnerungen an die Republik der Lobetrotter,* ed. Tobias Böhm (Berlin: Westermann-Kommunikation, 1992). In 1995, the same museum mounted an exhibit of *Brigadetagebücher* (brigade diaries).

4   Rutschky sees this "new" GDR identity as emerging from a specific "community of experience and narrating." This was impossible before 1989: "In the GDR, culture in this specific sense could not arise; for this to happen, free exchange and communication are needed"; Michael Rutschky, "Wie erst jetzt die DDR entsteht," *Merkur* 9/10 (Sept./Oct. 1995): 858, 856.

5   Barbara Köhler, "A la recherche de la révolution perdue," *German Monitor,* No. 31 (1994): 2. This is an allusion to a question which a former concentration camp inmate asks the narrator's mother at the end of the war in Christa Wolf's *Kindheitsmuster/Patterns of Childhood:* "Where on earth have you all been living?" (431/332). It is also an allusion to Brecht's poem about socialism's "Mühen der Ebenen," that is, the effort required once the basic structures of socialism are in place (see *Die Gedichte von Bertolt Brecht,* 960).

6   Caruth, "Introduction," in *Trauma,* 5. I am well aware of the problems inherent to using categories developed in the context of the Holocaust and its survivors for a description of German events.

7   Slavoj Žižek, *Tarrying with the Negative* (Durham: Duke University Press, 1993), 1.

8   Ina Merkel describes a more specific shock: the assault of images celebrating the Western world of commodities—and its femininity. For this "campaign of images, symbols, and fetishes of consumption ready to take a damaged world-view by storm" also introduced a new image of woman which appealed to East German women to change, to become "real women" (. . . *und Du, Frau an der Werkbank,* 7).

9   Quoted in Klaus Scherpe, "Erzwungener Alltag: Wahrgenommene und gedachte Wirklichkeit in der Reportageliteratur der Nachkriegszeit," in *Nachkriegsliteratur in Westdeutschland 1945–49,* ed. Jost Hermand, Helmut Peitsch, and Klaus Scherpe (Berlin: Argument Verlag, 1982), 45. As Scherpe points out, this statement also resonates with the shock of the loss of authority after the defeat of Nazism.

10   Ibid., 45. Scherpe talks about two "nodal points of the formation of ideology": on the one hand, a "do-it-yourself mentality" and, on the other, a sense of the postwar life-world "as lacking both a social order and classes" (47). The frequently used trope of Robinson Crusoe and the quaint but racist designation of the occupied zones as *Trizonesien* were part of this ideological formation.

11   Most importantly, the GDR was not characterized by a resolution of social conflict through war, sustained government racial persecution, or mass murder. Although I would not compare the depth and extent of the trauma experienced by National Socialism's victims with that of its perpetrators or even its bystanders, the structure of trauma as the inability to understand what was happening nevertheless applies to such non-victims as well.

12 Wolf then recalled that she went through an intense religious phase ("Auf mir bestehen," 243–44).

13 An enthusiasm quickly tempered by the realization of the extent of destruction to both the country and its people. Anna Seghers's statement that the destruction inside of people's heads was much greater than the destruction of Germany's cities is typical in this respect; see Anna Seghers, "Neue literarisch-künstlerische Probleme. Rede auf dem II. Deutschen Schriftstellerkongress 1950," in *Die Macht der Worte: Reden–Schriften–Briefe* (Leipzig and Weimar: Kiepenheuer Verlag, 1979), 221. This is testimony to the isolation of exiles from events inside of Germany; nor was there much enthusiasm at first on the part of political prisoners liberated from the concentration camps.

14 Wolf, "Für unser Land," in *Im Dialog,* 170.

15 On the emerging memorial landscape of Berlin, see Caroline Wiedmer's excellent article "Designing Memories," in Fascism and Its Ghosts, a special issue of *Alphabet City* 4/5 (December 1995): 6–22.

16 Two years before the publication of *Kassandra,* the last volume of another historical epic appeared, Peter Weiss's *Die Ästhetik des Widerstands* (The Aesthetics of Resistance) (Frankfurt a.M.: Suhrkamp Verlag, 1986 [1975–81]). Written outside of East Germany, this monumental novel provided an incisive radical critique of Stalinist antifascism. Its writing forced its author (very much against his own inclinations, I believe) into a radical gesture, namely, to leave the place of power empty, refusing to (re-)construct yet another mythical figure of the heroic fighter. I am referring to the celebrated final paragraph of Weiss's novel, the moment when its protagonist imagines returning to the Pergamon altar in Berlin sometime after 1945, at the end of his engagement with Europe's antifascist movement. Standing in his imagination before the relief, the narrator again reads the altar as an allegory of class struggle, but this time with respect to the period after 1945 rather than with respect to 1937. He would, he imagines, reencounter his parents. He also hallucinates the presence of his friends Coppi and Heilmann, who were executed for their participation in the clandestine anti-Nazi activities of the Rote Kapelle. As his gaze runs over the freeze, it comes to a stop at the lion's paw. Where the image of Heracles (who in this novel comes to represent the party of the oppressed, their "leader") should appear, he now sees an empty spot (3: 267–68). In Weiss's novel, the structure of the proletarian family narrative plays an important organizing role. It is one of the elements through which the novel is linked to the GDR's antifascist discourse. On this topic, see my "Rosa oder die Sehnsucht nach einer Geschichte ohne Stalin: Zur vergeschlechtlichten Textproduktion in Peter Weiss' *Ästhetik des Widerstands,*" *Peter Weiss Jahrbuch* (forthcoming).

17 This appeal was indeed partly justified by the Communists' resistance under the Nazis—but only partly because the Communists did not play the leading role that the S E D later claimed and because the Stalinist character of this resistance makes it a deeply problematic legacy. This legacy is still operative, rendering neofascism a most opaque and complex phenomenon. An interview with

a former model GDR schoolgirl-turned-neo-Nazi demonstrates with startling clarity that beneath her neofascist identity lies an identification with the F D J (Free German Youth) as a military vanguard in the style of the old K P D: "Our flag," Hanna says, "was always red"; see Robin Ostow, " 'Ne Art Bürgerwehr in Form von Skins': Young Germans on the Streets in the Eastern and Western States of the Federal Republic," *New German Critique* 64 (Winter 1995): 94–96. All of Hanna's neo-Nazi friends are former F D J members. The right-wing rock group Radikahl calls on its listeners to "raise the red flag with the swastika"; quoted in George Steinmetz, "Fordism and the (Im)moral Economy of Right-Wing Violence in Contemporary Germany," *Research on Democracy and Society* 2 (1994): 305, 304.

18 In many interviews conducted after 1989, East Germans have thematized sexuality in specific ways: in comparing their own supposed prudishness and backwardness to the sophistication of their Western counterparts, for example, they reproduce the dominant dichotomy of premodernity/modernity on the level of their bodies (see, e.g., *Ohne uns ist kein Staat zu machen: DDR-Frauen nach der Wende* [Cologne: Kiepenheuer and Witsch, 1990], 37).

Works Cited

Abusch, Alexander. *Der Irrweg einer Nation.* Berlin: Aufbau-Verlag, 1946.

———. "Drei Briefe an Anna Seghers." *Sinn und Form* 5 (1975): 885–93.

———. "Willi Bredels Roman-Trilogie einer proletarischen Familie." *Willi Bredel: Dokumente seines Lebens.* Berlin: Aufbau-Verlag, 1961. 33–41.

Ackermann, Anton. "Gibt es einen besonderen deutschen Weg zum Sozialismus?" *Einheit* 1 (1946): 22–32.

Adelson, Leslie. *Making Bodies, Making History: Feminism and German Identity.* Lincoln: University of Nebraska Press, 1993.

Adorno, Theodor W., and Max Horkheimer. *Dialektik der Aufklärung.* 1947. Frankfurt a.M.: Fischer Taschenbuch Verlag, 1984.

Agde, Günther, ed. *Kahlschlag. Das 11: Plenum des ZK der SED 1965.* Berlin: Aufbau-Verlag, 1991.

Ankum, Katharina von. "Christa Wolfs Poetik des Alltags: Von *Juninachmittag* bis *Was bleibt.*" *Zwischen gestern und morgen: Schriftstellerinnen der DDR aus amerikanischer Sicht.* Ed. Ute Brandes. Berlin and New York: Peter Lang, 1992. 183–98.

———. *Die Rezeption von Christa Wolf in Ost und West: Von "Moskauer Novelle" bis "Selbstversuch".* Amsterdam: Rodopi, 1992.

———. "Sibirien liegt (nicht) bei Ravensbrück: Gender and the Deconstruction of the Anti-Fascist National Narrative in the GDR." *History and Memory* 7 (1996): 41–69.

Anz, Thomas, ed. *"Es geht nicht um Christa Wolf": Der Literaturstreit im vereinten Deutschland.* Munich: Edition Spangenberg, 1991.

Anzieu, Didier. "L'Enveloppe sonore du Soi." *Nouvelle Revue de Psychanalyse* 13 (1976): 161–79.

Arac, Jonathan, ed. *Postmodernism and Politics.* Minneapolis: University of Minnesota Press, 1986.

Artaud, Antonin. *Antonin Artaud: Selected Writings.* Ed. Susan Sontag. New York: Farrar, Straus and Giroux, 1976.

Ashaev, Vassili. *Fern von Moskau.* Berlin: Verlag Kultur und Fortschritt, 1951.

Assoun, Paul-Laurent. *Leçons psychanalytiques sur le Regard et la Voix.* Paris: Anthropos, 1995. 2 vols.

Auer, Annemarie. "Proletarischer Familienroman und Nationalliteratur." *Kritik in der Zeit.* Ed. Klaus Jarmatz. Halle/Saale: Mitteldeutscher Verlag, 1969.

"Aufruf für eine eigenständige DDR." *"Wir sind das Volk".* Ed. Charles Schüddekopf. Reinbek: Rowohlt Taschenbuch Verlag, 1990. 240.

Azaryahu, Maoz. *Von Wilhelmplatz zu Thälmannplatz: Politische Symbole im öffentlichen Leben der DDR.* Gerlingen: Bleicher Verlag, 1991.

Bachmann, Ingeborg. "Frankfurter Vorlesungen." *Gesammelte Werke.* Munich: Piper Verlag, 1978. 4: 182–297.

Bammer, Angelika. "The American Feminist Reception of GDR Literature (with a Glance at West Germany)." *GDR Bulletin* 16 (1990): 18–24.

Bangerter, Lowell A. "Anna Seghers and Christa Wolf." *Germanic Review* 58 (1993): 127–32.

Barthes, Roland. *The Pleasure of the Text.* Trans. Richard Miller. New York: Hill and Wang, 1994. Originally published as *Le Plaisir du Texte* (1973).

———. *Image–Music–Text.* New York: Hill and Wang, 1985.

Bathrick, David. "Geschichtsbewusstsein als Selbstbewusstsein: Die Literatur der DDR." *Neues Handbuch der Literaturwissenschaft.* Ed. Klaus von See. Wiesbaden: Athenaion, 1979. 21: 273–314.

———. *The Powers of Speech.* Lincoln and London: University of Nebraska Press, 1996.

Batt, Kurt. *Anna Seghers: Versuch über Entwicklung und Werke.* Leipzig: Verlag Philipp Reclam, 1973.

———. "Der Dialog zwischen Anna Seghers und Georg Lukács." *Weimarer Beiträge* 5 (1975): 105–39.

Baudin, Antoine, Leonid Heller, and Thomas Lahusen. "Le réalisme socialiste sovietique de l'ère Jdanov: Compte rendu d'une enquête en cours." *Etudes de Lettres* 10 (1988): 69–103.

Beckwith, Sarah. *Christ's Body: Identity, Culture, and Society in Late Medieval Writings.* London and New York: Routledge, 1993.

Beicken, Peter. "Nachfolge nicht Nachahmung: Zur Beziehung Anna Seghers— Christa Wolf." *Deutsche Exilliteratur.* Ed. Wolfgang Elfe et al. Bern/Frankfurt/Las Vegas: Peter Lang, 1981. 114–32.

Beizer, Janet L. *Family Plots: Balzac's Narrative Generations.* New Haven and London: Yale University Press, 1986.

Benjamin, Walter. "Ein Familiendrama auf dem epischen Theater." In *Materialien zu Bertolt Brechts Die Mutter.* Ed. Werner Hecht. Frankfurt a.M.: Suhrkamp Verlag, 1969. 22–26.

Benseler, Frank. "Anna Seghers Treffen." In *Anna Seghers Materialenbuch.* Ed. Peter Roos and Friderike J. Hassauer-Roos. Darmstadt and Neuwied, 1977.

Bilke, Jörg. "Auf der Suche nach Netty Reiling." *Blätter der Carl-Zuckmayer Gesellschaft* 6 (1980): 186–201.

Bischoff, Joachim, and Christoph Lieber. "Woran der Staatssozialismus scheiterte." *Sozialismus* 3 (1993): 15-19.

Blanchot, Maurice. *Lautreamont et Sade*. Paris: Editions de Minuit, 1963.

Bloch, Ernst. *Erbschaft dieser Zeit*. 1935. Frankfurt a.M.: Suhrkamp Verlag, 1985.

Bloom, Harold. *The Anxiety of Influence*. New York: Oxford University Press, 1973.

Böck, Dorothea. " 'Ich schreibe, um herauszufinden, warum ich schreiben muss': Frauenliteratur in der DDR zwischen Selbsterfahrung und ästhetischem Experiment." *Feministische Studien* 1 (1990): 61-74.

Bock, Sigrid. "Erziehungsfunktion und Romanexperiment. Anna Seghers: 'Die Toten bleiben jung.' " *Erfahrung Exil. Antifaschistische Romane 1933-1945: Analysen*. Ed. Sigrid Bock and Manfred Hahn. Berlin and Weimar: Aufbau Verlag, 1979. 394-471.

———. "Die Farbe der Sonne und der Nacht: Gespräch mit Lenka Reinerova." *Argonautenschiff: Jahrbuch der Anna-Seghers-Gesellschaft* 3 (1994): 127-39.

Boden, Petra. "Ornamente und Tabus: Antifaschismus als Herrschaftsdiskurs." *Weimarer Beiträge* 41 (1995): 104-19.

Bogdal, Klaus-Michael. "Wer darf sprechen? Schriftsteller als moralische Instanz— Überlegungen zu einem Ende und einem Anfang." *Weimarer Beiträge* 37 (1991): 597-603.

Böhm, Tobias, ed. *Kurzwort. Ewig blühe: Erinnerungen an die Republik der Lobetrotter*. Berlin: Westermann-Kommunikation, 1992.

Bohrer, Karl-Heinz. "Kulturschutzgebiet DDR?" *Merkur* 500 (October/November 1990): 1015-18.

Borbely, Antal, and John Erpenbeck. "Vorschläge zu Freud." *Deutsche Zeitschrift für Philosophie* 35 (1987): 1016-24.

Bornemann, John, and Jeffrey M. Peck. *Sojourners: The Return of German Jews and the Question of Identity*. Lincoln: University of Nebraska Press, 1995.

Böthig, Peter, and Klaus Michael, eds. *MachtSpiele: Literatur und Staatssicherheit im Fokus Prenzlauer Berg*. Leipzig: Reclam-Verlag, 1993.

Bovenschen, Silvia. *Die imaginierte Weiblichkeit*. Frankfurt a.M.: Suhrkamp Verlag, 1979.

Brandes, Ute. *Anna Seghers*. Berlin: Colloquium Verlag, 1992.

Braun, Volker. *Hinze-Kunze-Roman*. 1985. Leipzig: Reclam-Verlag, 1990.

Brecht, Bertold. *Die Gedichte von Bertolt Brecht in einem Band*. Frankfurt a.M.: Suhrkamp Verlag, 1981.

Bredel, Willi. *Die Enkel*. 1953. Dortmund: Weltkreis Verlag, 1981.

———. *Die Prüfung*. 1934. Dortmund: Weltkreis Verlag, 1981.

———. *Die Söhne*. 1949. Dortmund: Weltkreis Verlag, 1981.

———. *Die Väter*. 1941. Dortmund: Weltkreis Verlag, 1981.

Bredel, Willi, and Michael Tschesno-Hell. *Ernst Thälmann. Führer seiner Klasse: Literarisches Szenarium*. Berlin: Henschelverlag, 1955.

———. *Ernst Thälmann. Sohn seiner Klasse: Literarisches Szenarium*. Berlin: Henschelverlag, 1954.

Brekle, Wolfgang. *Schriftsteller im Antifaschistischen Widerstand 1933–1945 in Deutschland.* Berlin and Weimar: Aufbau-Verlag, 1985.

Brennan, Teresa. *The Interpretation of the Flesh: Freud and Femininity.* London: Routledge, 1992.

Brockmann, Stephen. "Introduction: The Unification Debate." *New German Critique* 52 (1991): 3–30.

———. "Preservation and Change in Christa Wolf's *Was bleibt.*" *German Quarterly* 67 (1994): 73–85.

Brooks, Peter. *Body Work: Objects of Desire in Modern Narrative.* Cambridge, Mass.: Harvard University Press, 1993.

———. *Reading for the Plot: Design and Intention in Narrative.* New York: Vintage, 1985.

Bunge, Hans. "Im politischen Drehpunkt." *Christa Wolf: Ein Arbeitsbuch.* Ed. Angela Drescher. Berlin and Weimar: Aufbau-Verlag, 1989. 13–17.

Byg, Barton. "What Might Have Been: DEFA Films of the Past and the Future of German Cinema." *Cineaste* 17 (1992): 9–15.

Caruth, Cathy. "Introduction." *Trauma: Explorations in Memory.* Ed. Cathy Caruth. Baltimore and London: Johns Hopkins University Press, 1995. 3–12.

Cixous, Hélène, and Catherine Clément. "Exchange." *The Newly Born Woman.* Minneapolis: University of Minnesota Press, 1991. 135–60.

Clark, Katerina. *The Soviet Novel: History as Ritual.* Chicago: University of Chicago Press, 1985.

Claudius, Eduard. *Menschen an unserer Seite.* Berlin: Volk und Welt, 1951.

Cowie, Elizabeth. "Fantasia." *The Woman in Question.* Ed. Parveen Adams and Elizabeth Cowie. Cambridge, Mass.: MIT Press, 1990. 149–96.

———. "Representations." *The Woman in Question.* Ed. Parveen Adams and Elizabeth Cowie. Cambridge, Mass.: MIT Press, 1990. 110–16.

Cramer, Sibylle. "Eine unendliche Geschichte des Widerstands: Zu Christa Wolfs Erzählungen 'Kein Ort. Nirgends' und 'Kassandra.' " *Christa Wolf: Materialienbuch.* Ed. Klaus Sauer. Darmstadt and Neuwied: Luchterhand Verlag, 1983. 121–42.

Danyel, Jürgen. "Politische Rituale als Sowjetimporte." Unpublished ms. Potsdam: Zentrum für Zeithistorische Forschung, n.d.

Darnton, Robert. *Berlin Journal 1989–1990.* New York and London: W. W. Norton, 1991.

Deiritz, Karl, and Hannes Krauss, eds. *Der deutsch-deutsche Literaturstreit oder "Freunde, es spricht sich schlecht mit gebundener Zunge".* Hamburg: Luchterhand Literatur Verlag, 1991.

Diersen, Inge. "Jason 1948—Problematische Heimkehr." *Unerwünschte Erfahrung: Kriegsliteratur und Zensur in der DDR.* Ed. Ursula Heukenkamp. Berlin and Weimar: Aufbau-Verlag, 1990. 72–99.

———. "Kompositionsfragen in Anna Seghers' Romanen." *Kritik in der Zeit: Der Sozialismus-seine Literatur-ihre Entwicklung.* Ed. Klaus Jarmatz. Halle/Saale. Mitteldeutscher Verlag, 1969. 464–75.

Dölling, Irene. "Between Hope and Helplessness: Women in the GDR after the Turning Point." *Feminist Review* 39 (1991): 3-15.

Drawert, Klaus. *Spiegelland: Ein deutscher Monolog.* Frankfurt a.M.: Suhrkamp Verlag, 1992.

Drescher, Angela, ed. *Christa Wolf — Ein Arbeitsbuch.* Berlin and Weimar: Aufbau-Verlag, 1989.

————, ed. *Dokumentation zu Christa Wolf "Nachdenken über Christa T".* Frankfurt a.M.: Luchterhand Literaturverlag, 1991.

————. "In der blauen Höhle: Mutter-Tochter-Beziehungen in Büchern von Christa Wolf." *Christa Wolf in feministischer Sicht.* Ed. Michel Vanhelleputte. Frankfurt a.M.: Peter Lang, 1992.

————, ed. *Sei gegrüsst und lebe: Eine Freundschaft in Briefen, 1964-1973.* Berlin: Aufbau-Verlag, 1993.

Eickhoff, F.-W. "Identification and Its Vicissitudes in the Context of the Nazi Phenomenon." *International Journal of Psycho-Analysis* 67 (1986): 33-44.

Einhorn, Barbara. *Cinderella Goes to Market: Citizenship, Gender, and the Women's Movements in East Central Europe.* London: Verso, 1993.

————. "Women in the Federal States after the *Wende:* The Impact of Unification on Women's Employment Opportunities." In *Women and the Wende: Social Effects and Cultural Reflections of the German Unification Process.* Proceedings of a conference held by *Women in German Studies,* September 9-11, 1993, University of Nottingham. Ed. Elizabeth Boa and Janet Wharton. Amsterdam and Atlanta, Ga.: Rodopi, 1994. 18-29.

Elsaesser, Thomas. *New German Cinema: A History.* New Brunswick, N.J.: Rutgers University Press, 1989.

Emmerich, Wolfgang. "Affirmation–Utopie–Melancholie: Versuch einer Bilanz von vierzig Jahren DDR-Literatur." *German Studies Review* 14 (1991): 325-44.

————. "Antike Mythen auf dem Theater: Geschichte und Poesie, Vernunft und Terror." *Die andere deutsche Literatur: Aufsätze zur Literatur aus der DDR.* Opladen: Westdeutscher Verlag, 1994. 79-114.

————. "Für eine andere Wahrnehmung der DDR-Literatur." *Die andere deutsche Literatur: Aufsätze zur Literatur aus der DDR.* Opladen: Westdeutscher Verlag, 1994. 190-207.

————. "Gleichzeitigkeit: Vormoderne, Moderne und Postmoderne in der Literatur der DDR." *Die andere deutsche Literatur: Aufsätze zur Literatur aus der DDR.* Opladen: Westdeutscher Verlag, 1994. 129-50.

————. *Kleine Literaturgeschichte der DDR.* 1981. Rev. ed. Frankfurt a.M.: Luchterhand Literaturverlag, 1989.

————. "Der verlorene Faden: Probleme des Erzählens in den siebziger Jahren." *Die andere deutsche Literatur: Aufsätze zur Literatur aus der DDR.* Opladen: Westdeutscher Verlag, 1994. 46-78.

Eschwegge, Helmut. *Fremd unter meinesgleichen: Erinnerungen eines Dresdner Juden.* Berlin: Links, 1991.

Euringer, Richard. *Deutsche Passion 1933*. Oldenburg i. O. and Berlin: G. Stalling, 1933.

Fehervary, Helen. "Christa Wolf's Prose: A Landscape of Masks." *New German Critique* 27 (1982): 57–88.

———. "Die erzählerische Kolonisierug des weiblichen Schweigens: Frau und Arbeit in der DDR-Literatur." *Arbeit als Thema in der deutschen Literatur vom Mittelalter bis zur Gegenwart*. Ed. Reinhold Grimm and Jost Hermand. Königstein/Ts: Athenäum, 1979. 171–95.

———. "The Gender of Authorship: Heiner Müller and Christa Wolf." *Studies in Twentieth Century Literature* 5 (Fall 1980): 41–58.

Felman, Shoshana. "The Return of the Voice: Claude Lauzmann's *Shoah*." *Testimony: Crises of Witnessing in Literature, Psychoanalysis, and History*. Ed. Shoshana Felman and Dorri Laub. New York and London: Routledge, 1992. 204–83.

Femia, Joseph V. *Gramsci's Political Thought*. Oxford: Oxford University Press, 1988.

Feyl, Renate. *Bau mir eine Brücke*. Berlin: Verlag Neues Leben, 1972.

Fischer, Erica, and Petra Lux, eds. *Ohne uns ist kein Staat zu machen: DDR-Frauen nach der Wende*. Cologne: Kiepenheuer und Witsch, 1990.

Fischer, Sibylle Maria. "Representation and the Ends of Realism." Ph.D. Dissertation. Columbia University, 1995.

Fradkin, Ilja. *"Lehren der Geschichte."* Special issue of *Sinn und Form* on Willi Bredel. Berlin: Rütten und Loenig, 1965. 220–32.

Freud, Sigmund. "The Dissolution of the Oedipal Complex." *The Standard Edition of the Complete Psychological Works of Sigmund Freud*. Ed. James Strachey. London: Hogarth Press, 1961. 19: 173–79.

———. "The Economic Problem in Masochism." *The Standard Edition of the Complete Psychological Works of Sigmund Freud*. Ed. James Strachey. London: Hogarth Press, 1961. 19: 159–70.

———. "The Ego and the Id." *The Standard Edition of the Complete Psychological Works of Sigmund Freud*. Ed. James Strachey. London: Hogarth Press, 1961. 19: 12–59.

———. "Family Romances." *The Standard Edition of the Complete Psychological Works of Sigmund Freud*. Ed. James Strachey. London: Hogarth Press, 1961. 9: 238–39.

———. "Fetishism." *The Standard Edition of the Complete Psychological Works of Sigmund Freud*. Ed. James Strachey. London: Hogarth Press, 1961. 21: 152–57.

———. "Fragment of an Analysis of a Case of Hysteria." *The Standard Edition of the Complete Psychological Works of Sigmund Freud*. Ed. James Strachey. London: Hogarth Press, 1953. 7: 7–122.

———. "Hysterical Phantasies and Their Relation to Bisexuality." *The Standard Edition of the Complete Psychological Works of Sigmund Freud*. Ed. James Strachey. London: Hogarth Press, 1959. 9: 159–66.

———. "Lecture XXXI: The Dissection of the Psychical Personality." *New Intro-*

ductory Lectures on Psychoanalysis. Ed. James Strachey. New York: W. W. Norton, 1965. 57–80.

———. "On the Universal Tendency to Debasement in the Sphere of Love." *The Standard Edition of the Complete Psychological Works of Sigmund Freud.* Ed. James Strachey. London: Hogarth Press, 1910. 11: 179–90.

———. "Some General Remarks on Hysterical Attacks." *The Standard Edition of the Complete Psychological Works of Sigmund Freud.* Ed. James Strachey. London: Hogarth Press, 1959. Vol. 9.

Frieden, Sandra. " 'Falls es strafbar ist, die Grenzen zu verwischen': Autobiographie, Biographie, und Christa Wolf." *Christa Wolf—Ein Arbeitsbuch.* Ed. Angela Drescher. Berlin and Weimar: Aufbau-Verlag, 1989. 121–39.

———. "A Guarded Iconoclasm: The Self as Deconstructing Counterpoint to Documentation." *Responses to Christa Wolf.* Ed. Marilyn Sibley Fries. Detroit: Wayne State University Press, 1989. 266–78.

Friedlaender, Saul. *Kitsch und Tod: Der Widerschein des Faschismus.* Munich: Karl Hanser Verlag, 1984.

Friedman, E. "Where Are the Missing Contents? (Post)Modernism, Gender, and the Canon." *PMLA* 2 (1993): 240–53.

Fries, Marilyn Sibley, ed. *Responses to Christa Wolf.* Detroit: Wayne State University Press, 1989.

Fulbrook, Mary. *Anatomy of a Dictatorship: Inside the GDR 1949–1989.* Oxford: Oxford University Press, 1995.

Fühmann, Franz. *Briefe 1950–1984.* Ed. Hans-Jürgen Schmitt. Rostock: Hinsdorff Verlag, 1994.

Gallas, Helga. *Marxistische Literaturtheorie: Kontroversen im Bund proletarisch-revolutionärer Schriftsteller.* Darmstadt and Neuwied: Luchterhand, 1971.

Geertz, Clifford. "Centers, Kings, and Charisma: Reflections on the Symbolics of Power." In *Local Knowledge: Further Essays in Interpretive Anthropology.* New York: Basic Books, 1983. 121–46.

———. "Ideology as a Cultural System." *The Interpretation of Culture.* New York: Basic Books, 1973. 193–233.

———. *Local Knowledge: Further Essays in Interpretive Anthropology.* New York: Basic Books, 1983.

Geist, Peter. "Nachwort." *Ein Molotowcocktail auf fremder Bettkante.* Leipzig: Reclam-Verlag, 1991.

Gerlach, Ingeborg. *Bitterfeld: Arbeiterliteratur und Literatur der Arbeitswelt in der DDR.* Kronberg/Ts.: Scriptor-Verlag, 1974.

Gibas, Monika, and Rainer Gries. " 'Vorschlag für den ersten Mai: Die Führung zieht am Volk vorbei!' Überlegungen zur Geschichte der Tribüne in der DDR." *Deutschlandarchiv* 5 (1995): 481–94.

Gidion, Heidi. "Wer spricht? Beobachtungen zum Zitieren und zum Sprechen mit der eigenen Stimme an Christa Wolfs Günderrode- und Kassandra-Projekt." *Christa Wolf—Ein Arbeitsbuch.* Ed. Angela Drescher. Berlin and Weimar: Aufbau-Verlag, 1989. 204–15.

Gilbert, Sandra M., and Susan Gubar. *The Madwoman in the Attic*. New Haven: Yale University Press, 1984.

Gilpin, Heidi. "*Cassandra:* Creating a Female Voice." *Responses to Christa Wolf.* Ed. Marilyn Sibley Fries. Detroit: Wayne State University Press, 1989. 349–77.

Gladkow, Fjodor, and Heiner Müller. *Zement*. Ed. Fritz Mierau. Trans. Olga Halpern. Leipzig: Verlag Philipp Reclam, Jun., 1975.

Glaser, Georg K. *Geheimnis und Gewalt: Ein Bericht*. Stuttgart and Hamburg: Scherz und Coverts, 1953.

Glasser, Mervin. "Identification and Its Vicissitudes as Observed in the Perversions." *International Journal of Psycho-Analysis* 67 (1986): 9–17.

Goebbels, Joseph. *Michael: Ein deutsches Schicksal in Tagebuchblättern*. Munich: Zentralverlag der NSDAP, 1929.

Goodbody, Axel, Dennis Tate, and Ian Wallace. "The Failed Socialist Experiment: Culture in the GDR." *German Cultural Studies: An Introduction*. Ed. Rob Burns. Oxford: Oxford University Press, 1995. 147–207.

Gorky, Maksim. *Mother*. 1906. Secaucus, N.J.: Citadel Press, 1991.

Görner, Eberhard. "Ich trage eine Fahne . . . Nachdenken über eine untergegangene Partei und ihre Lieder." *Deutschland Archiv* 3 (March 1992): 264–73.

Gotsche, Otto. *Die Fahne von Kriwoj Rog*. Halle: Mitteldeutscher Verlag, 1959.

———. "Literatur und Geschichtsbewusstsein: Interview mit Otto Gotsche." *Auskünfte: Werkstattgespräche mit DDR-Autoren*. Berlin and Weimar: Aufbau-Verlag, 1974. 61–79.

———. *Zwischen Nacht und Morgen*. Halle/Saale: Mitteldeutscher Verlag, 1964.

Greiner, Bernhard. "Der Bann der Zeichen: Anna Seghers' Entwürfe der Identitätsfindung." *Jahrbuch zur Literatur in der DDR* 3 (1983): 131–55.

———. "DDR-Literatur als Problem in der Literaturwissenschaft." *Jahrbuch zur Literatur der DDR* 3 (1983): 233–54.

———. "Das Dilemma der 'Nachgeborenen': Paradoxien des Brecht-Gedichts und seiner literarischen Antworten in der DDR." *Frühe DDR-Literatur*. Ed. Klaus R. Scherpe and Lutz Winkler. Hamburg: Argument-Verlag, 1988. 174–93.

———. " 'Kolonien liebt, und tapfer Vergessen, der Geist': Anna Seghers' zyklisches Erzählen." *Argonautenschiff: Jahrbuch der Anna-Seghers-Gesellschaft* 3 (1994): 155–71.

———. " 'Mit der Erzählung geh ich in den Tod': Kontinuität und Wandel des Erzählens im Schaffen von Christa Wolf." *Christa Wolf—Ein Arbeitsbuch*. Ed. Angela Drescher. Berlin and Weimar: Aufbau-Verlag, 1989. 331–70.

———. "Die Schwierigkeit, 'ich' zu sagen: Christa Wolfs psychologische Orientierung des Erzählens." *Deutsche Vierteljahresschrift für Literaturwissenschaft und Geistesgeschichte* 55 (1981): 323–42.

———. *Von der Allegorie zur Idylle: Die Literatur der Arbeitswelt in der DDR*. Heidelberg: Quelle und Meyer, 1974.

Greiner, Ulrich. "Die deutsche Gesinnungsästhetik." *Die Zeit* 45 (November 2, 1990): 15–16.

———. "Keiner ist frei von Schuld." *Die Zeit* 45 (July 27, 1990): 1.

———. "Mangel an Feingefühl." *Die Zeit* (June 1, 1990): 13.

Groehler, Olaf. "Juden erkennen wir nicht an." *Konkret* 3 (1993): 50–54.

Grundriss der Geschichte der deutschen Arbeiterbewegung. Special issue of *Einheit* (August 1962): 58–186.

Grunenberg, Antonia. *Antifaschismus — ein deutscher Mythos.* Reinbek bei Hamburg: Rowohlt, 1993.

———. "In den Räumen der Sprache: Gedankenbilder zur Literatur Gert Neumanns." *Die andere Sprache: Neue DDR-Literatur der 80er Jahre.* Ed. Heinz Ludwig Arnold. Munich: Text und Kritik, 1990. 206–13.

Gutjahr, Ortrud. " 'Erinnerte Zukunft': Gedächtnisrekonstruktion und Subjektkonstitution im Werk Christa Wolfs." *Erinnerte Zukunft.* Ed. Wolfram Mauser. Würzburg: Königshausen und Neumann, 1985. 53–80.

Gutzmann, Gertraud. "Zum Stellenwert des Spanischen Bürgerkriegs in Anna Seghers' Romanen 'Die Entscheidung' und 'Das Vertrauen.' " *"Wen kümmert's, wer spricht?" Zur Literatur und Kulturgeschichte von Frauen aus Ost und West.* Ed. Inge Stephan. Cologne: Bohlau, 1991. 195–210.

Haas, Erika. " 'Post ins gelobte Land' — Ein Requiem." *Argonautenschiff: Jahrbuch der Anna-Seghers-Gesellschaft* 4 (1995): 139–50.

Habermas, Jürgen. "Bemerkungen zu einer verworrenen Diskussion: Was bedeutet 'Aufarbeitung der Vergangenheit' heute?" *Die Zeit* 15 (April 10, 1992): 17–19.

Halberg, Robert von, ed. *Literary Intellectuals and the Dissolution of the State: Professionalism and Conformity in the GDR.* Chicago: University of Chicago Press, 1996.

Haug, Frigga. "Ökonomie der Zeit, darin löst sich schliesslich alle Ökonomie auf. Neue Herausforderungen an einen sozialistischen Feminismus." *Das Argument* 184 (1990): 879–94.

Haug, Wolfgang Fritz. "Liberalität, die sich selbst aufhebt." *Freitag,* May 6, 1994.

———. "The Surrender of the Fortress: Did the East German People Vote for the Restoration?" *Rethinking Marxism* 4 (1991): 24–28.

Hauser, Kornelia. *Patriarchat als Sozialismus.* Hamburg: Argument-Verlag, 1994.

Hein, Christoph. *Die fünfte Grundrechenart: Aufsätze und Reden.* Frankfurt a.M.: Luchterhand, 1990.

Hell, Julia. "At the Center an Absence: Foundationalist Narratives of the GDR and the Legitimatory Discourse of Antifascism." *Monatshefte* 84 (1992): 23–45.

———. "Christa Wolf's *Divided Heaven* and the Collapse of (Socialist) Realism." *Rethinking Marxism* 7 (1994): 62–74.

———. "Christoph Hein's *Der Fremde Freund/Drachenblut* and the Antinomies of Writing under 'Real Existing Socialism.' " *Colloquia Germanica* 25 (1992): 307–37.

———. "Crisis Strategies: Family, Gender, and German History." Ph.D. Dissertation. University of Wisconsin–Madison, 1989.

———. "Rosa oder die Sehnsucht nach einer Geschichte ohne Stalin: Zur vergeschlechtlichten Textproduktion in Peter Weiss' *Ästhetik des Widerstands.*" *Peter Weiss Jahrbuch* (forthcoming).

———. "Soft-Porn, Kitsch, and Post-Fascist Bodies: The East German Novel of Arrival." *South Atlantic Quarterly* 94 (1995): 747–72.

Hell, Julia, Loren Kruger, and Katie Trumpener. "Dossier: Socialist Realism and East German Modernism—Another Historians' Debate." *Rethinking Marxism* 7 (1994): 36–44.

Heller, Leonid. "A World of Prettiness: Socialist Realism and Its Aesthetic Categories." *South Atlantic Quarterly* 94 (1995): 687–714.

Heller, Leonid, and Thomas Lahusen. "Palimpsexes: Les metamorphoses de la thématique sexuelle dans le roman de F. Gladkov 'Le Ciment.' " *Wiener Slavistischer Almanach* 15 (1985): 211–54.

Hensel, Kerstin. *Im Schlauch.* Frankfurt a.M.: Suhrkamp Verlag, 1993.

Herf, Jeffrey. "East German Communists and the Jewish Question: Fourth Alois Mertes Memorial Lecture." Occasional Paper No. 11. Washington: German Historical Institute, 1994. 7–27.

———. "German Communism, the Discourse of 'Antifascist Resistance' and the Jewish Catastrophe." *Resistance Against the Third Reich 1933–1990.* Ed. Michael Geyer and John W. Boyer. Chicago: University of Chicago Press, 1992. 257–94.

Hermand, Jost. "Das Gute-Neue und das Schlechte-Neue: Wandlungen der Modernismus-Debatte in der DDR seit 1956." *Literatur und Literaturtheorie in der DDR.* Ed. Peter Uwe Hohendahl and Patricia Herminghouse. Frankfurt a.M.: Edition Suhrkamp, 1981. 73–99.

Herminghouse, Patricia. "Confronting the 'Blank Spots of History': GDR Culture and the Legacy of 'Stalinism.' " *German Studies Review* 2 (May 1991): 345–65.

———. "Vergangenheit als Problem der Gegenwart: Zur Darstellung des Faschismus in der neueren DDR-Literatur." *Literatur der DDR in den siebziger Jahren.* Ed. Peter Uwe Hohendahl and Patricia Herminghouse. Frankfurt a.M.: Suhrkamp Verlag, 1983. 259–94.

———. "Whose German Literature? GDR Literature, German Literature, and the Question of National Identity." *GDR Bulletin* 16 (1990): 6–10.

———. "Wunschbild oder Portrait? Zur Darstellung der Frau im Roman der DDR." *Literatur und Literaturtheorie in der DDR.* Ed. Patricia Herminghouse and Peter Uwe Hohendahl. Frankfurt a.M.: Edition Suhrkamp, 1981. 281–334.

Hermlin, Stephan. *Mansfelder Oratorium.* Leipzig: Verlag C. F. Peters, 1953.

Herting, Herta. *Geschichte für die Gegenwart.* Berlin: Dietz Verlag, 1979.

Herzinger, Richard, and Heinz-Peter Preusser. "Vom Äussersten zum Ersten: DDR-Literatur in der Tradition deutscher Zivilisationskritik." *Literatur in der DDR: Rückblicke.* Ed. Heinz Ludwig Arnold. Munich: Edition Text und Kritik, 1991. 195–209.

Heukenkamp, Ursula. "Ein Erbe für die Friedenswissenschaft: Das Konzept der kulturellen Erneuerung in der SBZ (1945–1949)." *Unerwünschte Erfahrung: Kriegsliteratur und Zensur in der DDR.* Berlin and Weimar: Aufbau-Verlag, 1990. 9–71.

———. "Das Frauenbild in der antifaschistischen Erneuerung der SBZ." *"Wen kümmert's, wer spricht": Zur Literatur und Kulturgeschichte von Frauen aus Ost und West.* Ed. Inge Stephan, Sigrid Weigel, and Kerstin Wilhelms. Cologne and Vienna: Böhlau Verlag, 1991. 3–13.

———. "Soll das Vergessen verabredet werden? Eingenständigkeit und Eigenart der DDR-Literatur." *Aus Politik und Zeitgeschichte* B41–42 (1991): 3–12.

Hilbig, Wolfgang. *Ich.* Frankfurt a.M.: S. Fischer Verlag, 1993.

———. "Literatur als Dialog." *Zwischen den Paradiesen.* Leipzig: Reclam-Verlag, 1992. 198–202.

———. *Eine Übertragung.* Frankfurt a.M.: Fischer Taschenbuch Verlag, 1992.

———. *Die Weiber.* Frankfurt a.M.: S. Fischer Verlag, 1987.

Hilzinger, Sonja. *Kassandra: Über Christa Wolf.* Frankfurt a.M.: Haag und Herchen, 1984.

———. "Weibliches Schreiben als eine Ästhetik des Widerstands: Über Wolf's 'Kassandra'-Projekt." *Christa Wolf—Ein Arbeitsbuch.* Ed. Angela Drescher. Berlin and Weimar: Aufbau-Verlag, 1989. 216–32.

Hilzinger, Sonja, ed. *"Das siebte Kreuz" von Anna Seghers: Texte, Daten, Bilder.* Darmstadt and Neuwied: Luchterhand, 1990.

Hirsch, Marianne. *The Mother/Daughter Plot: Narrative, Psychoanalysis, Feminism.* Bloomington and Indianapolis: Indiana University Press, 1989.

Hobsbawm, Eric. "Man and Woman: Images on the Left." *Workers: Worlds of Labor.* New York: Pantheon Books, 1984. 83–102.

Hofmann, Gunter. "Schmerzen einer deutschen Familie: Die neue Unversöhnlichkeit unter den Schriftstellern ist eine Chiffre für den Zustand der Republik." *Die Zeit* (October 6, 1995): 3.

Hörnigk, Frank. " 'Texte, die auf Geschichte warten . . .': Zum Geschichtsbegriff bei Heiner Müller." *Heiner Müller Material: Texte und Kommentare.* Ed. Frank Hörnigk. Leipzig: Verlag Philipp Reclam, 1989. 123–37.

Hörnigk, Therese. *Christa Wolf.* Berlin: Aufbau-Verlag, 1989.

———. "Das 11. Plenum und die Folgen: Christa Wolf im politischen Diskurs der 60er." *Neue Deutsche Literatur* 38 (1990): 50–58.

Hunt, Lynn. *The Family Romance of the French Revolution.* Berkeley: University of California Press, 1992.

Hüppauf, Bernd. "Moral oder Sprache: DDR-Literatur vor der Moderne." *Literatur in der DDR: Rückblicke.* Ed. Heinz-Ludwig Arnold. Munich: Edition Text und Kritik, 1991. 220–31.

Huyssen, Andreas. "After the Wall: The Failure of German Intellectuals." *New German Critique* 52 (1991): 109–43.

———. "Auf den Spuren Ernst Blochs: Nachdenken über Christa Wolf." *Basis: Jahrbuch für Deutsche Gegenwartsliteratur* 5 (1975): 100–116.

———. "The Politics of Identification: 'Holocaust' and West German Drama." *After the Great Divide: Modernism, Mass Culture, Postmodernism.* Bloomington and Indianapolis: Indiana University Press, 1986. 94–114.

———. *Twilight Memories.* New York and London: Routledge, 1995.

Iversen, Margret. "Das Frauenbild bei Anna Seghers: Und dann ihr. Eure kalten Augen." *Spuren: Zeitschrift für Kunst und Gesellschaft* 3 (1979): 38–40.

Jacobsen, Wolfgang, ed. *Babelsberg: Ein Filmstudio, 1912-1992*. Berlin: Argon, 1992.

Jacobsen, Wolfgang, Anton Kaes, and Hans Helmut Prinzler, ed. *Geschichte des deutschen Films*. Stuttgart: Verlag J. B. Metzler, 1993.

Jameson, Fredric. "Beyond the Cave: Demystifying the Ideology of Modernism." *The Ideologies of Theory: Essays 1971-1986*. Minneapolis: University of Minnesota Press, 1988. 2: 115-32.

———. "Foreword." *The Postmodern Condition* by Jean-Francois Lyotard. Minneapolis: University of Minnesota Press, 1984. vii-xxi.

———. *The Political Unconscious: Narrative as a Socially Symbolic Act*. Ithaca: Cornell University Press, 1981.

———. "The Realist Floor-Plan." In *On Signs*. Ed. Marshall Blonsky. Baltimore: Johns Hopkins University Press, 1986. 373-83.

Janka, Walter. *Spuren eines Lebens*. Reinbek bei Hamburg: Rowohlt Taschenbuch Verlag, 1992.

Jarmatz, Klaus, ed. *Ravensbrücker Ballade oder Faschismusbewältigung in der DDR*. Berlin: Aufbau-Verlag, 1992.

Jäger, Manfred. *Kultur und Politik in der DDR*. Cologne: Edition Deutschlandarchiv, 1982.

———. "Wem schreibe ich?" *Die andere Sprache: Neue DDR-Literatur der 80er Jahre*. Ed. Heinz Ludwig Arnold. Munich: Edition Text und Kritik, 1990. 61-71.

Jay, Martin. *Marxism and Totality: The Adventures of a Concept from Lukács to Habermas*. Berkeley and Los Angeles: University of California Press, 1984.

Jessen, Ralph. "Die Gesellschaft im Staatssozialismus." *Geschichte und Gesellschaft* 21 (1995): 96-110.

Johnson, Uwe. *Begleitumstände: Frankfurter Vorlesungen*. Frankfurt a.M.: Suhrkamp Verlag, 1992.

———. *Mutmassungen über Jakob*. Frankfurt a.M.: Suhrkamp, 1959.

Kaes, Anton, ed. *Weimarer Republik: Manifeste und Dokumente zur deutschen Literatur 1918-1933*. Stuttgart: Metzler, 1983.

Kantorowicz, Ernst. *The King's Two Bodies: A Study in Medieval Political Theology*. Princeton, N.J.: Princeton University Press, 1957.

Kaplan, Alice Yaeger. *Reproductions of Banality: Fascism, Literature, and French Intellectual Life*. Minneapolis: University of Minnesota Press, 1986.

Kershaw, Ian. *The Nazi Dictatorship*. London: Edward Arnold, 1993.

Kirschey-Feix, Ingrid. *Brigitte Reimann Hermann Henselmann Briefwechsel*. Berlin: Verlag Neues Leben, 1994.

Klein, Alfred. "Werkstattcharakter oder ideologische Repression?" *Sinn und Form* 42 (1990): 467-78.

Klessmann, Christoph. "Opposition und Dissidenz in der Geschichte der DDR." *Aus Politik und Zeitgeschichte* B5 (1991): 52-62.

Kluge, Alexander, and Oskar Negt. *Öffentlichkeit und Erfahrung: Zur Organisationsanalyse von bürgerlicher und proletarischer Öffentlichkeit*. Frankfurt a.M.: Suhrkamp, 1972.

Knabe, Hubertus, ed. *Aufbruch in eine andere DDR*. Reinbek bei Hamburg: Rowohlt Taschenbuch Verlag, 1990.

Koch, Gertrud. "Vom Verschwinden der Toten unter den Lebenden: Holocaust und Identitätskonfusion in den Filmen von Konrad Wolf." *Babylon* 12 (1993): 97–112.

Koch, Hans. "Referat auf der Vorstandssitzung des Deutschen Schriftstellerverbandes am 30. 10. 1969." *Dokumentation zu Christa Wolf "Nachdenken über Christa T."*. Ed. Angela Drescher. Hamburg and Zürich: Luchterhand Literaturverlag, 1991. 154–59.

Köhler, Barbara. "A la recherche de la révolution perdue." In *Women and the Wende: Social Effects and Cultural Reflections of the German Unification Process*. Proceedings of a conference held by *Women in German Studies,* September 9–11, 1993, University of Nottingham. Ed. Elizabeth Boa and Janet Wharton. Amsterdam and Atlanta, Ga.: Rodopi, 1994. 1–5.

Kohon, Gregorio. "Reflections on Dora: The Case of Hysteria." *The British School of Psychoanalysis: The Independent Tradition*. Ed. Gregorio Kohon. New Haven and London: Yale University Press, 1986. 362–80.

Koonz, Claudia. *Mothers in the Fatherland*. New York: St. Martin's Press, 1987.

Koziol, Andreas, and Rainer Schedlinski, ed. *Abriss der Ariadnefabrik*. Berlin: Edition Galrev, 1990.

Krauss, Angela. *Der Dienst*. 1988. Frankfurt a.M.: Suhrkamp, 1990.

Krause, Barbara. *Gefesselte Rebellin: Brigitte Reimann*. Berlin: Verlag Neues Leben, 1994.

Kristeva, Julia. *The Kristeva Reader*. Ed. Toril Moi. New York: Columbia University Press, 1986.

———. *Powers of Horror: An Essay on Abjection*. Trans. Leon S. Roudiez. New York: Columbia University Press, 1982.

Kuhn, Anna S. *Christa Wolf's Utopian Vision: From Marxism to Feminism*. Cambridge: Cambridge University Press, 1988.

———. " 'Eine Königin köpfen ist effektiver als einen König köpfen': The Gender Politics of the Christa Wolf Controversy." *Women and the Wende: Social Effects and Cultural Reflections of the German Unification Process*. Proceedings of a conference held by *Women in German Studies,* September 9–11, 1993, University of Nottingham. Ed. Elizabeth Boa and Janet Wharton. Amsterdam and Atlanta, Ga.: Rodopi, 1994. 200–215.

———. "*Was bleibt:* (Re)Assessing Christa Wolf Scholarship after the *Wende:* A Review Essay." *Germanic Review* 4 (Fall 1992): 173–80.

LaBahn, Kathleen J. *Anna Seghers' Exile Literature*. New York: Peter Lang, 1986.

Lacan, Jacques. "The Function and Field of Speech and Language in Psychoanalysis." *Ecrits: A Selection*. New York: Norton, 1977. 30–113.

Lahusen, Thomas. *How Life Writes the Book: Real Socialism and Socialist Realism in Stalin's Russia*. Ithaca: Cornell University Press, 1997.

———. "L'Homme nouveau, la femme nouvelle et le héros positif ou De la semiotique des sexes dans le réalisme socialiste." *Revue des Etudes Slaves* 50 (1988): 839–54.

———. "Socialist Realism in Search of Its Shores: Some Historical Remarks on the 'Historically Open Aesthetic System of the Truthful Representation of Life.' " *South Atlantic Quarterly* 94 (1995): 661–85.

———. "Thousand and One Nights in Stalinist Culture: *Far from Moscow.*" *Discourse* 17 (1995): 56–74.

Langermann, Martina. "Dieter Nolls 'Die Abenteuer des Werner Holt I': Entstehung und wirkungsästhetische Aspekte des Romans." *Weimarer Beiträge* 35 (1989): 1640–54.

Langner, Maria. *Stahl.* Berlin: Verlag Volk und Welt, 1952.

Laplanche, Jean. "Panel on 'Hysteria Today.' " *International Journal of Psycho-Analysis* 55 (1974): 459–69.

Laplanche, Jean, and Jean-Bertrand Pontalis. "Fantasy and the Origins of Sexuality." *Formations of Fantasy.* Ed. Victor Burgin, James Donald, and Cora Kaplan. London and New York: Methuen, 1986. 5–34.

Lautreamont, Isidore Ducasse Comte de. *Les Chants de Maldoror.* 1869–74. Paris: Editions Gallimard, 1973.

Lefort, Claude. "The Image of the Body and Totalitarianism." *The Political Forms of Modern Society.* Ed. John B. Thompson. Cambridge, Mass.: MIT Press, 1986. 292–306.

———. "The Logic of Totalitarianism." *The Political Forms of Modern Society.* Ed. John B. Thompson. Cambridge, Mass.: MIT Press, 1986. 273–91.

Lennox, Sara. " 'Der Versuch, man selbst zu sein': Christa Wolf und der Feminismus." *Die Frau als Heldin und Autorin.* Ed. Wolfgang Paulsen. Bern and Munich: Francke Verlag, 1979. 217–22.

Leonhard, Wolfgang. *Die Revolution entlässt ihre Kinder.* Cologne and Berlin: Kiepenheuer und Witsch, 1955.

Lewis, Allison. " 'Foiling the Censor': Reading and Transference as Feminist Strategies in the Works of Christa Wolf, Irmtraud Morgner, and Christa Moog." *German Quarterly* 66 (1993): 372–86.

Liebmann, Irina. *In Berlin.* Cologne: Kiepenheuer und Witsch, 1994.

Lindenberger, Thomas. "Projektvorstellung: Herrschaft und Eigen-Sinn in der Diktatur—Studien zur Gesellschaftsgeschichte in Berlin-Brandenburg 1945–1990." *Potsdamer Bulletin für Zeithistorische Studien,* No. 5 (December 1995): 37–52.

Linn, Marie-Luise. "Doppelte Kindheit—Zur Interpretation von Christa Wolfs *Kindheitsmuster.*" *Der Deutschunterricht* 30 (1978): 52–66.

Literatur der DDR: Geschichte der deutschen Literatur 11. Berlin: Volk und Wissen Volkseigener Verlag, 1977.

Love, Myra. "Christa Wolf and Feminism: Breaking the Patriarchal Connection." *New German Critique* 16 (1979): 31–53.

Lukács, Georg. "A Correspondence with Anna Seghers." 1938–39. *Essays on Realism.* Ed. Rodney Livingston and trans. David Fernbach. Cambridge, Massachusetts: MIT Press, 1981. 167–97.

———. *Schicksalswende: Beiträge zu einer neuen deutschen Ideologie.* Berlin: Aufbau-Verlag, 1956.

Lutjeharms, Madeline. " 'Doch schreiben wir weiter in den Formen, an die wir gewöhnt sind': Überlegungen zum 'weiblichen Schreiben' aus sprachwissenschaftlicher Sicht am Beispiel der *Kassandra* von Christa Wolf." *Christa Wolf aus feministischer Sicht.* Ed. Michel Vanhelleputte. Frankfurt a.M.: Peter Lang, 1992. 115–26.

Maaz, Hans-Joachim. *Der Gefühlsstau: Ein Psychogramm der DDR.* Munich: Knaur, 1992.

Macherey, Pierre. *Pour une théorie de la production littéraire.* Paris: Seuil, 1966.

Maetzig, Kurt. *Filmarbeit.* Berlin: Henschelverlag Kunst und Gesellschaft, 1987.

Mammach, K. *Die deutsche antifaschistische Widerstandsbewegung 1933–1939: Geschichte der deutschen Widerstandsbewegung im Inland und in der Emigration.* Berlin: Dietz, 1974.

Mann, Thomas. *Buddenbrooks: The Decline of a Family.* Trans. H. T. Lowe-Porter. New York: Knopf, 1964 [1910].

Marchwitza, Hans. *Die Heimkehr der Kumiaks.* Berlin and Weimar: Aufbau-Verlag, 1964.

———. *Die Kumiaks.* 1934. Berlin and Weimar: Aufbau-Verlag, 1965.

———. *Die Kumiaks und ihre Kinder.* Berlin: Verlag Tribüne, 1959.

———. *Roheisen.* Berlin: Verlag der Tribüne, 1955.

Maron, Monika. "Ich war ein antifaschistisches Kind." *"Die Geschichte ist offen".* Ed. Michael Naumann. Frankfurt a.M.: Fischer Verlag, 1991. 117–35.

———. *Stille Zeile Sechs.* Frankfurt a.M.: Fischer Verlag, 1991.

Mauser, Wolfram. "Das 'dunkle Tier' und die Seherin: Zu Christa Wolfs Kassandra-Phantasie." *Freiburger Literaturpsychologische Gespräche.* Frankfurt a.M.: Peter Lang, 1985. 139–57.

———, ed. *Erinnerte Zukunft: Elf Studien zum Werk Christa Wolfs.* Würzburg: Königshausen und Neumann, 1985.

Mayakovsky, Vladimir. "Toi storone." *Complete Collection of His Works in 12 Volumes.* Moscow: Pravda, 1978.

Merkel, Ina. "Charme, Zement und Schwefelsäure: Frauenbilder in der DDR der 50er." *Alltäglicher Stalinismus.* Ed. Ostberliner Geschichtswerkstatt. Hamburg: Ergebnisseverlag, 1992. 48–50.

———. *. . . und du, Frau an der Werkbank: Die DDR in den 50er Jahren.* Berlin: Elefantenpress, 1990.

Merker, Paul. "Das Echo: Diskussion über 'Hitlers Antisemitismus und wir.' " *Freies Deutschland* 2 (1943): 33.

Messerschmidt, Beate. "Neue Wege, von Arbeitern zu erzählen: Hans Marchwitza's *Die Kumiaks.*" In *Erfahrung Exil: Antifaschistische Romane 1933–1945.* Ed. Sigrid Bock and Manfred Hahn. Berlin: Aufbau-Verlag, 1979. 73–93.

———. "Sozialistische Literatur im Exil: Das Beispiel Hans Marchwitza." *Internationales Archiv für Sozialgeschichte der deutschen Literatur* 12 (1987): 213–36.

Meuschel, Sigrid. *Legitimation und Parteiherrschaft: Zum Paradox von Stabilität und Revolution in der DDR 1945–1989.* Frankfurt a.M.: Suhrkamp Verlag, 1992.

————. "Überlegungen zu einer Herrschafts- und Gesellschaftsgeschichte der DDR." *Geschichte und Gesellschaft* 19 (1993): 5–14.

Michael, Klaus. "Feindbild Literatur: Die Biermann-Affäre, Staatssicherheit und die Herausbildung einer literarischen Alternativkultur in der DDR." *Aus Politik und Zeitgeschehen* B22–23 (1993): 23–31.

Mickel, Karl. "Bericht über meinen Vater." *Neue deutsche Literatur* 7 (1958): 45.

Mieth, Matias. " 'Der Mensch, der nicht geschunden wird, wird nicht erzogen': Johannes R. Becher und die Gewalt des Stalinismus." *Weimarer Beiträge* 5 (1991): 764–72.

Mitchell, Juliet. "Introduction I." *Feminine Sexuality.* Ed. Juliet Mitchell and Jacqueline Rose. New York: Norton, 1985. 1–26.

————. *Psycho-Analysis and Feminism.* New York: Vintage, 1975.

Mitscherlich, Alexander, and Margarete Mitscherlich. *Die Unfähigkeit zu trauern.* 1967. Munich: Piper Verlag, 1987.

Mitscherlich-Nielsen, Margarete. "Gratwanderung zwischen Anspruch und Verstrickung." *Christa Wolf—Ein Arbeitsbuch.* Ed. Angela Drescher. Berlin and Weimar: Aufbau-Verlag, 1989. 114–20.

Moi, Toril. "Appropriating Bourdieu: Feminist Theory and Pierre Bourdieu's Sociology of Culture." *New Literary History* 22 (1991): 1017–49.

————. "Psychoanalysis, Feminism, and Politics: A Conversation with Juliet Mitchell." *South Atlantic Quarterly* 93 (1994): 925–49.

————. *Simone de Beauvoir: The Making of an Intellectual Woman.* Oxford and Cambridge: Blackwell, 1994.

Mommsen, Wolfgang J. "Die DDR in der deutschen Geschichte." *Aus Politik und Zeitgeschehen* B29–30 (1993): 23, 29.

Morgner, Irmtraud. *Leben und Abenteuer der Trobadora Beatriz.* Darmstadt and Neuwied: Luchterhand, 1976.

Müller, Heiner. "Bericht vom Grossvater." 1950. *Geschichten aus der Produktion.* Berlin: Rotbuch Verlag, 1974. 7–9.

————. *Germania: Tod in Berlin.* Berlin: Rotbuch Verlag, 1977.

————. "Geschichte und Drama: Ein Gespräch mit Heiner Müller." *Basis: Jahrbuch für deutsche Gegenwartsliteratur.* Vol. 6. Ed. Reinhold Grimm and Jost Hermand. Frankfurt a.M.: Suhrkamp Verlag, 1976. 48–64.

————. *Die Hamletmaschine. Die Hamletmaschine. Heiner Müllers Endspiel.* Ed. Theo Girshausen. Cologne: Prometh Verlag, 1978. 11–23.

————. *Krieg ohne Schlacht: Leben in zwei Diktaturen.* Cologne: Kiepenheuer und Witsch, 1992.

————. "Reflections on Post-Modernism." *New German Critique* 16 (1979): 198–200.

————. "Der Vater." 1959. *Germania: Tod in Berlin.* Berlin: Rotbuch Verlag, 1977. 20–26.

————. "The Walls of History." *Semiotexte: The German Issue* 4 (1982): 36–76.

Mundstock, Karl. *Helle Nächte.* Halle/Saale: Mitteldeutscher Verlag, 1952.

Nägele, Rainer. "Trauer, Tropen, und Phantasmen: Ver-rückte Geschichten aus der

DDR." *Literatur der DDR in den siebziger Jahren*. Ed. Peter Uwe Hohendahl and Patricia Herminghouse. Frankfurt a.M.: Suhrkamp Verlag, 1983. 193–222.

Naumann, Michael, ed. *Die Geschichte ist offen: DDR 1990—Hoffnung auf eine neue Republik*. Reinbek bei Hamburg: Rowohlt Taschenbuch Verlag, 1990.

Neumann, Gerhard. "Christa Wolfs *Kassandra:* Die Archäologie der weiblichen Stimme." *Erinnerte Zukunft*. Ed. Wolfram Mauser. Würzburg: Königshausen und Neumann, 1985. 233–64.

Neumann, Gert. *Die Klandestinität der Kesselreiniger*. Frankfurt a.M.: S. Fischer Verlag, 1989.

Neutsch, Erik. *Der Friede im Osten*. Vol. 1. Halle: Mitteldeutscher Verlag, 1974.

———. *Spur der Steine*. 1964. Munich: Damnitz Verlag, 1975.

Niethammer, Lutz, Alexander von Plato, and Dorothee Wierling. *Die volkseigene Erfahrung*. Berlin: Rowohlt, 1990.

Noll, Dieter. *Die Abenteuer des Werner Holt: Roman einer Heimkehr*. 1963. Berlin and Weimar: Aufbau-Verlag, 1983.

———. *Die Abenteuer des Werner Holt: Roman einer Jugend*. Berlin and Weimar: Aufbau-Verlag, 1960.

———. *Kippenberg*. Berlin and Weimar: Aufbau-Verlag, 1979.

Noll, Hans. *Der Abschied: Journal meiner Ausreise aus der DDR*. Hamburg: Hoffmann und Campe, 1985.

Noll, Hans (Chaim). *Nachtgedanken über Deutschland*. Reinbek bei Hamburg: Rowohlt, 1992.

Ostow, Robin. "Being Jewish in the Other Germany: An Interview with Thomas Eckert." *New German Critique* 38 (Spring/Summer 1986): 73–87.

———. *Jews in Contemporary Germany: The Children of Moses in the Land of Marx*. New York: St. Martin's Press, 1989.

———. " 'Ne Art Bürgerwehr in Form von Skins': Young Germans on the Streets in the Eastern and Western States of the Federal Republic." *New German Critique* 64 (1995): 87–103.

Peukert, Detlev. *Inside Nazi Germany: Conformity, Opposition, and Racism in Everyday Life*. New Haven and London: Yale University Press, 1987.

Philipsen, Dirk. *We Were the People: Voices from East Germany's Revolutionary Autumn of 1989*. Durham: Duke University Press, 1993.

Pischel, Joseph. "Gewebe der Gesittung—Gewebe des Erzählens: Christa Wolfs Verhältnis zu Anna Seghers." *Christa Wolf—Ein Arbeitsbuch*. Ed. Angela Drescher. Berlin and Weimar: Aufbau-Verlag, 1989. 371–97.

Raddatz, Fritz J. "Von der Arbeiterkorrespondenz zur Literatur: Willi Bredel, F. C. Weiskopf." *Traditionen und Tendenzen: Materialien zur Literatur der DDR*. Frankfurt a.M.: Suhrkamp Verlag, 1972. 254–87.

———. "Von der Beschädigung der Literatur durch ihre Urheber." *Die Zeit* (February 5, 1993): 17–18.

Radvanyi, Pierre. "Einige Erinnerungen." *Argonautenschiff: Jahrbuch der Anna-Seghers-Gesellschaft* 3 (1994): 185–92.

Radvanyi, Ruth. Untitled. *Anna Seghers: Eine Biographie in Bildern.* Ed. Frank Wagner, Ursula Emmerich, and Ruth Radvanyi. Berlin: Aufbau-Verlag, 1994. 30.

Radway, Janice. *Reading the Romance.* Chapel Hill: University of North Carolina Press, 1984.

Rapisarda, Cettina. "Women and Peace in Literature and Politics: The Example of Anna Seghers." *German Writers and the Cold War 1945–61.* Ed. Rhys W. Williams, Stephen Parker, and Colin Riordan. Manchester and New York: Manchester University Press, 1992. 159–79.

Rathenow, Lutz. " 'Schreiben Sie doch für uns': Was sich die Staatssicherheit einfallen liess, um die Literatur zu bändigen." *Frankfurter Allgemeine Zeitung,* November 27, 1991, 36.

Rehmann, Ruth. *Unterwegs in fremden Träumen.* Munich: C. Hanser, 1993.

Reich, Ines. "Geteilter Widerstand: Die Tradierung des deutschen Widerstands in der Bundesrepublik und der DDR." *Zeitschrift für Geschichtswissenschaft* 42 (1994): 635–43.

Reich, Wilhelm. *Die sexuelle Revolution.* Frankfurt a.M.: Fischer Taschenbuch Verlag, 1973.

Reich-Ranicki, Marcel. "Ja, ich habe dran geglaubt." *Die Zeit* (June 17, 1994): 13–14.

Reiling, Netty (Seghers, Anna). *Jude und Judentum im Werke Rembrandts.* Intro. Christa Wolf. Leipzig: Reclam-Verlag, 1990.

Reimann, Brigitte. *Aber wir schaffen es, verlass Dich drauf! Briefe an eine Freundin im Westen.* Ed. Ingrid Krüger. Berlin: Elefanten Press, 1995.

———. *Ankunft im Alltag.* Berlin: Verlag Neues Leben, 1961.

———. *Franziska Linkerhand.* 1974. Munich: Deutscher Taschenbuch Verlag, 1984.

———. "Die Frau am Pranger: Erzählung." 1956. Berlin: Verlag Neues Leben, 1962.

———. *Die Geschwister.* 1962. Munich: Deutscher Taschenbuch Verlag, 1988.

Reimann, Brigitte, and Christa Wolf. *Sei gegrüsst und lebe: Eine Freundschaft in Briefen 1964–1973.* Berlin: Aufbau Taschenbuch Verlag, 1995.

Remmler, Karen. "Deciphering the Body of Memory: Writing by Former East German Women Writers." *Postcommunism and the Body Politic.* Ed. Ellen E. Berry. New York and London: New York University Press, 1995. 134–63.

Reso, Martin, ed. *"Der geteilte Himmel" und seine Kritiker.* Halle: Mitteldeutscher Verlag, 1965.

Roggausch, Werner. *Das Exilwerk von Anna Seghers 1933–1939.* Munich: Minerva Publikation, 1979.

Rohrwasser, Michael. *Saubere Mädel, starke Genossen: Proletarische Massenliteratur?* Berlin: Verlag Roter Stern, 1975.

Romero, Christiane Zehl. " 'Remembrance of Things Future': On Establishing a Female Tradition." *Responses to Christa Wolf.* Ed. Marilyn Sibley Fries. Detroit: Wayne State University Press, 1989. 108–27.

———. " 'Weibliches Schreiben' — Christa Wolfs *Kassandra." Studies in GDR Culture and Society* 4 (1984): 15–27.

Roscher, Achim. "Wirkung des Geschriebenen: Gespräche mit Anna Seghers." *Neue deutsche Literatur* 10 (1983): 61–75.

Rose, Jacqueline. *The Haunting of Sylvia Plath.* Cambridge, Mass.: Harvard University Press, 1993.

———. "An Interview with Jacqueline Rose." *Why War?* Oxford and Cambridge: Blackwell, 1993. 231–55.

———. "Introduction: Feminism and the Psychic." *Sexuality in the Field of Vision.* London and New York: Verso, 1991. 1–23.

Rosenfeld, David. "Identification and Its Vicissitudes in Relation to the Nazi Phenomenon." *International Journal of Psycho-Analysis* 67 (1986): 53–64.

Rosenhaft, Eve. *Beating the Fascists? The German Communists and Political Violence.* Cambridge: Cambridge University Press, 1983.

———. "The Uses of Remembrance: The Legacy of the Communist Resistance in the German Democratic Republic." *Germans Against Nazism: Essays in Honor of Peter Hoffmann.* Ed. Francis R. Nicosia and Lawrence D. Stokes. New York and Oxford: Berg, 1990. 369–88.

Rosolato, Guy. "La voix: Entre corps et language." *Revue Française de Psychanalyse* 38 (1974): 75–94.

Rutschky, Michael. "Wie erst jetzt die DDR entsteht." *Merkur* 9/10 (September/October 1995): 851–64.

Saeger, Uwe. *Der Kakerlak.* Munich and Zurich: Piper, 1990.

———. *Nöhr.* Rostock: Hinsdorff Verlag, 1980.

Santner, Eric. "History Beyond the Pleasure Principle: Some Thoughts on the Representation of Trauma." *Probing the Limits of Representation.* Ed. Saul Friedlander. Cambridge, Mass.: Harvard University Press, 1992. 143–54.

———. *Stranded Objects: Mourning, Memory, and Film in Postwar Germany.* Ithaca and London: Cornell University Press, 1990.

Sayre, Robert, and Michael Löwy. "Romanticism as a Feminist Vision: The Quest of Christa Wolf." *New German Critique* 64 (1995): 105–34.

Scarry, Elaine. *The Body in Pain.* New York and Oxford: Oxford University Press, 1985.

Schedlinski, Rainer. "Dem Druck, immer mehr sagen zu sollen, hielt ich nicht stand." *Frankfurter Allgemeine Zeitung,* January 14, 1992, 25.

Scherpe, Klaus. "Erzwungener Alltag: Wahrgenommene und gedachte Wirklichkeit in der Reportageliteratur der Nachkriegszeit." *Nachkriegsliteratur in Westdeutschland 1945–49.* Ed. Jost Hermand, Helmut Peitsch, and Klaus Scherpe. Berlin: Argument Verlag, 1982. 35–102.

Schirrmacher, Frank. "Abschied von der Literatur der Bundesrepublik." *Frankfurter Allgemeine Zeitung,* October 2, 1990, L1–2.

———. "Dem Druck des härteren, strengeren Lebens standhalten: Auch eine Studie zum autoritären Charakter." *"Es geht nicht um Christa Wolf": Der Literaturstreit im vereinten Deutschland.* Ed. Thomas Anz. Munich: Edition Spangenberg, 1991. 77–89.

———. " 'Meine Mutter hat für Mielke Schmalzstullen geschmiert': Ein Gespräch mit Monika Maron über ihre Kontakte zur 'Hauptverwaltung Aufklärung' des Staatssicherheitsdienstes der DDR." *Frankfurter Allgemeine Zeitung,* August 7, 1995, 25.

Schlegel, Friedrich H. *Die Romanliteratur der DDR: Erzähltechniken, Leserlenkung, Kulturpolitik.* Opladen: Westdeutscher Verlag, 1991.

Schlenstedt, Dieter. "Motive und Symbole in Christa Wolf's Erzählung 'Der geteilte Himmel.' " *Weimarer Beiträge* 10 (1964): 77–104.

———. *Die neuere DDR-Literatur und ihre Leser: Wirkungsästhetische Analysen.* Munich: Damnitz Verlag, 1980.

Schneider, Manfred. "Väter und Söhne, posthum.: Das beschädigte Verhältnis zweier Generationen." *Den Kopf verkehrt aufgesetzt oder Die melancholische Linke.* Darmstadt and Neuwied: Luchterhand, 1981. 8–64.

Schrade, Andreas. "Der Schriftsteller als Propagandist des sozialistischen Aufbaus: Standortbestimmung nach der Rückkehr aus dem Exil." *Argonautenschiff: Jahrbuch der Anna-Seghers-Gesellschaft* 2 (1993): 57–63.

Schulz, Genia. "Abschied von Morgen: Zu den Frauengestalten im Werk Heiner Müllers." In *Text und Kritik: Sonderband Heiner Müller.* Ed. Heinz Ludwig Arnold. Munich: Edition Text und Kritik, 1982. 58–69.

———. *Heiner Müller.* Stuttgart: Metzlersche Verlagsbuchhandlung, 1980.

———. "Kein Chorgesang: Neue Schreibweisen bei Autorinnen (aus) der DDR." *Bestandsaufnahme Gegenwartsliteratur.* Ed. Heinz Ludwig Arnold. Munich: Edition Text und Kritik, 1988. 212–25.

Schulz, Gerda. "Ein überraschender Erstling." *Neue deutsche Literatur* 9 (1961): 128–30.

Schulz, Martin. "Arbeiterdichter aus dem Kohlenpott." *Kritik in der Zeit.* Ed. Klaus Jarmatz. Halle/Saale: Mitteldeutscher Verlag, 1969. 140–42.

Schulz, Max Walter. "Das Neue und das Bleibende in unserer Literatur." *Dokumentation zu Christa Wolf "Nachdenken über Christa T.".* Ed. Angela Drescher. Hamburg and Zürich: Luchterhand Literaturverlag, 1991. 112–14.

Schütz, Friedrich. "Die Familie Seghers–Reiling und das jüdische Mainz." *Argonautenschiff: Jahrbuch der Anna-Seghers-Gesellschaft* 2 (1993): 151–73.

Schütz, Stefan. "Kekse und Totenschädel: Ein Gespräch mit Stefan Schütz von Axel Schnell." *Die Zeit* 15 (April 13, 1990): 26.

Scott, Joan. "Gender: A Useful Category of Historical Analysis." *Gender and the Politics of History.* New York: Columbia University Press, 1988. 28–50.

Segert, Dieter. "Fahnen, Umzüge, Rituale: Die Macht der Rituale und Symbole." *DDR–Ein Staat vergeht.* Ed. Thomas Blanke and Rainer Erd. Frankfurt a.M.: Fischer Taschenbuch Verlag, 1991. 25–35.

Seghers, Anna. "Agathe Schweigert." *Die Kraft der Schwachen.* Neuwied and Berlin: Luchterhand Verlag, 1966. 7–31.

———. *Anna Seghers–Wieland Herzfelde: Ein Briefwechsel 1939–1946.* Berlin and Weimar: Aufbau, 1985.

———. "Aufgaben der Kunst." 1943–44. *Glauben an Irdisches: Essays.* Ed. Christa Wolf. Leipzig: Reclam, 1974. 167–72.

————. *Aufsätze, Ansprachen, Essays: 1927–1953.* Berlin: Aufbau-Verlag, 1980.

————. "Der Ausflug der toten Mädchen." 1946. *Der Ausflug der toten Mädchen: Erzählungen.* Darmstadt and Neuwied: Luchterhand Verlag, 1989. "The Outing of the Dead Girls." *Three German Stories.* Trans. and ed. Michael Bullock. London: Oasis Books, 1984. 13–45.

————. "Briefwechsel mit Lukács." *Über Kunstwerk und Wirklichkeit.* Vol. 2. Berlin: Akademie-Verlag, 1971.

————. "Deutschland und wir." *Glauben an Irdisches: Essays.* Ed. Christa Wolf. Leipzig: Reclam, 1974. 16–23.

————. *Die Entscheidung.* 1959. Neuwied and Darmstadt: Luchterhand Literaturverlag, 1985.

————. "Frauen und Kinder in der Emigration." 1938. *Argonautenschiff: Jahrbuch der Anna-Seghers-Gesellschaft* 2 (1993): 319–27.

————. "Für Christa Wolf," *Sinn und Form* 31 (1979): 282; repr. as "Anna Seghers: Ein Brief," in *Christa Wolf—Ein Arbeitsbuch.* Ed. Angela Drescher. Berlin and Weimar: Aufbau-Verlag, 1989. 11–12.

————. *Der gerechte Richter.* Berlin: Aufbau-Verlag, 1990.

————. "Maerz 1933—Verhaftung Thälmanns." *Freies Deutschland* 2 (1943): 12.

————. "Neue literarisch-künstlerische Probleme. Rede auf dem II: Deutschen Schriftstellerkongress 1950." *Die Macht der Worte: Reden–Schriften–Briefe.* Leipzig and Weimar: Gustav Kiepenheuer Verlag, 1979. 215–28.

————. "Post ins gelobte Land." 1946. *Erzählungen (I): Auswahl 1926–1946.* Darmstadt and Neuwied: Luchterhand Verlag, 1977. 1: 155–75.

————. *Das siebte Kreuz.* 1942. Frankfurt a.M.: Luchterhand Literaturverlag, 1988. *The Seventh Cross.* Trans. James A. Galston. New York: Monthly Review Press, 1987.

————. "Die Toten auf der Insel Djal." *Über Kunstwerk und Wirklichkeit: Erganzungsband.* Ed. Sigrid Bock. Berlin: Akademie Verlag, 1979. 4: 205–9.

————. *Die Toten bleiben jung.* 1949. Neuwied and Darmstadt: Luchterhand, 1981. *The Dead Stay Young.* London: Eyre and Spottiswoode, 1950.

————. "Das Unsterbliche was in ihm verkörpert." *Neue deutsche Literatur* 4 (1953): 5–6.

————. "Vaterlandsliebe. Rede auf dem I. Internationalen Schriftstellerkongress zur Verteidigung der Kultur 1935." *Die Macht der Worte: Reden–Schriften–Briefe.* Leipzig and Weimar: Gustav Kiepenheuer Verlag, 1979. 29–33.

————. "Vierzig Jahre der Margarete Wolf." 1958. *Frauen in der DDR.* Ed. Lutz-W. Wolff. Munich: Deutscher Taschenbuch Verlag, 1990. 46–57.

————. "Volk und Schriftsteller." 1942. *Die Macht der Worte: Reden–Schriften–Briefe.* Leipzig and Weimar: Gustav Kiepenheuer Verlag, 1979. 48–56.

————. "Vorwort zum Roman 'Die Rettung.' " 1947. *Die Macht der Worte: Reden–Schriften–Briefe.* Leipzig and Weimar: Gustav Kiepenheuer Verlag, 1979. 14–15.

————. "Wird der Roman überflüssig?" 1973. *Die Macht der Worte: Reden–Schriften–Briefe.* Leipzig and Weimar: Gustav Kiepenheuer Verlag, 1979. 115–18.

Semler, Christian. "Gestrenge Ansichten der Henker Christi." *TAZ,* December 8, 1993, 12.

Sereny, Gitta. *Into That Darkness.* New York: Vintage, 1983.

Shils, Edward. "Center and Periphery." *The Constitution of Society.* Chicago: University of Chicago Press, 1982. 93–109.

VII. Schriftstellerkongress der Deutschen Demokratischen Republik: Protokoll. Berlin and Weimar: Aufbau-Verlag, 1974.

Silberman, Marc D. *Literature of the Working World: A Study of the Industrial Novel in East Germany.* Bern/Frankfurt: H. Lang, 1976.

————. "Remembering History: The Filmmaker Konrad Wolf." *New German Critique* 49 (Winter 1990): 163–85.

Silverman, Kaja. *The Acoustic Mirror: The Female Voice in Psychoanalysis and Cinema.* Bloomington and Indianapolis: Indiana University Press, 1988.

————. *Male Subjectivity at the Margins.* London: Routledge, 1992.

Simon, Annette. "Ich und sie: Versuch, mir und anderen meine ostdeutsche Moral zu erklären." *Kursbuch* 111 (February 1993): 25–34.

Soden, Kristine von. "Sexualität als Produktionskraft." *Irmtraud Morgners hexische Weltfahrt.* Ed. Kristine von Soden. Berlin: Elefanten Press, 1991. 101–8.

Soholm, Kirsten. "Mythos, Moderne und die Teilung Deutschlands." *Weimarer Beiträge* 36 (1990): 1513–23.

Spies, Bernhard. "Georg Lukács und der sozialistische Realismus in der DDR." *Literatur in der DDR: Rückblicke.* Ed. Heinz Ludwig Arnold. Munich: Edition Text und Kritik, 1992. 34–44.

Spira, Steffi. *Rote Fahne mit Trauerflor.* Freiburg: Kore, 1990.

Spittmann, Ilse, and Gisela Helwig, eds. *DDR-Lesebuch: Stalinisierung 1949–1955.* N.p.: Edition Deutschland Archiv, 1989.

Staritz, Dietrich. "Ein 'besonderer deutscher Weg' zum Sozialismus." *Was war: Historische Studien zu Geschichte und Politik der DDR.* Berlin: Metropol, 1994. 55–84.

Steinmetz, George. "Fordism and the (Im)moral Economy of Right-Wing Violence in Contemporary Germany." *Research on Democracy and Society* 2 (1994): 277–315.

————. "German Exceptionalism and the Origins of Nazism: The Career of a Concept." *Dictators Unleashed: Historical Approaches to Nazism and Stalinism.* Ed. Ian Kershaw and Moshe Lewin. Cambridge: Cambridge University Press, forthcoming.

Stephan, Alexander. *Anna Seghers im Exil: Essays, Texte, Dokumente.* Bonn: Bouvier, 1993.

————. *Christa Wolf.* Munich: Edition Text und Kritik, 1976.

————. " 'Ich habe das Gefühl, ich bin in die Eiszeit versetzt' . . . Zur Rückkehr von Anna Seghers aus dem Exil." *Germanic Review* 12 (1987): 143–52.

————. "Pläne für ein neues Deutschland: Die Kulturpolitik der Exil-KPD vor 1945." *Basis: Jahrbuch für Deutsche Gegenwartsliteratur.* Ed. Reinhold Grimm and Jost Hermand. Frankfurt a.M.: Suhrkamp Verlag, 1977. 7: 54–74.

Stites, Richard. *The Women's Liberation Movement in Russia.* Princeton: Princeton University Press, 1990.

Streiter, Gudrun. "Diary of an SA Man's Bride." *Nazi Culture.* Ed. George Mosse. New York: Schocken, 1981. 122–26.

Strittmatter, Erwin. *Der Laden.* Berlin: Aufbau-Verlag, 1992.

Suleiman, Robin. *Subversive Intent: Gender, Politics, and the Avantgarde.* Cambridge, Mass.: Harvard University Press, 1990.

Szemere, Anna. "Bandits, Heroes, the Honest and the Misled: Exploring the Politics of Representation in the Hungarian Uprising of 1956." *Cultural Studies Reader.* Ed. Lawrence Grossberg, Cary Nelson, and Paula A. Treichler. New York: Routledge, 1992. 623–39.

Teraoka, Arlene. *The Silence of Entropy or Universal Discourse: The Postmodernist Poetics of Heiner Müller.* New York: Peter Lang, 1985.

Theweleit, Klaus. *Male Fantasies.* 2 vols. Minneapolis: University of Minnesota Press, 1987, 1989.

Thompson, John B., ed. Editor's Introduction. *The Political Forms of Modern Society.* Cambridge, Mass.: MIT Press, 1986. 1–27.

Thürk, Harry. *Die Stunde der toten Augen.* Berlin: Das Neue Berlin, 1957.

Tobin, Patricia. *Time and the Novel: The Genealogical Imperative.* Princeton: Princeton University Press, 1978.

Trommler, Frank. "DDR-Erzählung und Bitterfelder Weg." *Basis* 3 (1972): 61–97.

———. "Die Kulturpolitik der DDR und die kulturelle Tradition des deutschen Sozialismus." *Literatur und Literaturtheorie in der DDR.* Ed. Peter Uwe Hohendahl and Patricia Herminghouse. Frankfurt a.M.: Edition Suhrkamp, 1981. 13–72.

———. *Sozialistische Literatur in Deutschland: Ein historischer Überblick.* Stuttgart: Metzler, 1976.

———. "Von Hölderlin zu Stalin: Über den Entwicklungsroman in der DDR." *Zum Roman in der DDR.* Ed. Marc D. Silberman. Stuttgart: Klett Verlag, 1980. 23–39.

Tröger, Annemarie. "Between Rape and Prostitution: Survival Strategies and Chances of Emancipation for Berlin Women after World War II." *Women in Culture and Politics: A Century of Change.* Ed. Judith Freidländer and Carroll Smith-Rosenberg. Bloomington: Indiana University Press, 1986. 97–118.

Trumpener, Katie. "On the Way to Socialist Realism: Teleology, Subject Formation, and Anna Seghers' 'On the Way to the American Embassy.' " *Rethinking Marxism* 7 (1994): 45–52.

Ulbricht, Walter. "Sozialistische Ethik und Moral (1958)." *Kurzwort: Ewig blühe Erinnerungen an die Republik der Lobetrotter.* Catalogue, ed. Tobias Böhm. Berlin: Westermann, 1992. 20.

Vanhelleputte, Michel, ed. *Christa Wolf in Feministischer Sicht.* Frankfurt a.M.: Peter Lang, 1992.

———. "Christa Wolf und der Bankrott des patriarchalischen Prinzips, oder die Voraussetzungen ihres Entwurfs eines weltverändernden Feminismus." *Christa Wolf aus Feministischer Sicht.* Ed. Michel Vanhelleputte. Frankfurt a.M.: Peter Lang, 1992. 13–22.

Vinke, Hermann, ed. *Akteneinsicht Christa Wolf: Zerrspiegel und Dialog.* Hamburg: Luchterhand Literaturverlag, 1993.

Viollet, Catherine. "Nachdenken über Pronomina: Zur Entstehung von Christa Wolfs 'Nachdenken über Christa T.' " *Christa Wolf — Ein Arbeitsbuch.* Ed. Angela Drescher. Berlin and Weimar: Aufbau-Verlag, 1989. 101–13.

Vogt, Jochen. "Langer Abschied von der Nachkriegsliteratur? Ein Kommentar zur letzten westdeutschen Literaturdebatte." *Der deutsch-deutsche Literaturstreit oder "Freunde, es spricht sich schlecht mit gebundener Zunge".* Ed. Karl Deiritz and Hannes Krauss. Hamburg: Luchterhand Literatur Verlag, 1991. 53–77.

Vollmer, Antje. "Die SPD nach dem Tod Willi Brandts." *Tageszeitung,* October 17, 1992, 10.

Wagner, Frank. "Deportation nach Piaski: Letzte Stationen der Passion von Hedwig Reiling." *Argonautenschiff* 3 (1994): 117–26.

Wagner, Frank, Ursula Emmerich, and Ruth Radvanyi, eds. *Anna Seghers: Eine Biographie in Bildern.* Berlin and Weimar: Aufbau-Verlag, 1994.

Walther, Joachim. *Sicherungsbereich Literatur: Schriftsteller und Staatssicherheit in der Deutschen Demokratischen Republik.* Berlin: CH. Links Verlag, 1996.

Walther, Joachim, Wolf Biermann, and Günter de Bruyn et al., eds. *Protokoll eines Tribunals: Die Ausschlüsse aus dem DDR-Schriftstellerverband.* Reinbek bei Hamburg: Rowohlt Verlag, 1991.

Wander, Maxie. *Guten Morgen, du Schöne. Frauen in der DDR: Protokolle.* Darmstadt and Neuwied: Luchterhand Verlag, 1978.

Wangenheim, Inge von. "Die Geschichte und unsere Geschichten: Gedanken eines Schriftstellers auf der Suche nach den Fabeln seiner Zeit." *Von Zeit Zu Zeit: Essays.* Halle: Mitteldeutscher Verlag, 1975. 7–137.

———. *Das Zimmer mit den offenen Augen.* Halle: Mitteldeutscher Verlag, 1965.

Weber, Heinz-Dieter. " 'Phantastische Genauigkeit': Der historische Sinn der Schreibart Christa Wolfs." *Erinnerte Zukunft: Elf Studien zum Werk Christa Wolfs.* Ed. Wolfram Mauser. Würzburg: Königshausen und Neumann, 1985. 81–106.

Weber, Hermann. *Die DDR 1945–1986.* Munich: R. Oldenbourg Verlag, 1988.

Weber, Samuel. *Return to Freud: Jacques Lacan's Dislocation of Psychoanalysis.* Cambridge: Cambridge University Press, 1991.

Weigel, Sigrid. " 'Blut im Schuh' — Körper-Gedächtnis und Körper-Sprache in Christa Wolfs Prosa." *Bilder des kulturellen Gedächtnisses.* Dülmen: Tende, 1994. 58–77.

———. "Die im Stand der Ähnlichkeit entstellte Welt: Vorbemerkung." *Bilder des kulturellen Gedächtnisses.* Dülmen: Tende, 1994. 9–17.

———. " 'Das Theater der weissen Revolution': Körper und Verkörperung im Revolutions-Theater von Heiner Müller und Georg Büchner." *Die Marseillaise der Weiber.* Ed. Inge Stephan and Sigrid Weigel. Berlin: Argument Verlag, 1989. 154–74.

———. "Väterbücher — Töchterschriften." *Die Stimme der Medusa.* Dülmen: Tende, 1987. 160–67.

———. "Vom Sehen zur Seherin: Christa Wolfs Umdeutung des Mythos und die Spur der Bachmann-Rezeption in ihrer Literatur." *Christa Wolf — Ein Arbeitsbuch.* Ed. Angela Drescher. Berlin and Weimar: Aufbau-Verlag, 1989. 169–203.

Weiss, Peter. *Die Ästhetik des Widerstands.* Frankfurt a.M.: Suhrkamp Verlag, 1986.

———. "Meine Ortschaft." *Rapporte.* Frankfurt a.M., 1968. 113–24.

Wenzel, Kurt. "Die Stasi-Debatte als Vorgang." *Neue deutsche Literatur* 6 (1993): 160–70.

Westphal, Anke. "Mein wunderbarer Plattenbau. Hoppla, wir leben noch. Ob Puhdys, Oktoberclub, Ernst Busch, Franke-Echo-Quintett oder Theo Schumann-Combo — das Ostlied wird wieder nachgefragt: Alles nur gestaut? Oder kommen jetzt die Liebhaber und Historiker?" *Die Tageszeitung,* August 25, 1995, 15–16.

Wiedmer, Caroline. "Designing Memories." *Alphabet City* 4/5 (December 1995): 6–22.

Wilke, Sabine. "Körpers als Schauplatz der Inzenierung der Weiblichkeit." *"Ausgraben und Erinnern": Zur Funktion von Geschichte, Subjekt und geschlechtlicher Identität in den Texten Christa Wolfs.* Würzburg: Königshausen und Neumann, 1993.

Winckler, Lutz. " 'An der Zerstörung des Faschismus mitschreiben': Anna Seghers' Romane *Das siebte Kreuz* und *Die Toten bleiben jung."* *Antifaschistische Literatur.* Ed. Lutz Winkler. Königstein/Ts.: Athenäum, 1979. 3: 172–201.

Witte, Karsten. "Film Im Nationalsozialismus: Blendung und Überblendung." *Geschichte Des Deutschen Films.* Ed. Anton Kaes, Wolfgang Jacobsen, and Hans Helmut Prinzler. Stuttgart and Weimar: Verlag J. B. Metzler, 1993.

Wolf, Christa. "Anmerkungen zu Geschichten (1970)." *Die Dimension des Autors.* Frankfurt a.M.: Luchterhand Literaturverlag, 1990. I: 323–31.

———. *Auf dem Weg nach Tabou: Texte 1990–1994.* Cologne: Kiepenheuer und Witsch, 1994.

———. " 'Auf mir bestehen': Christa Wolf im Gespräch mit Günter Gaus." *Akteneinsicht Christa Wolf: Zerrspiegel und Dialog.* Ed. Hermann Vinke. Hamburg: Luchterhand Literaturverlag, 1993. 242–63.

———. "Eine Auskunft." *Akteneinsicht Christa Wolf: Zerrspiegel und Dialog.* Ed. Hermann Vinke. Hamburg: Luchterhand Literaturverlag, 1993. 143–44.

———. "Befund." *Auf dem Weg nach Tabou.* Cologne: Kiepenheuer und Witsch, 1994. 189–93.

———. "Bei Anna Seghers." 1970. *Die Dimension des Autors.* Frankfurt a.M.: Luchterhand Literaturverlag, 1990. 1: 332–38.

———. "Berührung. Maxie Wander." 1977. *Die Dimension des Autors.* Frankfurt a.M.: Luchterhand Literaturverlag, 1990. 1: 196–209.

———. "Ein Brief." *Dokumentation zu Christa Wolf's "Nachdenken über Christa T."* Ed. Angela Drescher. Hamburg: Luchterhand Literaturverlag, 1991. 189–92.

———. "Ein Deutscher auf Widerspruch: Rede für Hans Mayer." *Auf dem Weg nach Tabou.* Cologne: Kiepenheuer und Witsch, 1994. 23–32.

———. "Dienstag, der 27. September 1960." *Neue deutsche Literatur* 22 (1974): 11–

22. "Tuesday, September 27." *What Remains and Other Stories.* Chicago: University of Chicago Press, 1995. 23–39.

———. *Die Dimension des Autors.* Frankfurt a.M.: Luchterhand Literaturverlag, 1990. 2 vols.

———. "Dokumente." *Im Dialog: Aktuelle Texte.* Frankfurt a.M.: Luchterhand Literaturverlag, 1990. 169–70.

———. "Erinnerung an Friedrich Schlotterbeck." 1985. *Die Dimension des Autors.* Frankfurt a.M.: Luchterhand Literaturverlag, 1990. 1: 243–51.

———. "Erinnerungsbericht." *Kahlschlag. Das 11. Plenum des ZK der SED 1965.* Ed. Günter Agde. Berlin: Aufbau-Verlag, 1991. 263–72.

———. "A Few Notes about My Work as a Writer." 1965. *The Author's Dimension: Selected Essays.* Ed. Alexander Stephan. Trans. Jan van Heurck. New York: Farrar, Straus and Giroux, 1993. 11–15.

———. "Fortgesetzter Versuch." 1974. *Die Dimension des Autors.* Frankfurt a.M.: Luchterhand Literaturverlag, 1990. 1: 339–46.

———. "The Fourth Dimension: A Conversation with Joachim Walther." *The Fourth Dimension: Interviews with Christa Wolf.* Trans. Hilary Pilkington. London and New York: Verso, 1988. 1–16.

———. "Fragen an Anna Seghers." 1959. *Die Dimension des Autors.* Frankfurt a.M.: Luchterhand Literaturverlag, 1990. 1: 255–62.

———. "From a Discussion at Ohio State University: A conversation with Christa and Gerhard Wolf." 1983. *The Fourth Dimension: Interviews with Christa Wolf.* Trans. Hilary Pilkington. London: Verso, 1988. 103–15.

———. "Für Unser Land." *Im Dialog: Aktuelle Texte.* Frankfurt a.M.: Luchterhand Literaturverlag, 1990. 170–71.

———. "Gesichter der Anna Seghers." *Anna Seghers: Eine Biographie in Bildern.* Ed. Frank Wagner, Ursula Emmerich, and Ruth Radvanyi. Berlin and Weimar: Aufbau-Verlag, 1994. 6–9.

———. "Gesichter der Anna Seghers—zu einem Bildband." *Auf dem Weg nach Tabou: Texte 1990–1994.* Cologne: Kiepenheuer und Witsch, 1994. 221–31.

———. "Ein Gespräch mit Anna Seghers." 1965. *Die Dimension des Autors.* Frankfurt a.M.: Luchterhand Literaturverlag, 1990. 1: 279–92.

———. *Der geteilte Himmel.* 1963. Munich: Deutscher Taschenbuchverlag, 1973. *The Divided Heaven.* Trans. Joan Becker. Rochester, N.Y.: Adler's Foreign Books, 1983.

———. "Glauben an Irdisches." 1968. *Die Dimension des Autors.* Frankfurt a.M.: Luchterhand Literaturverlag, 1990. 1: 293–322.

———. "Heine, die Zensur und wir: Rede auf dem ausserordentlichen Schriftstellerkongress der DDR." *Im Dialog: Aktuelle Texte.* Frankfurt a.M.: Luchterhand Literaturverlag, 1990. 163–68.

———. "I Admire a Certain Lack of Restraint: A Conversation with Wilfried F. Schoeller." 1979. *The Fourth Dimension: Interviews with Christa Wolf.* Trans. Hilary Pilkington. London and New York: Verso, 1988. 80–89.

————. *Im Dialog: Aktuelle Texte*. Frankfurt a.M.: Luchterhand Literaturverlag, 1990.

————. "Interview with Myself." *The Author's Dimension: Selected Essays*. Ed. Alexander Stephan. Trans. Jan van Heurck. New York: Farrar, Straus and Giroux, 1993. 11–15.

————. "Kann mann über alles schreiben?" *Neue deutsche Literatur* 6 (1958): 3–16.

————. *Kassandra: Erzählung*. 1983. Darmstadt: Luchterhand Literaturverlag. 1988. *Cassandra: A Novel and Other Essays*. Trans. Jan van Heurck. New York: Farrar, Straus and Giroux, 1984.

————. *Kein Ort, nirgends*. 1979. Darmstadt and Neuwied: Luchterhand Verlag, 1981. *No Place on Earth*. Trans. Jan van Heurck. New York: Farrar, Straus and Giroux, 1982.

————. *Kindheitsmuster*. 1976. Berlin and Weimar: Aufbau-Verlag, 1985. *Patterns of Childhood*. Trans. Ursule and Hedwig Rappolt Molinaro. New York: Farrar, Straus and Giroux, 1980.

————. "Land, in dem wir leben." *Neue deutsche Literatur* 5 (1961): 49–65.

————. "Leben oder gelebt werden." 1989. *Im Dialog*. Frankfurt a.M.: Luchterhand Literaturverlag, 1990. 101–18.

————. "Lesen und Schreiben." 1968. *Die Dimension des Autors*. Frankfurt a.M.: Luchterhand Literaturverlag, 1990. 2: 463–503. "Reading and Writing." *The Author's Dimension: Selected Essays*. Ed. Alexander Stephan. Trans. Jan van Heurck. New York: Farrar, Straus and Giroux, 1993. 20–48.

————. "Literary Work in the GDR." 1978. *The Fourth Dimension: Interviews with Christa Wolf*. Trans. Hilary Pilkington. London: Verso, 1988. 74–79.

————. "Margarete in Santa Monica: Interview Christa Wolf mit Fritz-Jochen Kopka (Wochenpost, 28.1.93)." *Akteneinsicht Christa Wolf: Zerrspiegel und Dialog*. Ed. Hermann Vinke. Hamburg: Luchterhand Literaturverlag, 1993. 164–67.

————. "A Model of Experience: A Discussion on *A Model Childhood*." 1975. *The Fourth Dimension: Interviews with Christa Wolf*. Trans. Hilary Pilkington. London and New York: Verso, 1988. 39–63.

————. *Moskauer Novelle. An den Tag gebracht: Prosa junger Menschen*. Ed. Heinz Sachs. Halle: Mitteldeutscher Verlag, 1961. 145–222.

————. *Nachdenken über Christa T.* 1968. Hamburg and Zurich: Luchterhand Literaturverlag, 1991. *The Quest for Christa T.* Trans. Christopher Middleton. New York: Farrar, Straus and Giroux, 1970.

————. "Nagelprobe." 1992. *Auf dem Weg nach Tabou*. Cologne: Kiepenheuer und Witsch, 1994. 156–68.

————. "Nun ja! Das nächste Leben geht aber heute an: Ein Brief über die Bettine." 1979. *Die Dimension des Autors*. Frankfurt a.M.: Luchterhand Literaturverlag, 1990. 2: 572–610.

————. "Romanticism in Perspective: A Conversation with Franke Meyer-Gosau." 1982. *The Fourth Dimension: Interviews with Christa Wolf*. Trans. Hilary Pilkington. London and New York: Verso, 1988. 90–102.

————. "The Sand and Pines of Brandenburg: A Conversation with Adam Krzeminski." 1976. *The Fourth Dimension: Interviews with Christa Wolf.* Trans. Hilary Pilkington. London and New York: Verso, 1988. 64–73.

————. "Der Schatten eines Traumes: Karoline von Günderrode—ein Entwurf." 1978. "The Shadow of a Dream: A Sketch of Karoline von Günderrode." *The Author's Dimension: Selected Essays.* Ed. Alexander Stephan. Trans. Jan van Heurck. New York: Farrar, Straus and Giroux, 1993. 131–75.

————. "Schreiben im Zeitbezug: Gespräch mit Aafke Steenhuis." 1989. *Im Dialog: Aktuelle Texte.* Frankfurt a.M.: Luchterhand Literaturverlag, 1990. 131–57.

————. "Selbstversuch: Traktat zu einem Protokoll." *Sinn und Form* 2 (1973): 301–23.

————. "The Sense and Non-Sense of Being Naive." 1973. *The Author's Dimension: Selected Essays.* Ed. Alexander Stephan. Trans. Jan van Heurck. New York: Farrar, Straus and Giroux, 1993. 49–57.

————. "Das siebte Kreuz." 1963. *Die Dimension des Autors.* Frankfurt a.M.: Luchterhand Literaturverlag, 1990. 1: 263–78.

————. "Sozialistische Literatur der Gegenwart." *Neue deutsche Literatur* 5 (1959): 3–7.

————. "Subjektive Authentizität: Gespräch mit Hans Kaufmann." 1973. *Die Dimension des Autors.* Frankfurt a.M.: Luchterhand Literaturverlag, 1990. 2: 773–805. "Subjective Authenticity: A Conversation with Hans Kaufmann." *The Fourth Dimension: Interviews with Christa Wolf.* Trans. Hilary Pilkington. London and New York: Verso, 1988. 17–38.

————. "Transit: Ortschaften." 1985. *Die Dimension des Autors.* Frankfurt a.M.: Luchterhand Literaturverlag, 1990. 1: 364–77.

————. "The Truth You Can Expect: The Prose of Ingeborg Bachmann." *The Author's Dimension: Selected Essays.* Ed. Alexander Stephan. Trans. Jan van Heurck. New York: Farrar, Straus and Giroux, 1993. 99–109.

————. "Unerledigte Widersprüche: Gespräch mit Therese Hörnigk." 1977–78. *Im Dialog: Aktuelle Texte.* Darmstadt and Neuwied: Luchterhand Verlag, 1990. 24–68.

————. "Ursprünge des Erzählens: Gespräch mit Jacqueline Grenz." 1983. *Die Dimension des Autors.* Frankfurt a.M.: Luchterhand Literaturverlag, 1990. 2: 912–28. "The Origins of Narration: A Conversation with Jacqueline Grenz." *The Fourth Dimension: Interviews with Christa Wolf.* Trans. Hilary Pilkington. London and New York: Verso, 1988. 116–27.

————. *Voraussetzungen einer Erzählung: Kassandra. Frankfurter Poetik Vorlesungen.* 1983. Darmstadt and Neuwied: Luchterhand Verlag, 1984. *Cassandra: A Novel and Other Essays.* Trans. Jan van Heurck. New York: Farrar, Straus and Giroux, 1984.

————. *Was bleibt.* Frankfurt a.M.: Luchterhand Literaturverlag, 1990. *What Remains and Other Stories.* Trans. Heike Schwarzbauer and Rick Takvorian. Chicago: University of Chicago Press, 1995.

————. "Zeitschichten." 1983. *Die Dimension des Autors.* Frankfurt a.M.: Luchter-hand Literaturverlag, 1990. 1: 353–63.

Young, James E. *The Texture of Memory.* New Haven and London: Yale University Press, 1993.

Zahlmann, Christel. "*Kinderheitsmuster:* Schreiben an der Grenze des Bewusst-seins." *Erinnerte Zukunft.* Ed. Wolfram Mauser. Würzburg: Verlag Königs-hausen und Neumann, 1985. 141–60.

Zehl Romero, Christiane. *Anna Seghers.* Reinbek: Rowohlt Verlag, 1993.

————. " 'Weibliches Schreiben'—Christa Wolfs 'Kassandra.' " *Studies in GDR Culture and Society* 4. Ed. Margy Gerber. Lanham, Md.: University Press of America, 1984. 15–29.

Zima, Peter V. "Der Mythos der Monosemie: Parteilichkeit und künstlerischer Standpunkt." *Literaturwissenschaft und Sozialwissenschaften 6: Einführung in Theorie, Geschichte und funktion der DDR-Literatur.* Ed. Hans-Jürgen Schmitt. Stuttgart: Metzler Verlag, 1975. 77–108.

Žižek, Slavoj. *For They Know Not What They Do: Enjoyment as a Political Factor.* London: Verso, 1991.

————. *The Sublime Object of Ideology.* London and New York: Verso, 1992.

————. *Tarrying with the Negative.* Durham: Duke University Press, 1993.

Index

Julia Hell is Associate Professor of Germanic Literature
at the University of Michigan.

Library of Congress Cataloging-in-Publication Data

Hell, Julia.
Post-fascist fantasies : psychoanalysis, history, and the literature of
East Germany / Julia Hell.
p.   cm. — (Post-contemporary interventions)
Includes bibliographical references and index.
ISBN 0-8223-1955-1 (cloth : alk. paper). — ISBN 0-8223-1963-2
(paper : alk. paper)
1. German literature—Germany (East)—History and criticism.
2. German literature—20th century—History and criticism.
3. Psychoanalysis and literature—Germany (East)   4. Fascism and
literature—Germany (East)   5. Germany (East)—In literature.
I. Title.   II. Series.
PT3705.H4   1997
833'.9109355—dc21   96-52157